A SHORT HISTORY
OF ANTI-SEMITISM

A
SHORT HISTORY
OF
ANTI-SEMITISM

Vamberto Morais

W · W · *Norton & Company · Inc ·*

NEW YORK

Copyright © 1976 *by W. W. Norton & Company, Inc.*
Originally published in Portuguese under the title *Pequena Historia
do Anti-Semitismo* (São Paulo, 1972)

Library of Congress Cataloging in Publication Data

Morais, Vamberto.
  A short history of anti-Semitism.

  An updated and expanded translation of Pequena
história do anti-semitismo, published in 1972.
  Bibliography: p.
  Includes index.
  1. Antisemitism—History. I. Title.
DS145.M6713   301.45′29′6   75-37914
ISBN 0-393-05567-1

Published simultaneously in Canada
by George J. McLeod Limited, Toronto

DESIGN BY M FRANKLIN-PLYMPTON

PRINTED IN THE UNITED STATES OF AMERICA
2 3 4 5 6 7 8 9

To my father
who first encouraged my historical interests

To my brother
who first taught me to challenge
established ideas

Contents

Acknowledgements

I am greatly indebted to my friend Graham Connell for revising the English text, which is an up-dated, somewhat expanded version of the original Brazilian book.

In all my research work and further reading I am deeply grateful to the staff of several libraries in London, and most particularly to the Wiener Library (absolutely invaluable for anyone engaged in Jewish studies in England), the British Museum Library, the BBC Library, and Canning House Library.

I wish to thank the following publishers and authors for kind permission to quote from the books mentioned:

Addison-Wesley Publishing Co., Reading, Mass.: *The Nature of Prejudice*, by Gordon W. Allport, 1954.

Andre Deutsch Ltd., London: *Notes from a Journal*, by Maxim Livinov.

East and West Library, London: *A Short History of the Jewish People*, by Cecil Roth.

Eyre & Spottiswoode Ltd., London: *Warrant for Genocide*, by Norman Cohn.

Granada Publishing Ltd., St. Albans: *The Saving Remnant*, by Herbert Agar.

Harkabi, Prof. Y., Jerusalem: *Arab Attitudes to Israel*.

Harper & Row, Inc., New York: *Racial and Cultural Minorities*, by George E. Simpson and J. Milton Yinger; *History of New Testament Times* and *Introduction to the Old Testament*, by Robert Pfeiffer.

The Jewish Publication Society of America, Philadelphia: *A History of the Marranos*, by Cecil Roth.

Macmillan Publishing Co., New York: *The Anguish of the Jews*, by Edward H. Flannery, 1965; and *Israel without Zionists*, by Uri Avnery, 1968.

Oxford University Press, Oxford: *The Legacy of Israel*, by E. R. Bevan and Charles Singer, 1927; *The Non-Jewish Jew and Other Essays*, by Isaac Deutscher, 1968; *The Jews in Soviet Russia since 1917*, edited by Lionel Kochan, 1972.

Penguin Books Ltd., Harmondsworth: *The Politics of Experience*, by R. D. Laing.

Prentice-Hall, Inc., Englewood Cliffs, N. J.: *The Study of Man,* by Ralph Linton.

Routledge & Kegan Paul Ltd., London: *History of Anti-Semitism,* by Léon Poliakov, 1974.

Weybright and Talley, New York: *A Peculiar People,* by Barnet Litvinoff.

Yale University Press, New Haven, Conn.: *The Jews in Russia,* by Louis Greenberg.

A SHORT HISTORY
OF ANTI-SEMITISM

Introduction

How This Book Came to Be Written

When I was about five years old, Adolf Hitler was an obscure demagogue whose *Putsch* had failed at a Munich beer hall in 1923. As far as I can remember, there was very little talk about anti-Semitism in Brazil at the time and I only began to hear the word about 1935.

My first playfellow, apart from my brother and sister, was a Jewish girl called Rachel who lived in the house next door in Recife Although our families never visited each other, I do not remember that anybody ever opposed our playing together. It is difficult to imagine any *apartheid* in the quiet, gentle atmosphere of Brazilian life at that time. I remember hearing disparaging remarks about the food habits of Jewish families. It was said the children smelled of onions because they took onion sandwiches to school, and there was talk of 'peculiar methods' of killing chickens. When a Jew with a long beard (*schachter*) appeared down the street, the children would shout, 'Here comes the hen-killer!' It was said he used to come to Jewish houses to kill the hens according to kosher regulations.

I do not think there was much malignity about all this. After all, the Jews were the largest group of 'gringos' (in Brazil a vague popular term for foreigners that was often applied to Jews) in a not very cosmopolitan town. The Jew was 'funny' because he was different. In fact, I think it is fair to say that the average Brazilian is more open and amiable to foreigners, and more interested in them, than most Europeans.

On the other hand, even in the easygoing atmosphere of those days, without many of the present tensions, the image and stereotype of the Jew were very much present, perhaps more on the religious plane than on any other. I remember vaguely that the grownups used to make puns about the word 'synagogue'. Nobody ever told me that the first Christians had preached at synagogues, and that Jesus himself had been a devout Jew, who used to follow the food precepts of his religion much more strictly than my Jewish neighbours in Recife. More than that: not many Chris-

1

tians nowadays are aware of the facts I stressed in a letter published by the English weekly *New Statesman* in a debate about the views of Professor Allegro:

> The Gospels talk of him [Jesus] eating with 'Publicans and sin-
> ners', but there is absolutely no mention of meals with gentiles;
> nor was he ever accused of eating 'impure' food or of breaking
> any of the segregation precepts (see for instance Mark 2:16).
> This was hardly conceivable since Jesus himself had forbidden
> contact with gentiles and Samaritans (Matt. 10:5). . . . He also
> criticised the gentiles for excessive worry over food and clothing
> (Luke 12:30; Matt. 6:32), long and repetitive prayers (Matt. 6:7)
> or rigid notions of authority (Mark 10:41–47 and parallels).[1]

Nor had I at that time any idea that the Jews still looked upon all non-Jews as Gentiles and that in their eyes I myself was a *goy*. It was only very gradually that I began to be aware of a 'game' which is probably as old as mankind—the old, cunning game of excluding people from in-groups, or

> I am the king of the castle
> You are a dirty rascal.

One of the earliest phrases I learned to use was 'Don't jew [don't torment] the little thing!' (In Portuguese: 'Não judie com o bichinho!') And one of the first children's books I read was the old morality story of a 'wicked' boy turned good, entitled *Tony the Jew* (*Totó Judeu*).

'Jew' was therefore a synonym for 'wicked' in Portuguese, and later I shall mention similar negative meanings in other languages. The whole idea of *judiação* (in the sense of ill-treatment and often used in the case of animals) was intimately linked with the mockery and torments suffered by Jesus—with the scenes we get familiar with very early in our childhood; particularly Catholics, who are brought up with the 'strip-cartoon' story of the Passion in churches and books.

It is true that by that time the image of the 'wicked Jew' had become rather faded and deprived of emotional charge. Jewish friends in Brazil have often told me that they themselves use the verb *judiar* (to 'jew' = to be cruel to) and the noun *judiação* (ill-treatment) without thinking of their anti-Semitic origin. This shows once more the mechanical character of so much that goes under the name of 'thought.' And it shows how much our so-called education is little more than a conditioning process to all sorts of distorted mental attitudes.

So no teacher of mine talked to me of Father Flannery's 'twenty-three centuries of anti-Semitism.' In my schoolbooks, as in his, there was no word on the subject:

Histories of the Middle Ages—and even of the Crusades—can be found in which the word 'Jew' does not appear, and there are Catholic dictionaries and encyclopaedias in which the term 'Anti-Semitism' is not listed. There seems to be only one conclusion: the pages Jews have memorized have been torn from our histories of the Christian era.[2]

But at least for one thing I and those of my generation in Brazil may be grateful: we were not given direct lessons in anti-Semitism, nor indeed in anti-Communism or any such indoctrination, as has become so common in the world today. Many school children elsewhere were less fortunate. And there was something more positive than this: the easy fraternization we had with Jewish boys and girls. I remember the delight we took in their very names, which sounded pleasantly exotic to our ears: names like Lispector (a prominent one now in Brazilian literature), Shapiro, or Ludmer. I remember my sister saying, 'Listen, Mummy, to the name of a girl at school. It is Zipporah Passarinho!' (Zipporah Bird). That might have been a fine chance for their teacher to explain to her class that Zippor means 'bird' or 'sparrow' in Hebrew, and that Zipporah was the name of Moses' wife. Be that as it may, I heard this name when I was about five and I never forgot it. It was only much later, of course, that I realized it was only another example of the age-old Jewish habit of translating their names into other languages, often adding the translation to the original (compare Desiderius Erasmus of Rotterdam).

When I entered the medical school at Recife, there was a strong Jewish element among the students. Most of them came from families which had emigrated from the Ukraine, Bessarabia, or Poland—in short, from the territories of the old tsarist empire. Although I did not know it at the time, they were living evidence of Russian anti-Semitism—of the persecutions and pogroms that are related in Chapters 11 and 12 of this book. But here I came across something which so far I had only known through newspapers and books: the militant anti-Semitism of a few 'Integralist' students (the 'Integralist', or Greenshirts, were the Brazilian version of the Fascist party), who used to bully some of the more timid Jewish boys. While they were playing at anti-Semitism, a more sinister game was taking place in Eastern Europe. There, in the western part of the Soviet Union, the Nazis killed something like a million Jews—in the very lands where my colleagues' families had come from.

Many years later, in 1956, I had just taken a degree in ancient history at London University, and had learned to know better the first part of Jewish history—and also the beginnings of Christianity. That year saw the celebration in Britain of the tercentenary of the readmission of Jews to the country. It was then that I became aware of a curious link between that event, the expulsion of the Dutch from Brazil in 1654 (that tercentenary had been commemorated in Recife two years earlier), and the establishment of the Jewish community in New York, today the largest in the world. So the migration of the Portuguese Jews, with names similar to mine and speaking then the same tongue, embraced in a vast transatlantic triangle three towns—London, Recife, and New York. And just as Recife (or Mauritsstadt, as it was then) had been refounded by Prince John Maurice of Nassau, in a similar way New York had begun as New Amsterdam. Again, just as Amsterdam had once been the great refuge of Portuguese Jews, Recife was to become the centre of the first synagogue in the New World, and the first town in America where Jews had (for a time) full freedom of worship.

It was only in October 1960 that I entered for the first time one of those synagogues which in my childhood were little more than a name. It was the famous Bevis Marks synagogue, in London, the oldest in the country, founded by those same Portuguese Jews, refugees from the Inquisition, who from 1656 onwards had been admitted into England by Cromwell: some had come from my native town, Recife, fleeing from the restoration of Portuguese (and therefore Catholic) rule. It was there that I attended the first day of *Sukkoth* (Tabernacles), the same festival that Jesus, according to John's Gospel, went to celebrate in Jerusalem. I was given a very friendly welcome, and the prominent scholar Dr. Richard Barnett kindly presented me with the history of the Bevis Marks synagogue, with documents and minutes in Portuguese. In the congregation there were several men with Portuguese names, and the old sexton, judging that my name indicated Jewish descent, asked me what he termed 'a delicate question': 'Are you still a Jew?' He explained that if I was he could 'call me to the Law'—that is, invite me to read the lesson from the Torah (Pentateuch): the old call to the *aliyah* made to a visitor, and to which Jesus himself had responded in the Nazareth synagogue (Luke 4:16–20).

In fact, I felt at Bevis Marks as if I were re-establishing a contact lost three centuries ago, picking up the thread broken by hatred and intolerance between the synagogue and the church in which I was brought up.

In the same year I helped to produce two programmes for the BBC, with Francesca Wilson—one of those admirable English Christians who did so much work for the refugees. The programmes were entitled 'Island of Refuge', and one of them was devoted to the Jews who had been coming to England from the time of Cromwell to that of Hitler: three centuries, it should be pointed out, almost free from persecution (except for the attacks of Mosley's Fascists), in which the Jewish community, in that democratic climate which Voltaire was one of the first to admire, enjoyed growing freedom.

In that programme I included one of the most moving documents I have ever heard: a recording of the first Jewish service held at the Belsen concentration camp immediately after liberation by British troops in the last weeks of World War II. It was directed by the army rabbi, and at one moment one could hear the sobs of some Jewish women as the word 'Adonai' (My Lord) was uttered during the service. In another recording of the BBC Sound Archives, the Jewish inmates of Belsen sang the beautiful song of welcome Shalom Aleichem, the ancient greeting that Jesus and his disciples must have used so often. Many Christians and Jews do not seem aware of the fact that its translation has been echoing in churches in many languages, particularly in the Pax Vobiscum of the Catholic mass. Is it not ironical now that its exact counterpart should be *Salaam aleikum* (Peace be with you) and that Arabs and Jews should be closely related in language and religion?

One year later—in fact, about the time of the Jewish New Year in 1961 —I gave a course of lectures at Recife University on 'The History of Anti-Semitism', arranged by Professor G. Freyre. I owe a great deal to those who attended that course, both Jews and non-Jews, who, apart from their many suggestions, stimulated me to write it all in book form.

My field of study has been above all ancient history and the history of religions, and so it is not surprising that the present book should emphasize these aspects of the problem. But what I believe to be shown in this book—and I make no claim of originality—is the continuity of the phenomenon. Between Graeco-Roman anti-Semitism, that of the Christian era, and modern National Socialism there is a continuous, uninterrupted thread: whether it runs through ancient Alexandria or Rome, medieval Metz, Seville or Lisbon, Recife in colonial Brazil, Vienna at the time of Hitler's youth, the Warsaw ghetto in 1943, or Buenos Aires in the 1960s, the phenomenon presents essentially similar features.

Although this book is fundamentally a historical study, the emphasis is not on the events as such, which in most cases are not in doubt. The reader will not find here a complete account of all the massacres and persecutions the Jews have suffered, though in my view I have included a very representative selection. When we hear Christians repeating defamatory stories that were already current before Christ, when we see the Nazis imitating anti-Jewish medieval practices, it becomes quite clear that in this matter there is not much that is new 'under the sun'.

What interests me most is to try to understand mental attitudes and emotions and inquire how the Jew has been seen at various times, without forgetting that side by side with hostility there has also been attraction, admiration, and particularly conversion. For this task of understanding we have now a growing arsenal of techniques of psychological interpretation. It is to be regretted that many historians still seem to be content with an elementary, superficial psychology.

I would never claim—as perhaps some do—that anti-Semitism is now a phenomenon as well understood and easy to explain as some diseases. On the contrary, I believe its essence still eludes us, because, as in the case of every great human problem, its cause may well lie in our deepest feelings about human relations and human identity.

As anti-Semitism is primarily a gentile phenomenon, his psychology necessarily takes precedence over that of the Jew, and I do not feel qualified to undertake a detailed profile of the latter, except in the (very considerable) measure in which it has been conditioned by anti-Jewish persecution. If there is a psychology of the Jew (and the whole question of 'national character' is most complex and full of pitfalls), whoever wants to engage in it should try and remove first of all the anti-Semitic mote from his eye, which we all inherit like a kind of original sin.

Some well-intentioned opponents of anti-Semitism have made the mistake of idealizing the Jews or at least of trying to present them without their 'warts' and black spots. This is neither more nor less than to fall into the trap set by the anti-Semite. It amounts to saying, 'Oh no, you are wrong, the Jew is not wicked at all, he is a splendid fellow!' They are not aware that in so doing they are in fact keeping intact the basic assumption that it is possible to postulate 'the Jew' or 'the Jews' as a well-defined entity which may be subject to clear-cut judgements, and that such judgements in turn are helpful in assessing any individuals belonging to the group. So the syllogism of the anti-Semite would be:

All Jews are crooks (or malignant, unreliable, etc.).
Jacob is a Jew.
Therefore he is a crook, etc.

The fault of such 'reasoning' lies not only in the negative statement but, more basically, in the validity of any such judgements. Once you reject the absurd premise about 'the Jews' (or 'the Americans', 'the Catholics', etc.), you demolish at one stroke not only anti-Semitism but also all labels, stereotypes, and barriers in which we all try to imprison ourselves and others, all the narrow and stifling compartments that exist above everything in our minds. Only after such 'purification' or 'purgation' could we aim at something like the world citizenship that is so much talked about.

In fact, those Jews who have reached a higher stage of mental development and insight are the first to reject the false idealization of their people and the rather complacent pride of many of their fellows. Jewish ethnocentrism, for instance, is neither better nor worse than that of other peoples. A Jew once wrote these penetrating words, in friendly criticism of a Christian:

> You dangerously overestimate us Jews, and you insist on loving our entire people. I do not ask, I decidedly do not wish, that we

be loved in this fashion (we, or for that matter, any other people). All I ask of you is justice, nothing else, nothing more. In
the name of that justice I proclaim our right to number among
us professional and emotional criminals, brutes of every description, ignoble men and women. A man who would refuse us this
inalienable right, given to all other peoples, condemns us to a
shameful death.

The pitiless battle against anti-Semitism is your concern. For if
this hatred is sometimes a mortal danger to us, for you it is a disease, a cancer, that you carry within yourselves.[3]

This is indeed the heart of the matter, which lays bare the basic mental
distortion not only of the anti-Semite but of every prejudiced person. More
dangerous than the violent, raving fanatic is the moderate, 'reasonable' per-
suader, the 'polite bigot' as Melvin Tumin has called him, who talks in a
quiet voice. He begins by denying his anti-Semitism and then goes on to
enumerate the faults he sees in the Jew. What is he trying to do in fact?
He is simply demanding that the Jews be superior to all other peoples in
the world: there must not be among them any criminals, greedy, dishonest,
or selfish people. In a world full of fierce nationalisms they are accused of
helping only each other; in societies dominated by the profit motive and
the cash nexus they are accused of 'worshipping the golden calf'; in a world
that stimulates competition to the highest degree they are condemned for
'disloyal competition'. Finally, in a world that has been persecuting them
for centuries, the Jew has often been labelled as malevolent and revenge-
ful. We come back, in fact, to the magnificent speech Shakespeare wrote
for Shylock.

Therefore, to reject anti-Semitism is not to build up a false and idealized
image of the Jews; it is simply to accept them as human beings as they are
and have been made by their history, 'with warts and all'—as Cromwell
wanted to be painted. It is not even to try and see them as 'a people like
all others', for no doubt there is something unique and tragic in their destiny: and this peculiarity has to be fully accepted as part of the infinite
variety of mankind. But is not every people, like every individual, unique?
And is not freedom really the right to be different?

Many Gentiles and Jews have talked of assimilation as the 'final solution'
of the problem. It is quite possible it will go on in many countries, just as
it has taken place to a limited extent in the case of Jewish communities in
countries like China, Peru, and some parts of modern Brazil—in none of
which was there ever serious anti-Jewish persecution. But there is little reason to consider assimilation as something necessary or ideal. Increase in
tolerance should not lead to uniformity but to a maximum of variety.

But there is a deeper sense in which we have to try and assimilate ourselves—not to the patterns of behaviour and narrow mental attitudes of

some in-group or other, not according to some limited idea of 'healthy so-cial adjustment'—but in the wide and generous terms of a true world citi-zenship. Everything else has now become too narrow. But tribalism, 'my country right or wrong', and the accumulated prejudices which they per-petuate are the deadly enemies of world citizenship, just as they are of world peace. It is a ridiculous contradiction to say '*Shalom*' or '*Salaam*', or to moan wearily, 'Why do they go on with these silly wars?' and at the same time to stick to attitudes which perpetuate such wars.

Anti-Semitism is only one—perhaps one of the most destructive—of such prejudices. The anti-Semite has often claimed that the Jews are a 'pest' or a kind of cancer. In his testament written just before committing suicide, Adolf Hitler described 'international Jewry' as 'the world poisoner of all peoples' (*Weltvergifter aller Völker*). The facts related in this book show quite clearly that it is anti-Semitism that has constituted one of the great poisons and plagues of history. Once more the condemnation is turned against the self-styled judge, as in the famous Biblical scene in which the prophet Nathan pointed at King David: 'Thou art the man!'

The present study is a contribution to the understanding of this plague and to its final eradication. But you cannot hit at one prejudice without attacking them all. It is easy for people to protest against prejudices when they hurt their own group. It is shortsighted and narrow-minded to stop there without looking at what other groups suffer, or—even more impor-tant—at one's own attitudes to different groups. And you cannot do that without asking some big questions about human mental evolution and edu-cation. I have tried to do that—very inadequately, I know—in the last two chapters of this book.

I

In the Beginning

And you shall become a horror, a proverb, and a byword, among all the peoples where the Lord will lead you away.

—Deut. 28:37

ISRAEL IN HISTORY

On the fifth of the month of Iyar, Anno Mundi 5708—or, if you prefer, 14 May 1948 A.D.—in the afternoon, a group of men were assembled in the Tel Aviv Museum. If you looked at them closely, you would probably describe them as 'Europeans', or perhaps, in view of the prevalence of certain facial features, you might specify 'East European' or 'Slav'. But you could not fail to see the duplicated symbol on the wall behind the table at which the presiding committee sat: the interlocking triangles of the Star of David (*Magen David*). Nobody really knows how or where this symbol appeared, but for many centuries it has become associated with the Jewish people. The men who met in this room, all very mixed racially, considered themselves Jews, although the Jews of David's kingdom or even those living in Judaea two thousand years ago would certainly have looked upon them as very un-Jewish.

These men were there because of history and to enact history. They were fulfilling a dream at once old and new. Their aim was very modern, very Western: the proclamation of a new state, for which America had set the pattern in 1776. They were following an age-old search for collective security, a security that still eludes them today. And they were trying to find it there because of their identification with the past, and particularly because of the Bible. One can also say that they were there because of certain hostile attitudes and patterns of behaviour which we have come to call 'anti-Semitism'.

As one looks back from this landmark when the modern state of Israel was founded, it is easy to find certain striking historical parallels. If we discount two rebellions against Roman rule and the vassal state of the Herods,

9

there had not been a Jewish national state for over two thousand years: since 63 B.C., when the Roman general Pompey took Jerusalem and put an end to the kingdom founded by the Maccabees.

In that year Palestine had become part of the Roman Empire. In 1948 A.D. it became independent of a much larger state—the British Empire. But Jerusalem, holy to three religions, the most fought-for city in history, was to fall, to be conquered and reconquered on many occasions before our own century, when it changed hands three times and was for a period both physically and symbolically divided.

There are rich emotional and legendary associations in the history of the Wandering People and of their longing for Jerusalem. The anti-Semitic legend of the Wandering Jew had its parallel in the Messianic 'hope of Israel'. 'Next year in Jerusalem!' was the final verse of the Seder or Passover service. Or in that splendid Psalm:

> If I forget you, O Jerusalem,
> Let my right hand wither . . . (Ps. 137:5).

For the Christians, too, Jerusalem had become the heavenly city, the splendid spiritual vision of a prophetic poet like Blake, the New Jerusalem in which the meek should inherit the earth at last.

There is an extraordinary, tragic unity in the history of Israel. The Jews make their first entrance with the invasion of Canaan after a long period of oppression in Egypt and the Exodus. This migration gave rise to their first organized state, that of the Judges, which, following the usual pattern in the ancient East, became established as a strong kingdom. The modern state of Israel was founded very largely as a reaction to something more than oppression: to large-scale extermination, the most deliberate in history, which required the coining of a new word—'genocide'. Again, in both cases the Jews had to fight 'the people of the land', their relatives at least in language, Canaanites and Arabs.

From the probable date of the Exodus in the thirteenth century B.C. to 1948 we have over three thousand years of history, very poorly documented at times and with many gaps. But two features stand out during a large part of that period: the wide migrations of the Jewish people and the series of persecutions they have suffered. As a result, any history of anti-Semitism becomes, to a large extent, a history of the Jews.

HOW PREJUDICE WORKS

So much has been written against racialist mythology that it is hardly necessary to go over some well-established facts. First of all, it is current knowledge that 'anti-Semitism' is a euphemistic and incorrect term coined by the anti-Semites themselves to give their prejudice a pseudo-scientific façade. Although writers still loosely use such expressions as 'Semitic peoples', the only precise or scientific meaning that the words 'Semite' or 'Semitic' can have is in the field of linguistics. It is perhaps unfortunate that the German philologist Schlözer should have chosen in 1781 a term taken from Biblical genealogy to describe an important family of languages (now called Hamito-Semitic).

Obviously, a consistent 'anti-Semite' who wanted to do justice to the appellation would have to dislike not only Jews (most of whom do not speak Hebrew anyway) but also Arabs, Ethiopians, and the small communities who still speak Aramaic or Syriac. It is significant that even in Nazi Germany some leaders tried to avoid the term 'anti-Semitism' so as not to cause offence to the Arabs, whose favour German diplomacy thought it worth while to court.[1]

Both the words 'Semite' and 'anti-Semite' seem to have become current in Europe in the 1870s, while the coining of 'anti-Semitism' is usually attributed to the German journalist Wilhelm Marr, who in 1873 published his anti-Semitic best seller *The Victory of Judaism over Germanism* (see Chapter 11). A term like 'Judaeophobia' (actually used by the Jewish writer Leo Pinsker in 1882) would be preferable, but unfortunately 'anti-Semitism' has come into general use and it is too late to try and replace it.

It is not within my scope to analyze in detail the concept of prejudice, of which anti-Semitism is such a blatant example. For the purpose of this study I shall accept Allport's definition:

> . . . an avertive or hostile attitude toward a person who belongs to a group, simply because he belongs to that group, and is therefore presumed to have the objectionable qualities ascribed to the group.

Or, put more simply:

> Ethnic prejudice is an antipathy based upon a faulty and inflexible generalization.[2]

The essence of prejudice, then, is that the attitude towards an individual is subordinated to a judgement that embraces the whole group, as in the saying quoted in one of the Pauline epistles: 'Cretans are always liars, evil beasts, lazy gluttons' (Titus 1:12).

As this was actually said by a Cretan writer called Epimenides, it gave rise to a famous paradox: 'Epimenides says that all Cretans are liars. Now, Epimenides is a Cretan, therefore he is a liar. But if he is lying, then all Cretans are not liars. Now, Epimenides is a Cretan, therefore he is telling the truth, and all Cretans are liars, and so on.' The paradox itself shows the absurdity of such generalizations, but that does not prevent people from making them everywhere and about all sorts of groups. So anti-Semites go on repeating the syllogism:

All Jews are swindlers (or money-grabbers, etc.).
Jacob is a Jew.
Therefore he is a swindler.

It is easy to show that prejudices are not normally the result of some previous experience, but experience is in fact interpreted in terms of prejudice, as in the well-known case of 'selective perception': i.e., one sees only what one wants to see, just as in the opposite case of 'being blind' to someone's faults. For instance, if one is angry with someone, one is more likely to 'discover' all sorts of faults in him that did not seem so apparent before, and similarly a pessimistic mood tends to spread to everything in a sort of psychological chain-reaction. It is therefore extremely difficult for an anti-Semite to become aware of positive contributions made by Jewish communities, such as those mentioned in Chapter 8.

The generalization about the group being all-embracing, it will still be preserved even if exceptions are admitted. Even the most anti-Semitic Nazis accepted the existence of 'decent Jews' and went as far as to point out examples, but that did not diminish their anti-Semitism one jot.

Prejudice can also flourish very well at a distance. For instance, when Shakespeare staged his famous anti-Semitic play *The Merchant of Venice* in London (according to experts before 1598), few English people would have had the opportunity of meeting Jews. Apart from a few who lived there clandestinely, the Jewish community had been expelled by King Edward I three centuries earlier. Yet there is evidence of marked anti-Semitism in Elizabethan England, just as in other European countries, and not only on the stage. A few years earlier, in 1594, Dr. Rodrigo Lopez, a Portuguese Jew, was tried and executed for plotting to poison the queen, and there is little doubt that anti-Jewish prejudice exerted a powerful influence on the verdict.[3]

The greater the distance, the more fanciful can prejudice become, and ignorance is an excellent breeding ground. Before tourism became widespread, most people in the West had never been to Africa, and even now journeys south of the Sahara are not at all frequent. And yet the popular image of 'an African Negro' was much cruder than the anti-Semitic stereotype of a Jew. Westerners used to think, and still do, of cannibalism, witchcraft, and frantic dances, or have wild notions of people 'living up in trees'. The accent has always been on cruelty, savagery, and superstition, and it has been suggested with some plausibility that such an image is largely a projection of the darker side of the Western mind.[4] The horrors of the slave trade and of plantation slavery, or the atrocities committed by the agents of King Leopold II in the former Belgian Congo are not part of the popular image.

The force of the popular Western stereotype of the African was eloquently shown when French troops, including African contingents, occupied the Ruhr in 1923 in order to force Germany to fulfil the Versailles Treaty. It was not long before vociferous German nationalists (including the Nazi party) clamoured against the crime of letting loose on the population 'the savagery of African Negroes'. Some people swore they had seen an African soldier eating the brains of a German child,[5] a story that reminds one of the accusation of ritual murder made against the Jews (see Chapter 6). As would be expected, German anti-Semites like Hitler invented the story that the African occupation was yet another devilish plan concocted by the Jews. When one thinks of what the Germans did in occupied Europe, particularly in Russia, one might well ask who was the savage.

But prejudices and national stereotypes are not only found on the popular level. It is only lately that we have become more aware of how schools, schoolbooks, and even universities help to disseminate and strengthen national or racial prejudices. In fact, some work has been done on anti-Semitism in religious education,[6] but this is just one example among many. Although the better schools and teachers are trying their best to develop habits of questioning accepted ideas and creative thinking (what some are calling nowadays 'lateral' thinking), it is still true in many countries, as Margaret Mead tried to show,[7] that education is very largely an inculcation of 'orderly sets of prejudices'. More than that, schools have often served as centres for fostering a militant, rabid nationalism, and the statement that World War I was prepared by French and German schoolmasters is not a very exaggerated one. Even now, what seems to be going on in Israeli and Arab schools is not encouraging for peace in the Middle East.

While anti-Semitism is just one case of prejudice for which many instructive parallels can be found, yet it presents some special features in its strength and persistence, which can be partly explained by historical circumstances, including religious history.

Take the pogrom, for instance. Many examples can be quoted of outbursts of violence against an unpopular minority which serves as a scapegoat, such as the massacre of Flemish merchants during the Peasant Revolt of 1381 in England or the Armenian massacres in modern Turkey. The Jews, however, have remained particularly vulnerable for, apart from having no established national state that could afford them protection, they were for many centuries the only people of any importance that could be found scattered all over the world. There is also the case of the Gypsies, but their dispersion, although great, has been on a smaller scale than that of the Jewish Diaspora. Considered an enigma for so long, they are in fact an Indian tribe which migrated to Persia before 1000 A.D. and from the four-teenth century onwards was scattered throughout Europe. It is interesting to note that the Gypsies (*gitanos, tziganes, ciganos, Zigeuner, zingari, romani*) have often been the victims of prejudice, discrimination, persecu-tion, and superstitious accusations which are in some ways similar to those found in anti-Semitism. For instance, Gypsies have been charged with, and sometimes executed for, alleged kidnapping of children, cannibalism, and so on. During Nazi rule it is estimated that over 400,000 of them were ex-terminated in occupied Europe as a measure of 'racial purity'.[8]

But in most cases the Gypsies' nomadic way of life, affording only mar-ginal participation in the social and economic life of Western communities, together with their comparatively low level of culture, has to some extent protected them against aggression. With the Jews it is different: they have usually played an important part in the countries where they live and so could easily become the targets of envy and resentment.

It may be useful at this stage to understand how the Jewish Diaspora came about, and therefore I propose to give a very brief summary of early Jewish history.

A BRIEF HISTORICAL SUMMARY

The word 'Jew' (Hebrew *Yehudi*, Greek *Ioudaios*, Latin *Judaeus*) comes from the name of the most important of the twelve traditional Jewish tribes, Judah (Hebrew *Yehuda*): the tribe that gave Israel the glorious Davidic dynasty. The more general use of this term dates from the time when the Israelites began to spread in the Mediterranean world, first under Hellenistic and later under Roman rule. The usual expression in the Bible is 'the people of Israel' or 'the children of Israel' (*Bene Israel*), and it is only natural that it should have been adopted as the name of the new state founded in 1948.

In history almost every beginning is obscure and it is unavoidable that it should be so. A new nation, like a new religion, does not begin its career as a fully self-conscious entity: this consciousness comes slowly by degrees and then is projected into the past, giving rise to a myth or a series of myths. That this pattern of development applies to Israel is clear from even a cursory examination of the Bible, and scholars have distinguished in it a number of layers as in the evolution of rocks.

It would seem that the Bene Israel came from a group of semi-nomadic tribes which, by language at least, were related to the Phoenicians, Ara-maeans, and Arabs. Their way of life is reflected in the pages of Genesis, and just as modern Bedouin tribes have names preceded by *Banu* (children of), several Semitic peoples in antiquity followed this immemorial practice. For instance, in the eighteenth century B.C. cuneiform tablets at the time of King Hammurabi of Babylon mention the Bene-Yamina (children of the South, or children of the Right Hand) as an aggressive people threatening urban centres. Now, Bene-Yamina is exactly the same as Benjamin (Hebrew *Ben-Yamin*), the tribe of Israel which, according to tradition, descended from Jacob's youngest son. There may not be the slightest relation between the two, but at least here we have evidence that already at that time tribes with a Semitic name were wandering in the Fertile Crescent, as, indeed, we can see from the legendary traditions of the 'Jewish' or Hebrew patriarchs Abraham, Isaac, and Jacob. These tribes were considered 'barbarians' by the more advanced peoples of the area, Egyptians and Babylonians. They lived on the periphery of organized states, sometimes coming to the agricultural centres for food in time of famine (hence the Biblical stories about the journeys of Abraham and Jacob's sons to Egypt in search of grain) or at other times attacking such centres.

There is reason to believe that during the second millennium B.C. some of these Semitic tribes were collectively known as *Habiru* or *Apiru*, which occurs in the Egyptian and cuneiform records of the time. Although we do not know the exact origin of the word, two things can be said about it: first, it was used by the more advanced peoples and not by the tribes themselves; and, secondly, it was applied more or less indiscriminately to such peoples, perhaps vaguely as the words 'barbarian' or 'nomad'. From *Habiru* came very probably the Hebrew word *Hebrim* (*Hevrim*), which is not very often used in the Bible, and gave the Greek *Hebraioi* (Hebrews).

Every people has traditions about crucial events, experiences shared in common which help to form national consciousness. In the case of the Jews it is clear that the basic event was the period of servitude in Egypt and the Exodus under the leadership of Moshe, or Moses. It was this ordeal that turned a group of wandering Hebrews into the People of Israel. The Biblical narrative is, of course, a splendid myth, but under it there must be a core of solid truth.

It may have happened something like this: some 'Hebrew' tribes of Semitic language settled in Egypt to escape famine. In the course of time their condition worsened and came very near slavery, during a period when the pharaohs were engaged in great building works. One of the Hebrews who had received an Egyptian education and name, Moshe, had an overwhelming religious experience in some ways comparable to that of Joan of Arc, and was inspired to lead his people out of Egypt and to cross the desert to the 'Land of Canaan'. The date of the Exodus has been one of the most controversial problems of Jewish history, but most historians nowadays place it in the thirteenth century B.C., in the reign of the famous pharaoh Ramses II. The event is not mentioned in any other document apart from the Bible and does not seem to have had immediate repercussions.

It is generally thought that not all the tribes which constituted the people of Israel joined the migratory movement to Egypt. But in any case the Egyptians exerted a powerful influence over them: on leaving the country the Israelites must have carried with them not only 'borrowed' objects (as the Biblical tradition mentions) but also no doubt a number of Egyptian customs and practices, perhaps including circumcision. Some have even seen Egyptian influence in Moses' fervent monotheism, and no doubt there are similarities between the language of the Psalms and the religious hymns of the time of the pharaoh Akhenaten, who tried in vain to reform Egyptian religion. But this is pure conjecture, and the origin of the cult of Yahweh is still very obscure. In any case, there is no doubt as to the force and originality of Moses' religious experience or to its great importance in religious history.

The Jewish conquest of Canaan, or Palestine, was slow and uphill work, interrupted by serious setbacks and internal disputes. But it did contribute to strengthen the precarious unity of the Israelite tribes. They were led at first by chieftains called *Sophetim* (Judges), who are also found in Phoenician cities. Later, as military efficiency became more imperative, particularly under the pressure of the aggressive Philistines, the Israelites followed the example of other Eastern peoples by adopting a centralized monarchy. The *Melek*, or king, was made sacrosanct through the ceremony of anointing and so came to be called the 'Anointed of the Lord' (Hebrew *Mashiah Yahweh*, Greek *Christos Kyriou*). The name was to be given a new, apocalyptic dimension with the later Messianic hope and the various forms of Christian millenarism.

It was the second king, David, from the tribe of Yehuda, or Judah, who consolidated the state about the year 1000 B.C. Under his leadership Israel became a formidable military power which attained its height of prosperity under his son, Solomon. But the northern tribes seceded soon after his death, and this led to a breakup into two kingdoms: that of Israel to the north, later with the capital at Samaria, and that of Judah to the south, centred at Jerusalem.

These two small, quarrelling states led a difficult life, under the pressure of stronger powers like renascent Egypt, Damascus, and particularly Assyria. For a long period they were vassals of the Assyrians. Political division led to a religious schism: the northern tribes no longer attended the great temple of Jerusalem, but their king had new shrines built in his own territory. It is a development comparable to the protest against the centralization of Christianity at Rome, first by the Eastern or Byzantine schism and later by the Protestant Reformation.

In 721 B.C. Samaria was taken by Sargon II of Assyria, the kingdom of Israel disappeared as a political unit, and a large part of its population was deported. The smaller kingdom of Judah resisted for over a century but it also succumbed in 587 B.C. Nebuchadnezzar of Babylon took Jerusalem, destroyed the temple, and carried out a final deportation of the Jewish people to the area which is now Iraq. This great disaster, the first fall of Jerusalem and the end of the 'First Temple', was an important crisis in Jewish history and marked the beginning of the 'Babylonian Captivity'. It was the first stage of the Jewish Dispersion, or Diaspora (*Golah* or *Galuth*).

The history of the Israelites from this period to the time of the Maccabees (second century B.C.) is rather obscure. In 538 the Babylonian Empire was conquered by the Persians, who were greeted as liberators by the Jews and certainly proved to be more liberal rulers. In fact, this pattern would be repeated several times in Jewish history; for instance in Spain, when the Sephardic Jews, persecuted by the Visigoths, co-operated with the invading Muslims. Under Persian rule several groups were allowed to go back to Palestine and were granted a certain degree of autonomy. The Second Temple was built, and the whole of this period, which provides the background for the Books of Ezra and Nehemiah, set the pattern for repeated returns to the land of Israel. It was also a time for strengthening and reaffirming religious unity, when the first part of the Bible (Torah) probably received its final recension.[9] The Jews, who had then no political unity, were becoming 'the People of the Book', and that unique institution in the ancient world, the synagogue, was already established.

THE 'FIRST POGROM'?

With the fall of Jerusalem, groups of Jews (including for a time the prophet Jeremiah) took refuge in Egypt, whose rulers had used Judah more than once as an ally or cat's-paw against Assyria or Babylon. Later Egypt also fell under Persian domination, and many of these Jews served in the Persian army.

In the fifth century B.C. there was a Jewish community established at Elephantine (Aswan), in Upper Egypt, who had built a temple to Yahweh. In one of the Aramaic documents discovered at this place the Jews complain to the Persian authorities that the Egyptians attacked and sacked their temple. Some historians have seen in this attack the first recorded example of 'anti-Semitic' aggression. But the circumstances are not well known, and it would be impossible to say whether the Egyptian attack resulted from intolerance against an exotic cult or from hostility to the Jews for serving the hated Persian Empire.

On the other hand, the Jewish historian Josephus (see Chapter 3) would say much later that the Egyptians had been the first to spread hostility and invent stories against the Jews and their religion. Certainly at a later period, when Egypt fell under Macedonian rule, there is clear evidence of anti-Semitism there.

That period was inaugurated by the conquests of Alexander the Great, who between 334 and 323 B.C. overthrew the Persian Empire and opened the way for the diffusion of the Greek civilization and language in western Asia. The Jews, who were already settled in several regions of Asia and Africa, were an important element in the population of a new city, Alexandria, which was to become one of the largest and most important in the world.

Before the Macedonian conquest, most Jews already spoke Aramaic, which was a lingua franca in parts of the Persian Empire. Hebrew became more and more restricted to Jewish worship and the Bible. But in the Hellenistic period a growing number of Jews, particularly the large Egyptian community, adopted Greek as their everyday language. About 270 B.C. it became necessary to translate the Jewish scriptures into Greek, an important task which was carried out in Alexandria: hence the fact that so many common Biblical terms are in fact Greek, like 'Exodus', 'prophet', 'proselyte', 'blasphemy', 'synagogue', and the very word 'Bible'.

THE FIRST GREAT PERSECUTION

It was also from that time that the Israelites, who previously were little known and were usually bundled together with their neighbours of Syria and Palestine (Palestine itself, significantly, means 'country of the Philistines', not of the Jews), began to stand out as 'a peculiar people': a fervently religious community whose life was ruled by very strict precepts like a host of dietary prohibitions and the Sabbath rest. Judaism attracted a number of 'proselytes' from other peoples, and even many of the proud Greeks saw in it a fascinating new 'philosophy'.

Although it is also during the Hellenistic period that we can discern the first signs of a specific anti-Jewish reaction, most of our evidence comes in fact from the Roman period. In any case, it was a Hellenistic monarch who made the first recorded attempt to stamp out the 'peculiarity' of Jewish worship.

When the vast empire conquered by Alexander of Macedon was broken up among his generals, Palestine fell first to the Ptolemaic dynasty of Egypt, whose last representative was to be the famous Cleopatra. But in 200 B.C. Antiochus III the (Great) of the rival Seleucid dynasty took Palestine from Ptolemy IV of Egypt. In 168 B.C. one of his successors, Antiochus IV (Epiphanes, or 'the God Manifest') tried to 'assimilate' the Jews by forcibly imposing Greek worship and Greek customs. A section of the Jewish aristocracy, who were already Hellenized, co-operated with this policy, but soon there was a fierce outburst in favour of the national religion which was led from the start by a family of south Judaea, Judas Maccabee and his brothers (their real dynastic name was Hasmonaean, and Maccabee was only the nickname of Judas). The Maccabees waged successful guerrilla warfare—in fact, one of the first such cases in history—and after a long struggle, taking advantage of the internal quarrels in the reigning Seleucid dynasty and of growing intervention by Rome, succeeded in establishing an autonomous Jewish state. At its head stood a high priest of the Hasmonaean family, and at the end of the second century B.C. the small theocratic state had enlarged its territory and even imposed Judaism on some neighbouring peoples, including the Idumaeans (which would give Judaea the dynasty of the Herods).

Increase in secular power led the Hasmonaeans away from their popular and religious basis. They became increasingly Hellenized, and often oppressive, even adopting the Greek title of *basileus* (king), which was frowned upon by the more orthodox Jews. Divided by dynastic quarrels and religious disputes, the kingdom fell an easy prey to the Romans. Caesar's rival Pompey took Jerusalem in 63 B.C., the same year in which Cicero was pronouncing his famous speeches against Catiline in the Roman Senate. Once more defeat widened the Diaspora, and thousands of Jews were enslaved and taken to the imperial capital, where later Caesar freed a good number of them.

THE FINAL DISASTERS

Pompey had left in Jerusalem a prince of the Hasmonaean dynasty, Hyrcanus II, limited to the title and functions of a high priest. He soon fell under the influence of an Idumaean adventurer whose son, Herod, succeeded later in making himself 'king' of a sizable part of Palestine (then called Judaea) with Roman help and protection. Herod and his descendants were generally hated by the Jews as foreign usurpers and Rome's puppet rulers. Although they did enjoy a certain autonomy, everybody knew that these princes were no more than vassals or 'clients' of the Roman generals and emperors, always ready to flatter them and to further imperial interests. The names of the new towns built by Herod and his sons, like Caesarea and Tiberias, are an eloquent illustration of such subservience.

The first Herod, sometimes called 'the Great' (the wicked king in the 'slaughter of the innocents' recounted in the Gospel of Matthew), died in 4 B.C., and a few years later Judaea became a Roman province administered by an imperial official usually called 'procurator' or 'prefect'. Meanwhile, the other territories of the vassal kingdom, such as the turbulent Galilee, cradle of guerrilla fighters, were divided among Herod's sons. Except for the period 37–44 A.D. (coinciding with the first part of the Acts of the Apostles) when Agrippa I ruled most of the territory with the title of king, Judaea remained under Roman governors with their seat at Caesarea on the coast.

The oppressive, inept, often corrupt rule of these officials—like Pontius Pilate, an anti-Semite whom the Jewish philosopher Philo described as 'inflexible, impious, and obstinate'—created growing tension, which was made worse by considerable disproportion of wealth, unemployment, and other problems endemic in the region. Such evils are apparent in John the Baptist's and Jesus' preaching on behalf of the oppressed poor and their radical condemnation of the rich. Rebellions, terrorism, and even urban guerrilla activities, which look strikingly modern, became increasingly frequent, as well as fierce Roman repression. At last, in the year 66, in the reign of Nero, there was an unplanned rebellion led by some extremist popular leaders, while the priestly class either kept aloof or lent lukewarm support.

The Jewish rebels succeeded in holding Jerusalem and a great part of the country, but thanks to their disunity and lack of discipline, Roman military efficiency triumphed once more. After heroic, suicidal resistance, Jerusalem was taken once more in the tragic year 70. The siege and conquest were accompanied by hideous scenes of massacre, famine, and even cannibalism, which are described in detail in Josephus' classic work *The Wars of the Jews* (see Chapter 3). Thousands of Jewish rebels received the infamous punishment of the cross. The splendid Second Temple, sumptuously rebuilt by Herod, which Jesus had pointed out as something ephemeral that should not imprison the spirit of religion, was destroyed for ever.

Meanwhile, the annual tribute, or 'half shekel', which every devout Jew had to pay towards the temple came to be collected by the Romans. On that occasion it was used to rebuild the temple of Jupiter Capitolinus in Rome. This *fiscus judaicus*, as it came to be called, although comparatively light, served later as a precedent for a considerably heavier tribute in the Middle Ages.[10]

In 115–16 A.D. there was again trouble in several centres of the Diaspora, including Egypt, Cyrene, and even Cyprus. The mutual hostility between Jews and Greeks exploded in violent riots with massacres on both sides until the Romans intervened with fierce repression.

Finally, in the following reign, the emperor Hadrian gave orders for the establishment of a Roman colony in Jerusalem with the name of Aelia Capitolina and the erection of a temple there dedicated to Jupiter. Circumcision was also forbidden as a 'barbarian practice'. A final rebellion broke out, this time a carefully planned one and led by Simon bar Kokhba (Son of the Star) who was proclaimed Messiah by the rabbi Akiba. The war lasted three years, 132–35 A.D., and the Roman legions were fully stretched before the revolt was finally quelled. Perhaps it should be pointed out that there was nothing unusual in such stubborn rebellions in the Roman Empire: nobody likes foreign rule, and the Romans had to fight repeatedly in countries like Spain, Gaul, Britain, and so on.

But what we have given in the previous pages is no more than the bare bones of history. In the following chapters I shall try to clothe them with some flesh and to indicate the kinds of attitudes and prejudices people had towards the Jews in the Roman Empire.

2

Alexandria, the Cradle of Anti-Semitism

The chief priests of the Jews then said to Pilate: 'Do not write THE KING OF THE JEWS, but THIS MAN SAID, I AM KING OF THE JEWS'. Pilate answered: 'What I have written I have written'.

—John 19:21–22

AGRIPPA, 'THE WANDERING JEW'

In the second year of the reign of the emperor Gaius (nicknamed Caligula), 38 A.D., a few years after the crucifixion of Jesus, a Jewish king by the name of Agrippa arrived in Alexandria with a special guard and a certain pomp. He was the grandson of Herod the Great, who had always been hated by the Jews. The hostility of the Christian tradition towards Herod and his dynasty, which finds its expression in the probably legendary story of the Slaughter of the Innocents, derives in part from Jewish hostility. But with Agrippa (thus named in honour of a prominent friend and helper of the emperor Augustus) it was different: he had the blood of the royal dynasty of the Hasmonaeans, champions of Jewish nationalism and religion. In spite of his Roman upbringing, Agrippa soon showed himself to be a fervent devotee of the faith of Israel. Of Herod's successors he was perhaps the only one to win the support of at least a part of the Jews, and the Talmud speaks well of him.

It is thus not surprising that in the year 38, when he came from Rome and stopped in Alexandria on the way to his kingdom, Agrippa should have received a warm welcome from the Jewish community. Alexandria was the capital of Egypt—the 'granary of Rome'—and one of the largest and most famous cities in the world, with perhaps half a million inhabitants. A great cultural and commercial centre, its population was cosmopolitan and turbulent.

The Alexandrian Jews were a large and prosperous community and may have been the biggest urban Jewish settlement of the period, at least outside Palestine. Their proportion in the population of the city is not exactly known, but it cannot have been much less than that of New York today, where the Jews account for nearly one-fourth of the population (just under 2 million out of 8 million). Philo,[1] the eminent Jewish philosopher from Alexandria and our chief witness for the events narrated in this chapter, estimates the number of Jews in the whole of Egypt at around one million, which is probably an exaggeration.

It appears that the Alexandrian Jews were not full citizens but enjoyed a certain degree of autonomy. But if they lived in 'a city that was not theirs'—as the emperor Claudius was to remind them later in an edict addressed to the Alexandrians—the passage of Agrippa was for them an auspicious event: it meant that once again there was a king of Jewish 'blood' (although one-quarter only, as he was three-quarters Idumaean). Agrippa arrived quietly at night, but he was coming with the emperor's full favour —they had been companions from early youth—and escorted by a guard in splendid armour.

THE ALEXANDRIAN SATIRE OF 'THE BEGGAR KING'

It was perhaps natural that the Jews should make a fuss of him and identify themselves with his glory: since the fall of Jerusalem in 63 B.C. (exactly a century earlier) they had not had a national sovereign. It was also natural that the Alexandrian Greeks and Egyptians should have felt envious, because since the death of the famous Cleopatra in 30 B.C. they also had not had a monarch of Hellenic race and language in Alexandria. There was some hostility between the two groups, probably an old one, and anti-Jewish feeling and propaganda were then nothing new. In any case, Agrippa's arrival exacerbated matters.

Was he not the same wretched man who stayed in Alexandria like a beggar, borrowing money from the Jewish community there? Had he not lived as a dependent of his uncle Antipas the tetrarch? Had Caligula not released him from the prison in Rome where Tiberius had thrown him, to send him now bedecked with honours? In the ups and downs of his eventful life Agrippa already foreshadowed the Wandering Jew.

So it was that the Alexandrians circulated all kinds of jokes and satires at the expense of the new sovereign and of his coreligionists. According to Philo they also resorted to a sort of parody of the popular theatrical farces or pantomimes. There was in the city a poor, harmless feebleminded man by the name of Carabas, who was the butt of the jests and practical jokes of the idlers at the marketplace. A gang of anti-Semitic Alexandrians seized Carabas, placed him on a seat of honour near the gymnasium, and wrapped him up in a mat as if it were a royal cloak. Then they put a sheet of papyrus on his head, pretending it was a diadem, and thrust another piece of papyrus into his hand to serve as a sceptre. As an escort the boys, armed with sticks, like the children in Bizet's *Carmen* playing at soldiers, formed a royal guard around him. Finally, to complete the parody, the crowd surrounded Carabas like courtiers, pretending to flatter him, presenting petitions to him, and respectfully greeting him as *Marin* ('Lord' in Aramaic).[2]

It was a piece of clowning typical of the Greek Kronia or of the Roman Saturnalia—the festival that later became the European carnival. In Rome the cry of '*Io Saturnalia*' was the signal for the temporary removal of class barriers and the reversal of social status: the slaves gained a temporary freedom, the beggar became 'king for a day'. A *princeps Saturnalicius* was elected (a carnival king like the 'Lord of Misrule' in Elizabethan England). Masquerades of this kind were performed for a long time in Christian Europe, even in churches and with priests taking part.

But there was a much closer and immensely more significant and tragic parallel: there too the triumphal entry of a 'king' had been followed by a cruel jest. Perhaps some Alexandrian Greek or Egyptian knew—the affair had not then caused any significant repercussions outside Palestine—that not many years earlier a certain Yeshu or Jesus of Nazareth had been arrested and crucified in Jerusalem as a dangerous agitator. He too had been greeted by some of his people as the awaited Messiah, the King of the Jews. And Pilate's soldiers had subjected him to the same Saturnalian masquerade that was now being repeated in Alexandria: they had dressed him in a purple cloak, and placed a crown of thorns on his head and a reed in his hand to serve as a sceptre. 'And kneeling before him they mocked him, saying, "Hail, King of the Jews!"' (Matt. 27:29; cf. Mark 15:18; in Luke 23:11 the mockery was done by Antipas and his soldiers).

It was very similar to the title of *Marin*, or Lord, by which the beggar Carabas was addressed. In fact, the soldiers' merciless masquerade was directed not only against Jesus but against the Jews, whom many of them despised. Josephus mentions similar incidents in which the Roman legionaries of the Jerusalem garrison made fun of the Jewish religion, particularly during the Passover.[3] Sneering at the religious faith of foreigners is typical of a low mental level. Centuries later, 'Christian' mobs were to show the same crassness and ignorance, by humiliating rabbis and desecrating synagogues, while the Nazis carried this sadism to new heights of refinement.

Pontius Pilate, who was perhaps as anti-Jewish as his colleagues of Alexandria, gave his official stamp to the sneer campaign by having the famous legend IESUS NAZARENUS REX JUDAEORUM nailed to the cross. According to John's Gospel it was written in the three languages spoken in Palestine—Greek, Aramaic, and Latin—so that it could be read by as many people as possible. And there is a tradition that the Jewish religious leaders complained to Pilate about the insulting inscription, to which he replied, 'What I have written I have written'.

This incident seems at least plausible. The priests would have understood the anti-Jewish intention of the inscription on the cross, which is now overlooked by most people simply because we are accustomed to regarding Jesus' crucifixion as a sacred drama, unrelated to the historical background of the period.

Christ on the cross was, therefore, not only a brutal warning against any rebellion but also an anti-Jewish 'tableau' on the part of the Romans. They were saying—somewhat like the citizens of Alexandria later—'There is your King, a beggar in rags from Galilee whom we have punished in the infamous manner befitting a slave'. The cross—*supplicium servilis*—was the usual deterrent for the runaway or rebel slave or for the provincial who rebelled against Rome. A century before, the Appian Way near Rome had been adorned with the crosses of the prisoners taken in Spartacus' rebellion, and something similar was to occur in 66–70 A.D. in Palestine during the great Jewish rebellion.

THE ALEXANDRIA POGROM

It is now time to return to the events in Alexandria. If the Roman soldiers' masquerade had a tragic ending, the Alexandrians' clowning with King Agrippa was not pure comedy. The new ruler hastened to continue his journey to Ituraea, the vacant tetrarchy Caligula had granted him. But this was not the end of the affair. The Roman governor, instead of maintaining a certain sense of fairness which was one of the qualities of the better Roman administrators, openly sided with the enemies of the Jews.

It is true that our only witness, Philo, was a Jew and thus liable to be biased. But when all allowances are made for this fact, the story he tells seems trustworthy and similar to what we know about other pogroms. Unfortunately, like most apologetic works, *Against Flaccus* has gaps and omissions. The most important one is that we are not told the alleged reasons or pretexts for the Alexandrians' outburst against the Jewish minority, since Agrippa's visit by itself was clearly not sufficient to account for it. Some historians suppose that the Jews attempted to use Agrippa's prestige to demand full rights of citizenship in Alexandria, which would surely have raised violent opposition.

Be that as it may, Philo says that the populace (most of them Egyptians) began to desecrate the synagogues, setting up images of Caligula there. Flaccus not only failed to control this violence but published an edict severely restricting the rights of the Jewish community. It is not quite clear how this was done, but the practical result was very serious.

The city was divided into five districts named by letters of Greek alphabet, and it seems that two of them—Beta and Delta—had a Jewish majority. It was then decided, with the governor's sanction, to concentrate all the Jews in an area of one of the districts—a curious foretaste of the ghetto system in medieval and modern Europe. The other district, from which the Jews were expelled, was looted by the crowd, who openly shared the booty in the marketplace.

The Jews, hemmed in in their new quarters, had to improvise dwellings on the beaches and even in cemeteries. The merchants had lost their stocks, and the community began to suffer hunger. Any Jews who dared to leave were stoned, beaten, or burnt to death and even nailed to the cross.

Meanwhile, Flaccus ordered the arrest of thirty-eight members of the 'Council of the Elders', which was responsible for governing the community, and had them publicly whipped in the theatre. Some were beaten to death. Not content with this, he staged a whole spectacle of Jews being whipped and tortured. Jewish women were captured by the populace and made to eat pork in front of the public; those who refused were also tortured, as in the episodes narrated in II Maccabees.

This is the first pogrom of which we have a detailed account (what happened in Palestine at the time of Antiochus Epiphanes was more in the nature of religious persecution). Just as the Books of the Maccabees served as the prototype for Christian martyrology, so Philo's pamphlet inspired the traditional belief that those who persecute the faithful always come to a 'bad end': the same theme was adopted by the Christian writer Lactantius in his *De mortibus persecutorum* (Deaths of the Persecutors). In fact, Flaccus did receive his punishment. Perhaps at King Agrippa's instigation, Caligula suspected that he was wooing the Alexandrians with the design of rebelling against Rome, and sent an envoy to dismiss and arrest the governor. Flaccus was exiled to the Greek island of Andros, where he was later executed.

PHILO'S MISSION TO ROME

Meanwhile calm had not been restored in Alexandria. The people not only continued setting up images of the emperor in the synagogues but also went as far as to burn some of them down. The Jews then decided to send a delegation to Caligula, whereupon their opponents promptly did likewise. This mission is known in some detail, for it was reported on by its leader, Philo himself, in another pamphlet—*Embassy to Gaius*. In the opposing delegation the most important figure was the Egyptian Apion, a fervid Alexandrian anti-Semite, to whom we shall return later (see Chapter 3).

Nothing has survived of his writings, and we possess, unfortunately, only the Jewish version of the events given by Philo and Josephus.

The two delegations appear to have reached Rome in the year 39. In order to understand clearly the matter in dispute, one must remember that the religion of Israel forbade (as it still forbids) and abominated not only the use of images in cult but the very depiction of creatures of any sort. Now, the Roman government did not force the Jews to worship the 'pagan' gods. But the empire had brought with it an innovation that must have shocked the more conservative adherents of the republic: the deification of the ruler, following the precedent set by Alexander the Great and several of his successors, who in their turn had imitated the pharaohs of Egypt and other Eastern monarchies. Thus, Caesar had been deified after his assassination, becoming posthumously known as Divus Julius. His heir, Octavian, the 'founder' of the empire, took the semi-religious title of Augustus (in Greek *sebastos* = 'the reverend', later much used in the Church). With his posthumous deification under the name of Divus Augustus, a divine genealogy was invented according to which his real father had been the god Apollo. Tiberius, Augustus' successor, did not take the cult seriously, but it encouraged the next emperor, Caligula, in his delusions of grandeur. The whole empire had to worship him as a god, erecting images in his honour, with special priests in charge of the cult.

In these conditions it is easy to understand how the turbulent Alexandrians, flatterers like so many people under such a regime, should have taken advantage of Caligula's madness to embarrass the hated Jews. As Philo says, their hatred was an old one.[4] They lost no time in loudly denouncing the Jews, accusing them of disloyalty and of refusing to pay due homage to the emperor.

The initial reception of the Jewish delegation in Rome was apparently favourable. Philo and his companions delivered a memorial to Caligula and followed the court to Puteoli (now Pozzuoli), the port on the Bay of Naples. Their main purpose was to persuade the emperor to protect their synagogues from desecration, and they were just discussing their chances of success when a messenger suddenly appeared, pale and haggard as in a Greek tragedy, with the appalling news: Caligula had ordered his own statue to be set up not in a synagogue but in the temple at Jerusalem! According to Philo, the suggestion had come from a group of anti-Semites from Judaea and Syria. Petronius, the imperial legate in Syria, was entrusted with the mission: he had orders to have a colossal golden image of Caligula made and to enthrone it solemnly in the Holy of Holies, where only the Jewish high priest could enter.

It was then that the terrified ambassadors had their audience with the emperor, about the rights of the Jewish community at Alexandria. Caligula, after much procrastination, received them in the rooms of a villa on the outskirts of Rome, where he had gone to receive the administrators' rendering of accounts.

The scene, which has more than a touch of comedy, is described vividly by Philo: it reminds one a little of Chaplin's *The Great Dictator*, or of *Alice through the Looking-Glass*. The Jews entered and greeted the emperor with a low bow. Caligula, showing his teeth in a sneering grin, received them with these words: 'So you are the enemies of the gods—the only people who refuse to recognize my divinity, and yet you worship a god whose name you dare not pronounce'.

Then, to the horror of the delegation, he pronounced the name 'Yahweh'. Philo says that at this point the Greeks from Alexandria, who were also present, began to show their satisfaction with insulting gestures. One of them accused the Jews of being the only people who refused to offer sacrifice on behalf of the emperor. The Jews protested, claiming that they had already made a sacrifice three times, and had been the first to do so on Caligula's accession to the throne.

The latter promptly retorted, 'Yes, you make a sacrifice *for* me, but not *to* me!'

Caligula then began running from one room to another, opening and closing doors, criticizing everything, and accompanied to and fro by the poor Jewish delegates. Suddenly he turned to them and shouted, 'Why don't you eat pork?'

The Jews replied that each people had its own customs: some dislike lamb.

In the end, after some further inconclusive discussion, Caligula dismissed them with the words: 'They're not so bad after all. They're just a poor, stupid people unable to believe in my divinity'.

THE JEWS' NON-VIOLENT RESISTANCE

What followed showed how firm and obstinate Jewish faith could be, just as the Christian martyrs would demonstrate later to the highest degree.

Petronius, the legate entrusted with Caligula's insane mission, ordered the statue from the Phoenician craftsmen of Sidon, and travelled to Tiberias, the capital of Galilee. As soon as the news spread, the Roman was besieged by pathetic processions. Crowds of Jews flocked to him from all parts of the country, filling the roads, all completely unarmed—men, women, and children dressed in the sackcloth of penitents with their heads covered with ashes. They came to beg Petronius not to obey the order. It is not known whether any of Christ's followers, still few in number at the time, took part in the demonstration. Then began a long, dramatic debate between the power of Caesar and the power of God, in which the

Jews seem to have effectively applied Gandhi's principles of non-violent resistance.

When Petronius asked them whether they were prepared to disobey the emperor and defy Rome, they replied, 'We do not want war, but we would rather be killed than infringe our Law'.

They then prostrated themselves and offered their necks to the Roman legionaries' swords. According to Philo, the debate went on for the traditional Biblical period of forty days. It was sowing time, but the fields were left empty: the peasants had abandoned them.

Petronius may not have been very imaginative, but he seems to have been a sensible and humane man. The decision he took, after some hesitation, shows the extent to which the Jews' faith had impressed him. He wrote to Caligula, pointing out the people's resistance to the order, the inevitable bloodshed it would cause, and the harm it was already producing. He announced his decision at a mass meeting of the Jews and exhorted them to disperse peacefully. The weather had been exceptionally dry and the expected rains had not yet arrived, but no sooner had Petronius finished speaking than the sky clouded over and the rain suddenly came down in sheets. The Jews regarded this as a sign of divine approval, and even the Roman legate, brought up to believe in 'auguries' and other signs, was deeply impressed.

In the meantime, however, King Agrippa [5] was in Rome meeting his old friend the emperor, who had just given him the tetrarchy of his uncle Antipas, who had been deposed and banished. It is said that Agrippa offered Caligula a banquet, and the emperor, in a flash of generosity—and, one may suspect, under the influence of the best Roman wine—made him the classic offer of rulers: 'Ask whatever you like of me'. Agrippa, instead of requesting some extra territory, begged him not to have the statue erected in the temple at Jerusalem.

Caligula, carried away by the atmosphere of the feast, promptly agreed. But this did not prevent him from being furious when shortly afterwards he received Petronius' letter containing the same request, and he even went as far as to order the legate's execution. Philo adds that he also changed his mind about the statue, but this is not confirmed by Josephus. In any case, it would not have made the least difference. The order to execute Petronius was accidentally delayed, and before this he and the Jews had received the great news: Caligula had been murdered by a group of Praetorian officers.

It seemed like another divine punishment for the persecutors of Judaism. Pontius Pilate had been dismissed by Tiberius, and Flaccus executed: now it was the turn of the impious emperor himself.

Meanwhile, Alexandria remained agitated for some time, and it is not known in detail how the conflict was settled. Caligula's successor, Claudius, was much more sensible, and he pacified the city, addressing edicts to the people of Alexandria. We know at least that the Jewish community recovered their security and freedom of worship.

But anti-Semitism remained latent, and during the following hundred years there would often be communal unrest. And one day the Alexandrian crowds would attack Jews no longer on behalf of Caesar but claiming to act in the name of a 'King of the Jews', Jesus Christ.

3

Judaism and Anti-Judaism in the Roman Empire

'There is a certain people scattered abroad and dispersed among the peoples in all the provinces of your kingdom; their laws are different from those of every other people, and they do not keep the king's laws, so that it is not for the king's profit to tolerate them'.

—Esther 3:8

THE FIRST DEFENCE AGAINST ANTI-SEMITISM

In the year 67 A.D., when the Roman forces under the command of Vespasian invaded Galilee to quell the Jewish rebellion, the rebels in the area were led by a Pharisee called Joseph bar Matthiah (Joseph the son of Matthias). After playing a rather ambiguous part in the struggle, this Joseph became what some might call nowadays a collaborationist: he surrendered to the Romans and ingratiated himself with Vespasian by prophesying, truthfully as it turned out, that he would become emperor. In Roman eyes this became associated with what they had heard vaguely about the Messiah—'the ruler who would come from the East'. Suetonius, the biographer of the Caesars, had this to say:

> An ancient superstition was current in the East, that out of Judaea would come the rulers of the world. This prediction, as it later proved, referred to two Roman Emperors, Vespasian and his son Titus.[1]

Naturally, no right-thinking Roman (and few orthodox Jews, for that matter) would entertain the idea that the real 'Rex Judaeorum' had been an obscure carpenter crucified in Jerusalem. Least of all the Pharisee Flavius Josephus (he adopted the family name of his imperial patron), a strong believer in the 'powers that be' who followed Vespasian and Titus till the final tragedy—the siege and capture of Jerusalem. He may not be an attractive character, but we owe to him not only an excellent account of the Jewish war but an invaluable (if biased) document about Jewish relations with the Graeco-Roman world.

The Wars of the Jews by Josephus must have appeared between the years 75 and 79, first in the language spoken by Jesus and his disciples—Aramaic—and later in a translation into Greek, which was the literary and international language of the empire. Later still Josephus wrote other important works, all in Greek: a short autobiography; The Antiquities of the Jews, a long account tracing the history of his people from early Biblical times until the war with the Romans; and finally a pamphlet in two parts which has come down to us under the title Against Apion.

The latter has a very special interest for our story, for it is one of the earliest works of propaganda we know and in fact the first specific document of the history of anti-Semitism. The great Alexandrian philosopher Philo also wrote an Apology of the Jews, but it has not been preserved in the collection of his works. As we have seen, he was a contemporary of Apion, the anti-Semitic writer who comes under special attack by Josephus. Again, Against Apion is also the prototype of a rather popular kind of Christian literature—apologetic works, such as Against Celsus by Origen and works by Justin Martyr, Tertullian, and St. Augustine himself, all of which were aimed at refuting and discrediting anti-Christian prejudices current at the time. Josephus says himself that he writes 'in order to reconcile other people' to the Jews, 'and to take away the causes of that hatred which unreasonable men bear to us'.[2]

When Josephus wrote Against Apion, in the reign of Domitian, the successor of Titus, the Jews had been for a long time a people widely scattered on what the Greeks and Romans called 'the inhabited earth', i.e., the part of the world they knew (just as 'the world' even nowadays very often means 'the Western world' for people in the West). For instance, in The Wars of the Jews, Josephus makes King Agrippa II (son of the Agrippa mentioned in the preceding chapter, who governed certain territories north of Palestine) say in his speech persuading the Jews against revolt:

> Again, the danger threatens not only ourselves here but also those who live in other cities; for there is not a region in the inhabited earth [Greek oikoumene] without its Jewish colony. All these, if you go to war, will be massacred by your opponents, and through the folly of a few men every city will run with Jewish blood.[3]

And that is exactly what happened in many Greek or Hellenized cities in the area. The parallel with the present situation, when Jewish minorities in Arab countries have suffered because of the conflict with Israel, is rather obvious. But let us detain ourselves over this interesting idea of oikoumene, which gave the Christian vocabulary the word 'ecumenical'. At the time of Josephus *oikoumene ge* (the inhabited earth), or simply the *oikoumene*, meant either the territories of the empire or, more broadly, all the known world. The expression had been used by Aristotle in the fourth century, but it was only later that its use became more generalized, expressing in fact the broader, more cosmopolitan outlook of the age.

With the conquests of Alexander the Great from 334 B.C. onwards there had begun the great process of the 'Hellenization' of the East. Then came the Romans, and their empire, as is well known, became the great vehicle of cultural standardization, unifying the peoples of the Mediterranean through Graeco-Roman languages and civilization—not forgetting the new Roman roads. All this would considerably help the spread of Christianity.

In 1943 the American Wendell Willkie proclaimed that we now live in 'one world'—McLuhan's global village. In a similar way, about the middle of the second century B.C., the Greek historian Polybius stressed in the first book of his *Histories* that the Mediterranean world—the *oikoumene* in its stricter sense—had become a single whole with a single historical destiny.[4]

THE JEWS OF THE DIASPORA

Now, as Josephus remarked, there were Jews all over that *oikoumene*. This was already known as the Diaspora (dispersion), another Greek term, which has been used since that time to translate the Hebrew *Golah* or *Galuth*. Very approximate (and to some extent conflicting) estimates made by historians seem to show that the Jews—including many Gentiles converted to Judaism—constituted quite a sizable element in the population of the empire. Pfeiffer's estimate is one of the most conservative:

> The numerical increase of the Jews during the last three centuries B.C. is due, in part, to the influx of proselytes. In the time of Nehemiah (444 B.C.) the total number of Jews was considerably less than one million (probably little more than half a million), while in the first century of our era the Jews of the Dispersion probably numbered about two millions, while those in Palestine are estimated to have been at least one million (Juster's figure of five millions is incredible).[5]

As I tried to show in Chapter 1, the question 'When did it all start?' may be answered with what we know of the classical world. Certainly 'anti-Semitism' did not begin in the nineteenth century when Wilhelm Marr coined the term in 1873. On the other hand, the concept would become too vague if we were to trace back its earliest manifestations to a very hazy past. A line must be drawn somewhere, and we can say with some confidence that the signs of a specific prejudice against the Jews only began to emerge when the Diaspora reached its full extent: and, equally important, when the classical world gained that cultural unity and cosmopolitan character which I have just mentioned, thereby throwing into relief the singularity of the Jewish minority. And it is significant that the first acute symptoms should have broken out in the most cosmopolitan city of the *oikoumene*, Alexandria: just as in the Vienna of Hitler's youth. From that time up to the present anti-Semitism has remained a phenomenon, as Arnold Rose has rightly called it, of city hatred.[6]

In the classical world the Jews found themselves in a culture which in spite of its great variety had certain common features and to which they (apart from religious proselytism) had contributed little. Outside their Law, Israel was an obscure people whose fame could not be compared to that of the Egyptians or Babylonians, let alone the Greeks. In the world at large the ephemeral glories of David's and Solomon's reigns had not at that time become a legend like those of the pharaohs or the Assyrian kings and queens. In his apology *Against Apion* Josephus takes great pains to explain the few appearances of his people in the works of the Greek classical authors, who set the standards of good taste among the educated classes of the empire. Homer, Herodotus, Euripides, Plato—what had they ever said about Israel?

In the empire the Jews found themselves in the midst of a busy city life, with its temples, gymnasia, public baths, religious festivals, processions, athletic competitions, and soon—with the spread of the more vulgar tastes of the Roman crowds—chariot races and gladiatorial fights.

Some Hellenized (or Romanized) Jews had shared to some extent in that kind of life. In Jerusalem itself, at the time of Antiochus Epiphanes, young Jews had scandalized the orthodox by taking exercise in the gymnasia, adopting Greek fashions, and even trying to hide circumcision through a kind of plastic surgery.[7] This trend was severely resisted; and one of the treatises of the Talmud, the 'Avoda Zara, lays down very detailed precepts to prevent Jews from sharing in the festivals and 'abominations' of the Gentiles and establishing a kind of *cordon sanitaire* or hedge for the orthodox.

In matters of religion the Graeco-Roman world had an entirely different outlook and usually favoured a free and tolerant interchange of gods and cults. The average Greek had always practised syncretism, combining and fusing together deities of various sources and giving them new attributes. Oriental cults were introduced in the West and vice versa. Athens, like other Greek states, welcomed gods and rituals of other countries, an example later followed (at times reluctantly) by Rome. If, for instance, the Greeks came across a Babylonian goddess called Mylitta, they would immediately identify her with one of their own and say, 'The Babylonians worship Aphrodite under the name of Mylitta'.[8]

This is not surprising since Aphrodite herself (later identified with the Roman Venus), a goddess of partly Oriental origin, was related to the Phoenician Astarte or Ashtoreth, whom King Solomon is said to have worshipped (I Kings 11:5). To an orthodox Jew, of course, the very idea of a goddess was a blasphemous absurdity, and later the cult of the Virgin Mary would be viewed in the same way. Judaism was a very masculine religion (it still is, in spite of reform).

THE PECULIAR RELIGION

So only one cult resisted the religious assimilation (we might almost say promiscuity or permissiveness) of the ancient world. To the average citizen of the empire this was a very strange and austere religion, without images or sacrifices (except in the temple of Jerusalem) and without gay festivals. Until the destruction of the temple in 70 A.D. many conjectures used to be made about the contents of its Holy of Holies. If it followed the normal practice, it should contain a statue of the Jewish god—the mysterious Yahweh: perhaps a super-Zeus like the famous statue of Zeus at Olympia or that of Jupiter Capitolinus in Rome, whose copy would be one day erected in Jerusalem to the scandal of all Israel. But the better informed knew that it was no such thing. The Jews, with surprising restraint, had never represented their deity, whose name could not even be pronounced and who was invoked simply as 'My Lord' (*Adonai*). A more curious Gentile could read the Greek translation of the Jewish scriptures, and the prohibition was there very clearly:

> You shall not make for yourself a graven image, or any likeness of anything that is in heaven above, or that is in earth beneath or that is in the water under the earth; you shall not bow down to them or serve them (Exod. 20:4–5).

And the Bible did not stop there. As we shall see later, the Jews are instructed to destroy the 'false idols' of other cults. When they did not have the power to do so, they took to mocking them, just as the Gentiles might return the mockery at any time of Jewish misfortune with the taunting question 'Where is your God?' (Ps. 42:3).

But what did the Jews really do in their worship? Wherever there is a minority that keeps itself apart, all sorts of fantastic stories are likely to be invented about it. For instance, some Greek authors like Apion of Alexandria himself, spread the story that when King Antiochus Epiphanes entered and desecrated the temple of Jerusalem, he found there a golden statue of the head of an ass. Even the Roman Tacitus, a serious historian, repeated the legend:

To establish his influence over this people for all time, Moses introduced new religious practices, quite opposed to those of all
other religions. The Jews regard as profane all that we hold sacred;
on the other hand, they permit all that we abhor. They dedicated,
in a shrine, a statue of that creature whose guidance enabled them
to put an end to their long and thirsty wanderings.[9]

This was an allusion to a curious legend that during the Exodus the Jews
had been guided to water by a herd of wild asses. The story of the golden
statue itself might well have been a distorted account of the Cherubim—
the winged celestial figures that stood as guardians in the temple. Nobody
really knows what they looked like.

We have already seen the kind of anti-Semitic satire that was current in
Alexandria. There is also later evidence for the legend of ass worship. In
the remains of an ancient Roman house, a series of graffiti was found which
the experts date to the third century A.D. One of them pictures a young
man facing an ass-headed figure nailed to a cross. The legend, in ungram-
matical Greek, says, 'Alexamenos worships his God'. Young Alexamenos
was perhaps a house slave, a follower of Christianity, and the author of the
graffito who wanted to mock his religion seems to be saying, 'Here's the
god you adore: it has the head of an ass and on top of that he died on the
cross!' In fact, as we shall see later, many people tended to confuse Judaism
with its 'heretical sect', Christianity. And we know that similar stories about
both Jews and Christians were current in the empire.

A little more serious, but even more absurd, was the accusation of can-
nibal rites, which, according to Josephus, Apion had got from other authors. It was said that the same King Antiochus found in the temple of
Jerusalem a Greek who was being fattened for human sacrifice. The Jews,
it was said,

. . . would capture a Greek traveller, fatten him for a year and
then kill him in a certain wood; they slew him according to their
rites, tasted of his entrails and at the same time swore an oath of
eternal enmity to the Greeks.[10]

This story may well have continued in Christian times with the myth
of the ritual slaughter of a child. Cecil Roth, with unconscious humour,
points out that human flesh was implicitly forbidden as 'impure' by Mosaic
law, and the Bible strictly prohibits the sacrifice of children practised by
the Phoenicians.

'THEY DO NOT WORSHIP OUR GODS'

That the singularity of Jewish religion was already the target of criticism
and resentment at the time of the Maccabees (second century B.C.) is clear

from certain books of the Bible, particularly Esther. Modern commentators regard this book as pure fiction, and it certainly has a flavour of the Arabian Nights, but every work of fiction reflects real social conditions and real mental attitudes. A famous passage in which Haman, the villain of the story, addresses the king of Persia is a kind of archetype of anti-Semitism, and in fact of every prejudice against minorities:

> 'There is a certain people scattered abroad and dispersed among the peoples in all the provinces of your kingdom; their laws are different from those of every other people, and they do not keep the king's laws, so that it is not for the king's profit to tolerate them' (Esther 3:8).

Here you have very clearly set out the irrational animal basis of the prejudice: the Jews are different from all the rest, so they must be suspect. Their peculiarity is emphasized in religious matters because religion pervaded the whole of life in an ancient city—perhaps as much as in medieval Europe. 'They do not worship the same gods' meant in fact being antisocial, not belonging; keeping themselves apart from all sacrifices, festivals, processions, and so on. It also meant a denial of city patriotism. Josephus gives a direct quotation from Apion, who had asked, 'If the Jews are citizens of Alexandria, why don't they worship the same gods as the Alexandrians?' [11]

One sees here the intimate connection between worship and citizenship, which in fact was almost universally accepted until the emergence of the first laicized Western states in the eighteenth century—the United States and the French republic. Even in a tolerant democracy like Athens, Socrates was charged with and executed for 'introducing new gods'. Jesus was condemned, among other things, for blasphemy against the national temple of Jerusalem, while St. Paul was brought to justice for 'attacking our people, our Law' and for 'bringing Greeks into the temple and polluting it' (Acts 21:28). The famous episode in which an Ephesian crowd chanted for two hours the slogan 'Great is Artemis of the Ephesians!' when faced with an attempt to introduce 'a new god' is an eloquent proof of the connection between local cults and city patriotism.

Just as in Roman times the Jews were accused of scorning the city gods, later on they would be charged with disrespect or worse for the Virgin Mary (whose cult came to have many local variants, identified with local patriotism) or some patron saint. In Catholic countries especially, *Vivas* to Our Lady or to the patron saint still echo 'Great is Artemis of the Ephesians!' in every local festival, and even in comparatively tolerant Brazil a popular eucharistic hymn states that 'the unbeliever is no true Brazilian' (*Quem não crê brasileiro não é*).

Judaism was so austere, so averse to images and external representations, that the Jews were inevitably accused of atheism, as in fact the Christians themselves were: the same charge, indeed, that has often been made against men and women of very lofty religious spirit, like Socrates, for instance. Tacitus does not make that mistake and says more correctly:

> The Jews conceive of one god only, and that with the mind alone: they regard as impious [*profanos*] those who make from perishable materials representations of gods in man's image; that supreme and eternal being is to them incapable of representation and without end. Therefore they set up no statues in their cities, still less in their temples.[12]

Here Tacitus achieves some understanding of the essence of Judaism, and seems to be saying the same as the great message of the Kena Upanishad: 'That alone is the eternal Brahman and not what people here adore' (I.5). But unless the story of the ass-headed statue really refers to the Cherubim, he seems to be contradicting himself: the more so as a little later he says that when Pompey entered the temple he found 'that the secret shrine contained nothing'.[13] On the other hand, Tacitus does not hide his contempt for the Jewish cult. What nonsense to say, he adds, that the Jews really worship a form of Liber (identified with Dionysos or Bacchus). The Bacchic cult is full of gaiety and colour while that of the Jews is 'preposterous and mean' (*sordidus*).

In other words, many people in the empire showed towards Judaism a distaste similar to that often voiced by Catholics against most forms of Protestant worship. It is a commonplace of Christian history that the Reformation, with its return to the Bible, became much more Jewish in character than either the Catholic or the Orthodox Church, and Luther (see Chapter 10) even hoped to convert the Jews at last.

But the complaints of the 'Gentiles' were not limited to religion. Let us hear Tacitus once more:

> They sit apart at meals, and they sleep apart, and although as a people [*gens*] they are particularly prone to lust [*libido*], they abstain from intercourse with foreign women; yet among themselves they consider nothing illicit.[14]

Here we have one of the earliest manifestations of the old complaint that Jews 'do not mix' (note also the silly statement about lust, which would be taken up and enlarged upon by Christians and later by Nazi mythology). It is quite clear that this segregation has always made them more vulnerable, more easily identifiable as a peculiar minority, and therefore more apt to serve as scapegoats whenever the occasion arose.

Think only of the enormous social importance of meals. If the Mosaic precepts are followed even with moderate strictness, that prevents any orthodox Jew from eating (on most occasions) with a non-Jew. Now, to share a meal, 'to break bread together,' to eat salt with a guest (the old

Arab custom) is a very old ritual of great emotional value, which among both Jews and Christians—and others—acquired a sacramental character. A teetotaller who refuses to drink with someone may be considered a spoilsport, and vegetarians are often regarded as joyless prigs. Even a man like Shakespeare, who can have had very little opportunity of observing Jewish customs, makes Shylock say: 'I will buy with you, sell with you, talk with you, walk with you, and so following: but I will not eat with you, drink with you, nor pray with you'.[15]

Very few Christians seem to realize, as I stressed in the Introduction, that Jesus never ate with Gentiles; he broke other taboos—like eating with the despised publicans and also with people attacked by skin diseases and therefore regarded as 'impure'—but there is no recorded instance of a meal with a Gentile. And he also recommended segregation from the Gentiles: 'Go nowhere among the Gentiles, and enter no town of the Samaritans'.[16]

More than that: the Gospels (like the Bible in general) provide good evidence for a strong and ingrained Jewish prejudice against the Gentiles, of which Jesus gives us only the more moderate part. The stereotype is all there, and the mockery and hatred are strong in several books of the Old Testament. On the other hand, in spite of the passage I have just quoted, Jesus, like all great masters, was a demolisher of prejudices, as is shown by his wonderful parable of the Good Samaritan. Perhaps it was not his fault that the word 'Pharisee' became 'a proverb and a byword'.

Nevertheless, contact with non-Jews, as we shall see, was to become a crucial question and the subject of burning disputes among the early Christians.

MOCKERY OF CIRCUMCISION

Even more crucial was the question 'to circumcise or not to circumcise', which to many people today would be more a matter for Dr. Spock than for the Acts of the Apostles. If Judaism is a very masculine religion, the Jew may be briefly defined as a circumcised man: and circumcision stands symbolically for restriction and discipline. Tacitus says significantly: 'They adopted circumcision as a mark of distinction from other peoples'.[17]

The statement may be absurd from the historical or anthropological point of view, but it is very revealing all the same for the psychology of prejudice—and of Judaism as well. 'You want to be different from everybody else' is still used as a criticism in all sorts of cases. In *Against Apion*, Josephus rightly replies that the Jews were far from being the only people who practised that custom. And he quotes a famous passage of Herodotus saying that the Egyptians were supposed to have taught circumcision to 'the Syrians of Palestine', the Ethiopians, and others.[18] But in the Roman

Empire the Jews were the only circumcised men who could normally be seen in many cities. And for them it had a tremendous religious significance: it was the mark on the flesh of the Covenant with their God. A Gentile was above everything uncircumcised and therefore outside the pale —a term of contempt.

As the Jews were a minority in the cities of the empire, even if they tried to take some share in certain customs, circumcision could well be a stumbling block. Greek men—and 'Greek' had become much more a cultural or linguistic category than a racial one—were used to exercising naked: gymnasia and public baths were important meeting places in many cities. The Jews, like other Eastern peoples, were averse to nudity, as one can see in strict prohibitions laid down by the Bible. And if a Jew frequented a gymnasium—in spite of criticism from the orthodox, who considered such establishments impious, as the Christians would later condemn both the theatre and the circus—he might be subject to ridicule from a people much given to jokes of a sexual nature. This is obvious from the satirical poetry of Horace, Martial, or Juvenal, in which the Jew is often called *curtus* (short or defective, gelded) or *verpus* (from *verpa* = penis, as in Greek *psolos* from *psole*).

'BARBAROUS SUPERSTITION'

Although such criticisms and mockery do not amount to a very malignant anti-Semitism, nevertheless the evidence for a strong prejudice among many Greeks and Romans is unmistakable. We know Apion's propaganda only through his opponent Josephus, but the opinions of the Roman authors may be read in their own works. Themselves a very proud and ethnocentric people, they had learned cultural snobbery from the Greeks and came to use the same Greek term *barbarus* for those who did not share their customs and culture: nonetheless, the Romans themselves, in the eyes of the Greeks, were also considered 'barbarians', at least initially. Here is how Tacitus describes the religious persecution and attempt at forced Hellenization carried out by Antiochus Epiphanes: 'King Antiochus endeavoured to abolish Jewish superstition and to introduce Greek civilization [*mores Graecorum*]'.[19]

It is like a European or an American in modern times talking about 'civilizing the African savages'. Cicero calls Judaism *barbara superstitio*, and Seneca is not much kinder. If cultured men like these had such attitudes, what could one expect of more ignorant and narrow-minded officials like the prefects or procurators of Judaea? Pontius Pilate, Felix, and Festus could not hide their contempt and boredom on being called upon to intervene in Jewish religious disputes. The image some intellectuals have of Pilate as 'a subtle sceptic'—just because John's Gospel attributes to him the cynical question 'What is truth?'—is a silly and false one. We know from Josephus that this man, a callous anti-Semite, could order the massacre of crowds of Jewish demonstrators in Jerusalem, and was finally dismissed by the emperor for cruelty and incompetence. Perhaps he was momentarily impressed by Jesus, but this is probably just one more sign of that tremendous magnetic force which could penetrate even the hardened skin of a Roman prefect.

On the other hand, one must try to be fair to the Roman rulers, with all their limitations. Their perplexity was the result of their own attitudes to religion. They found it difficult to believe that people could engage in interminable disputes about beliefs and persecute or kill on that account. To the average Roman of the ruling classes religion was a matter of habit and ritual, hardly ever of fervour or passion.

SOCIAL PREJUDICE: THE 'FOETOR JUDAICUS'

Besides, the attitude people have towards a certain group is powerfully influenced by the first individuals they meet. And the first Jews many Romans encountered were slaves, beggars, or street sellers in Rome. In a similar way American attitudes to Italians or Latin Americans have been strongly conditioned by seeing poor Puerto Rican, Mexican, or Italian immigrants in towns like New York: hence, derogatory names like 'greasers', 'wet-backs', and so on. The same happens in England, where racial prejudices are reinforced by the fact that most black residents are poor immigrants from the West Indies, descended from slaves. In all such cases the social prejudice is added to the racial one: the hostile reaction that comfortable and 'respectable' people usually have towards the underprivileged, the poor, the shabbily dressed.

Now, as we have seen, a large number of Jews had been brought to Italy as slaves. Although there is some evidence for an earlier community, most of the Roman Jews had been brought over by Pompey after the fall of Jerusalem in 63 B.C. Later, Julius Caesar liberated many of them, but the rebellion from 66 to 70 A.D. was to produce a further wave of Jewish slaves. For instance, in the Epistle to the Romans, written perhaps before 60 A.D., Paul mentions by name several Christians in the capital—both Jews and proselytes—who were slaves.[20]

Even the freedmen seem to have led a very precarious life. In the works of Martial and Juvenal the Jews of Rome appear as rather wretched, sordid figures.

To the Greeks as to the Romans, it was 'natural' to despise slaves and their like, to consider them as subhuman: according to Aristotle's teaching, the 'barbarian' was made by nature to be a slave. Even the princes of Judaea, the Hasmonaeans or the descendants of Herod—what would they come to Rome for? To beg favours and territories. That was one of the points of the Alexandrian mockery of King Agrippa. One feels that the contempt expressed by Tacitus and other upper-class Romans comes from the same source: he calls the Jews 'the most despicable of all slavish peoples' and 'a most vile nation' (*teterrima gens*). As to the emperor Marcus Aurelius—an exponent of Roman virtue and Stoic philosophy—it is said that when he went through Judaea and saw himself surrounded by a crowd of 'stinking and tumultuous Jews', he exclaimed that he would rather have the company of the barbarians his troops had just been fighting.[21]

Here there are two noteworthy features. The first is the importance of smells in the formation of prejudices. The *foetor judaicus* has a long history which stretches from Marcus Aurelius to Hitler and Streicher, with a long passage through medieval Europe.

It is possible that Greeks and Romans may have bathed more frequently than the Eastern peoples at the time, but one may be certain that a crowd of Romans, hustling in the amphitheatre or the circus, must have produced very unpleasant smells. In any case, dirt has usually been the bedfellow of poverty. Smells as a factor in prejudice are a good instance of what psychologists call 'selective perception'. They are more noticed in the target group because the finger is already pointed at it. Fundamentally, it is the same mental mechanism that has produced generalizations like 'All Jews are crooks' or 'All Jews are Communists'.

In a similar case, that of the Negroes, a research worker carried out experiments in which subjects were asked to identify the race of two coloured and two white individuals by smell alone, first after strenuous exercise and then after a shower bath. In all cases identification by smell proved impossible.[22]

The other interesting feature in the incident of Marcus Aurelius is the tendency to link the group which is prejudiced against with a strong negative adjective, such as 'dirty Jew' (or Yid), 'nigger trash', with the implication that there is something especially abominable in the particular vice or fault of that group. But here we touch not only on the concept of the stereotype but also on the fascinating question of the role of language in the formation of prejudices.

As we have seen (see Introduction and also Chapter 6), the word 'Jew' became itself a weapon of insult and aggression, with its later form 'Yid' (compare Russian *Zhid*) and other slang words (such as 'kike' or 'sheeny') frequently used by Jew-haters. In fact, the Anglo-Saxon peoples seem to have a special tendency to coin such popular terms of ethnic contempt— like 'dago', 'mex', 'greaser', 'nigger', 'frog', 'wop', 'wog' (loosely applied in

Britain but usually with reference to Arabs: English observers have re-marked on its psychological importance in whipping up hatred for the Egyptians in the Suez War of 1956), and a host of others. It is important to notice that, particularly in English, such terms, like 'obscene' words, have the force of powerful expletives: they are a very primitive (or de-generate) form of language and go back to animal aggression—like the hiss of a snake or the spitting of a cat.

In fact, as hatred and contempt become sharper, comparisons with ani-mals are often used (like 'dog', used by both Jew-haters and Jews, or the imagery used by the Nazis, as we shall see in Chapter 12). But the idea held by some Romans of the Jews as a 'slavish' or 'vile' people had its support in a myth of Egyptian or Graeco-Egyptian origin which Tacitus does not fail to quote. It was 'the expulsion of the impure'—which is like the Exodus story seen in a distorting mirror. A certain pharaoh had cleansed the country of all lepers and sufferers from 'impure' diseases, and these—the dregs of the nation—would have been the ancestors of the Jews. Josephus attributes this defamatory story to the famous Egyptian historian and priest Manetho.[23]

A PEOPLE APART

But unlike the Roman Jews, those of Alexandria and other Eastern cities outside Palestine were not beggars, nor were they scorned by their neighbours. On the contrary, many of them were very prosperous, and even Tacitus mentions their wealth, which might easily become a source of envy. On the other hand, the later type of Jewish merchant or money-lender had not appeared, and in the anti-Semitic attacks of the time there are no accusations of greed and love of money, which only emerge in the Middle Ages. And Josephus was able to say, trying to explain the com-parative obscurity of his people in earlier times: 'We do not inhabit a maritime land nor do we like trade with the contact with foreigners it entails'.[24]

That is probably the best comment that could be made of the deeply rooted idea that Jews and buying and selling are somehow inseparable. In Egypt, at least, about whose life in Roman times we have more intimate knowledge, the Jews seem to have been widely distributed in all sorts of occupations, which is a very different situation from what came to prevail later in the West.

But the above quotation by Josephus acknowledges one of the oldest complaints: 'We don't like contact with foreigners'. This leads us back to the tendency to segregation. It results initially from Jewish religious practices and strict customs and produces a hostile reaction of intolerance among the Gentiles. This in turn reinforces Jewish segregation as a defence mechanism, and so we have the classic vicious circle of mutual suspicion and hostility.

The Jews were proud of their Law and of their unique character, and so it was easy to accuse them of atheism and misanthropy, as did Apollonius Molon, Cicero's teacher and the author of a lost book called *Against the Jews*. Tacitus, although he knew better than to call them atheists, repeated the accusation of misanthropy and selfishness:

> The Jews are extremely loyal toward one another, and always ready to show compassion [*fides obstinata, misericordia in promptu*], but toward every other people they feel only hate and enmity [*hostile odium*].[25]

But one should remember that the Christians were also tarred with the same brush of 'atheism' and 'misanthropy', and Tacitus himself used about them the famous phrase 'hatred of the human race' (*odium humani generis*). Juvenal accuses the Jews of showing the way or a water fountain only to a compatriot, never to be Gentile. According to Josephus, Apion had invented the story that the Jews used to swear a strong oath never to show any good will towards Gentiles, 'especially towards Greeks'.[26] This seems to be linked to the legend of human sacrifice.

But if the Jews in the ancient world provoked such delusions of persecution, we have to admit that Jewish religious pride could be at times provocative. Robert Pfeiffer says with some justification:

> In a measure Gentile writers merely reciprocated Jewish contempt for heathenism. In the ancient world the Jews alone claimed that theirs was the only true religion and that eventually it would conquer the world. By setting themselves apart from all other nations as the chosen people of the only God in existence, and by ridiculing Gentile religions as a foolish worship of wooden and stone idols, as some Jews had done since the days of the Second Isaiah (Isa. 40–55) and Cyrus the Great, they invited pagan resentment both as a people and as a religious community.[27]

This is acceptable as long as one remembers that 'the Jews' is just a shorthand term for a wide variety of individuals that embraced, as it does now, all sorts of attitudes to Judaism and their Jewishness, ranging from devotion or bigotry to downright apostasy or even anti-Jewish hatred. What Isaac Deutscher calls 'the non-Jewish Jew' has always existed, just as has the non-English Englishman and so on. You have only to skim the Bible to feel the continuous tension and conflict, the strain, the zealot's anger against the erring Jews who 'whored after other gods' or married gentile women, who fell for the attraction of Canaanite, Syrian, or, later, Greek customs.

On the other hand, the Jewish claim to practise the only true religion, which would be inherited by both Christians and Muslims and then be turned against the Jews themselves, was entirely opposed, as we have seen, to the current attitudes of Greeks, Romans, and Eastern peoples generally. None of them would condemn the others for worshipping *dei falsi e bugiardi* (Dante's 'false and deceitful gods'). Certainly those who talked of Jewish (or Christian) 'atheism' did not realize that in many ways it was a higher level of religious experience. But most Jews or Christians could not recognize, in their intolerance, that there was something positive and valuable, and even deeper streams of mysticism, in 'pagan' cults. And they were almost entirely ignorant of the great Hindu and Buddhist traditions, where 'polytheistic' image worship has coexisted to this day with a very deep and original spiritual life and the revolutionary practices of Yoga.

For instance, if a Gentile picked up the Greek version of the Jewish Law, or Torah, he could read the proud and magnificent Chapter 7 of Deuteronomy:

> You shall make no marriages with them [the peoples of the land of Canaan]. . . . For they would turn away your sons from following me, to serve other gods. . . . But thus shall you deal with them: you shall break down their altars, and dash in pieces their pillars, and hew down their Asherim [sacred poles], and burn their graven images with fire. For you are a people holy to Yahweh your God; Yahweh your God has chosen you to be a people for his own possession, out of all the peoples that are on the face of the earth (Deut. 7:3-6; cf. Num. 25:6ff.).

Such passages were later invoked by the Christians to justify their destruction and vandalism of 'pagan' temples. As to the Jews, not having the power of an organized state, they could still hit at the idols with the weapon of their religious propaganda or weave mythical stories (also imitated later by the Christians) in black-and-white terms in which the devout Jews always triumph in the end over gentile villains who want to destroy them or to make them bow to false idols. The Book of Daniel and its additions, like the more belligerent Esther, were followed by the later and inferior Third Book of Maccabees.[28]

If many Romans despised the Jews as a 'vile people', the Jewish aversion for the *goyim* could be physical at times. Jewish education tended to produce a strong conditioned reaction to everything considered 'impure' or 'abominable'. A devout Jew could really feel nauseated by things like pork or idols and have all the symptoms of an allergic reaction. The intense religious feelings cultivated by Judaism were double-edged: they could lead to great spiritual depth and at the same time to fierce intolerance, *odium theologicum*, and acts of furious condemnation. On reading the Bible, one may be struck by the contrast between splendid passages of religious inspiration, which sound like the thunder at Mount Sinai, and outbursts of hatred and aversion. The Hebrew expression translated as 'his bowels were moved' is perhaps typical of some Jewish reactions of that time.

The Book of Esther gives us the fierce backlash to ancient anti-Semitism:

> So the Jews smote all their enemies with the sword, slaughtering and destroying them, and did as they pleased to those who hated them. In Susa the capital itself the Jews slew and destroyed five hundred men (9:5).

This is probably pure fiction, but in the rebellion of 66 A.D. and in others during Roman rule, certain Jewish communities did take revenge for the pogroms they suffered. And it is significant that the fictitious Esther episode should be celebrated in the joyful festival of Purim, in which the punishment of the anti-Semite Haman became a popular ritual—as in Brazil groups of children still 'hang the Judas' on the Saturday of Holy Week, or as in England they burn Guy Fawkes. Pfeiffer says about Esther: 'Nationalistic to the core, it extols utter devotion to one's kindred, even at the cost of one's life (4:16), and implacable, undying hatred for the enemy'.

It is interesting that he should stress exactly what Tacitus called *fides obstinata* to the in-group and *hostile odium* to the stranger. But he also adds:

> It is unfair to regard the book as evidence of the Jewish *odium generis humani* (hatred for the human race), for its ferocity is that of the battlefield, and it mirrors primarily the Jewish state of mind in the reign of Hyrcanus. Christians have written far too much in this viciously bellicose vein, to be the first to 'cast a stone' at Esther.[29]

On the other hand, it would be entirely absurd to imagine that there was only hostility between Jew and Gentile in many parts of the Roman world. The picture of anti-Semitism has to be tempered with that of friendly attraction and particularly with that of Jewish proselytism: and this is the theme of the next chapter.

4

Jewish Proselytism
and Assimilation

Aquila said to King Hadrian: 'I wish to get converted and to become an Israelite'. Hadrian answered: 'What, would you belong to this nation and become part of the vilest of peoples? . . . 'The smallest of them', replied Aquila, 'knows how the Lord (blessed be He!) created the world . . . And their Torah [Law] is the truth'. 'Learn then the Torah', said Hadrian, 'but do not get circumcised'.

—Shemoth Rabba, 30

THE ITALIAN 'JEWS' OF SAN NICANDRO

In 1944, when Nazi Germany was not very far from its final collapse, Jewish troops from Palestine attached to the British Eighth Army occupied a small village in Apulia, Italy, called San Nicandro. To their amazement they met there a group of semi-literate Italian peasants who claimed to be strict followers of Judaism. Their conversion had occurred in 1931, when Donato Manduzio, a man widely respected in the community as a faithhealer, began to read an Italian Bible. He concluded that he had been misled by both Catholic and Protestant preachers and that the true religion was that of the Old Testament. He began to follow Mosaic precepts to the letter, and one of the first things he did was to burn his household images of Christ, the Madonna, and the archangel Michael.

Thenceforward Manduzio considered himself a Jew and changed his name to Levi. He soon attracted followers and ruled his sect like a patriarch. As in similar religious movements in other areas, there must have been an element of social and economic protest in this, particularly when we remember the poverty of south Italy and Sicily. The Sabbatini, as they came to be called locally, were so cut off from the wider world that they thought the Biblical Hebrews were an extinct race. When contact was finally made, difficulties began to arise: much had happened to Judaism

47

after 'the Law and the Prophets', and the new prophet regarded new accretions, like the Talmud, with great suspicion. The rabbinical authorities in Rome, on their side, were more embarrassed than flattered by these ardent and demanding proselytes, but at last sent them a *mohel* to perform the required circumcision.

On meeting the Palestinian soldiers, 'Levi' and his followers heard some more thrilling news: many Jews had gone back to the 'land of Canaan' and it was possible to join them. Like Moses, the leader died before he could set foot in the Promised Land. His followers made the journey and were soon fighting with the Hagana for the independence of Israel, reliving what they had read in the Bible. But with the years the Sabbatini became somewhat frustrated and split into factions. They found most Israelis either irreligious or very lax in their practice of the Law, while on the other hand they were not accepted as Jews but only as *gerim* (proselytes). Nevertheless, they did stay in their adopted land.[1]

JUDAISM AS A MISSIONARY RELIGION

This is obviously a very exceptional case, of proselytism through the Bible alone, but it did produce a genuine, permanent conversion. Many people find it surprising that men or women educated in other religions should become 'Jews'. This is largely due, as we shall see later, to the ambiguity of the word 'Jew', which in fact has never been resolved and continues to be hotly debated, in Israel and elsewhere. Again, for historical reasons which will soon become clear, one does not see rabbis or devout Jews preaching Judaism in a militant way. And yet this was not always so.

Many Christians and Jews are not aware that Judaism was once a fervently missionary religion, and that the word 'proselyte' itself acquired its present meaning as a result of these efforts. As far as I know, the word *proselytos* is not found in Greek classical authors and seems to have come into use in order to translate the Biblical Hebrew word *ger* (plural *gerim*), which was applied in very early times to foreigners living among Jewish communities. Etymologically *proselytos* means one who 'comes to' (from outside) or joins, and it is often translated in the Latin Vulgate as *peregrinus*.[2]

When the Jews began to convert Gentiles to their religion, the word came to have something like its present meaning—both the Hebrew *ger* and its Greek translation *proselytos*. Nobody knows exactly when this happened, but it must have been during the Hellenistic period, when a growing number of Jews came to speak Greek as their ordinary language. The first Greek translation of the Bible, made in Alexandria during the rule of the Ptolemies (third century B.C.), may have had conversion of Gentiles to Judaism as one of its aims, thus pioneering the great linguistic effort of Christian' missionaries, which goes on even now. Every great international language is an instrument of proselytism, and also of syncretism—of fusion and cross-fertilization of different beliefs and cults.

Language can be a bridge or an obstacle. The Catholic Church lost much in the past by prohibiting or discouraging vernacular translations of the Bible. As to the great religions of the Far East, Hinduism and Buddhism, they only began to make converts in the West when their scriptures, in modern times, appeared in European languages.

In the case of Jewish proselytism, it is somewhat curious that Christians should tend to forget its importance when there is a very well-known saying by Jesus which bears witness to it: 'Woe to you, scribes and Pharisees, hypocrites! for you traverse sea and land to make a single proselyte . . .' (Matt. 23:15).

Now, to 'traverse sea and land' implies missionary journeys—precisely the kind of thing that became an accepted practice among Christians, beginning with St. Paul—himself a good Pharisee. It was also, one may add, what Buddhist monks had done earlier, carrying Buddha's message 'over sea and land', to China or Japan, many centuries before the great Jesuit missionaries like St. Francis Xavier.

There is yet another reason for regretting Christian ignorance of this matter: Christian proselytism, one of the most vigorous and 'aggressive' in history, was in fact an heir and a rival of Jewish proselytism. It was precisely among the proselytes and sympathizers of Judaism that the Christian faith began to spread more widely, getting away from its early narrow Galilean or Judaean environment. It is as if missionaries like St. Paul used the proselytes as a bridge to span the gap between the Jews and the gentile world. But the remarkable thing—which Paul and his co-workers could not foresee—is that the bridge, once used, had to disappear. The Christian sect passed over to the gentile world, as in a new Exodus, and broke entirely with orthodox Judaism. It is as if we were watching over the emergence of a new species.

CHURCH AND SYNAGOGUE AS RIVALS

But there is a plausible, if only partial, explanation of the Christian tendency to forget Jewish proselytism: it is the secular rivalry between the two religions, a factor that must not be forgotten in the development of Christian anti-Semitism. Legislation against Jewish proselytism was enacted very frequently after the triumph of Christianity. For instance, in Visigothic Spain, during the reign of Sisebut (612 A.D.), it became a capital offence for a Jew to circumcise a Christian,[3] and there are well-recorded instances of Christians, even among the clergy, who 'Judaized' more or less openly. Aquila, well known as one of the Greek translators of the Bible (second century A.D.), was an early example of this, because he first became a Christian convert and then a Jewish proselyte. Much later there was the case of Deacon Bodo, at the time of Emperor Louis the German, who became a circumcised Jew in 839, adopted the name of Eleazar, and fled to Muslim Spain.[4] Even in Italy the friar Corneglio de Montalcino was punished for apostasy to Judaism in the pontificate of Pope Julius III (1550–55). In Russia there was a Judaizing sect in the fifteenth century (see Chapter 10), and several English Puritans were accused of Judaism in the early seventeenth century, and some went as far as to cross over to Holland and join the Amsterdam synagogue.[5] So one can see that the Sabbatini of San Nicandro are not such an odd phenomenon as it might appear.

Even today, although Judaism (like the Christian churches) continues to lose many followers, it still gains converts. According to one estimate, some 3,000 Americans join Jewish communities every year, although the great majority of these conversions are through marriage.[6]

A special case was that of Christian slaves or servants in Jewish households. The Mosaic law regarding the Passover banned all foreign slaves and *gerim* from participation (Exod. 12:43–51) unless they were circumcised. We must not forget that the ancient family was strongly patriarchal, and in the Roman Empire the word *familia* meant the whole household, including slaves. So the Jewish practice of circumcising family slaves was quite natural, just as much later American or Brazilian plantation owners baptized their Negro slaves. This was in fact one of the sources of Jewish proselytism, and it went on for some time, in spite of frequent legislation enacted by Christian kings and the Church.

JEWISH PROSELYTES IN THE ROMAN EMPIRE

At one time there had also been 'forced conversion' ('those who are afraid of lions', as the Talmud puts it).[7] In the militant age of the Hasmonaean dynasty Hyrcanus I imposed circumcision on the Idumaeans in the south (who later gave Judaea the Herodian dynasty), and his successor, Aristobulus I (104–103 B.C.), did the same to many of the Ituraeans, who lived in Lebanon to the north.

The precarious character of such use of compulsion would be well demonstrated later by the Jews themselves when official Christianity tried at various times to bring them by force into the fold. When talking of Jewish proselytes, we naturally think mainly of those who were spontaneously attracted. To what extent was Jewish proselytism successful?

To take the Roman Empire first, it is obviously impossible to give any precise numbers or percentages, but proselytism was undeniably an important factor in the growth of the Jewish population (see Chapter 3). The contempt shown by Roman authors like Tacitus, together with certain passages of the New Testament, seems to indicate that a good number of proselytes were from the working classes, the same kind of humble people among whom Christianity would thrive. Tacitus says: 'The worst among other peoples, renouncing their ancestral religions, always kept sending tribute and contributions to Jerusalem, thereby increasing the wealth of the Jews'.[8]

This is an allusion to the contributions sent to the temple at Jerusalem, including the compulsory 'half shekel'. Certainly the proselytes, whether rich or poor, did send money there, just as foreign devotees of the Greek gods made donations to the various temples. In the first century B.C. a Roman governor of Asia Minor banned the sending of contributions to Jerusalem from his province, and defending him in a Roman court, the famous orator Cicero protested against such a drain of gold to promote a *barbara superstitio*. It was a little like the clamour that would arise later against the flow of money to the pope in Rome.

But even among the Romans themselves there is evidence that Judaism made converts among the upper classes. Juvenal, for instance, pokes fun at Roman families where the fathers begin by keeping the Sabbath and abstaining from pork, and the sons 'look down on Roman law' and end up by getting themselves circumcised.[9] Seneca goes even further and parodies Horace's famous phrase about the cultural triumph of Greece, saying that 'the vanquished [the Jews] gave laws to the victors' (*victi victoribus leges dederunt*).[10]

For people insensitive to religious values, like Juvenal, the popularity of Judaism was no more than a silly fashion, just as nowadays a smilar lack of understanding is often shown to the growing number of Western converts to forms of Hindu Yoga or Buddhism. In Roman times, just as now, the source of attraction was not only the exotic or 'esoteric' element; that could also be found in the popular mystery cults like those of Isis or Serapis. To many earnest seekers and cultured minds, Judaism offered something that 'pagan' cults lacked.

On the other hand, Jewish proselytism, like that of Christianity, was often helped by the conversion of women, who at times prove to be particularly sensitive to new influences. That Roman lady (see Chapter 5) who gave some Jews gold and jewels for the temple of Jerusalem may have been one of many, and Nero's wife, Poppaea, was strongly attracted to Judaism. At the time of the Jewish rebellion, according to Josephus,[11] most of the women of Damascus followed Judaism. Women had one obvious advantage: they did not have to undergo the painful and disturbing ritual of circumcision. To the average Roman such a custom would probably appear much more distasteful than to the average American of today. At one time it was estimated that 85 percent of babies born in maternity wards in America were being circumcised 'for hygienic reasons'.[12] But in the Roman Empire the ban on castration (practised especially by the priests of the Asiatic goddess Cybele) was at times extended to circumcision. In the repressive reign of Hadrian in the second century A.D. Jews were even forbidden to circumcise their own sons, which was a complete reversal of the consistent imperial policy of toleration towards Judaism and most other cults.

It does seem that circumcision was also a barrier to many who felt an attraction to Judaism strong enough to overcome other possible disadvantages—strict discipline, social ostracism, and so on. To be circumcised as a baby was one thing; to have it done as an adult, long before the days of anaesthesia, was quite a different matter. On the other hand, it was always possible to follow certain practices without going the whole hog.

'PARTIAL CONVERSION'

Josephus goes as far as to say: 'There is no Greek city or barbarian [non-Greek] people which has not adopted in some measure our practice of Sabbath rest, our fasts, our lighting of lamps or many of our food precepts'.[13]

There may be some exaggeration in this, and Josephus is speaking with the ethnocentric zeal of an apologist, but Roman sources (most of them hostile, as we have seen) confirm the wide diffusion of practices like the Sabbath rest and abstention from pork. Research carried out on the origin of the week has shown the great influence of the Jewish Sabbath in the growing acceptance in the empire of the 'Planetary Week'.[14] In Rome Saturday was exactly what its English name means—Saturn's Day (*dies Saturni*), usually considered a day of bad omen. In one of Horace's satires he tries to avoid a bore by pretending to be a Sabbath-keeper and asks: 'Do you want to insult the circumcised Jews?' (literally 'to fart at the shortened Jews', *curtis Judaeis oppedere*).[15]

As the only true Jewish converts were those who followed the whole of the Law, there had to be a distinction between them and semi-converts. It seems that the former were called 'proselytes of justice' (*gerim ha-Tzedeq*), while the others must be those described in the Acts of the Apostles as 'the God-fearing' (Greek *hoi phoboumenoi ton theon*), who in the synagogues would have occupied a position similar to that of the catechumens in the early Church. One gets the impression that there were a good number of them in some places.

These proselytes were a marginal group who obviously hesitated to take the final step of circumcision. They longed for salvation, and no doubt some of them at least had sought it among the many Oriental or other mystery cults of the time. It was a situation comparable to that of today in the West, where many dissatisfied souls, brought up in some Christian church, turn to Zen Buddhism, Theosophy, transcendental meditation, or the Hare Krishna cult.

EXPANSION OF JUDAISM IN ASIA

But there is good evidence for more substantial and complete conversions to Judaism. It is known, for instance, that some prominent rabbis were converted Jews. Josephus gives a detailed account of the conversion of the royal house of Adiabene, a small buffer state of the time which comprised part of ancient Assyria.

Among the Arab neighbours, whose language was similar, and who also practised circumcision, it is not surprising that Judaism should also have made progress, although some Arab tribes are reported by the Romans as being anti-Jewish.[16] When Muhammad began his conquest of the Arabian peninsula in about 630 A.D., he came across several tribes of Jews and Judaizing Arabs. In the south the king of the Hymiarites (Yemen) became converted to Judaism in the fifth century A.D., but his kingdom was conquered by the Ethiopians with local help from Christians.

As to Muhammad himself, there is no need to emphasize the influence that Judaism and Jewish traditions exerted on the development of Islam. In his first period, when the Prophet still hoped to attract the Arabian Jews, he adopted the fast of Yom Kippur and the prostration in the direction of Jerusalem (later changed to Mecca).[17] As Muhammad gave up hope in that direction, he became a fierce persecutor of Jewish tribes, and the massacre of the Banu Quraiza, who were slaughtered in a large ditch ready to serve as a grave, has an obvious resemblance to Nazi methods. But one should remember that this was after a war, and during long periods Muslim states were often more tolerant than Christian kingdoms. From the religious point of view Jews had more in common with Muslims than with Christians.

While Islam was making its remarkable conquests, a curious case of conversion occurred in the Tartar kingdom of the Khazars on the Volga. The story is told in a correspondence between the king of the Khazars and a prominent Jew of the tenth century, Hasdai ibn Shabrut, who was physician and adviser to the caliph of Cordoba, Abder-Rahman III. There are many doubts about the authenticity of these documents, but even if the story is largely mythical, it reveals something of the missionary zeal of the three 'Semitic' religions. The king relates to Hasdai that at the time of one of his predecessors, Bulan (eighth century), the Khazar court had received visits from a Christian monk and a Muslim *cadi*. They both tried to convert him, but Bulan 'in his wisdom' also invited representatives of Israel and held a debate, each trying to extol the merits of his own religion (it is well known that similar debates used to take place in medieval Europe between rabbis and Christian theologians). After some time the king turned to the representative of 'Edom' (the Christian monk) and asked, 'If you had to choose between the religions of Israel and Ismael [Islam], which would you prefer?' The monk chose Israel. The king then asked the Muslim, 'Would you rather choose the religion of Edom or that of Israel?' The *cadi* replied, 'I find the faith of Israel preferable to that of the Nazarenes'. In view of this, Bulan chose Israel too, asked for a number of rabbis to come and give instruction to his people, and submitted to circumcision. So Judaism won on a sort of 'second ballot', as the mediator between the Cross and the Crescent, a role that some Jews were actually destined to play.

The history of the Khazars is so obscure that it is not exactly known to what extent they accepted Judaism, whether the people as a whole embraced it or only the ruling classes.[18] The kingdom was destroyed by the Russians of Kiev in the tenth century, but there is evidence of the Khazars' survival in later periods and of their connections with the Jews. For instance, Cecil Roth points out the Mongoloid traits of many Russian Jews.

PROSELYTISM AND ANTI-JUDAISM

I think we have said enough to show, first, that Jewish proselytism has been an important factor in religious history and, secondly, that anti-Semitism in the Roman Empire was not so widespread as one might think by reading hostile authors like Tacitus or Apion. In fact, hostility to the Jews seems to have been greater in certain important Greek or semi-Greek cities of the East, like Alexandria, Antioch, or even Caesarea, built by Herod himself. In spite of proselytes and admirers, there was often antagonism between the Jewish and the Greek mentality, which probably went back to their earlier contact and to the violent conflicts of the Maccabaean period. Several authors have emphasized the conflicting outlooks of the two peoples in ancient times: the austere Jew with his religious fervour and strict obedience to the Law, and the Greek with his intellectual curiosity, his lighter and more volatile mind. There may be some truth in this, as long as we remember that in both peoples one would have found a wide variety of types and that there is no such thing as 'a typical Jew'.

But we have reason to believe that such tension or cultural antagonism between Jew and Greek (already reflected in the Acts of the Apostles) played an important role in the doctrinal disputes inside early Christianity. More than this: we may say that the Oriental Greeks—and Hellenized Egyptians, the first anti-Semites of history to produce a specific propaganda—are the connecting link, so to speak, between pre-Christian and Christian Jew-baiting. It is significant that the mobs of Alexandria went on carrying out pogroms after their conversion to Christianity, just as before they had killed Jews in the name of the gods and the emperor.

On the other hand, from the Jewish point of view it is clear that Christianity developed in ways which were increasingly distant from the Old Testament, and this the orthodox Jews could only attribute to gentile (Greek or Oriental) influence, which had introduced the cult of images and of the Virgin Mary, so foreign to Judaism.

There is also evidence for marked Jewish hostility to the Greeks at the time. This is clear from recorded acts of violence, the strong militant tone of the Maccabees and other writings, and the Talmudic precept: 'To teach Greek to a son is the same as to eat pork'.

WHAT IS A JEW?

To return to proselytism: apart from its intrinsic interest, it is a strong challenge to the whole concept of the 'Jew', whether put forward by anti-Semites or by the Jews themselves. Are the Italian Sabbatini Jews? Are the Black Jews of Harlem 'real' Jews?

What made Israel unique in history is the fact that it was at the same time a 'nation' and a religion (one could perhaps say the same of groups like the less influential Parsees). So in order to become converted to Judaism the proselyte had, so to speak, to get 'naturalized' as a Jew and enter a more or less segregated group within which he or she would still be, at least in the first generation, something like a foreign element (it also meant abandoning affiliation to 'gentile' groups and, in social and religious terms, being 'born anew'). The Christian sect also had this character in its early period, but soon it began to embrace Gentiles who were not proselytes. By dispensing with the need for circumcision (and also with Mosaic food precepts), Paul and those who thought like him cut the Gordian knot and resolved the ambiguity of Jewish proselytism. As Edmund Fleg says, he wiped out the distinction between the 'God-fearing' and the 'proselytes of justice'.

'There is neither Jew nor Greek, there is neither slave nor free, there is neither male nor female; for you are all one in Christ Jesus' (Gal. 3:28). It is the great and revolutionary message of Christian universalism, but like so much else in Christianity it lost its edge later, and its full social implications were never fully understood or put into practice.

It was therefore due to this ambiguity, this strong link between the religious and the ethnic element, that Judaism, although a missionary and fervent religion, did not have a success comparable to that of Buddhism or Islam, not to mention Christianity. Jewish proselytism was soon to be restricted and suppressed by Christian legislation, and also by the Jews' own fear of provoking their persecutors. Israel had to remain on the defensive, cultivating knowledge and an intense inner life from which several mystical trends would emerge.

PROSELYTISM AND RACIAL ASSIMILATION

But Jewish proselytism also had an anthropological importance which should not be forgotten, particularly in view of the now discredited racialist myths: it contributed to diversify a people which was already considerably mixed.

I do not have to repeat here that the claim to recognize Jews by their physical traits has been proved completely baseless. A number of both popular and more specialized works, including the excellent tracts of UNESCO, have now established that the features popularly attributed to Jews (especially by anti-Semites) are neither exclusively Jewish nor found in most of the Jewish population. It is clear that each Jewish community is racially more similar to the people of the country where it has lived (often for many centuries) than to other Jewish groups, and this has been confirmed by blood-group investigations.

Several of these communities lost contact altogether with each other, and when they met again it was as strangers, with all the accompanying feelings of alienation, prejudice, and mutual hostility. For instance, the Sephardim of Spain and Portugal, proud of their ancient prosperity and aristocratic tradition, tended to look down on the Ashkenazim from Eastern Europe (originally from German territories; hence the Yiddish dialect, which is essentially German) and called them *Tudescos*. Sometimes they would even deny that those poor, shabby immigrants (at least when they arrived) were real Israelites: they were said to descend from the Russian Khazars. This happened in England, in the United States, and in other countries, where the Ashkenazim were generally the later arrivals. Here again one sees in action the social, class prejudice (reinforced by racial differences) which we observed in Roman anti-Semitism. Speaking of France, Philippe Erlanger says:

> The great Sephardic families preferred to speak fifteenth-century Spanish amongst themselves, and deplored Yiddish. At the end of the nineteenth century the first marriages between Sephardis and

Ashkenazis created a greater sensation in Jewish society than did the Gramont-Rothschild match. Complete assimilation took time, and in 'mixed' homes children were ashamed of grandparents stained with 'teutonism' and referred only to their Sephardic blood.[19]

And here is what Bernard Weinryb says about the situation in America:

Socially, the Sephardim (and Sephardized Ashkenazim) had added to their usual pride (a consideration of themselves as a sort of Jewish aristocracy), the 'right' of first-comers and of wealth. They despised the poorer Ashkenazim and looked down upon the uncouth and uneducated small-town German Jews.[20]

He adds that the Ashkenazim 'who succeeded in amassing fortunes tried to achieve status by "Sephardization" ': a social process comparable to passing as white among Negroes, or to what has been somewhat pedantically called 'hypergamy', i.e., rising from the working class to the middle class through marriage.

Among the German Jews, who had dropped Yiddish, contempt for Jewish immigrants from Eastern Europe was also common: they tended to identify themselves with the supposedly 'higher' Western culture, and the assimilated ones shared German attitudes to Eastern European Jews. Similarly, a group of fair-skinned Jews from Baghdad who settled in Bombay considered themselves part of the white (British) rulers of India and looked down on the 'Bene Israel' (see below)—the dark-skinned local Jews —as a subject, lower people.[21]

As the latter example shows, the Sephardim and Ashkenazim are far from exhausting the bewildering variety of the Diaspora. Scattered all over the world today (although some have emigrated to Israel) are many communities which lived in isolation for a long time and represent the furthest outposts of Jewish migrations and also of Jewish proselytism. All or nearly all are very similar racially to the populations among whom they have lived, generally speak the local languages, and, apart from Judaism, also follow local customs.

The Falashas of Ethiopia who live north of Lake Tana were 'discovered' in 1790, just at the time when Jewish emancipation was making progress in the West. They are very dark, much like the Ethiopians, and before making contact with the main stream of Judaism knew nothing about post-Biblical literature and the Talmud. Their number is estimated at about 26,000.

The Yemenite Jews (south Arabia) who descend from converts made at the time of the Hymiarite kingdom (see above) closely resemble the Arabs. They lived through many centuries of oppression until the great majority (about 46,000) were transported by plane to Israel in 1949–50 in the so-called Operation Magic Carpet. As in the case of other non-European Jews, their adjustment to Israeli life has produced, as could be expected, all sorts of problems and social tensions.

On the other hand, the Jews of India seem never to have suffered any persecution. This country of great religious tolerance received them as well as the last remnants of Zoroastrianism from Persia, the Parsees (fleeing from Muslim persecution), who, because of their commercial prosperity and their practice of marrying only among themselves, have sometimes been called 'the Jews of India'. From a total of about 16,000 Indian Jews, the most interesting community is that of Bene Israel, who until recently were divided into two rigidly segregated castes—Whites (*Gora*) and Blacks (*Kala*). They claim to descend from members of the Ten Tribes of Israel. The less numerous Cochin Jews still maintain their division into three endogamous subgroups: the White Jews, the Black Jews, and the Meshuararim. The former consider themselves the only 'pure', genuine Jews and do not admit the 'Blacks' to their worship.[22]

One of the most remarkable cases is that of the Jews of China, who were 'discovered' by Father Ricci and other Jesuit missionaries in the sixteenth and seventeenth centuries. It appears that they had come from Persia towards the year 1000. In the eighteenth century they were concentrated in the city of Kai Feng Fu (central province of Honan), which at the time of their migration was the capital of the Chinese Empire. There was an imposing synagogue in the town, maintained and renovated by Chinese potentates. At that time the Jewish community was being completely assimilated, and by the nineteenth century the synagogue was in ruins. In the few pictures we have of them, these Chinese Jews show clear Mongoloid features. In modern times other Jewish groups, mostly of Sephardic origin, have settled in China.

This case shows that the Jews can be completely assimilated, and it is by no means the only one. There is the more recent example of Peru, where a colony of Alsatian Jews who settled there after 1870 'became entirely assimilated within half a century'.[23] I have also been informed of a few small communities in north Brazil which disappeared in the same way.

In the case of some groups like the Falashas and Yemenites, it is almost certain they descend from converts made in their respective areas. But the distinction between a 'Jew by blood' (an expression which is practically meaningless) and a 'Jew by conversion' is entirely academic, since we know that those of the main stream (whether Sephardim or Ashkenazim) must also contain a strong element of gentile proselytes.

Apart from the Italian Sabbatini, there are at least two other communities entirely made up of converts, both in North America.

One is the Black Jews of Harlem (New York) comprising various groups or congregations. Most of them claim to be descendants of the Ethiopian

Falashas, which is almost certainly a status-raising myth. A more likely hypothesis is that they descend from circumcised slaves of Sephardic Jews in the West Indies, but there is no proof for this. Howard Brotz, who has made a study of the Black Jews,[24] shows how they have used the Jewish affiliation in order to acquire a new collective identity (and dignity), thus trying to break away from their past as slaves.

Even before they appeared, there was a strong Judaizing tendency among the Negro slaves of America, immersed as they were in the Old Testament atmosphere and imagery. They found consolation and meaning in comparing their own oppression with that of the Hebrews in Egypt; and already in 1900 Negro preachers claimed that the former slaves were in fact 'the lost tribes of Israel' (see Chapter 9 for other versions of this myth).

From this point of view, Black Judaism has some similarity with the more recent Black Muslim movement: both seek a new collective identity and both reject Christianity as the religion of the white oppressors. On the other hand, the prevalence of anti-Semitism among American Negroes is well known.

The other group is that of Mexican Indians who live in Mexico City and Venta Prieta. Again, they claim to descend from Spanish Marranos (see Chapter 8) but ethnically are of Indian or mestizo type.

This fascinating gallery of communities scattered throughout the world is not only a collection of exotic curiosities. It reinforces the central themes of this chapter: on one side the proselytizing force of Judaism, and on the other the great racial diversity of the Jews and the tensions and prejudices it produces. What makes a Jew is not the mythical 'blood' of the racialists but the cohesive strength of cultural and religious tradition; and—we must not forget—anti-Semitism itself.

Even at a not very represenative assembly like the First Zionist Congress of 1897, a Jewish observer was surprised by the diversity of racial types, faces, and complexions.[25] It is easy to imagine what would happen if all those scattered communities were assembled: they would present such a kaleidoscope of racial types as one finds today in New York, London, or a Brazilian town like São Paulo. But it is just this 'ingathering of exiles' (what the Israelis call the *kibbutz galuyoth*) that has been taking place in Israel, like a new melting pot in miniature. And there again one finds the gulf and resulting tensions between European' and Oriental Jew. In short, as Schifra Strizower says, Jews 'show almost every physical variation that is to be found among human beings'.[26]

'THE JEWISH SOUL'

If the Jews have no racial unity and are not distinguishable by common physical features, many (and the anti-Semites particularly) tend to regard them as having certain common psychological traits. In fact, a large part of this national pseudo-psychology is as mythical as physical racialism and tends to fall into rigid stereotypes. Nevertheless, there is a genuine social psychology of the Jews, to which they themselves have contributed with some penetrating analyses. It is not my aim to go into this subject, which may be studied in detail in such books as Gordon Allport's *The Nature of Prejudice*. No group can be persecuted for centuries without developing certain defensive traits, but these, as Allport shows, are not specific and may be found in any persecuted minority. What may be special in the case of the Jews is their combination with very particular historic circumstances and with a special brand of ethnocentrism.

One such trait (found, of course, in varying degree) is what some psychologists have called the obsessive concern with Jewishness. The more a group is persecuted, the more clannish it tends to become. The more the Jews are labelled and discriminated against, the more Jewish they feel (naturally, some may have the opposite reaction of becoming 'renegades'). So in the end anti-Semitism and Jewish ethnocentrism agree in one thing: an idolatrous obsession with 'the Jew'. Bernard Lazare, an early Jewish student of the problem, was well aware of this fact when he remarked shrewdly that 'the anti-Semites do the work of philo-Semites':

> It is absurd to turn Israel into the centre of the world, the ferment of peoples, the subverter of all nations: but that is exactly what is done by both the friends and enemies of the Jews. They attach an excessive importance to them, which Jewish vanity, that wild and characteristic vanity [*cette vanité sauvage et characteristique*], has accepted willingly. But of this vanity we must be rid.[27]

If the Jews have become widely diversified physically, it is only to be expected that they should have also undergone the deepest changes in their way of life, outlook, and psychology. It is easy to contrast the subjects of Solomon's reign, the fierce guerrilla fighter of the Maccabaean period, the Pharisee or Galilean fisherman of the time of Jesus, the adventurous merchant of the Dark Ages in the West, the hated usurer of medieval Europe, the humble shopkeeper or artisan of some European ghetto two centuries ago, or the Israeli *sabra* working in his *kibbutz* or patrolling the desert. In fact, there probably have been more varied types of Jews than of most peoples, and the way they have reacted to their Jewishness is equally variable.

The very qualities many anti-Semites attribute to the Jews (always with a connotation of danger or malevolence) such as an ingrained talent for business, cunning, competitiveness, have nothing special about them: in fact, they appear in varying degrees in many immigrant groups. In the first century A.D., as we have seen, Josephus could say that his compatriots had no liking for trade.

Accusations of low cunning, dissimulation, treachery, and devilish tricks have been made against many other groups besides the Jews and often mutually, which is an obvious case of what the psychoanalysts have called 'projection'. As Gordon Allport says: 'The Egyptian Moslem so accuses the Christian Copts . . . the Turk points at the Armenians, and the Armenian at the Turks'.[28]

A Levantine proverb does not give pride of place to the Jews: 'It takes three Jews to cheat a Greek, three Greeks to cheat a Syrian, and three Syrians to cheat an Armenian'.

A. A. Roback, in his *Dictionary of International Slurs* (a mine of precious information for students of ethnic prejudices), also gives the more popular French variant: 'Trust a serpent before a Jew; trust a Jew before a Greek; but never trust an Armenian'.[29]

No doubt such sayings must have helped the Turks to perpetrate their Armenian massacres, which were in no way distinguishable from pogroms.

THE POWER OF THE NAME

Anti-Semites have made Jewishness into a kind of metaphysical (or demonological) entity.[30] There is, in fact, something very primitive in this, for a name has always had magic or power attached to it. When somebody says 'I am a Jew' or 'I am an American', he is attaching to himself something more than a mere label. It is almost like the tattoo marks of a tribe, or circumcision itself, which is the indelible mark on the flesh of being a Jew. The power of the collective name has its dangers but has also a protective value. If you have a collective identity you are something or somebody (a need which has already been noticed in the case of the American Negroes, who protect themselves against the idea of nonentity or inferiority by claiming to be Muslims or Jews: one of Muhammad Ali's favourite taunts is 'You are nothing!'). This is shown in a very revealing way in Genesis, in the story of the Tower of Babel: 'Let us make a name for ourselves, lest we be scattered abroad upon the face of the whole earth' (Gen. 11:4).

This is a very deep human fear, which operates on both the individual and the collective level. People feel lost if they have 'nothing to hang on to', no clear image of themselves as individuals or as a group. And yet the higher stages of human development, as I shall try to show in the last chapters, inevitably entail letting go these crutches, which are in fact obstacles to evolution. The 'self-annihilation' of higher religions and mysticism also involves going beyond any attachments to caste or nation.

Naturally, the fear of losing collective identity, which pervades the whole of the Old Testament, has been very deeply felt by many Jews, even when that identity meant suffering and persecution. On the other hand, the name is powerful in another way, for it is linked with aggression: it means 'pointing the finger' at somebody or at a whole group. In fact, both expressions are part of the powerful language of the Bible. Anti-Semitism, like any other form of prejudice, consists exactly in pointing the finger at and giving people a (bad) name. That is the meaning of the Hebrew *mashal*, usually translated as 'proverb' or 'example': 'And you shall become a horror, a proverb [*mashal*], and a byword, among all the peoples where the Lord will lead you away' (Deut. 28:37).

To 'become a proverb' means to be identified or labelled with a certain quality (usually bad) or with some degrading act: a Judas, a Messalina, a Quisling. Commenting on *mashal*, the Bible scholar Eissfeldt says: 'It is characteristic of human nature to be more ready to mock at a fellow man than to acknowledge him, and thus *to become a proverb* normally or invariably means to be an object of mockery'.[31]

Obviously, this can apply both to the collective and to the individual name, and the former is what social psychologists have called a 'stereotype'. To prejudiced people there are few individual distinctions, and one could almost say that only collective identity exists. Hence the tendency to say simply: 'Jew!' 'Negro!' 'Communist!' (or, as I have tried to show in a study of anti-feminine prejudice, 'Woman!'). For instance, in *The Merchant of Venice* Shylock is addressed as 'Jew' precisely in the more aggressive scenes. What is behind this is the assumption 'they are all alike', actually a favourite phrase of people who hold national, racial, or class prejudices. So the name itself becomes a condemnation, like that of Christian at the time of Roman persecutions or that of Communist in countries that conduct political witch-hunting. For instance, the apologist Athenagoras, writing in the second century B.C., pleaded with the emperors for religious toleration: 'In our case we [Christians] are hated for our name. . . . Names are not deserving of hatred: it is the unjust act that calls for penalty and punishment'.[32] Later, when Christianity became the official religion, no people were more persecuted for their name than the Jews.

But the individual name too has been very important, and in spite of the well-known anti-Semitic boast, 'I would know a Jew anywhere', the fact is that in most cases identification is made by the name or by other external signs.

At the time of Jesus there was nothing like what we now call a surname, except among male Roman citizens, who usually had three names (like Caius Julius Caesar). Some Jews had two names—the Jewish and the Greek or Roman one. A good example is St. Paul himself, who was called Saul like the first Jewish king but, being a Roman citizen, also had a good Roman name, Paulus. Under the empire, as in other countries and at different times, many Jews seem to have followed this practice, perhaps as a kind of protective camouflage (even Daniel and his three young companions had Babylonian names, in Daniel 1:7). If there were two, the Jewish name would be regarded as the sacred and secret one. In fact, we know that proselytes usually took the name of Abraham or Sarah after conversion: just as Muslim converts came to adopt Arabic names and Christians 'Christian names' (*nom de baptême* in French, as in most Romance languages, like Portuguese). This may be compared with the case of monks (whether Christian, Hindu, or Buddhist), who receive a new, sacred name on being ordained.

Later the Jews acquired a great variety of names, according to the countries where they came to live: Arabic, Portuguese or Spanish, German, Polish, and so on. At one time 'Portuguese' and 'Jew' were regarded as synonymous in Europe at large, a fact which, as we shall see later, distressed the Portuguese greatly. Even recently I had personal experience of this when visiting the Bevis Marks synagogue (see Introduction).

Camouflage was particularly frequent at the time of the Inquisition in the Spanish and Portuguese empires, when baptized Jews often continued to practise Judaism in secret and therefore had a Jewish name apart from the official Iberian name. For instance, Rabbi Isaac Aboab da Fonseca, who presided at the first synagogue in the New World (see Chapter 9), was also called Manuel Dias Soeiro, a good Portuguese name. Some, in fact, had more than two names, and in the seventeenth century the Spanish consul in Amsterdam wrote to the Spanish ambassador in The Hague saying:

> It is the custom of members of the nation [Jews] to take as many
> names as they please, either for the sake of deceit or in order not
> to bear that name so as to jeopardize their parents who are known
> by that name in Spain.[33]

Modern Jewish surnames, at least in Europe, often originated from places. In the Frankfurt ghetto, for instance, each *Judengasse* (Jewry or Jewish Street) had a particular sign, and that of the Red Shield (Rothschild) gave its name to one of the most famous Jewish families of modern times, while the sign of the Eagle (Adler) provided a very common surname.

In modern Israel, of course, the fashion has been to discard the German or Slav surnames in favour of genuine Hebrew ones, as if the Jews wanted to throw off the disguises or protective shells of centuries. It was also a gesture of a new national pride.

But meanwhile the old camouflage has gone on in the Diaspora, particularly in countries where anti-Semitism or prejudice against foreigners is in evidence. It is well known that often the British 'Lewis' was in fact Levi, and I have heard of a family called Simulovitch who changed their name to Smith. As to America, a study made in Los Angeles about petitions for change of name revealed that 46 percent of the petitioners were Jews.[34] This is not surprising when social discrimination against Jews still occurs in both the United States and Canada. A Canadian research student sent letters in duplicate to one hundred hotels asking for a room reservation: one of the letters was signed 'Mr. Greenberg' and the other 'Mr. Lockwood'. While 'Lockwood' got 95 percent replies and 93 percent reservations, 'Greenberg' had only 52 percent replies and 36 percent offering him accommodation.

Obviously, if it were really possible to recognize Jews by their physical characteristics, such camouflage by change of name would not be effective.[35] In fact, in a country like Brazil (where anti-Semitism is very mild) the Jews, most of them Ashkenazim, stand out a little more because a good number have fair skins, while in the United States or Britain types like these blend more easily with the general population, unless, of course, they bear obviously Hebrew names (Cohen, Levi, Israel, etc.) or certain German surnames (Rosenberg, Finkelstein) which are already identified as Jewish. On the other hand, in countries like Britain or Holland the Sephardim may still be identified by their Portuguese names, like Henriques, Mesquita, or Costa.

But perhaps the best proof of the fallacy of the boast 'I'd know a Jew anywhere' is this: the most virulent anti-Semites, like those responsible for the strict medieval legislation or the Nazis in modern times, had to label and mark down the Jew. Whether it was the Jewish badge or hat, the segregation in the ghetto, the name *Jude* stamped on the passport or scribbled on shops, or even—the most dreadful of them all—the Star of David branded on the forehead: all this had the aim, apart from its inherent hatred, of permitting easy and immediate identification.

This is a significant and symbolic fact: the anti-Semite needs the Jew psychologically, as a separate, labelled entity. He has greatly contributed to maintaining the collective identity of Israel.

5

The Roots of
Christian Anti-Semitism

'They had certain points of dispute with him about their own superstition and about one Jesus, who was dead, but whom Paul asserted to
be alive'.

—Acts 25:19

WHO WAS CHRESTUS?

There is a famous passage of Suetonius' biography of the emperor Claudius
(in the *Lives of the Caesars*) which says: 'As the Jews at Rome caused continuous disturbances at the instigation of Chrestus, he [Claudius] expelled
them from the City'.[1]

As we shall see later, Claudius was particularly tolerant towards the Jews,
and there may not have been a true expulsion. The historian Dio Cassius,
who is a little more trustworthy than gossip writer Suetonius, only speaks
about a ban on public meetings. In any case, during the following reign of
Nero the Jews were still in Rome in appreciable numbers.

But the passage gives rise to other questions, which have been hotly debated. What were those disturbances? Who was this mysterious Chrestus?
Most scholars think that the name is nothing but a corruption of 'Christus'
and that here we have one of the very few and precious historical sources
about early Christianity outside the New Testament. It is perfectly understandable that Suetonius, writing some seventy years after the event (the
alleged expulsion would perhaps have taken place in 53 A.D., that is, about
twenty years after the crucifixion of Jesus), may have made a mistake
about an exotic religion which did not interest him. From his point of
view, those were tedious disputes 'about their own superstition', as Festus
(one of Pilate's successors) would say when he had to intervene in the
charges made against Paul by the priestly oligarchy of Jerusalem (but it
should be noted that *superstitio* in Latin, like the Greek word used in the

65

original, did not necessarily have a derogatory meaning and the New English Bible prefers to translate it as 'religion').

There is in fact a plausible explanation of Suetonius' mistake, which has been put forward by some scholars.[2] To a Greek-speaking person of the time (whether Greek, Roman, or any other) the name 'Christos' applied to a man would have sounded odd if not slightly ridiculous. Its principal meaning was medical: it meant an ointment for the skin, or, as a chemist would put it, 'for external use only'. When we talk today about 'anointing', we immediately think of sacraments or coronations, while to an ancient Greek or educated Roman 'Christos' would not mean so much 'the Anointed' as 'the ointment' or perhaps 'the smeared one'. So it was natural that ill-informed people should change it to 'Chrestos' ('good' or 'honest' in Greek), which might have sounded more likely as the title of a religious leader. Distortions and misunderstandings of this kind are the rule rather than the exception in reporting other people's religious beliefs.

So if a Roman asked a Jew what the trouble was about, the answer might well have been, 'Oh, it's all because of the Christ [Messiah]'. It would have been easy to think that the person in question was actually in Rome at that moment.

'THE NAZARENE HERESY'

Whatever the explanation, there is little doubt that Suetonius is giving us the Roman version of the type of disturbance between orthodox Jews and early Christians about which we read so much in the Acts of the Apostles. At the time the Romans could not make a clear distinction between the two groups for the simple reason that there had not yet been a final break, a schism. The Christians, originally called *Nazoraioi* (perhaps the same as 'Nazarenes'), were no more than a Jewish sect, like the Pharisees or Essenes. In a passage of the Acts Paul is called 'leader of the Nazarene heresy'.[3] Incidentally, it is interesting that in the same passage his accuser the high priest Hanan (Ananias) should charge the apostle, in the presence of the Roman prefect Felix and King Agrippa II, with being 'a fomenter of discord among the Jews all over the earth' (*oikoumene*). Now, this must have happened around the year 57 A.D. and so a few years after the supposed expulsion of the Roman Jews by Claudius because of 'agitation' of the same kind.

In translating 'leader of the Nazarene heresy' I was deliberately literal (and therefore wrong), for the Greek word *hairesis* was then very far from having the meaning (and emotional charge) it came to acquire in the Christian Church. It comes from the verb *haireō* (to choose), which certainly suggests the famous definition by Bossuet (a French anti-Semite, by the way): 'The heretic is a man with an opinion'. Both the Sadducees and

Pharisees are called 'heresies' in the Acts, while Josephus uses the same designation for the Essenes. Obviously, none of these was 'heretical' in the later sense, for the simple reason that Judaism at the time of Jesus had not yet crystallized into a firm doctrine or theology. On the other hand, there is no doubt that very soon Jews of various persuasions came to look upon the followers of Jesus (and particularly Paul's converts) as a *pernicious* heresy. As Judaism became more unified, the 'Nazarenes' ended up by being considered as abominable as the Samaritans, whom Jesus himself had forbidden his disciples to approach (at least, if we follow the Synoptic tradition rather than that of John's Gospel). They came to be called *Minim*, a term broadly corresponding to heretics in Talmudic literature.[4]

At the time of Claudius, however, the final break had not yet occurred, and therefore modern English translators tend to render the passage in question as 'the ringleader of the sect of the Nazarenes'. And that is exactly what the Christians were then: a Jewish sect which was gradually (from the orthodox viewpoint) becoming a heresy. This point, long ignored or forgotten before the emergence of a more objective religious history, is absolutely essential to a just understanding of the relations between the Church and the synagogue and of their mutual hostility.

No great religious movement in history has ever arisen with the express purpose of 'founding a new religion': the phrase itself is entirely modern and foreign to the outlook of people at the time of Christ (or of Buddha, for that matter). The first Christians were Jews who hoped to convert their coreligionists to the 'Good News' that the expected Messiah had already come and inaugurated a new revolutionary era of faith and love. The preaching of the message among the Gentiles and the opening of doors to them without imposing all the burdens of the Jewish Law may have been implicit in Jesus Christ's revolution, but were certainly not foreseen by his immediate disciples and shocked them a great deal. The famous phrase of the Bible scholar Wellhausen, 'Jesus was a Jew, not a Christian', may also be shocking to many and certainly is only a half-truth, for it ignores the universal aspect of the Christ: but at least it has the merit of reminding us that Jesus' preaching was exclusively among Jews and his contact with Gentiles was purely fortuitous.

JEWISH INTOLERANCE?

How did the Jews receive the 'Good News'? Jesus and later the Hellenized Jew Stephen accused the ruling classes of intolerance: they had persecuted or killed several prophets, who were known for the courage and bluntness with which they condemned the oppression of the poor: 'O Jerusalem, Jerusalem, the city that murders the prophets and stones the messengers sent to her' (Matt. 23:37).

Jesus mentions the case of Zechariah, who was stoned, but there were others.[5] In fact, the Mosaic law had harsh penalties against 'false prophets', and these may well have been invoked against Jesus:

> If a prophet arises among you, or a dreamer of dreams, and gives you a sign or a wonder, and the sign or wonder which he tells you comes to pass, and if he says, 'Let us go after other gods', which you have not known, 'and let us serve them', you shall not listen to the words of that prophet or to that dreamer of dreams. . . . But that prophet or that dreamer of dreams shall be put to death . . . (Deut. 13:1–3, 5).

Naturally, the charge or label of 'false prophet' (like that of 'heretic' later or that of 'Communist' or 'subversive' nowadays) could be very convenient to eliminate any awkward preacher who denounced abuses or oppressions. In some cases, it is true, suppression came from an unpopular ruler like Antipas the tetrarch (considered a foreign usurper by the Jews), who had John the Baptist beheaded because he was a dangerous agitator.

So when Cecil Roth, the late professor of Jewish studies at Oxford, claims for Judaism a long tradition of religious tolerance, we must consider this a nationalistic apology rather than sound historical judgement. It cannot be said that the Jews were a model of tolerance in antiquity, especially when the priestly class was powerful. If the modern state of Israel is exemplary in that respect—as I believe it is—one should remember that it was founded by people immersed in the liberal tradition and who had seen a great deal of persecution.

Even if we leave aside the killing of several prophets, there is enough evidence of intolerance in the Old Testament and other sources. The struggle against image worship, in which priests of the Phoenician cult of Baal were killed, the punishment of Jews who married foreign women at the time of Ezra and Nehemiah, the imposition of Judaism on foreign peoples like the Idumaeans, and finally the persecution of the early Christians—in all this it is fair to say that Judaism pointed the way to Christian intolerance, which was certainly more systematic and implacable.

The practice of Church excommunication, for instance, has clear roots in the synagogue. Jewish authorities came to distinguish a temporary exclusion (*niddah*) from the final one, called *herem* (compare Arabic *harem*, meaning the exclusion of women's quarters). *Herem* was translated as *anathema* (Greek and later also Latin), and *anathema sit* (let him be anathematized) became a set formula for the condemnation of heretics and heretical doctrines by the Church. The idea of anathema (like that of abomination) is typical of Biblical Judaism and has some connection with the primitive concept of taboo: *herem* is a thing or living object set apart, dedicated to Yahweh as a sacrifice and thus devoted to destruction.[6] As to Jewish excommunication, there are well-known instances of it in comparatively modern times, as in the case of the famous Jewish philosopher Spinoza, of Portuguese origin, who was expelled from the synagogue of Amsterdam and had to leave the town.

Here we have another great irony of Jewish history. Judaism had two spiritual daughters, both aggressive and militant like their mother, who both turned against her: Christianity and Islam.

'THE JEWS KILLED CHRIST'

At this stage something should perhaps be said about the trial of Jesus, for that would be the great libel thrown at the whole Jewish people throughout the centuries: THE JEWS KILLED CHRIST. And remember that Christ being God in Christian eyes, the Jews were considered guilty of the awful crime of deicide. That became indeed a licence to kill and persecute, an ironical denial of the whole way of life preached and practised by Jesus.

Much too much has been written on the trial of Jesus, and often from a narrow legalistic point of view which is hardly enlightening. In 1965 the Vatican Council for the first time in the history of the Church denied Jewish collective guilt, saying:

> The Jewish authorities and those who sided with them pressed for the death of Christ [cf. John 19:6]; still, what happened in His passion cannot be attributed without distinction to all Jews then alive, nor can it be attributed to the Jews of today. Certainly, the Church is the new people of God; nevertheless, the Jews are not to be presented as rejected or accursed by God, as if this followed from Holy Scripture.[7]

Better late than never, but such a timid and lukewarm statement (Jesus was never lukewarm), obviously the fruit of much discussion and compromise, is hardly to the credit of the Church. It is a little ludicrous that one should have solemnly to declare something that is obvious even to the most superficial examination. (A recent declaration by the Vatican, issued at the opening of the Holy Year in January 1975, condemns anti-Semitism more explicitly, but has been considered unsatisfactory by official representatives of Judaism.) Independent historical research, whether carried out by Christians, Jews, or agnostics (and, one may add, the more generous spirit of many Christian clergymen), had already gone far beyond this. It would be presumptuous to claim that we can understand in all detail the great drama that took place in Jerusalem nearly two thousand years ago. But there are certain facts that stand out clearly and give us insight into the kind of motivation that led to the condemnation of Jesus.

One of the important factors was the gulf or antagonism that existed in

Palestine between the common people and the priestly oligarchy, usually identified with the sect of the Sadducees, who normally controlled the ruling council, or Sanhedrin, at Jerusalem and the temple. The members of this ruling class tended to despise the lower classes and called them *Ham ha-eretz* (people of the country), and such hostility is clear from several passages in the New Testament.[8]

As has often been stated, an important element of the Jewish prophetic tradition was the social and moral protest against the oppression of the poor. Both John the Baptist and Jesus were right in the line of that tradition, and it would be hard to find in Isaiah or Amos such burning and penetrating denunciations of the rich and their greed as in the Gospels.

When Jesus made his entry into Jerusalem, he was received by a great popular demonstration. During the Jewish Passover the city was a boiling cauldron of agitation, very alarming for the ruling priests and their ally the Roman prefect (it was normal practice in the Roman Empire, as among modern imperialist powers, to give support to the ruling classes or the rich in general, in order to prevent any 'subversion'). When Jesus expelled the merchants from the temple and uttered some words which were repeated or distorted as amounting to blasphemy, this was seized upon as an open threat to the national religion and its authorities. As shown recently by S. G. F. Brandon in his book *The Trial of Jesus of Nazareth*, the temple of Jerusalem was also, in fact (like the great cathedrals and abbeys of the Middle Ages), an economic institution, the power base of the priestly oligarchy. On the other hand, he goes entirely astray when he practically equates Jesus and his disciples with the 'urban guerrillas' of today, and thinks they tried 'to occupy the Temple' in a bold coup. Such fantasy, like the popular Marxist interpretation that would see in the crucifixion of Jesus just another episode of social protest or class struggle, completely ignores the religious dimension of the event. Personally, I would rather follow those who believe that the (very important) element of social conflict was closely interconnected with a religious revolution.

Brandon, like others who have written on the subject (including the Jewish scholar Paul Winter), holds essentially a) that the movement led by Jesus was a social and political Messianism and therefore a direct threat to Roman rule, and b) that Jesus was arrested, condemned, and crucified by the Romans as a political rebel. Thus the Jews of that time are completely exonerated from any 'responsibility'.

Such a view goes entirely against the account in the so-called Synoptic Gospels (Matthew, Mark, and Luke), usually considered as more reliable than that of John's Gospel. In fact, the picture given in the first three Gospels makes perfect sense and on the whole agrees with what we know from Jewish sources. It seems clear that those responsible for the condemnation of Jesus were the leaders of the priestly oligarchy, belonging to the sect of the Sadducees (the role of their rivals the Pharisees is a more debatable point and maybe they were divided). Representing the interests of the upper classes and the rigidly orthodox point of view, the chief priests hated and feared Jesus as a revolutionary leader who was stirring the people with his dangerous Messianism and as a blasphemer who had attacked the temple, symbol of the national religion and of priestly power.

But there was more to it than that: Jesus represented a dynamic religious force, beyond rituals and temples, and the priests could only feel panic when faced with power that threatened to destroy them: just as the later Christian Church would react against its own prophets and mystics. There is, therefore, a deep truth in the phrase of the Gospels that Jesus was killed 'because of envy'.

In short, the essence of the trial from the legal point of view was that Jesus, after being condemned by the Sanhedrin as a 'false prophet' or 'blasphemer', was surrendered to the 'secular arm' represented by Pontius Pilate to receive the normal punishment meted out to the seditious or to rebel slaves: in fact, much the same practice as would later be followed by the Church in cases of heresy, except that the stake would replace the cross.

Again, although the Gospels may have idealized or distorted the behaviour of the Roman prefect, there is little reason to doubt the picture of a reluctant Pilate who did not want to get involved in 'points of dispute about their own superstition': for such would be the attitude of his successors when the same priestly caste demanded the condemnation of Paul, a good Pharisee who had 'gone astray' and followed the heretical Nazarenes.

If it is true to say that the Athenians killed Socrates, it would not be correct to state that the Jews (even if we specify 'the Jews of Jerusalem') killed Jesus. The difference is obvious: Socrates was condemned (although by a small majority) by a democratic popular court, while Jesus was condemned and executed by a small group of priests and elders, with the support (however reluctant) of a foreign governor and troops. Perhaps the best proof that his enemies were a minority, and also of his popularity among the crowds congregated in Jerusalem (which always included thousands of Diaspora Jews), is that the ruling council took the precaution to arrest him in a solitary place and late at night, the time always preferred by tyrannical regimes and the secret police.

Another interesting indication of the gulf between the ruling priesthood and the common people in Judaea was that in the great Jewish rebellion against the Romans in 66–70 A.D., admittedly an act of political suicide, most of the leadership was provided by popular guerrillas and other 'outsiders' (including Simon bar Giora, which means 'Simon the son of a proselyte'). Meanwhile, many of the ruling priesthood either remained passive or (like Josephus) took a lukewarm or doubtful part in the struggle.

In conclusion, in order to reject the absurd libel that the Jews killed Christ, there is no need to distort the facts and to try and shift the whole or most of the blame to the Roman authorities.

THE 'ANTI-SEMITIC GOSPEL'?

We can now try to understand how an act of intolerance on the part of a group of priests (in Roman eyes a trivial occurrence that would hardly have deserved a mention had newspapers then circulated in Rome) began to be magnified and finally become a great burden of collective guilt from which were to suffer all those who called themselves Jews. And the first step in this direction can already be seen in the fourth Gospel.

When the Gospels came to be written, the Christian sect was in open conflict with Judaism. Nobody knows exactly when they were written: most scholars think they were composed between the time of the Jewish rebellion and the beginning of the next century. At any rate, everybody agrees that John's Gospel is the latest of the four. Few Bible scholars accept that it was really written by 'John the brother of James', that is, one of the Galilean fishermen who became the Master's closest disciple. Nowadays only Catholic commentators and a minority of Protestant students accept this traditional authorship.

But any reader who is not interested in the interminable disputes of the scholars may carry out a simple practical test which I would recommend: it is to read the account of the trial of Jesus (and other incidents) in all four Gospels and to compare them. Whatever his beliefs or lack of belief, he will notice an interesting difference: John's Gospel is the only one where the enemies of Jesus are collectively described as 'the Jews.' In none of the three Synoptics do we have this picture of 'the Jews' demanding en masse the death of Jesus. In Mark, Matthew, and Luke the 'plot' to arrest and condemn him to death is always presented as springing from a small group —'the main priests and elders', which fully justifies the expression I have used of priestly oligarchy. In fact, only the fourth Gospel includes 'the Pharisees' in this group. As to the famous chanting of the slogan 'Crucify him!' to put pressure on Pilate, like a modern political demonstration (assuming the detail to be genuine), it has always been easy to assemble a crowd or claque in any town to shout something.

What conclusions can be drawn from this significant difference? First of all, the different tone of John's narrative reflects a later situation from that of the earlier Gospels, in which the Jewish element was gradually becoming a minority in the Christian sect, and the 'parting of the ways' between Church and synagogue was almost complete. So it is quite natural that the author of the Gospel should have projected retrospectively (a very common distortion in historical accounts) the growing anti-Jewish feeling among

Christians. Could a Jew have written it? It is not impossible, for the Jewish anti-Semite is a well-known type. But one must admit that it is not very likely. The author of the fourth Gospel may have been a gentile proselyte or perhaps a strongly Hellenized Jew. In the view of some scholars he was a priest of Ephesus called John the Elder.

But whoever he was, one thing is clear: the fourth Gospel must have contributed to fix and crystallize in the Christian mind, through the centuries, this black-and-white picture of the Jews acting collectively as the enemies of Jesus, contrary to the Synoptic tradition, which makes the ruling priests responsible. This is now admitted even by Catholic students like Father Flannery,[9] although he thinks that John's 'anti-Semitism' 'is only apparent'. His argument that the author had no intention of attributing the condemnation to the whole Jewish people is not very convincing. But in any case the practical result is undeniable: successive generations of Christians read in the Gospels the collective guilt of the Jews (naturally, this only applies to a literate minority who could read and had access to the Bible, as the great majority only had the popular graphic account of the Passion, repeated in innumerable pictures and also through the mouth of often ignorant preachers). And obviously they were not aware of the difference between the Synoptic Gospels and John.

THE QUESTION OF CIRCUMCISION

Nevertheless, as is well known, the intolerance of the priestly leaders to the Nazarene sect did not end with the Crucifixion. Persecution continued intermittently, either directly or through the intervention of the Roman prefects or of King Agrippa (Chapter 2), who ordered the execution of the apostle James, brother of the supposed author of the Gospel. Some middle-class Pharisees, like Paul himself before 'the road to Damascus', were active in this persecution.

But here we come to an interesting distinction. It is clear from the account of the Acts that in the eyes of official Judaism the more dangerous and innovating group was that of the so-called Hellenists, that is, Greek-speaking Jews who tended to have a more open attitude toward Gentiles. The first great conflict in the history of the Church was the clash between them and the more orthodox followers (in the Jewish sense) of Jesus.

The issue, which we know from Paul's Epistle and Galatians in particular, was this: did salvation through Christ (the New Covenant or New Testament) supersede or make optional obedience to the Mosaic law (the Old Covenant)? And most important in practice: if Gentiles or those who were already 'God-fearing' (half-proselytes) were converted to Christ, should they follow the whole of the Jewish Law, or not? The more orthodox Nazarenes said yes: this was the main group of the apostles, led by

Jacob the brother of Jesus, who presided at the 'synagogue' of Nazarenes at Jerusalem and became its first 'supervisor' or bishop. The Hellenists said no, and soon they would find an outstanding leader in a religious genius of the time—Saul, or Paul.

For a time a compromise seems to have been reached, under which Christian converts simply had to follow certain basic food precepts which were probably very widespread among the sympathizers of Judaism: abstention from meat that had been offered to the idols, from blood, and from anything that had been strangled. Nevertheless, the more strict seem to have continued to insist on circumcision and other essential practices of the Law. It was a difficult question because there was no relevant pronouncement by Jesus Christ (it had not arisen in his time because his preaching had been exclusively among 'the lost sheep of Israel', as he himself put it). Paul then took a bold step: what really mattered, he proclaimed, was 'circumcision of the heart'. Those who are circumcised should not hide it through any operation; those who are not should also remain as they are. He talks angrily about a kind of 'thought police': 'false brethren secretly brought in, who slipped in to spy out our freedom which we have in Christ Jesus . . .' (Gal. 2:4).

Even so, he had to circumcise his young disciple Timotheus, actually the son of a 'mixed marriage' between a Greek (hence his Greek name, like that of Stephen) and a Jewess (Acts 16:1–3).

Almost as important as the question of circumcision was that of kosher food. The Nazarenes were making converts not only among Jewish proselytes but among Gentiles who knew little or nothing of the Law. It was in Antioch, in a sense the real cradle of Christianity, that the segregation barrier began to fall: and it was also there, significantly, that the Jewish sect of Nazarenes began to be called in Greek *Christianoi*, followers of the Christ (Acts 11:19–26). It is clear that Christian missionaries in that cosmopolitan place, where there were a good number of proselytes but also a great deal of anti-Jewish feeling, began to fraternize with Gentiles and to share meals with them: the common supper (*agape*) was an important ritual of early Christianity. Nevertheless, this was a flagrant violation of Mosaic law, and the conservative wing protested. In a famous passage of the Epistle to the Galatians Paul tells the story:

> But when Kephas [Peter] came to Antioch I opposed him face to face, because he stood condemned. For before certain men came from James [Jacob the brother of Jesus], he ate with the Gentiles; but when they came he drew back and separated himself, fearing the circumcision party. And with him the rest of the Jews acted insincerely, so that even Barnabas was carried away by their hypocrisy (Gal. 2:11–13).[10]

Here we can see the groping and hesitations on a vital crossroads of religious history. The details of the controversy are obscure and controversial: we only hear some of the echoes and the final result. It is clear that there was a serious clash between the innovating or 'liberal' wing (compare with liberal or Reform Judaism of modern times, which no longer demands circumcision from converts) led by St. Paul, and the conservative or orthodox congregation of Jerusalem led by James or Jacob the Just and perhaps Peter too, although for some time he seems to have hovered uneasily between the two.

Now, the leaders of official Judaism seem to have persecuted more consistently the group led by Paul. In the 'great persecution' mentioned in the Acts the Jerusalem apostles do not seem to have been molested, and some scholars assume that this persecution effectively separated the two currents: the conservative wing remained at Jerusalem, while the 'Hellenists' were scattered through Syria.[11] From this small Diaspora, later galvanized by Paul's burning zeal, would have sprung the more vigorous branches of the Church. It is an attractive reconstruction, but the history of these early times of Christianity is full of uncertainty. As Teilhard de Chardin has said, the beginnings of anything important are necessarily obscure.

CHRISTIANS AND EBIONITES

It is clear that if the conservative Jews had won the dispute, that is, had the Nazarenes continued to demand strict obedience to the Law from their gentile converts, there would not have been a new religion at all: the Nazarenes might well have ended up as an obscure Messianic sect, like the Dead Sea Essenes, whom we know from their now famous scrolls. But we know how irrelevant are all these 'ifs' of history.

As to the congregation at Jerusalem, it went on attending the temple and following all Jewish precepts. Their bishop James or Jacob was so widely respected for his devotion that he received the cognomen of 'the Just' (*Sadiq*). It was only much later, a few years before the great Jewish rebellion, that the high priest had him stoned. This act committed against an aged man shocked many orthodox Jews (including the Pharisee Josephus, who does not fail to mention it) and cost the high priest his post: the Romans may have wished to prove that only they had the power to put people to death.

What became of Jacob's and Peter's followers—the Nazarenes of Jerusalem? Even if we follow popular Christian tradition in accepting that some, like St. Peter, went elsewhere, there is evidence that the others remained and held to their position of conformity. Eusebius, in his history of the Church, gives the list of bishops of Jerusalem, and remarks that until Bar Kokhba's rebellion they were all 'circumcised Jews', but after that they were Gentiles. Christian writers claim that Bar Kokhba persecuted the Christians, who had to leave Jerusalem. And when Roman rule was reimposed in 135 A.D., there was a ban on the entrance of Jews into the city: so the new congregation was completely gentile..

By that time the Jewish element was becoming a minority. The predominant language of the Church was Greek, thus superseding Aramaic, and as the historian Delisle Burns put it so well: 'A different language is not merely another way of saying the same thing. It is a different form of thought, emotion, even experience as a whole'.[12]

From that time onwards Christianity would develop its own vocabulary (in Greek and Latin) and ways of expression, which were increasingly divergent from those of Judaism.

By the time we hear of Jewish Christians again, it is as a distinct sect which occupied a kind of intermediate ground between the two religions. These Ebionites, as they were called (from *evionim* = 'poor' in Hebrew), lived on the west bank of the Jordan, just where the Jerusalem Christians are said to have taken refuge on account of the Bar Kokhba rebellion. They followed the Jewish Law and kept the Sabbath, but also celebrated Sunday as the day of Christ's resurrection. Apparently there were certain divergences among them as to the person of Christ, but they did not accept Mary's virginity. Eusebius' account about the Ebionites is worth quoting:

> They held him [Jesus] to be a plain and ordinary man who had achieved righteousness by the progress of his character and had been born naturally from Mary and her husband. They insisted on the complete observation of the Law and did not think that they would be saved by faith in Christ alone and by a life in accordance with it . . . [Others] thought that the letters of the Apostle [Paul] ought to be wholly rejected and called him an apostate of the Law. They used only the Gospel according to the Hebrews and made little account of the rest.[13]

It is possible that the name *Evionim* (poor) indicates that they, like the Essenes and the Jerusalem congregation, were faithful to the rejection of private property advocated by Jesus and 'held all things in common'.

THE FINAL BREAK

Maybe some readers will think that we are getting away from the subject of anti-Semitism and becoming too involved with 'disputes about their own superstition'. But I believe that we cannot understand the relations between Jews and Christians, and therefore Christian anti-Judaism, without looking at the evolution of the Church from the Jewish (and Ebionite) point of view. Both groups might agree on one thing: there had been a two-stage apostasy, and the man responsible for this had been Paul, 'the apostate of the Law'. He had opened the door to the Gentiles without requiring from them obedience to the Law; and they in turn had introduced into the new religion all their 'abominations'—the 'deification' of Christ, the cult of the Virgin Mary harking back to the great 'pagan' goddesses, the setting up of images in churches, which was an open infringement of the Second Commandment, and so on.

Paul and the other missionaries had begun preaching in the synagogues, like Jesus himself. And the hope of converting the majority of Jews to the 'Good News' would persist for a long time; indeed, it would recur in new, more aggressive or impatient forms in the Middle Ages and down to the time of Luther and later. But gradually the gulf become wider between Church and synagogue. The last tenuous links—the Ebionites and other Judaizing sects—became extinct. The Jewish element which had followed the Pauline revolution was assimilated and Christianity, although powerfully influenced by Judaism, ceased very largely to be Jewish in language and even outlook.

Threatened by the popularity of the new religion, Judaism closed its ranks, expelling or persecuting suspect groups. The Jews established a final canon of the Bible (Old Testament), excluding certain books which were accepted by most Christians (the Apocrypha) and condemning the writings of the Nazarenes. Apparently the final break occurred when the Jewish patriarch Gamaliel II included an imprecation against the Christians in the Shemoneh Esreh (Eighteen Benedictions), an important prayer of the Jewish cult.[14] This may have taken place in the Synod of Jabneh before 100 A.D. Later the Roman Easter service would also include a harsh condemnation of the Jews, using such expressions as 'Judaica perfidia' (see note 7).

The situation was in fact quite similar to the great schisms and conflicts that later divided Christianity into irreconcilable sects. Jews and Christians 'excommunicated' each other just as in 1054 the Pope and the Patriarch of Constantinople exchanged bulls of excommunication and later Catholics and Protestants anathematized each other; and, one might add, this was carried on in this century with the ideological war between capitalism and Communism and the mutual condemnations between different brands of Communism.

Catholic writers like Father Flannery admit that the Christian literature from the second century onwards is markedly anti-Jewish: warnings and condemnations of 'Judaizing trends' in the Church are fairly frequent. At the same time, the Christians accused the Jews not only of hating and persecuting them but also of inciting the Roman authorities against them. According to some Fathers of the Church like Origen, they helped to spread defamatory stories against the Christian cult, making accusations of orgies and cannibalism (similar to those that had been current about Judaism). In some cases, it is quite possible that the more bigoted Jews did co-operate with the Roman authorities in putting Christians to death. For instance, when St. Polycarp was burned in 155 A.D. at Smyrna, the traditional account says that a group of Jews collected faggots for the stake 'as is their custom'.[15] Given the intolerance and hatred between the two religions, there is little reason to doubt the truth of such persecution, which later, when Christianity was raised to the status of the official religion would be carried out with even greater ruthlessness by those who called themselves Christians.

THE PERSECUTIONS OF THE CHRISTIANS

It would perhaps be a little naïve to hope that Christianity would have 'learned tolerance' through the savage persecution its followers were subject to in the heroic age of martyrdom. Tolerance requires a high level of mental awareness and spiritual insight, and these were rare in the Jewish-Christian tradition but could be found in countries like India as early as the age of the emperor Ashoka (see Postscript).

As we have already indicated, the Christians were the victims of prejudices, stereotypes, and defamatory stories very similar to those that were current about the Jews, and many upper-class Romans also despised them as part of the rabble and the slavish elements that came from the East. Nero accused the Christians of having set fire to Rome in 64 A.D., just as the Europeans in the Middle Ages would accuse the Jews of having caused the Black Death in 1348 by poisoning the wells. The more popular stories about the Christians were about 'Oedipodean intercourse and Thyestean banquets', that is, incest and cannibalism. Later, heretical sects like the Albigenses, or Cathari, would be accused of various sexual sins, and in the twelfth century the rabbi Benjamin of Tudela, in a travel book, mentions the orgies of the Druses.

Christian writers like Tertullian were well aware that the martyrs served as scapegoats for popular anxieties or frustration:

> If the Tiber reaches the walls, if the Nile does not rise to the fields, if the sky does not move or the earth does, if there is famine, if there is plague, there is the cry at once: 'The Christians to the lion!' [*Christiani ad leonem*]. What, all of them to one lion?' [16]

Some Christians must have read this when the Jews were serving as scapegoats centuries later. But if they ever recognized the similarity of situations, they never put the idea into writing.

Savage and prolonged as the persecutions of Christians were, they tended to be somewhat exaggerated later, and even today, after *Quo Vadis* and the Biblical spectacular films, our imagination is too much occupied with 'the Christians to the lion'. We must not forget that there was a considerable measure of tolerance in the Roman Empire, which the Jews enjoyed particularly. They were exempted from paying divine honours to the emperor and also from sacrificing to the gods. The edicts that Claudius issued to the Alexandrians are a good example of this. The emperor determines that the Jews 'should not be forced to infringe' the precepts of their religion, and condemns 'the great madness' of Gaius (Caligula), his predecessor, whom we saw in action in Chapter 2. Claudius appeals to the Jews and Greeks that they should live in peace at Alexandria, and to the Jews especially he warns that they must 'use my kindness to them with moderation, and not show contempt for the religious observances of other nations, but be content with keeping their own laws'.[17]

Within its limitations, this can be compared to great proclamations of religious tolerance by the Indian emperor Ashoka three centuries earlier; there must be mutual respect between the followers of different religions.

THE 'GHETTO' OF ANCIENT ROME

But the Jews (and Christians) in Rome were in a very special case. Just as Pilate did not want tumult in Jerusalem during the explosive period of the Jewish Passover, the emperors were nervous of anything that looked like 'agitation', particularly among the working classes and slaves. Here the element of class conflict is obvious, and the fears of the Roman ruling classes were not fantastic when one remembers the recurring slave rebellions in Sicily and the great rebellion of Spartacus (gladiators and slaves) in the first century B.C.: all punished by the cross, as would be the later rebellion of the Jews in their own country.

We have already seen (Chapter 3) the low status of most Jews in Rome. Many of them lived in the quarter then called Transtiberinus (now Trastevere, south of the Vatican), and in fact the satirist Martial uses the word *transtiberinus* as a synonym for Jew, just as in modern times a Londoner would identify Whitechapel or Golders Green with its Jewish community. Both Martial and Juvenal talk with contempt about their activities as pedlars and fortune-tellers, much as until recently people would make fun of the Jewish old-clothes man.

The poverty of these Jews is confirmed by the fact that they shared in the distribution of free corn (the classic *panem et circenses*) made traditionally to placate the urban proletariat. At the time of Augustus they enjoyed a privilege which again shows Roman tolerance: if the distribution fell on the Sabbath, their share could be collected later.

In the following reign of Tiberius (who was a contemporary of Jesus and removed Pilate) a Roman lady called Fulvia, who had become a Jewish proselyte, seems to have been the victim of a confidence trick by four Jews: they persuaded her to give gold and purple to the temple of Jerusalem and then were accused of keeping the donation for themselves. In view of this, Tiberius decided drastically to expel the Jews from Rome, a sad precedent for many such deportations in the Middle Ages and later. It is said that about four thousand were sent to Sardinia in order to serve in the army. But this expulsion must have been incomplete or temporary, for, as we have seen, Claudius would renew it—if in fact he did—because of tumultuous debates with the Christians.

These facts, like the spectacles of refined cruelty invented by Nero to punish the 'abominable' Christians, show that Roman tolerance was indeed very 'relative'. The more conservative had a strong prejudice against any exotic cults from the East, which they considered barbarous or disreputable, shocking to Roman *gravitas:* just as Eastern cults brought by immigrants would be considered now by some as 'un-American' or 'un-English'. And if Roman women were often attracted by this 'nonsense', so much the worse for them. Thus there would be a mutual reinforcement of ethnic, social, and anti-feminine prejudices.

THE CHRISTIAN AND THE JEW IN ROME

We can now understand a little better the mental attitudes behind the passage of Suetonius quoted in the beginning of this chapter. Like so much 'tolerance' of our times, that of the Roman Empire was conditioned by the acceptance of certain standards of conformity. The Christians, for instance, could practise their cult provided they also paid the customary homage to the Roman gods and to the emperor (for some reason, they were never officially granted the special privileges the Jews had). The empire was full of exotic cults, like those of Isis, Cybele, Mithras, and so on, but their followers did not see anything incongruous in also sacrificing to Jupiter Capitolinus (the imperial divinity *par excellence*) or to the emperor himself as *Divus,* that is, a deified man.

But the God of Christianity, like that of Judaism from which it had sprung, was 'a jealous God', who could not become just another addition to the almost inexhaustible pantheon of the time. And the obstinate refusal by the Christian to sacrifice to the gods could only be taken as a hostile, anti-social act.

Later, of course, Christianity would show a very special genius for absorbing and assimilating what was best (and also some lower levels) of the 'pagan' cults, and this could make it more attractive and colourful than the austere Jewish monotheism.

In short, Christianity began as a salvation religion for the oppressed, like slaves, freedmen, or artisans, but was by no means limited to them, and, like Judaism, offered an incomparably higher level of religious experience and way of life. In the faith of Christ the uprooted and 'outsiders' found a new fraternity, above citizenship and class. That faith, scorned by the ruling classes of Rome, would one day triumph. But victory would bring with it not only a growing 'paganization' which would be abhorrent to the Jews but also the corrupting influence of power and official status. Being a universalist and unifying creed, Christianity was even more exclusive than Judaism and carried within it the seed of intolerance. We shall see now how that seed bore fruit in the case of the Jews.

6

The Church Militant
and the Jews

The Lord will bring a nation against you from afar, from the end
of the earth, as swift as the eagle flies, a nation whose language you
do not understand, a nation of stern countenance, who shall not regard the person of the old or show favour to the young.

—Deut. 28:49–50

THE CHRISTIANS TURN PERSECUTORS

When Pontius Pilate began his administration of Judaea, one of his first
acts was to introduce secretly into Jerusalem the eagles or insignia of the
Roman legions. As images they infringed the Second Commandment, and
the Romans, with exemplary tact, had until then refrained from introducing them into the city. And even now Pilate was faced with such a storm
of protest that very reluctantly he gave way and the eagles had to be withdrawn again.

What would he have said if somebody had predicted to him that less
than three centuries later the proud Roman army would hoist in battle a
sign used by that rabble whose leader he had crucified? In that fateful year
of 312 A.D. the emperor Constantine, just before the decisive battle against
his rival Maxentius, gave orders for a Christian symbol to be placed on his
standard—the *labarum*. It was the monogram XP formed by the first two
letters of the Greek word XPICTOC (*Christos*):

This famous incident became linked with the story of Constantine's vision or dream, in which he had seen the symbol in the sky and heard the
word: 'Conquer in this sign'. If we contrast this with the earlier affair of
the eagles, we can understand its historical significance a little better. The
alliance between 'the powers of this world' and the persecuted Church, be-

82

tween God and Caesar, which would have been inconceivable in the age of the martyrs, now became reality. The Church Militant was being born and one day it would fasten the cross on the armour of the fierce Crusaders: in flagrant contrast with the first Christians, who were pacifists and very often refused service in the legions. And when the last emperor fell in the West, there would still remain a figure with growing power, invested with one of Caesar's traditional titles: the Bishop of Rome, Pope, or 'Pontifex Maximus'. Among other things, he would inherit an old imperial problem: that awkward minority, the Jews.

Like many great historical changes, this one was so gradual and entailed such changes of outlook that it was not really perceptible. The Christianization of the empire, and the corresponding 'Romanization' of the Church, took several generations. Constantine and his immediate successors continued to use the title of 'Pontifex Maximus', which since Julius Caesar had been an attribute of the supreme ruler. It was only in the reign of Gratian, about 375, that the emperor gave it up, thus allowing it to be transferred to the Bishop of Rome.

The growth in power of Christianity as an official religion coincided with the final development of the empire into a rigid military autocracy. Constantine, the first Christian emperor, was also first to use the diadem, symbol of Eastern royalty, and to be regularly addressed as *dominus* (Lord), things that would have been most shocking in the days when the emperor still pretended to be the head of a republic.

Official Christianity did not take long to begin persecution of other cults. Acts of vandalism against 'pagan' temples became frequent, and freedom of worship was increasingly restricted. The rule of Julian the Apostate (so called because after being baptized and brought up as a Christian he became a convert to the old 'pagan' cult) was a brief interlude of comparative tolerance (361–63). In one of his epistles he condemned religious persecution as clearly as the Buddhist emperor Ashoka had done six centuries earlier:

> Men should be taught and won over by reason, not by blows, insults and corporal punishments. I therefore most earnestly admonish the adherents of the true religion not to injure or insult the Galilaeans [Christians] in any way, either by physical attack or by reproaches. Those who are in the wrong in matters of supreme importance are objects of pity rather than of hate . . .[1]

In his policy of tolerance and as an attempt to hold the advancing tide of Christianity, the emperor tried a kind of ecumenical gambit and offered his protection to Judaism. He revoked all the restrictive measures of his predecessor (Constantine's son Constans), who had forbidden marriage between Jews and Christians and banned Jewish entry into Jerusalem. Not content with this, Julian wrote a letter to the Patriarch of Tiberias, then the head of the Jews in the West, addressing him as brother, and even gave orders for the rebuilding of the temple at Jerusalem. But all this was interrupted by his death on an expedition against the Persians.

His disappearance meant the return to repressive measures, not only against paganism but against the Jews. It was in vain that the Roman writer Symmachus addressed a petition to the emperor Valentinian II in 384 A.D. asking for toleration of all cults.

At that time the crowds had already started the popular pastime of burning synagogues. This was too much for the emperor, and he ordered the rebuilding of a Roman synagogue which had been burned down.

The act provoked the wrath of St. Ambrose, bishop of Milan, although he was in fact much more tolerant than church leaders of later centuries. For instance, he opposed the execution of the first heretics in the Roman Empire, which had been ordered by another bishop, and also denied communion to Theodosius because of his massacre of the citizens of Thessalonica. But with Jews it was different. In a violent epistle which has been included in the collection of his works, Ambrose disapproves of the destruction of synagogues but condemns much more vigorously their restoration. He even says that a Christian bishop would not hesitate to declare himself the accomplice of such destruction:

> Noble falsehood! I, myself, would willingly assume the guilt; I,
> I say, have set this synagogue in flames, at least in so far that
> I have urged on you all that there should be no place left in
> which Christ is denied.[2]

In view of the bishop's protest the emperor did not insist that his order be obeyed. But when Ambrose died, he issued a decree assuring the Jews complete freedom of worship and threatening with severe punishment all those who burned synagogues.

'THEODORE, BELIEVE IN CHRIST!'

Christian tradition relates a curious case which is said to have occurred on the island of Minorca. The local bishop, Severus, was concerned about the great number of Jews there, particularly in the island capital Magona (now Port Mahon). Encouraged by the arrival of the relics of St. Stephen, he began to provoke the Jews to public debates. The Jewish champion in these discussions was a rabbi of great renown called Theodore.

One Saturday the bishop issued a new challenge to the Jews and invited them to present their case in the church. The Jews excused themselves, saying that they could not enter an impure place during the Sabbath. The bishop decided then to head a march to the synagogue and set out followed by a procession of the faithful singing a psalm. It was said that the Jews had collected a great store of arms, like stones, clubs, and arrows, and the fight was provoked by some Jewish women throwing stones from the windows. This was the sign for a full-scale riot in which the Christians had the upper hand and broke into the synagogue, setting it on fire and destroying all its furniture except the scrolls of the Law and the silver.

Three days later the Jews collected again sadly among the ruins of their synagogue, and a Christian crowd soon appeared. Theodore, the rabbi, began to preach an eloquent sermon and answered all the objections from his hecklers. He was such a brilliant speaker that, as the bishop himself confesses, his opponents fell into utter confusion. The Christian crowd then resorted to the argument of the Ephesians when confronted with St. Paul and the other missionaries: they began to chant the slogan 'Theodore, believe in Christ!' This went on for so long that those Jews who were farthest from the rabbi mistook the phrase and thought it was a cry of triumph: 'Theodore believes in Christ!' The women tore their hair in desperation, and all fled, leaving the rabbi alone. Theodore had not the strength to resist the arguments of converted Jews who pointed out the advantages of baptism. So he yielded and his example was followed by most of his congregation.

CHRISTIAN ATTITUDES TOWARDS THE JEWS

It might be useful at this stage to try to consider how the Christians came to regard the Jews from the time the Church triumphed. Obviously, the anti-Jewish legislation, burnings of synagogues, and persecutions of the late Roman and Byzantine period were child's play in comparison with what was to come later, with the Crusades.

It was easy for a Christian to assume, say from the fifth century onwards, that the victory of his religion was something final and universal. To him the 'world' (the *oikoumene*) meant the empire, and even those who were better informed knew that even in the rival Persian Empire there were many Christians. The earth was conceived to be a flat disc, and it was natural to imagine that very soon Christianity would reach its utmost confines.

Hardly anybody had the slightest idea that there were other important religions, much older than Christianity, in the Far East. When the first Christian monasteries were founded, their inmates knew nothing of the great ascetic tradition and religious orders which existed in India and Buddhist countries. The Persian cult of Zoroaster was little known, and the old cults of the Roman Empire were in utter decline. This tremendous victory of Christianity over 'paganism' could only fill the Christians with supreme confidence. The powers of this world had done their best to eradicate the faith of Christ by force: it had resisted all persecutions and finally had converted its persecutors.

And yet, apart from the so-called heretical sects, there remained that obstinate minority who 'perversely' refused to believe in the Gospel. 'Theodore, believe in Christ!': the cry of the crowds at Magona was more aggressive than had been that of the Ephesians. The latter, after all, were only defending the goddess of their city against what they considered to be the invasion of a new, foreign cult: nobody was trying to impose the worship of Artemis on the whole world. Christianity, on the contrary, had necessarily to be ecumenical and could not tolerate rivals.

'Theodore, believe in Christ!' was, then, the challenge that the Christians issued to the Jews from that time onwards. Particularly during periods of greater militancy they found it difficult to accept the existence of that minority which just 'would not enter the fold'. Partly, it was the old tribal reaction against nonconformists which is still enormously strong nowadays. '*Everybody* believes in Christ, why shouldn't you? *Everybody* goes to church, why not you? Why do you want to be different from everybody else?' This primal reaction may be as strong among schoolboys as in any tribe. In fact, it was very similar to the behaviour of the 'pagans' when they constituted the dominant majority, and also of the Jews themselves towards their own rebels or apostates.

Besides, the Christians thought they could find justification for the use of force and violence not only in the Old Testament but in the Gospels. The allegorical interpretation of Biblical texts had begun with Jewish scholars (like Philo) and now was developed into a fine art in the Church. Although it was often used in very inspiring and illuminating ways by theologians and mystics, it was also carried to ludicrous excesses that would later be ridiculed by Erasmus of Rotterdam.

Now, Jesus says in Matthew that he had come to save 'the lost sheep of Israel' (15:24). And John's Gospel attributes to him these words: 'And I have other sheep that are not of this fold; I must bring them also, and they will heed my voice. So there shall be one flock, one shepherd' (10:16).

This 'one flock, one shepherd' contained the unifying impetus of Christianity which could not tolerate exceptions. Likewise, Paul's Epistle to the Ephesians proclaims 'one Lord, one faith, one baptism' (4:5), and this text, like that of St. John, would be widely used by the Church: as in the famous bull *Unam sanctam* by Boniface VIII, in which the 'the Holy Catholic and Apostolic Church' is compared to Noah's ark, outside which there is no salvation.[3]

Soon there would also be found justification for bringing the sheep into the fold by force. In the famous parable of the Messianic banquet in Luke, the host orders his servant to bring in any passersby saying: 'Compel people to come in' (*compelle entrare* [Luke 14:23]). This may be the letter rather than the sense of the parable, but many Christians invoked such a text in order to justify 'forced conversion', particularly of the Jews. They obviously had not heard the English proverb 'You can lead a horse to water but you cannot make it drink', which is a good comment on the whole history of forced baptism of the Jews.

But there was another factor besides the dislike of the dissenter. Aggressive reactions are often stronger between those who are closely related, and a good example of this is the *odium theologicum* of sects issuing from the same source, like the hatred between Jews and Samaritans, Catholics and Protestants, or Sunnites and Shiites in Islam. The Christians had, so to speak, cut the umbilical cord between their faith and Judaism. The divergence was now so great that many were led to forget the Christian debt to Judaism or to remember only the element of conflict between the two faiths.

Anti-Jewish feeling had begun inside the synagogues in the fierce debates about the Christ and was to continue in the sermons and diatribes of the Church apologists. We have already seen that Christian literature was strongly anti-Jewish in the second century A.D. At least from the time of Origen in the third century Jewish misfortunes were attributed to divine punishment. The usual interpretation ran something like this: Israel had indeed been the Chosen People but had forfeited this privileged position by their own lack of faith and their crimes. God had therefore adopted gentile Christianity as 'the new Israel'. It was easy to find evidence for this not only in the New but in the Old Testament, with its recurring themes of acceptance, rejection, and punishment. Just as Jacob had supplanted Esau, the legitimate firstborn, just as Joseph had received divine favour rather than his elder brothers, so the Church (the good daughter) had triumphed over the synagogue (the wicked daughter). And the concept of a new branch, of an adopted child, is already well developed in Paul's theology. The comparison with acceptance and rejection within a family is not irrelevant, as God was above all the Father, and some psychoanalysts have interpreted anti-Semitism as aggression centered on 'the bad brother'.[4]

Condemnations of the Jews and of Judaism became more violent after Christianity became the official religion in the Empire. Particularly in its Eastern or Byzantine half, with its traditions of Greek and Egyptian anti-Semitism, Christian preachers launched into violent diatribes. This is St. John Chrysostom, for instance, in the sixth century:

> Brothel and theater, the synagogue is also a cave of pirates and the lair of wild beasts. . . . Living for their belly, mouth forever gaping, the Jews behave no better than hogs and goats in their lewd grossness and the excesses of their gluttony.

But already in the fourth century St. Gregory of Nyssa had been even more violent:

> Murderers of the Lord, assassins of the prophets, rebels and de-
> testers of God, they outrage the Law, resist grace, repudiate the
> faith of their fathers. Companions of the devil, race of vipers, in-
> formers, calumniators, darkeners of the mind, Pharisaic leaven,
> Sanhedrin of demons, accursed, detested lapidators, enemies of all
> that is beautiful . . .[5]

At the head of this inverted litany stands the accusation of *deicide*, which was to be for centuries the main theme of anti-Jewish hatred.[6] It would be a mistake to underestimate the importance of this cumulative propaganda, even in the case of modern anti-Semitism, which developed other themes.

JUDAS AS THE JEWISH ARCHETYPE

In the Christian world the Jew would in fact be magnified as a figure of apocalyptic dimensions, like the Beast or the Antichrist (Jean-Paul Sartre has rightly remarked that anti-Semitism is 'une conception du monde ma-nichéiste'). And this would be suitably personified in the person of Judas, the arch-betrayer, above all others 'an example and a byword'. The Hebrew Bible abounds in puns and purely verbal interpretations. Popular Chris-tianity was only following its example by seeing a symbolical similarity be-tween the names 'Judas' and 'Jew' (in most European languages the word 'Jew' was much closer in sound to the Latin *Judaeus*). It just could not be a coincidence. By a most unfortunate circumstance Judas had been marked as the essential, archetypal Jew. Philologically, that is exactly what Judas (Yehuda) means: or, rather, the name 'Judaean' or 'Jew' comes from the tribe of Judah or Yehuda. In the *Tol 'doth Yeshu* (see Chapter 10) Judas is called Yehuda Iskarioto.[7] So it was not surprising that in popular Chris-tianity Judas and Jew should become almost synonymous.

The intensity of the stereotype left a profound mark in all languages used or developed by Christian peoples. Just as Judas came to mean a be-trayer, the word 'Jew' soon acquired all sorts of negative connotations, like wicked, perverse, miserly, dishonest, and so on. I have already mentioned the verb *judiar* in Portuguese as meaning 'to torment' (see Introduction). In English 'to jew' (in America 'to jew down') came to mean another as-pect of the anti-Semitic stereotype—'to swindle'. In German *jüdeln* has meant 'to talk like a Jew'; 'to bargain like a Jew'; finally 'to smell like a Jew'. The classic German dictionary of the Grimm brothers give a number of proverbial idioms, such as 'dirty as an old Jew', 'he stinks like a Jew', or 'this food tastes like a dead Jew'. In Polish there are expressions like 'mangy

Jew' (*parchaty Żyd*) and 'the Jew stinks' (*Żyd śmierdzic*).[8] Naturally, *Jude*, like *Juif* in French or 'Jew' in English, became a synonym for 'usurer', and in German *Judenpiess* meant the same as *Wucher* ('usury').

As on this level of popular 'religion' there is hardly any historical sense, people were simply not aware that Jesus and the apostles had all been Jews. In fact, modern anti-Semites like the racialist Houston Chamberlain (see Chapter 11) drew the 'logical' conclusion: Jesus could not have been a Jew, so he was really an 'Aryan'.

This was like the naïve racial assimilation that made the Chinese and Japanese sculpture a Mongoloid Buddha or even depict a Chinese Jesus. In a similar way, it is amusing to see medieval and Renaissance painters represent Biblical scenes with the dress and social background of their own time. So Flavius Josephus may appear in a medieval book with the conical hat worn by many Jews in Europe, and Piero della Francesca, in his picture *Solomon Receiving the Queen of Sheba*, drew the king of Israel as a fifteenth-century Jew with the broad-brimmed hat which was compulsory in Italy.

More significant and more to the point are the representations of the apostles, as in *The Last Supper* or *The Kiss of Judas*. In these paintings Judas is normally the only one who is given the traditional 'Jewish' features: he usually appears with red beard and hair, yellow clothes (the distinctive colour many Jews were forced to wear), and—a detail that seemed ideally suited to the image of the greedy Jew—the bag of money.[9] One could also add a malignant expression, like that of the villain of a melodrama, and ugly or 'subhuman' features.

In short, the drama of the Passion, incessantly repeated like a slogan in innumerable pictures, and also acted on the popular stage, had characters as stereotyped as those of some folk stories, including that of Esther in the dramas of the Jewish Purim. Its conventions are as naïve and black-and-white as the old-fashioned Hollywood Western or strip cartoon. And they are as racialist as certain cheap British or American fiction in which the villain is some sinister 'dago' with a moustache or the 'fiendish Chinese'.

The formation of a 'villain', of a hated and despised figure, is an example of what psychoanalysts have termed 'projection'. We are all apt (but some more than others) to project onto others certain undesirable character traits or impulses which we do not like to acknowledge in ourselves. Carried to its extreme form, this mechanism has led to the segregation of despised pariah groups. This was at work in Judaea at the time of Christ where the Jews hated, for different reasons, the Samaritans and the 'publicans': the former because they were 'religious heretics' and the latter because they were the instruments of Roman taxation, a role, indeed, that would often be played by the Jews in European states, thus reinforcing anti-Jewish feeling. Jesus, as I shall try to show later (see Chapter 14), had a deep understanding of projection, and by his parable of the Good Samaritan and by consorting openly with publicans he tried to show the unfairness of such prejudices.

These examples show that the Jews are very far from being unique in playing the part of scapegoats in a given community. In Chapter 1 I gave some examples of outbursts of violence in which a community gives vent to its frustrations and negative feelings by attacking a vulnerable minority.

Admittedly, anti-Semitism has meant much more than these periodic outbursts. It led in fact to a permanent distortion of vision and behaviour in the whole Christian world, and the Jew was always seen through a distorting mirror.

DEMONOLOGY OF THE JEW

I stress this feature of distorted vision because of its psychological importance, which can be seen in more extreme degrees in psychotic cases. Schizophrenic or paranoid patients have a distorted view of the world or of certain people: for instance, a female patient saw her husband as a devil. This will immediately appear as pathological, but for most people it is more difficult to become aware of their own distorted ways of seeing the world or others.

The fear of the Devil has greatly faded nowadays, to the extent that he is often looked upon as a figure of fun, but for centuries he was extremely real and frightening to most people in Christian countries. One can even say that demons and devils were an integral part of medieval life, almost as if they belonged to every household. People often saw and felt the devilish element in things, animals, and human beings, and they often represented it visually or talked about it. The image of the Devil and the devilish, being so strong, could be easily projected onto individuals or groups. One has only to think of contemporary beliefs about mental illness being caused by demonic possession (which had behind it the authority of the Gospels), leading, of course, to cruel ill-treatment of patients, and of the savage persecution of the so-called witches, who suffered as much as the Jews.

It is revealing that Americans should have had the excellent idea of applying the term 'witch-hunt' to modern political persecution, particularly of Communists or supposed Communists. But the original witch-hunt has not died altogether, and some years ago Budapest television produced an excellent documentary about an old woman who was hounded out of her village in Hungary because she was thought to be a witch.

One can get some idea of the vivid fascination exerted for centuries by demonology from pictorial representations. For instance, many people nowadays will find Hieronymus Bosch's engravings revolting or pathological, but they were 'normal' for his time. In a simliar way, the average modern reader, who has very little experience of or feeling for religion anyway, will find the visions of the Book of Revelation a series of absurd delusions. And yet its influence over the mind and imagination of all Christianity has been enormous in the past, and not only among people of 'mystical' tendencies. For centuries the Antichrist, the Beast, and the Whore of Babylon have been very real figures and all pervaded with the devilish element. Apocalyptic thought, which came out of Judaism, has played an important part in the whole anti-Semitic movement, and we might remind ourselves that, in a purified form, it may still prove to be a valid way of looking at human history.

Not everybody, of course, looked upon the Jew as a devil. Some of the more humane clergy, like Pope Martin V (see Chapter 7), had to remind people that in spite of their 'faults 'or 'crimes' Jews were human beings and therefore 'made after the image of God'. But that is exactly what anti-Jewish hatred denied, at least in practice. In fact, every prejudice of this nature, taken to its logical conclusion (as the Nazis were to do), means the rejection of a whole group as being in some way subhuman. And if the Jew tended to be dark among a predominantly fair-skinned population, this fact could reinforce the process by the well-known psychological associations of dark colour.

In the eyes of Christian peoples during the Middle Ages and even later, the Jew was considered a devilish creature in both mind and body, and thus many of the features of Satan, such as horns and noxious odours, could easily be attributed to him. In Spain, at least, the belief that Jews had tails persisted until the nineteenth century—*los Judios rabudos*.[10] Like the goat (popularly considered a suitable vehicle of devilish action) he stinks; and like both the goat and Satan he is endowed with supernatural and dangerous virility. On the other hand, with the usual inconsistency of such beliefs, all sorts of dreadful illnesses and monstrosities were ascribed to the Jew as suitable to a subhuman being outside the plan of divine creation. Léon Poliakov gives some good examples:

> They are born misshapen, they are hemorrhoidal and, men as well as women, afflicted with menstruation. From this point of view they are women, that is, inframen, scorned, loathed, and mocked. Sometimes the description is even more circumstantial, and the ills the Jews suffer are differentiated according to their tribes. The descendants of Simeon bleed four days every year, those of Zebulun spit blood yearly, those of Benjamin have worms in their mouths, and so on.[11]

It is interesting to see the Jews being identified to some extent with women. This is not perhaps surprising, as in the Middle Ages most Jews were deprived of many normal 'male' attributes, such as the right to bear arms. In the last century a Jewish anti-Semite, Otto Weininger, wrote a book (*Sex and Character*) drawing an analogy between Jews and women (see Chapter 14).

From the religious point of view the Jewish cult (of which the great majority of people were almost totally ignorant) was also considered diabolical, 'the synagogue of Satan', and even the powers or magical skills often attributed to Jews were looked upon as deriving from association with the Devil. In fact, they were part of the whole mixed bag of demons, witches, and heretics that people had learned to fear and detest. Everything connected with the Jews was tainted with a dark and sinister element, or, more specifically, with God's curse.

THE ACCURSED PEOPLE

A fierce anti-Semite of the ninth century, Bishop Agobard of Lyons, used devastating Biblical language to lash the Jews:

> They are clothed with cursing as with a garment. The curse penetrates into their bones, their marrow, and their entrails, as water and oil flow through the human body. They are accursed in the city and the country, at the beginning and ending of their lives: their flocks, their meat, their granaries, their cellars, their magazines, are accursed.[12]

The first part is almost verbatim from the Vulgate (Ps. 108:18; 109:18 in the English versions), while the rest is a freer paraphrase from some of the terrible curses in Deuteronomy (28:16ff.). Here we have the tragic irony of the Biblical texts being used against the Jews themselves, as if they had provided their own condemnation in advance or signed their own confession of guilt. This chapter of the most hallowed part of the Old Testament was very clear: if the Jews followed all God's commandments they would be blessed, but if they transgressed them terrible curses would fall on them. Now, the blessings are given in fourteen verses, while the curses—the most thorough and terrifying of the whole Bible—comprise no less than fifty-four verses. Any Christian who read this and knew something about the sufferings and persecutions undergone by the Jews could not fail to conclude that it all tallied and made sense. Here was the wrath of God, prophesying that the Jews would be scattered, humiliated, persecuted, exploited, harassed, oppressed, smitten with all kinds of diseases, plagues, and disasters—that their children would be taken away from them, that they would find no peace anywhere. Here in the Hebrew Bible, long before the Crusades, the Inquisition, or Adolf Hitler, was a whole catalogue of persecutions, a blueprint for anti-Semitism. And not only there but in many other books of the Bible, Jewish anger against lack of faith, Jewish shame and sense of guilt, the prophetic thunder against backslidings and 'whoring after other gods'—all this now provided a terrible weapon for the Jew-haters. Here was the Bible itself proclaiming the Jews as a faithless, contemptible, 'stiff-necked', wicked people. The Bible was the word of God, Christ was the Son of God, and the Jews had brought upon themselves all those curses by killing Christ. Given these premises, the conclusion was unavoidable: it was not only right that the accursed people should suffer but it was positively a Christian duty to make them suffer, just as in earlier days God seemed to have given the Jews the right to oppress other peoples.

The idea of the 'accursed people' was to crystallize in the famous myth of the Wandering Jew (*der Ewige Jude*, or Eternal Jew, as the Germans called him), condemned to rove upon the earth until the second coming of Christ (see Chapter 9).

DELUSIONS OF PERSECUTION AGAINST THE JEWS

A 'logical' and frequent development of the whole mechanism of projection is to produce a delusion of persecution. If I hate a certain group, I am inevitably led to ascribe to it all kinds of sinister and malignant plots against me and to try and frustrate them. So those who imagine themselves persecuted turn logically into persecutors. Normally, this goes on on an unconscious level, but it may also be conscious and in that case it constitutes one of the oldest tricks in human history: that is, I accuse my 'enemy' of plotting exactly what I am planning against him and then proceed to attack him in alleged self-defence.

Politically, this is a very old ploy, and there are several recent examples in Latin American countries, in which a group accuse their opponents of 'subversion' and overthrow democracy under the pretext of defending it (or promote war 'in order to preserve peace').[13] For instance, Hitler quite consciously used the fear of an alleged Communist conspiracy in Germany in order to establish and consolidate his regime. But unconsciously he also used the ghost of 'international Jewry' in order to channel all the aggression and frustrations of the German people.

Here we are more concerned with the unconscious process, as applied to the Jews in Christian countries. Earlier in this book we saw the stories that were current in Alexandria and elsewhere about Jewish 'misanthropy' and the alleged oath of eternal enmity to the Greeks. With the triumph of Christianity this would be intensified and repeated on a much wider scale. Perhaps the old stories were not forgotten but only refurbished and given a 'Christian' content.

The Jews were considered implacable enemies of Christ and Christianity. Every segregated minority with peculiar customs is suspect. What mysterious rites did they practise? What was the meaning of those sinister characters they wrote? (Most people had no idea that the original Old Testament was written with those letters and that Jesus had used them.) In the Roman Empire the Jews, like the Christians themselves, had been accused of cannibalism. Now, under Christianity, the story began to spread that the Jews carried out a ritual sacrifice of Christian children. Kidnappings of children have been attributed to all sorts of people, like witches or Gypsies. In nineteenth-century China similar accusations were made against Christian missionaries, and in Madagascar at about the same time against agents of the French government. As Poliakov says, it seems to be 'a virtually universal theme'.[14]

Curiously enough, the earliest recorded instance of a charge of child murder against the Jews is the only one that may have been true. It occurred in the reign of the Eastern emperor Theodosius II (408–50) in a place called Immestar, between Chalcis and Antioch. It was said that a group of drunken Jews had fastened a Christian boy to a cross and beaten him to death.[15] Modern historians seem to accept the story as true, but it must be pointed out that it has nothing to do with the false libel of 'ritual murder', which only made its appearance several centuries later, and in Western Europe.

Two of the most famous cases of ritual murder occurred in England. The first was that of William of Norwich, a boy who was found dead at Easter time in 1144. The inhabitants of Norwich spread the story that the Jews had kidnapped and crucified him after synagogue service as part of their Passover ritual. On that occasion the Norwich Jews were protected by the civil authorities, and only one of the leaders seems to have been murdered. But at the death of Hugh of Lincoln in 1255 there was a full-scale trial and a number of executions. The boy was found dead near the house of a Jew after he had been missing for three weeks. The Jew was arrested and tortured until he 'confessed' that Hugh had been killed in a ritual murder. The full story, after all the embellishments had been added, was that the Jews had fattened the boy for ten days on bread and milk, and then crucified him with all the refined details of the Passion, in the presence of a large congregation who had assembled specially for that end. According to one version, one of the Jews had played the part of Pilate and condemned Hugh.

As a result of the accusation, nearly one hundred Jews were put on trial and many of them hanged. The boy's corpse was solemnly buried in Lincoln Cathedral, and he came to be venerated as the martyr St. Hugh of Lincoln. The story became part of folklore and was used by Chaucer in his *Canterbury Tales*.[16]

The similarity to the alleged fattening and ritual killing of Greeks spread

by Apion is obvious. It is hardly necessary to point out that when such accusations were the object of a comparatively fair trial in modern times their
falsity was fully proved. But the Jews continued to be periodically accused
of ritual murder, the latest case being in tsarist Russia as late as 1910. The
Nazis did not hesitate to unearth the libel, and even in America it gained
some currency. The case of the American Jew Leo Frank (see Chapter 11),
who was lynched in Atlanta, Georgia, in 1915 under the accusation of having killed a young girl, may perhaps be considered a late instance, although
ritual murder was not part of the charge.

'TORTURE' OF THE CONSECRATED HOST

In 1215 the Fourth Lateran Council officially approved the doctrine of
transubstantiation: i.e., the belief that the host of the Eucharist, on being
consecrated by the priest, is actually transformed into the body of Jesus
Christ, while the wine contained in the chalice becomes his blood. It was
just at that time that a new charge became current against the Jews, no
doubt the most fantastic and delusional of them all.

It was stated that they periodically stole a consecrated host and subjected it to all kinds of 'ill-treatment'. Thus Christ would be made to suffer
again all the torments of the Passion. The evidence for this was supposed
to be in certain mysterious drops of blood that would suddenly appear in
some wafers.

In 1243 a great number of Jews were burned at the stake in Beelitz, near
Berlin, on account of this charge. There were similar pogroms in 1290 in
Paris and in 1370 in Brussels.

A very likely explanation is that the alleged blood drops were in fact
caused by a bacterium, *Micrococcus prodigiosus*, which often attacks bakery
products and forms red colonies, hence the popular name of 'bleeding
bread'. Cecil Roth comments that the most ridiculous element of such an
accusation is that 'it postulates a degree of regard for, and belief in, the
consecrated elements which must be contradictory in any non-Catholic': [17]
in other words, it naïvely assumes a universal belief in transubstantiation.
Such inability to see a question from a different point of view is typical of
the prejudiced mind.

Even more striking, perhaps, in this delusional idea is its magic character, of the type that Frazer called 'homeopathic 'or 'imitative' magic: just
as in the well-known practice of sticking pins in an effigy representing the
person against whom the witchcraft is aimed.

Christian obsession with suffering and torment was almost inevitable in
a religion that made of the cross its main symbol. One must think of successive generations brought up on the vivid Passion story, which was re-

peated almost everywhere: in pictures in the Church and at home, in crucifixes, painted glass, illuminated manuscripts, through the passionate sermons of preachers, or as a story told by mothers to children (just as the Bible orders Jews to explain the Passover ritual to their own children). One must think of people being asked daily to meditate on the sufferings of the crucified Jesus, to concentrate on details like the nails tearing out the flesh, the scourging, the crown of thorns, the holy 'stigmata', and so on. One must think of generations brought up almost from the cradle to hate the Jew, to see in him the archvillain, the Judas, the murderer of the Lord, to 'point the finger' at him (in the Biblical sense), to cry 'It was he!' When one thinks of all this, one can form a pale idea of the tremendous cumulative force of Christian anti-Judaism.

Modern psychologists have shown that sadism and masochism are two sides of the same phenomenon. The obsession with blood and sacrifice can be turned inwards, leading to the well-known excesses of ascetic practices (which, after all, are common in almost every religion), to the desire to torment one's own flesh, as in the medieval Flagellants. Or it can be turned outwards in sadistic aggression, against convenient scapegoats like the Jews. That both impulses could go hand in hand is proved by the fact that at the time of the Black Death, as we shall see in the next chapter, the Flagellants carried out violent pogroms.

The drama of the Passion was so much an integral part of Christian life that people attributed to the Jews a similar obsession with it. Every year Jesus was crucified, every year Judas betrayed him and was ritually hanged. It seemed a cycle as natural as that of the seasons. It was not surprising that the Jews, being associated with the Devil, should also carry out a ritual but aiming at an opposite effect. There was hardly any distinction between past and present: the Passion was an eternal drama, belonging to what Alan Watts calls 'the eternal now'. Just as Christ, the Virgin, angels, and demons could appear in vision to many people, in a similar way the Jews, the villains of the drama, were those present now, not those of the time of Christ. As Milman rightly says: 'Every Jew was as deadly a foe as if he had joined in the frantic cry of Crucify him! Crucify him!'[18]

So again, it is not surprising that at Béziers, in the Languedoc (south of France), some priests should incite the faithful to stone the Jews at the beginning of Holy Week. The preacher would say from his pulpit:

> You have around you those who crucified this Messiah, who deny Mary the Mother of God. Now is the time when you would feel most deeply the iniquity of which Christ was the victim. This is the day on which our Prince has graciously given us permission to avenge this crime. Like your pious ancestors, hurl

stones at the Jews, and show your sense of his wrongs by the vigour with which you resent them.[19]

It seems that the crowds used this licence with great fervour. And when a bishop banned the old practice, he was accused of being bribed by the Jews. In fact, as in other kinds of witch-hunt, any man in authority who tried to protect the Jews was liable to be charged with this, if not with the worse accusation of being a crypto-Jew or Judaizer himself.

It is clear that such rituals as the hanging of Judas on the Saturday before Easter, still carried out by children in Portugal and some places in Brazil, though without any anti-Semitic connotation, must be very old. The practice of burning a hated character in effigy is very widespread, and one of the best known instances is that of Guy Fawkes on 5 November in England, also very popular with children and associated with fireworks and bonfires. This was in fact an anti-Catholic ritual, although now deprived of all emotional content, to celebrate the failure of the famous Gunpowder Plot in 1605, which aimed at overthrowing the regime and the Anglican Church. At the town of Lewes, at least until recently, people burnt the effigy of the Pope, not Guy Fawkes.

It is interesting that during the Purim festival some Jewish communities resorted to a similar ritual in order to give vent to their resentment against the persecuting Gentiles. The story of Esther, like that of the Passion, has often been put on the Jewish popular stage, and it was traditional that the audience should shout noisily their execration of Haman, the anti-Jewish villain of the play. In the fifth century, in the Eastern empire, certain Jewish communities used to hang an effigy of Haman on a kind of scaffold and subject it to all kinds of ill-treatment. Some Christians who saw this thought mistakenly that it had something to do with the Passion story (in fact, Purim is celebrated between February and March), and the Theodosian Code banned such customs.[20]

THE FOUR SOLUTIONS

One might think that the Jewish minority was in fact performing several 'useful' psychological functions, particularly for the ruling classes, if they were cynical enough to realize and admit it. But human societies are hardly ever consistent even in their hatreds, and it is clear that against a general background of anti-Jewish feeling there was a great deal of variation. In practice four solutions were possible to 'the Jewish problem': 1) conversion or, rather, forced baptism; 2) expulsion; 3) strict segregation; and 4) extermination. All four of these were tried in different ways by Christian communities. As recently as 1898 Pobyedonostzev, an influential Russian authority under Tsar Nicholas II, openly proposed to deal in the following way with the Russian Jews: to exterminate one third, to assimilate (convert) one third, and to provoke the emigration of one third.

Conversion was the first solution to be tried, and it was considered ideal, at least by many Church leaders. One should be fair to popes and bishops and recognize that on the whole they tended to favour less violent methods than Jew-baiting crowds or some fanatical clerics. On several occasions, as in the great pogroms of the First Crusade, some bishops did try to protect the Jews against popular fury; and as far as I have been able to ascertain, there never were pogroms in Rome. On the other hand, Church leaders also incited anti-Jewish hatred on many occasions, and the Church was largely responsible for the horrors of the Inquisition, which was officialized torture, and for many repressive measures like the ghetto, the Jewish badge, and so on.

There was a very widespread belief that the millennium, the triumphal Advent of Christ, would only come about when the Jews were converted at last. In fact, several of the medieval apocalyptic sects carried out pogroms, and some of them, as Norman Cohn has shown,[21] followed a brand of racialist German nationalism which anticipated National Socialism by several centuries.

In short, from the apocalyptic point of view the Jew was the missing character, the key figure who obstinately refused to take his cue in the staging of the magnificent drama of the Advent, so long awaited, so many times advertised and then postponed until further notice. This does not mean that there were not frequent conversions of Jews, often quite sincere. But as will be seen in the case of Spain and Portugal, even giving up Judaism and Jewish collective identity did not protect the Jews against persecution or discrimination. Christian anti-Semitism was not entirely devoid of racialism.

Expulsion was a policy adopted on many different occasions by European rulers, sometimes perhaps with the secondary aim of acquiring much booty. In a way it did 'solve' the problem locally, but it was not always strictly followed, and a Jewish community, expelled at one time, could always come back under a more tolerant regime. One should also note that these expulsions were often carried out with great callousness or cruelty, not only impoverishing the community concerned but also causing much distress and a good number of deaths.

Strict *segregation*, bound up with many humiliating restrictions and turning the Jews into pariahs of society, was imposed in many countries and continued throughout Europe until comparatively recent times, with the approval and often strict injunction of the Church. It was the egalitarian tide of radical thought, culminating with the French Revolution, that finally toppled the walls of the ghettos. One of the most oppressive of all segregations, that of tsarist Russia, was only abolished with the Revolution of March 1917. But the ghettos would still have a brief period of restoration under the Nazi Third Reich.

The fourth solution, termed under Hitler's regime the 'Final Solution', was *extermination*. Cecil Roth remarks that in the past the ghetto had the advantage of giving the Jews some protection against outbursts of popular violence. But it could also be attacked and sacked, and this was no rare occurrence. Although often condemned by popes and bishops, slaughter of Jews continued to be practised, but without the scientific thoroughness that only the Nazis were to bring to it. It is true that in many cases the Jew, like the Christian in the Roman Empire, was allowed to choose between martyrdom and conversion. But those who accepted baptism to save their lives or gain advantages, or, again, those who were forcibly baptized, might still practise Judaism secretly, and in that case came under the attention of the Inquisition as relapsed heretics.

One should not underestimate the efficiency of the Holy Office, for it practically eliminated the Jewish element in the Peninsula and tried its best in Latin America. Even so, we had to come to the twentieth century to see what the monstrous 'logic' of the Nazis could do, with all the advantages of modern technology and propaganda. The greatest evil of 'Christian' and ecclesiastical anti-Judaism, I repeat, did not lie in the destruction of human lives, great and criminal as it was, but in its permanent poisoning of entire generations, and in the mental distortion it produced not only among the Christian peoples but inevitably in the Jews themselves.

7

Crusades, Pogroms, and Ghettos

One evening several years ago, I walked north on Park Avenue in New York City in the company of a young Jewish couple. Behind us shone the huge illuminated cross the Grand Central Building displays each year at Christmas time. Glancing over her shoulder, the young lady—ordinarily well disposed toward Christianity—declared: 'That cross makes me shudder. It is like an evil presence'.

This disturbing comment evoked many questions in me, not least of which was: 'How did the cross, the supreme symbol of universal love, become a sign of fear, of evil for this young Jewess?'
—Father Flannery, *The Anguish of the Jews*, p. xi

'GOD WILLS IT!'

On 27 November 1095, in the town of Clermont in France, an important public meeting in European history took place. It could not be called democratic, but certainly it was popular and it was held in an open field. During a synod of the Church, Pope Urban II took this opportunity to make a general appeal. His message was something like this: 'Christians of Europe, unite! Take up your cross and sword and go and liberate the Holy Land, which is in the hands of the Muslim infidels'.

The appeal was made with a great deal of sincerity and fervour by a man of vision who was then at the height of his prestige and authority. He wished not only to see Jerusalem and the Holy Sepulchre back in Christian hands but desired also that the turbulent barons should stop fighting each other and oppressing their subjects. And in exchange for peace among Christians, the 'holy truce', he offered a prize for aggression that was religiously permissible, and indeed meritorious. Like Moses, he held up before his audience the vision of a Land of Promise flowing with milk and honey.

Whatever the motives that led individual Crusaders, there is no doubt that Urban's appeal was met with tremendous enthusiasm. Men of all classes promised to join the movement and as a token began to sew crosses on their right shoulders, while the famous cry went round—'Dieu le veult!' (God wills it).

The Crusades have been rightly considered the first great popular movement in Christian Europe, and the name became a synonym for any idealistic enterprise aimed at a better world. And yet the project that looked so splendid on that field in Clermont was fulfilled less than four years later, on 15 July 1099, with the hideous massacre that followed the conquest of Jerusalem. Not only were the Muslims slaughtered, but all the Jews of the city and even Christians of the Syrian Jacobite Church. The Christian chroniclers talk of the classic rivers of blood that reached up to the ankles.[1]

In contrast, when the famous Muslim ruler Saladin reconquered Jerusalem nearly a century later, in 1187, there was no massacre. Of the Christian prisoners, the rich were ransomed while the poor were abandoned to their fate, but Saladin freed most of those who could not ransom themselves and let them take their goods away.

This does not mean, of course, that the Muslims always showed such clemency or that the Western Christians were always barbaric. But the stereotype of the fanatical and cruel Muslim, which goes back at least to the age of the Crusades, is still being imprinted in Western minds. In a study of schoolbooks carried out for UNESCO, the English historian Joseph Lauwerys (who has done much to discredit the 'Europocentric' and colonialist view of history) showed that they tend to present the Arab in general (or the Muslim) as a fanatical warrior: 'In textbook illustrations he always appears as a bloodthirsty horseman with lifted sword, and the Crusades are interpreted as a struggle of civilized Christians against barbarians'.[2]

The historical truth is quite the opposite, for culturally Western Europe was then a less civilized part of the earth, which attacked the higher Arab civilization, and in the end also turned against the sophisticated Byzantine Empire. The Jewish minority was an important element of both these civilizations. In fact, it was the Crusaders who learned from the Muslims in the East. The rough Franks who settled in the Holy Land—which they called 'Outre Mer'—often adopted more refined Oriental habits and dress, married native women, and in the end shocked newly arrived Westerners with their new outlook and religious tolerance.

'A NATION OF STERN COUNTENANCE'

If this cultural interchange was something positive, the results of the Crusades were on the whole disastrous, for they inevitably provoked a

Muslim backlash and further embittered the relations between the two religions. But aggression was by no means confined to the Muslims. Like the sorcerer's apprentice, Pope Urban II had unleashed forces that neither he nor his successors would be able to control. This was always the fatal illusion of the Church in the Middle Ages: to imagine that it could guide the 'secular arm' in the execution of its grandiose but violent designs.

After the synod of Clermont many people in Western Europe began to ask themselves, with impeccable logic: 'Why go to Palestine to fight infidels and leave here in our midst the enemies of Christ, the synagogue of Satan? If it is meritorious to kill Arabs and Turks, why cannot we gain the same indulgences by killing Jews?'

As victims, the Jews had two strong qualifications: they were close at hand and defenceless. Besides, many of them practised usury, which was condemned by the Church, although a growing number of Christians were flouting this prohibition. Many people had fallen into debt in order to face the expenses of the journey to Palestine, placing their goods in pawn to Jews. Here was an excellent opportunity to get rid of the debt: it would not be the first or the last time that the Jewish creditors would be killed to settle mundane and celestial accounts at one blow.

It was the first unruly crowds of Crusaders en route to the Holy Land that began the attacks in 1096. Apart from the doubtful report of an attack at Rouen in France, all the pogroms seem to have been in German towns, and were carried out by contingents of German Crusaders.

At that time many of the Jewish communities in Germany were concentrated in the Rhineland, along one of the most important trade routes. The wave of attacks began at Speier, where the bishop placed the Jews under his protection and even captured some of the murderers and had them punished. Even so, several Jews were killed. In Worms it was much worse, for the crowd broke into the bishop's palace, where about five hundred Jews had taken sanctuary, and killed them all in spite of his protests.

At Mainz it was much the same story, except that the archbishop fled in alarm with all his retainers, and the number of victims was higher, being estimated at about 1,300. Many women committed suicide, while the older Jews covered themselves with their prayer shawls, repeating, 'He is a rock, His works are perfect'. Two of them, Uri and Isaac, together with the latter's two daughters, were forcibly baptized. But Isaac killed the two girls, 'defiled with the proud water', as a Jewish chronicle puts it, and set fire to his house as in atonement. Later the two friends committed suicide in the burning synagogue.

There were other massacres, at Cologne, Metz, and Regensburg (Ratisbon) in Bavaria. At Trier (Treves) on the Moselle the Crusaders launched a savage attack, murdering, sacking, and raping women. Many Jewesses threw themselves in the river with stones tied to their necks, in order to escape the twin threats of rape and baptism. Those who escaped tried, as usual, to take refuge in the bishop's palace, but he received them with these words: 'Wretches, your sins have come upon you; ye who have blasphemed the Son of God and calumniated his Mother. This is the cause of your present miseries!' [3]

The bishop promised the Jews their lives if they would be baptized, and under threat of death they accepted.

The chronicle compiled in the sixteenth century by the rabbi Joseph ha-Cohen, *The Vale of Tears,* gives an idea of how these pogroms were seen from the Jewish side:

> Crowds of German and French rose up against them, 'a nation of stern countenance, who showed no regard for the person of the old or favour to the young'. And they said: 'Let us be revenged for our Messiah upon the Jews that are among us, and let us destroy them from being a nation, that the name of Israel may be had no more in remembrance; so shall they change their glory and be like unto us; then will we go to the East'.[4]

Such passages show that the Jews, like the persecuting Christians, saw the event in Biblical terms, except that each side interpreted it in its own way. It is also striking that no voice was raised in Europe against the pogroms. There is no compassion, only callousness in the Christian chronicles of the time, often written by monks. Certainly, the Pope had not wanted the anti-Jewish attacks, and, as we have seen, several bishops did their best to protect the Jews. But there were no energetic protests from the Church leaders: in their eyes it was perhaps just a question of excess of zeal. The German emperor Henry IV, who had been excommunicated by the pope on account of a long dispute between the two powers, seems to have been the only one who took measures against the atrocities. In a decree issued in Ratisbon, he allowed the Jews who had been forcibly baptized to return to their religion and ordered the restitution of all property taken in the attacks.

There is no doubt that 1096 was a landmark in the history of anti-Semitism, separating a period of strong prejudice but with rare outbursts of violence from another in which pogroms became a more frequent occurrence. It is not surprising, therefore, that the Jews of the time should consider the synod of Clermont the beginning of an age of persecution: by a play of words which came so easily to readers of the Bible, Clermont (Mount of Light) became *Har Ophel* (Mount of Darkness). Cecil Roth says:

> Take any realistic description of the position of world Jewry down to the close of the last century; take any indictment drawn

up by anti-Semites in our own times; take any contemporary analysis of the weakness of the Jewish position or the alleged shortcomings of the Jewish character; and in almost every instance it will be possible to trace the origin, if not actually to the Crusades, to the currents which they stirred.[5]

A CATALOGUE OF POGROMS

Meanwhile the habit of slaughter, once begun, continued. When St. Bernard of Clairvaux preached the Second Crusade, there was a new wave of attacks, instigated by a monk called Rudolf, which spread from Germany to France. It was then, it seems, that the cry *Hep! Hep!* became a rallying-cry for killing Jews. It is usually interpreted as meaning *Hierosolyma est perdita* (Jerusalem is lost). This cry was still being used in Germany as late as the nineteenth century, in the attacks against the ghettos in 1819. St. Bernard himself opposed the massacres and succeeded in preventing them in some places, but other Church leaders were not so peaceful. Peter the Venerable, abbot of the famous monastery of Cluny, wrote to the king of France condemning tolerance towards the Jews. He did not go as far as to recommend killing, but he thought pillage of their goods perfectly justified: thus the 'ill-acquired' property of one race of infidels would help to finance war against the other—the Muslims.

It was about the same time that accusations of ritual murder of children (see Chapter 6) became more frequent. Popular imagination gave it different versions: it was said either that the child was crucified as an imitation of Christ's torment, or that the Jews used his blood in order to make their Passover bread, or again that they drank it to get rid of their bad smell (*foetor judaicus*). Any missing child could give rise to the accusation, and the Jews could not hope for a fair inquest since they were already condemned beforehand.

Later the other charge, about the consecrated host, also became widespread, and both of them provoked a series of pogroms. Boppard in 1179, Vienna in 1181, Speier again in 1185, Halle in 1205, Erfurt in 1221, Mecklenburg in 1225, Fulda in 1236, Frankfurt in 1241, Beelitz in 1243, Pforzheim in 1244, Paris in 1270, Würzburg and Nuremberg in 1298, Alsace, Swabia, and Franconia in 1336, Bavaria, Bohemia, and Moravia in 1337—the list is interminable. And once more German or Germanized places were prominent in the killing of Jews.

But England did not escape the scourge. In 1189, during the coronation of King Richard the Lion-Hearted, who was about to depart for the Third Crusade, the Jews were forbidden to attend the festivities (according to a chronicler, for fear of their 'magic arts').[6] Nevertheless, a Jewish deputation came to Westminster Hall bearing rich gifts to the king. In the confusion some managed to get in, but were brutally driven out. This provoked a riot among the crowd watching at the gates, and soon there was a rumour that the king had ordered a general slaughter of Jews. The people attacked the London Jewry, set fire to the houses, and killed a number of Jews. The next year there were further outbreaks of violence, the worst being at York. The Jews took refuge in the local castle, called Clifford's Tower, where they were beseiged. On the advice of their leader, a prominent rabbi, the man killed their wives and daughters and then slew each other. When the besiegers managed at last to enter the castle, they massacred the few who were left.

THE BLACK DEATH

In 1348 the Jews were accused of causing the great epidemic of bubonic plague, the Black Death, which according to some estimates killed about one-third of the population of Europe. That the scapegoat mechanism was not limited to them is clear from other stories recorded in contemporary chronicles: the Muslims in Spain were also blamed for spreading the plague, and so were Portuguese pilgrims in Aragon, and even lepers, who in the Middle Ages were treated with great cruelty. But even in 1321, before the real outbreak of the epidemic, a story became current in the south of France that the Jews used to pay the lepers to poison the wells so as to spread the disease. Another version was that Jews had been paid by the Muslim king of Granada to do the same.[7]

Suspicions were aroused when people saw Jews preferring to drink from running water in streams. Perhaps because of their strict hygienic habits they were somewhat less liable to catch the plague, at least in the beginning. At Chillon in the Savoy a Jew called Balavingus at last 'confessed' after torture that the wells had been poisoned. A popular version of the story even gave the full recipe, typical of a witches' cauldron: spiders, toads, lizards, hearts of Christians, and consecrated wafers.

Within a short time people were talking about a very complicated plot to spread the plague, with Muslim complicity and having its headquarters at Toledo in Spain. One may compare this to the more modern myth of a Jewish-Masonic plot and even to the famous *Protocols of the Elders of Zion* (see Chapter 12).

As a result there was a violent wave of pogroms which, in spite of condemnation by Pope Clement VI, spread from the south of France to Germany, Switzerland, Austria, and even Poland. At Strasbourg the whole Jewish community was burned in an enormous bonfire in their own cemetery, anticipating Nazi methods of mass execution. At Cologne the Jews, when threatened, decided to set fire to their own houses and perished in the conflagration, on a day that two centuries later would acquire an equally sinister fame—that of St. Bartholomew. At Mainz the Jews put up armed resistance, and it is said that they killed about two hundred of their attackers.

In the following year, 1349, the massacre was renewed in Frankfurt by a fanatical band of Flagellants, who went around the Continent carrying out collective whippings and terrifying the population. The pope again condemned them for 'shedding the blood of Jews' and threatened the ringleaders with excommunication. Even so, there was great loss of life and property, though it is impossible to get reliable estimates. There is a record of about 350 pogroms at the time of the Black Death in which 60 large and 150 small communities were attacked. A rabbi of Toledo calculated the total number of dead as 16,000.

One of the most important results of these Black Death pogroms was the flight of a great number of Jews to Eastern Europe, particularly to Poland. The community of Polish Ashkenazim, who later would become subjects of the tsarist empire, was to be one of the largest and most flourishing in the world.

THE MARTYRS OF JUDAISM

What many Christians considered to be the fruit of religious zeal (in many cases it was simply an opportunity to murder, pillage, and rob), to many Jews was martyrdom, dying for their faith. There again Biblical tradition came to their help with the glorious example of the victims of the time of the Maccabees. The medieval Christians, who by then had developed a full-grown cult of their own martyrs, with pilgrimages, relics, and miracles, were unable to understand that the Jews could feel in the same way: for instance, that the braver ones could sing hymns while being burned at the stake and accept the sacrifice as being 'for the sanctification of the Holy Name' (*kiddush ha-Shem*).

Many Christians at the time of the Roman persecutions had chosen death or torture rather than to offer incense to the gods or to curse the name of Christ. Their coreligionists of later centuries could not understand that the Jews found themselves in a similar situation: for them to worship an image of Christ or of the Virgin Mary would be as sinful or 'abominable' as for a Christian to sacrifice to Jupiter. But of course the Christians, like the Jews and Muslims, were convinced that theirs was the only true religion.

Again Christians have always considered one of their most precious privileges to be the right to educate their children in their parents' religion. In fact, the great majority of people have followed (to the extent to which they may be said to do so) the religious practices of their own group out of habit, not out of choice, and in Christian countries it was considered monstrous that children should be taken away by force or kidnapped and brought up as, say, Muslims. And yet many did not hesitate to do the same to Jewish children and baptize them.

As recently as 1858 a six-year-old child of Jewish parents called Edgardo Mortara was kidnapped at Bologna and brought up as a Christian under the pretext that he had been 'baptized' by a servant a few years earlier. The case aroused a great deal of protest in Jewish and liberal circles, but Bologna still belonged to the Papal States and Pius IX was inflexible. In the Middle Ages, of course, such cases were frequent and there was nobody to complain. The Christians could not understand that in Jewish eyes an uncircumcised Jewish boy was as shocking as an unbaptized child was to them.

WORSENING STATUS OF THE JEWS

But as we have already remarked, the worst consequence of Christian anti-Semitism was not the pogrom itself but its effect on the situation of the Jewish minority within medieval society. Similarly, the worst of African slavery was not the terrible loss of life as a result of the trade or of working conditions but the lasting effect on the Africans of cultural uprooting, human degradation, and the fact that they stayed in an oppressed condition even after Abolition.

Until the age of the Crusades the condition of the Jews in many parts of Europe and the Byzantine Empire had been 'tolerable'. At the time of the Carolingian empire, for instance (eighth and ninth centuries), there is evidence not only of Jewish prosperity but of reasonably good relations between Christians and Jews. It was against just such fraternization that intolerant Church leaders like Bishop Agobard of Lyons preached.

In that period of restricted trade the professional merchant was often a Jew or a Syrian, who might bring to Europe luxury goods like incense for the churches. In the eighth and ninth centuries the words *Judaeus* and *mercator* (merchant) became almost synonymous. They also trafficked in slaves, a practice which raised protest from the Church, not because it condemned slavery as such but because many of the slaves were Christian. But the Jews were not the only slave merchants, and Byzantine Greeks and Venetians took an important part in that trade.

In fact, the period of Jewish and Syrian predominance in trade was comparatively short. With the emergence of the great Italian merchant towns, like Venice and Amalfi, and later with the growth of important towns in much of Western Europe, a powerful middle class appeared which organized itself in corporations.

The whole medieval society was taking shape along hierarchical and corporate lines, leaving less and less room for that anomaly, the Jews.

Within the monopoly of faith and truth held by the Church, there was no margin for tolerated religions. Any freedom of worship the Jews might have was within very narrow limits. Within the feudal system there was little room for independent or peculiar groups.

What, then, was the Jew within the medieval order? He could not be regarded as a heretic, although many people looked upon him as something very similar. It should be noted that the Inquisition never proceeded against the Jew as such but only against those who had been baptized (often by force or at least under pressure) and went on practising Judaism in secret. The Jews were considered a kind of excrescence or anomaly which the official Church tolerated in view of their relationship with the Christian faith, always hoping for their eventual conversion.

Medieval society was a good example of what Müller-Lyer has called a 'function-centred' (not person-centred) society. Each individual had his position more or less rigidly determined within the social order, just as every planet or star had its fixed place in the 'celestial spheres' which were an integral part of the medieval conception of the universe, as we can see in works like Dante's *Divine Comedy*. The Jew did not quite belong to that order, or, rather, perhaps he helped paradoxically to maintain it by being a pariah and thus demonstrating the validity of the order by being excluded from it. Those who were 'inside' felt more accepted through looking upon them, just as the bliss of souls in Heaven, it was thought, was increased by contemplating the torments of those in Hell. Thomas Merton has expressed this with some penetration: 'I have what you have not. I am what you are not. . . . You are despised while I am praised. . . . And so I spend my life admiring the distance between you and me'.[8]

There was no place for the Jew in the feudal system, either as master or serf. It became generally accepted practice, often incorporated into laws, that he could not own land. Admittedly, there were many exceptions and variations, but in time this became general in the Christian world. And so the Jews were excluded from the then basic activity of economic life— agriculture.[9]

In the past, even outside Palestine the Jews had often served as mercenary soldiers, in the armies of the Great King of Persia, of Macedonian dynasties, or even of the Roman Empire. But during the Middle Ages military service became an integral part of the feudal system. The Jew could not be 'a man of arms', let alone a knight, who was a 'soldier of Christ'.[10] At the time of the Crusades the cross became an essential part of army dress and it was usually seen on flags, following the use of the crescent by Muslims. The new orders of knighthood in particular, like the Templars or the Teutonic Knights, belonged to the Church Militant and were often noted for their fierce anti-Semitism. It is no coincidence that the Nazi SS was supposed to carry on that tradition, and leaders like Himmler had a strong antiquarian interest in the Teutonic Knights.

In certain countries, such as Germany, the Jews preserved the right to bear arms until the end of the thirteenth century (and so were sometimes able to resist armed attacks). But they were usually deprived of military instruction and any share in sports and exercises. So they tended to become helpless victims, and therefore even more contemptible in the eyes of aggressive communities to whom bravery in combat was one of the most highly prized virtues.

THE JEWISH USURER

As commerce became more active and better organized, opportunities for Jewish participation decreased and many Jews were virtually forced into the only business that was open to them—the money market. Merchant and Jew were no longer synonymous; instead it was the hated practice of usury that became closely associated with him, and this in turn embittered anti-Jewish feeling. As in so many situations of this kind, a vicious circle was formed.

In the Middle Ages the Church periodically condemned usury, as in the Third Lateran Council (1179), which denied Christian burial to all those who practised it, and later in the sterner laws enacted by the Councils of Lyons (1274) and Vienna (1312).[11] Usurers were excluded from communion, confession, and absolution, and anybody who stated that usury was not a sin was declared a heretic and became subject to the Inquisition.

But the very severity of these laws, and the frequency with which they were enacted, show that the practice was becoming widespread among Christians, and that the Jews were only one of many groups to practice it. In Italy the Lombards became notorious in this respect (again the Biblical 'example and byword'), and Dante placed the Paduans in one of the circles of Hell on account of usury.[12]

Obviously, the resentment against the Jewish usurer (in fact, as is well known, the word 'Jew' itself became a synonym for usurer) was yet another example of 'selective perception': the fault of a minority which is prejudiced against becomes a special object of condemnation because the finger is already pointed at it. The final result was the classical stereotype of the Jew in the West: the miserly old man with his hooked nose and greedy claws, avidly grasping his moneybags—Shakespeare's Shylock, Isaac of York in Scott's *Ivanhoe*, or Fagin in Dickens' *Oliver Twist*. In studies of stereotypes carried out by social psychologists, the character trait most often associated with the Jews is love of money.[13] In fact, the alleged Jewish vocation for usury, capitalism, or lucre in general was precisely a result of anti-Semitism. The Jewish usurer was little known in Europe before the eleventh century, just as Josephus could say in his time that the Jews were not given to trade.

We can see here that the status of the Jews in the Middle Ages determined not only the choice of occupation (if choice is the right word) but also the conditions in which it was exercised. Jewish communities were subject to pogroms, decrees of expulsion, or crushing taxation. People living an insecure life, liable at any moment to be attacked or expelled, tended to become attached to money because this was one of the few means of wealth they could own and it was also easy to carry. They had in a way to make themselves easily portable. Hence Jewish interest in money and jewels, which permit concentration of wealth in comparatively small volume, although they also exert maximum attraction on thieves, as the Jew Jesus of Nazareth used to warn (Luke 12:33). Jesus, like the wiser of mankind, knew that economic security was a mirage.

BLACKMAIL AND SPOLIATION OF THE JEWS

This financial role played by many Jews in the Middle Ages became even more important through the use that kings and other rulers made of them. The *fiscus judaicus* [14] of the Roman Empire was inherited not only by Byzantine emperors but also by several monarchs in the West and by the Church itself. In a society ruled by the feudal system, any payment or tribute was bound to be regarded as a token of serfdom. The Jews were serfs of the emperor or of any other authority: in England they were described as *servi camerae regis* or the 'king's persons'. St. Thomas Aquinas went as far as to say that all Jews were collectively serfs of the Church.

It was an idea that tallied admirably with the outlook and concepts of the age. Bondage was considered a general condition: nobody had an inborn right to freedom (that was a revolutionary idea when it first emerged in the eighteenth century), for all mankind was tainted with original sin. The Jews particularly could be considered as paying with their serfdom for the collective sin of having murdered Our Lord. And those who knew their Bible would remember that the descendants of Esau (the rejected brother) had been condemned to serve those of Jacob.

The relation of dependence became even more pronounced when the Jews were forced to seek protection against violence from any ruler, whether Churchman or layman. Protection, as in the gangster world, had to be paid for in money. During the Middle Ages such tribute came to represent an important part of the income of kings and lords, and the Jews could even be transferred from one master to another as a fief. As Milman says: 'The Jew thus often became a valuable property; he was granted away, he was named in a marriage settlement, he was bequeathed, in fact he was pawned, he was sold, he was stolen'.[15]

Kings and feudal lords also used the Jewish usurers as a convenient sponge that absorbed wealth and then could be squeezed through exorbitant tribute or total spoliation. The idea of extracting from a human being all the value he can have was not a Nazi invention, but it was the Nazis who carried it to its 'logical' and gruesome conclusion; for instance, collecting the gold from their victims' mouths, women's hair, human fat for the manufacture of soap, and so on. On the other hand, there is some evidence in the Middle Ages that barons and other people who were indebted to Jews could instigate massacres in order to wipe out the debt.

The mechanism of the 'sponge' was clear in the case of England. King Edward I, after making repeated extortions from the Jewish community, concluded that no more could be got out of them, so he established contact with Christian capitalists in Europe and in 1290 ordered the expulsion of all Jews not only from the British Isles but from his French possessions. The expulsion was carried out in the most ruthless manner, and many Jews, after losing all they had, fell into the hands of ship captains, who in at least one case left them on a sandbank to be drowned.

The old scapegoat gambit could also work in a somewhat different way: the Jews were used as an instrument of extortion (as tax collectors and in other ways) and then received all the blame. Or the feudal lords could use them as a suitable target for giving vent to resentment against any abuses or oppression for which the upper classes were entirely responsible. Something very similar occurred in modern times when anti-Semitism became the weapon of the extreme right against social reform.

THE JEWISH BADGE

While the Church fought against usury, it had also to deal with various 'heretical' sects like the Albigenses (Cathari) and Waldenses, against whom the Third (1179) and the Fourth (1215) Lateran Councils enacted strong measures. The Albigenses flourished in the south of France and were especially tolerant towards the Jews, some of whom reached prominent positions in the Languedoc area. They were crushed in the terrible crusade carried out from 1209 onwards by order of Pope Innocent III and later by Louis IX of France.

Besides the establishment of the Inquisition in 1233 the Church approved several stricter repressive measures in the thirteenth century, particularly forbidding mixed marriages and preventing Christian nurses or midwives from looking after Jews. The Lateran Council of 1215 decreed for the first time that Jews should wear a special badge, apparently following a practice that had been started among Muslim states.

In Europe the Jewish badge was aimed especially at preventing Christians from unknowingly having sexual relations with Jews. Such an act could be severely punished: an interesting anticipation of the strict sexual segregation imposed in South Africa, Rhodesia, and the southern states of America. Jealousy and sexual fears play an important part in racial prejudice, and as we shall see later, Nazi propaganda would make use of this.[16]

The imposition of the badge is a very revealing aspect in the history and social psychology of anti-Semitism. It meant in fact branding the Jew with a mark as one brands cattle. It was the physical expression of the prejudice and of its condemnation: THIS MAN IS A JEW. One is reminded of the mocking title on the cross, THIS IS THE KING OF THE JEWS, or again the tunic or 'sanbenito' that the victims of the Inquisition had to wear in doing penance or in the procession to the stake.

People who use the scapegoat mechanism have to brand the object of their hatred aggressively with a word or a label: 'Jew!' 'Communist!' [17] Readers of Nathaniel Hawthorne will remember the scarlet letter 'A' which was sewn on the dress of women condemned for adultery. In medieval Europe prostitutes often had to wear special clothes; and the analogy is not farfetched, since Jews and courtesans were two classes of pariahs who in certain towns could only attend the public baths on certain specified days.

The Jewish badge tended to vary from country to country. It often consisted of a patch of yellow or red cloth sewn on the clothes, and in France, Germany, and a few other countries it was shaped as a wheel or 'O', hence the name *rouelle* or *rotella*. In England it represented the Tables of the Law. In Austria and Germany the Jews were often forced to wear a distinctive pointed hat (*Judenhut*).[18] In Italy it was a broad-brimmed hat, which gave rise to a story that may not be true but seems *molto bene trovata*. It was said that at one time the Jewish hat was red, and a short-sighted priest, as he walked the streets of Rome, thought he saw a cardinal and paid him a very respectful reverence. In fact it was a Jew, and to avoid such shocking mistakes the colour of the Jewish hat was changed from red to yellow.

On the island of Crete the badge was placed not only on individuals but on their houses, again in a curious anticipation of a practice to be followed by the Nazis in Germany.

THE EMERGENCE OF THE GHETTO

In Rome there was an old custom which in a way reveals a measure of tolerance. Whenever a new pope was enthroned, the Jews used to take part in the traditional procession as if they were just another corporation, carrying their own standard and singing psalms. They would go before the new pontiff as before a king and present him with the scroll of the Torah as a kind of tribute. The pope would return it with a gesture of contempt and renew the edict forbidding any interference with the Jewish cult.

Many popes in the Middle Ages and Renaissance were little more than Italian princes and used Jewish financiers just as other rulers did. In a way, as heirs of the Roman emperors, they were following the old tradition of tolerance and patronage. An example of this more humane policy is the bull of Mantua, issued by Martin V (1417–31), who was elected to put an end to the Great Schism. It begins thus:

> Since the Jews are made in the image of God, since a remnant of them shall be saved, since, further, their trading is profitable to Christians, and lastly, since they solicit our countenance and our compassion, thus will we, in the same sense as Calixtus, Eugenius, Alexander, Clement, Celestine, Innocent, Honorius, etc., and other former Popes of blessed memory.[19]

But another pope, in the militant and fanatical period of the Counter Reformation, showed himself one of the most implacable anti-Semites in history.

In 1555 Cardinal Caraffa was elected with the name of Paul IV. His fanatical zeal was aimed not only at the Protestants or any suspects of 'heresy' but also against the Jews. In the very first year of his reign he issued the bull *Cum nimis absurdum*, re-enacting several repressive measures of former periods. At the same time he withdrew the protection his predecessors had given to the Marranos of Portugal (see Chapter 8), who had taken refuge at Ancona, and had twenty-five of them burned at the stake.

On that occasion it seems that for the first time in history the weapon of commercial boycott was used, and the Jews of the Ottoman Empire placed an interdict on the Papal States. The sultan himself, Suleiman the Magnificent, sent a strong letter to the pope protesting against the persecution and demanding the release of the Jews who were Ottoman subjects. At that time, obviously, the Jews were a flourishing and prosperous community under Turkish rule.

Pope Paul IV also established the Roman ghetto, which was already in existence in many European cities in the Middle Ages. Again the Muslims, in spite of their toleration, seem to have pointed the way, for the earliest forced segregation we know of was in Morocco, where in 1280 the Jews were placed in special quarters called *millahs*.

The name 'ghetto' came into use in Venice and its origin is obscure. Some think it may be an abbreviation of *borghetto* (little borough) while others derive it from an iron foundry near Venice (*gettare* = to cast in metal). Another name, which even today is given to a Venetian canal, is *giudecca* (Jewry), corresponding to the Spanish *judería* and the Portuguese *judiaria*. It is significant that Dante in his *Divine Comedy* should have chosen that name for one of the areas of Hell reserved for traitors and naturally for their archetype Judas.[20]

In Verona the name used was *zuecca*, while in Germany the ghetto was called *Judengasse* or *Judenstadt* (respectively, street and town of Jews) and in France *carrière des Juifs* or simply *carrière*. In England there never was a real, segregated ghetto. In London until the expulsion by Edward I the Jews tended to concentrate in an area of the City where there is still a street with the name of Old Jewry. When they were readmitted to the country at the time of Cromwell, from 1656 onwards, it was on a new basis of tolerance, and their tendency to concentrate in certain districts, which is also found among other immigrant groups, has no character of segregation.

Ghettos prevailed for centuries in many European towns, great and small, and their existence was accepted as something quite natural and unavoidable. At least until World War II some of the old buildings could still be seen in towns like Frankfurt, Prague, Rome, or Venice.

The typical ghetto was a comparatively small area enclosed by walls and gates, which were kept locked at night and during festivals such as Easter, when violence against Jews was particularly liable to occur. The gates were massive, under a low arch, and there were watchmen who had to be paid by the Jewish community. After curfew any Jews found outside the ghetto could be severely punished, but so would Christians if found inside.

As the ghetto normally could not expand horizontally, its growth had to be vertical, and viewed from a distance it seemed to tower over the rest of the town. Its old, often ramshackle buildings tended to be dangerous and liable to catch fire. As one would expect, they were overcrowded and insanitary. But inside the ghetto at least the Jews felt reasonably secure and lived in their own way, with their own institutions. Inevitably, this produced a withdrawn, encapsulated kind of life and mentality, which even after the abolition of the ghettos they took a long time to outgrow.

Outside, the Jews were usually forced to wear the yellow badge, but even without it they tended to adopt a somewhat distinctive dress in many countries. The men wore a long cloak made with a strong, rough cloth—the gabardine, or gauvardine, also frequently worn by pilgrims and beggars.[21]

In Spain from 1412 onwards Jews and Moors had to wear a long cloak which came down to the feet. The broad-brimmed hat, whether compulsory or not, became a distinctive feature. In Eastern Europe, particularly in Poland, the Jews retained for centuries the long, dark tunic, or caftan, and the hat called *streimel*. Some types of costume, together with a long beard and sidelocks, came to acquire a religious significance, especially in the case of the rabbi, the *mohel*, the *shohet*, and other community officials. Their preservation became at the same time a distinctive feature and a token of loyalty to Judaism.

In other words, the Jews, whom the Bible describes as 'a holy people', became in some ways as distinctive a class as the clergy. In both cases there was a similar conservative tendency in matters of costume. Historians have often pointed out that the priest's cassock, as to a certain point the habits worn by monks and nuns, was not really a 'uniform' of special design like that of soldiers. What happened was simply that while among the people at large fashions were always changing, the clergy continued to wear the kind of costume worn in the late Roman Empire. In a similar way Greek or Russian Orthodox priests still wear long beards, like many Jewish rabbis, not as a distinctive feature but according to the custom of the Byzantine Empire and of early tsarist Russia.

THE JEW AS A STOCK TYPE AND CARICATURE

Here we see clearly at last that repressive measures on the one hand and Jewish religious conservatism on the other both contributed to shape the appearance of the Jew and to produce a distinctive type. It was this 'strange', outlandish creature, 'an apparition in a long caftan and black sidelocks', that the young Adolf Hitler was to 'discover' one day in the streets of Vienna and identify as the secret agent of all sorts of diabolical plans (see Chapter 11).

In fact, the Jew as a stock type was often put on the medieval stage as an object of mockery or hatred. In the traditional mystery plays it was normal to follow the same conventions that we have noticed in the case of paintings: that is, in Biblical scenes the 'bad characters' appeared dressed as medieval Jews, especially Judas, who always came on as a Jewish usurer with a red beard. In a German mystery cycle the stage introductions say that the main Jewish character, Archisynagogus, is 'to imitate the gestures of a Jew in all things'. This is a reference to the alleged wild gesticulation attributed to Jews in many European countries (for instance, the district of Whitechapel in the East End of London, where many Jews used to live, was jocularly known at one time as 'the land of waving palms'). Even when the scenes are taken from the Old Testament, as in a Latin play about Isaac and Rebecca from twelfth-century Austria, the characters are told to wear *pilea judaica*, i.e., typical Jewish headdresses.[22]

Even in modern times the stock type could still continue as the Jewish usurer or the old-clothes man, both images of social degradation. Like the 'murderer of Our Lord', such stereotyped images have exerted a deep influence on our imagination, and no doubt on the Jews themselves. There is a large measure of truth in what Jean-Paul Sartre says: 'Ce n'est pas le charactère juif qui provoque l'anti-sémitisme mais, au contraire, c'est l'anti-sémite qui crée le Juif'.[23]

8

Expulsions
and Autos-da-Fé

... And if I had no other merit save that I believe, as I always do,
firmly and truly in God, in all that the holy Roman Catholic Church
holds and believes, and that I am a mortal enemy of the Jews, as I
am, the historians ought to have mercy on me and treat me well in
their writings.
— Sancho Panza in Cervantes, *Don Quixote*, Part II, chap. 8

ONE STEP FORWARD AND TWO BACKWARD

'In the same month when they expelled all Jews from the country, Your
Highnesses commanded me to go with an adequate fleet to those parts of
India'.[1]

Thus wrote Christopher Columbus in the account of his famous journey
which led to the 'discovery' of America. The month is March 1492, and
the edict of expulsion mentioned by Columbus ends with these words:
'Given in the city of Granada on the 31st of the month of March in the
year 1492 of the birth of Our Lord Jesus Christ'.[2]

With the conquest of Granada by King Ferdinand and Queen Isabella,
the last bulwark of Islam on the Peninsula had fallen and Christian Spain
had been unified at last. With the expulsion of the Jews the task of achieving unity had been completed, and there would be 'no place left in which
Christ is denied'. 'One Lord, one faith, one baptism'.[3] One King, one God,
one Church. The cry was echoed by the Muslims themselves, who would
sometimes go into battle shouting, 'One! One!' (*Ahad*).

The year 1492 presents another symbolic contrast: the Spanish were taking a great step forward on the road that would one day lead human beings
to the moon, and at the same time retreating in matters of tolerance and
humanity. In the end the two steps backward would prevail and the whole
Peninsula would pay for its obscurantism.

Paradoxically, Spain had been a comparatively safe haven for the Jews, and looking back on those centuries the Sephardim would consider that period a true Golden Age: the feeling would be reflected even in the aristocratic pride that made them look down on Jews of other countries. They considered themselves more fortunate, for they had enjoyed a secure and respected position and even said that for six hundred years Spain had been like an earthly paradise.

We all tend to idealize the past, but there was an element of truth in this picture. It may be assumed that the six centuries referred to lasted from the Muslim conquest of the Peninsula (711–15) to the first serious pogroms (1320–29). Indeed, in that period the situation of the Sephardic Jews there had been far better than that of their coreligionists in other Christian countries. The policy of expulsion itself had never been adopted in Spain before Ferdinand and Isabella. England had already expelled its Jewish community in 1290 and France not long after, in 1306.

THE JEWS IN THE PENINSULA

The Jewish communities in the Peninsula were very ancient and dated at least from Roman times. We have seen how numerous they were in the Balearic Islands where forced conversions occurred in the fifth century.

The Visigoths who began their conquest of Spain the same century were Arians (the term derives from Arius, a bishop of Alexandria, and must not be confused with the linguistic name 'Aryan'): i.e., they followed the doctrine condemned as heretical by the Council of Nicaea (325), according to which the nature of the Son in the Holy Trinity was not identical with that of the Father. The heretical sects were as a rule more tolerant than the official Church, and while the Visigothic kings remained Arian the Jews lived in comparative peace.

In 587, however, with the conversion of King Reccared to Catholicism, the situation began to change. In 616 Sisebut issued repressive laws and went as far as to forbid circumcision. The practice of Judaism was forbidden and many Jews submitted to baptism. The Twelfth Council of Toledo (681) approved even more severe regulations: any Jewish parents who had their children circumcised would lose their noses and have their property confiscated. No Jew could travel in the country without permission from the local bishop or justice of the peace, and he also had to present a certificate of 'good behaviour' and a passport. The Jews were also required to eat and drink with the Christians, and on the Sabbath they had to assemble in the presence of the bishop.

In view of all this, it is not surprising that the persecuted minority should welcome the Muslim invasion. They were accused of giving active help to the invaders, just as when the Persians invaded the Byzantine Empire about a century earlier, or the Dutch invaded colonial Brazil in the seventeenth century.

It was in the interest of the Muslims to have Jewish support, and there was also some religious affinity between the two groups. Under the brilliant caliphate (earlier emirate) of Cordoba, founded in 756 by Abd-ar-Rahman I, the Jewish communities, besides having freedom of worship, were not under any major legal disability and could follow many professions. As the Jews were often of a higher level of education than the local population, they were much in demand as administrators, physicians, diplomats, and so on.

This is perhaps a good place to stress a historical fact which has an obvious interest for the study of anti-Semitism and has been often ignored by anti-Semitic writers. The Jews were the bearers of an ancient culture and an age-old literary tradition, which had been cross-fertilized by some of the highest civilizations of the ancient world, like the Greek, Egyptian, Babylonian, and Persian. They possessed a rich religious literature and folklore, which were constantly added to: to the Muslims the Jews were 'the people of the Book'.

The simple obligation to give religious instruction and 'to teach the Law' to new generations, so often reiterated in the Bible, had promoted a high level of literacy. Every boy was supposed to go through the Bar Mitzvah ceremony, and even if this was not always done, it meant that a reasonable level of education was maintained even in difficult periods. By contrast, during the so-called Dark Ages and even later, illiteracy was the rule in the West, and even great leaders like the emperor Charlemagne could not read.

There are reasons to believe that even in the Roman Empire the Jews had a good level of education. Seneca, whose anti-Jewish feelings have been mentioned, admitted that they were one of the few peoples in the empire well instructed in their own religion. Josephus could be relied upon to stress this point:

> Among ourselves, you can ask anybody about the Laws and he will explain them more promptly than his own name. Thus, since the awakening of reason we assimilate them so deeply that we have them as it were engraved on our souls.[4]

Even allowing for idealization, this passage is revealing about the strict conditioning of Jewish children. It was the secret of their survival as a religious and cultural entity. If it were not so deeply imprinted in childhood, Judaism would have disappeared and followed the fate of so many other cults.

Admittedly, ancient Jewish education was predominantly religious, and the Jews as a whole, apart from a more enlightened minority, lacked the concept of liberal education practised by the Greeks and which was to flourish later in the West. But there is little doubt that in the period of cultural disintegration and upheaval which followed the fall of the Roman Empire in the West, the Jewish minority played an important cultural role.

On the other hand, the emerging Arab civilization, which through Syrian, Jewish, or Nestorian Christian elements had absorbed much of value from the Persians and Byzantine Greeks, reached a high level. In the ninth and tenth centuries Baghdad in the East and Cordoba in the West stood among the most important cultural centres in the world, rivalling India and the China of the T'ang dynasty, while Western Europe remained backward and semi-barbaric. In Europe as a whole, until the creation of the first universities, cultivation of knowledge was restricted to the monasteries and some of the more enlightened courts.

Meanwhile, the Jews of the Peninsula, speaking and writing in Arabic, which was then one of the most important literary languages, produced a series of outstanding philosophers, astronomers, and doctors: men like Solomon ibn-Gabirol (Avicebron), Hasdai ibn-Shaprut, Abraham ben Ezra, and, most famous of all, Moses ben Maimon (Maimonides).

Jewish scholars and wise men played an important role in cultural transmission, translating Greek works into Arabic and Arabic works into Latin. In Spain and other areas of international contact (Sicily, the south of France), they acted as intermediaries between the Muslim world and the Christian West. They played the part of diplomats as well, and when Charlemagne sent a mission to the court of the famous caliph of Baghdad, Harun al-Rashid, his envoy was a Jew.

Some modern Jewish scholars like Charles Singer go as far as to say that the Jewish carriers represent perhaps the most continuously civilized element in Europe'. And he adds:

> European Jewish thinkers in numbers were consciously developing Hellenic philosophy and discussing Plato and Aristotle, the Stoics and Plotinus, while the rest of Europe was, as yet, in its barbaric incoherent childhood. A reasonable claim may be made for the Jewish communities of Southern France, the Iberian Peninsula, and the Rhineland, as having had the longest and most ancient continuous civilized history in Europe outside the classical zone. In a cultural sense the Jews were the first Europeans.[5]

While some may question this for Europe as a whole, there is little doubt as to the role played by prominent Jews in the Peninsula. Like Joseph in ancient Egypt, they were called upon to fill important posts in the court as ministers, treasurers, physicians, or diplomats. This was common practice in the caliphate of Cordoba and was imitated by the Christian kingdoms, together with so many other things they borrowed from their opponents. In fact, when the Almohades (a fanatical Muslim sect from North Africa) conquered Muslim Spain, it was the turn of the Jews to seek refuge in the Christian states from Mohammedan persecution. For instance, the family of Maimonides had to leave Cordoba because freedom of worship no longer existed there.

On the other hand, people who climb high become more vulnerable, and envy or jealousy could easily reinforce anti-Jewish feelings. The emergent European monarchies needed capable administrators and officials, and very often could only get them either from the Church or from the Jewish community. This 'rivalry' is not surprising since Israel was also, in a way, a church, an organized religious community, while Christianity had claimed for itself the Jewish inheritance, that is, the claim to be 'the true Israel'.

As a result the Christian clergy were both religious and 'professional' rivals of the Jew. The Church leaders were concerned with Jewish proselytism, which might take away followers from Christianity, and feared any growth in Jewish power and influence. Bishops and priests put pressure on rulers suspected of favouring Jews and tried to remove the latter from any important positions, sometimes going to the extent of recommending expulsion.

In the Iberian Peninsula, however, at least until the fourteenth century, the forces of hatred and intolerance had not given rise to active persecution. Even between Christians and Muslims there was a measure of peaceful coexistence, in spite of frequent wars. The mere fact that the Peninsula (like Sicily) was an area of contact between the three religions did produce more tolerant attitudes: Muslims, Christians, and Jews could see with their own eyes that the 'infidels' of other religions were people much like themselves.

Even during the struggles of the *Reconquista* (the Christian reconquest of Muslim territories), this tolerance remained for a period, and some kings of Castile called themselves 'Kings of the Three Religions'. The first to do so seems to have been Ferdinand III (1217–52). His successor, Alfonso the Wise (Alfonso X), renowned for his learning and religious tolerance, gave protection to Judaism in his famous code of *Las Siete Partidas* and promoted the active work of translation at Toledo in which Jewish scholars took an important part.

More concrete evidence is found in a bull issued by Pope Honorius III in 1219. As we have seen, the Lateran Council of 1215 had made the Jewish badge compulsory. But in Spain there was such an outcry from the Sephardic Jews that the pope addressed a bull to the archbishop of Toledo suspending the enforcement of the regulation in Castile. The letter says that the Jews had threatened 'to withdraw to the lands of the Moors', and the Castilian king Ferdinand III may have feared the loss to himself this would represent. In the thirteenth century there were in Castile alone three hundred Jewish communities, usually called *juderías* or *aljamas*, which contributed a good sum of money to the royal treasury.

THE SPANISH POGROMS

In the fourteenth century the situation began to change, though it is difficult to see exactly why. One should take into account, of course, the cumulative effect of the long wars of the *Reconquista*, real crusades in which Spanish and Portuguese sometimes received the help of foreign contingents. And there were external influences too.

In fact, the first waves of violence seem to have come from France. In 1320 an apocalyptic French sect called the Pastoureaux (shepherds) crossed the Pyrenees and attacked Jewish communities in Aragon. In 1328 a new wave exterminated a large part of the Jews in Navarre.

In the reign of Pedro I of Castile (1350–69), called 'the Cruel' by his enemies, the Jews suffered greatly in the long dynastic struggle between the king and his brother Henry of Trastamara (later Henry II). Pedro favoured them so much that he was accused of being a Judaizer or even a Jew: it was said that the queen his mother, having given birth to a girl, had her replaced by a Jewish boy.

Pedro infringed the law that banned the Jews from filling public offices, and made Samuel Abulafia his treasurer, who had a splendid synagogue built at Toledo that outshone the Christian churches. The wealth and power of some Jews stirred envy and resentment among the people who accused them of extortion through taxation.

In the end the king himself had Abulafia arrested for embezzlement and had him executed after torture. The pattern of the Jewish grandee who achieves power and influence at a court only to fall from favor and lose his head was to be repeated several times in history.

When the dynastic war began between Henry of Trastamara and the king, the Jews took the king's side and suffered several massacres. One of the worst was at Toledo, where according to a contemporary chronicle the troops of Prince Henry 'killed about 1,200 men and women and did not do worse damage because they were not able to enter the larger of the ghettos (*judería mayor*)'.[6]

With Henry's victory in 1369 the repressive anti-Jewish Church legislation was strictly enforced for the first time in Castile. This did not prevent Henry from appointing a Jewish minister, Joseph Pichon, who became his chief accountant. This time Pichon was the victim not of anti-Jewish hatred but of his enemies inside the Jewish community, who according to one version suspected him of Christian leanings. There was a curious and involved plot in which John I, Henry's son and successor, confirmed the

Jews' death sentence without knowing that it was aimed at his own minister (1379). Pichon's execution caused great indignation and John had the culprits beheaded, also depriving the Jewish community of all legal autonomy.

During the same reign a fierce anti-Semite, the archdeacon of Écija, Martinez, began to preach violent sermons against the Jews. His theme was twofold: the Jews were the murderers of Jesus Christ, and they were exploiting the people through their activities as tax collectors and usurers.

The more extremist groups took advantage of King John I's death, his successor being an eleven-year-old boy, Henry III. Easter was commonly a time for more militant fervour. On Ash Wednesday in 1391 the crowds at Seville, at the instigation of Martinez, began to attack the *juderías* of the town. After an interlude of quiet when the Jews asked in vain for the punishment of the ringleaders, the pogroms started again in June and this time spread to a large part of Spain. For the first time the Sephardim experienced all the horrors they had heard about in other lands: arson, rape, ruthless slaughter. The *juderías* or *aljamas* of Cordoba, Toledo, Burgos, and Barcelona were all destroyed. It was said that in the province of Valencia not a single Jew escaped. The synagogues were either burned down or converted, like the two most magnificent in Seville, into churches. The neighbouring reigns of Aragon and Navarre were contaminated with the same virus, and John I of Aragon seems to have been the only one who punished the ringleaders (he had twenty-six of them beheaded). The historian Amador de los Ríos points out the impoverishment caused by the pogroms, for many shops were sacked and several lines of trade where the Jews were active suffered greatly. In the Peninsula only the Portuguese Jews escaped.

EMERGENCE OF THE 'MARRANOS'

The massacres of 1391–92 had another important consequence. 'For the first and only time in history', Cecil Roth claims, 'the Jewish morale broke' and many thousands accepted baptism in order to escape slaughter. Contemporary estimates, never very reliable, exaggerated their numbers, but they must have been great.

That it occurred in Spain is perhaps not very difficult to understand. The very wealth and prosperity of the Sephardic Jews had undermined their faith and steadiness (Jesus would have understood that), and obviously they wanted to hold on to the position they had achieved. Probably not all became Christians entirely out of expediency. Some may have been sincere, and there were others who turned persecutors and violently anti-Jewish. An example of that was the rabbi Solomon ha-Levi who was baptized as Pablo de Santa Maria and lived to be bishop of Burgos, his native city, and a member of the regency council of Castile.

In the beginning of the fifteenth century, and so a few years after the Spanish pogroms, another Jewish apostate, Master Jerome of Santa Fe (called by the Jews *Megadef*, 'the blasphemer'), helped the fanatical Dominican Fray Vincent Ferrer carry out the forcible conversion of Jews, breaking into synagogues at the head of a tumultuous crowd. He also incited the Avignon pope Benedict XIII to stage a formal dispute (such as were common in the Middle Ages) between Jewish scholars and Christian priests.

But the majority remained 'Christians' only for appearance' sake. So one had this curious phenomenon in religious history: thousands of people pretending to follow one religion and practising a different one in secret. This had also happened to a number of Christians in Roman times, but to a much lesser degree. In Muslim Spain a number of Jews (*Anusim*) became outwardly converts to Islam. But nothing could compare with the minute examination of habits, gestures, words, or even thoughts carried out by the Inquisition: the very name would become 'an example and a byword'.

The double life led many Jews in Spain (later in Portugal as well and Latin America) could apply to many events and rituals. If Jewish parents had to take their child to the baptismal font in church, they immediately tried to wipe out all traces of the ceremony on arriving home, and whenever possible had the boys circumcised. They would marry in church, but also celebrate a Jewish wedding in secret. Marriages with Gentiles were mutually avoided, for the Gentiles also were prejudiced against marrying those 'of impure blood'.

There were all sorts of tricks and subterfuges devised by the Marranos, as the 'converted' Jews came to be called. For instance, the members of a family would loudly call each other to go to church, for the benefit of their neighbours, who, after all, might always act as informers. They would all go out and after a long detour go back home without setting foot in the church. Or if they attended mass, some way could be found of not actually taking part in the sacrifice: at the elevation of the host they might, for example, pretend a speck of dust had fallen in their eyes. Who knows what similar tricks the Roman Christians may have invented so as in some way to invalidate the sacrifice to the gods?

Some Jews would attend the synagogue in secret or send donations of oil for the lamps. Or again they would found religious associations camouflaged under the name of Catholic saints but in fact for the secret practice of Judaism. Extraordinary as it may seem, a number of Jewish communities managed to keep up this dissimulation for generations, and in some cases only dropped the mask after the Reformation, when they came to live under a Protestant regime, usually less intolerant to Judaism.

One of the most curious and ironical incidents occurred at the end of the sixteenth century when a group of Marranos from the Peninsula settled in Amsterdam. The Dutch were at the time fighting Spain for their religious and political freedom, and the authorities proceeded to arrest the Spanish Jews as Catholics. As they could not speak any Dutch, it was very difficult to explain the real situation. At last, one of the leaders, Manuel Rodrigues Vega (or to give his secret Jewish name, Jacob Tirado), who had lately been circumcised at an advanced age, had the happy idea of trying Latin, which was still the international language of the West. He explained that they were all Jews and were as much persecuted by the Inquisition as the Protestants. Not only were they released but the Dutch authorities allowed them freedom of worship. This was in fact the beginning of a very flourishing community, and, as we shall see, a springboard for settlements in other countries.

Amsterdam—or the New Jerusalem, as some came to call it—would be the great refuge for the Sephardim. It welcomed Jews from Spain and Portugal, Flemish merchants from Antwerp, and French Huguenots, thus expanding as a commercial and industrial centre. From there would depart expeditions to Brazil, leading to the opening of the first synagogue in the New World. In fact, the success of the Dutch would abundantly show that intolerance, besides being morally wrong, is bad business.

Nor should one forget the cultural consequences of persecution. Refugees, whether political or religious, tend to be distinguished by a higher level of energy, initiative, and education: such was the case of many Sephardic Jews and of the Pilgrim Fathers who sailed to America in the *Mayflower*. It is not surprising that Amsterdam was also enriched as a cultural centre, and like Alexandria she was to produce a Philo—the Portuguese Jew Spinoza.

POGROMS AGAINST THE MARRANOS

But the Diaspora of the Sephardic Jews was still in the future: it occurred exactly one hundred years after the pogroms of 1391–92. The acceptance of baptism and religious dissimulation might bring advantages to the Jews, but there were always people on the watch and eager to begin the witch-hunt. Soon they found out that the old suspicions and resentment had not died. A baptized Jew was released from all the restrictions of his previous status and he could enter any profession, including the one that afforded most advancement and influence, the Church. But the very success and prosperity that many of them acquired soon aroused envy and resentment among the native Christians.

If the Jews have always been accused of marrying only among themselves, the Spanish had their own racial pride. The converted Jews were called in Spain *Marranos*, an offensive term which probably means 'swine'. In Portugal the more neutral name 'New Christian' (*Cristão Novo*) came to be used. Old Spanish families which admitted Marranos to their midst through marriage could be considered 'polluted' with *mala sangre* (bad blood). Many of the most aristocratic families of Aragon and Castile came to have 'Jewish blood', and there were few who could take pride in their *limpieza* (clean or pure blood). Later there were attempts to impose disabilities on Marranos or New Christians, and these seem to have been stricter in Portugal.

It was not long before the Jews learned that baptism or even a sincere conversion was no protection against popular violence. In 1473 a new Catholic brotherhood was founded in Cordoba which did not admit Marranos. During processions and religious festivals (as during the Passover at Jerusalem at the time of Jesus) fanaticism is more liable to explode. At the inaugural procession of the new brotherhood the rumour went round that a little Marrano girl had thrown dirty water on the image of the Virgin. This was the sign for a fierce attack on the houses of the New Christians, with shouts of '*Viva la fe de Dios*' (Long live the faith of God), and in spite of strong reaction there was the usual wave of slaughter, rape, and pillage. The riots spread to other towns in Andalusia, and in the following year there was a similar wave of pogroms in the north.

THE SPANISH INQUISITION

In that same year of 1474 the Infanta Isabella succeeded to the throne of Castile: she and her husband, Ferdinand, who later inherited Aragon, would for the first time unify Spain. Their confessor was the Dominican friar Tomás de Torquemada.

Torquemada, whose name has become closely associated with the Inquisition, was a fanatical Catholic, a supreme expression of that spirit of monolithic unification that would characterize the reign of 'Their Catholic Majesties'. Two 'problems' obsessed him: the Marranos, or New Christians, and the *Moriscos*, i.e., people of Muslim origin who would later be faced with the same dilemma—baptism or expulsion. Just as Hitler believed that 'international Jewry' was poisoning the life and racial purity of Germany, so Torquemada was fully convinced that the Marranos and Moriscos (particularly the former) constituted a very grave threat to Catholic life in Spain.

In 1478, under his influence, Ferdinand and Isabella asked Pope Sixtus IV for permission to establish the Inquisition in the country. This was granted, and in 1480 the first Inquisitors were appointed in Spain. In 1483 Torquemada was given the famous title of Grand Inquisitor.

The Portuguese have a proverb that 'the devil is never as ugly as he is depicted'. Certainly the Inquisitors were not the bloodthirsty, sadistic monsters some people imagine, and a picture like that given by Bernard Shaw in his play *Saint Joan* is probably nearer the truth. Compared with Hitler and his followers, the Inquisition was a model of moderation and good intentions. But as has often been remarked, 'good intentions' have produced some of the most monstrous crimes in history, and there is no doubt that the Inquisition was responsible for an amount of suffering and oppression that cannot be estimated by mere figures of people burned at the stake.

Following the official establishment of the inquisitorial process by Pope Gregory IX in 1233, mainly with the aim of suppressing the Albigenses, another pope, Innocent IV, approved the use of torture in 1252. It was only abolished by a papal bull of 1816. This has not, of course, prevented its frequent and sometimes systematic use for political ends in the present day, by military regimes like those of Greece or South America and in Communist countries.

Torquemada's Code of Instructions (1484) only permitted torture when there was serious presumption of guilt. In practice such restrictions were of little value, since they depended entirely on the interpretation of individual tribunals.

What distinguished the Spanish Inquisition was the fact of being under state control and its special aim of suppressing the crypto-Judaism of the Marranos and later of the Moriscos as well. In 1480 it was solemnly inaugurated at Seville, and the following year the first *auto-da-fé* (Portuguese for act or sentence of faith) took place and six Marranos were burned for Judaism. Henceforward Torquemada and his successors would work continuously at their task, and the Spanish Inquisition would last for over three centuries.

THE ANOMALY OF THE UNCONVERTED JEWS

A curious situation emerged. There were now in Spain two kinds of 'Jews': those who had remained faithful to their religion and the baptized Marranos, or New Christians. The first group had suffered great losses in number, wealth, and position, but it was still important. The Marranos seem to have been more numerous and to have enjoyed a much better position in Spanish society, and a large proportion of them were really secret Judaizers.

Now, although the Church had often condemned forced baptism, and implicitly baptism under threat of death, still the sacrament was considered irrevocable: once a Christian, Christian for ever. What did this mean? Simply that every baptized Jew who practised Judaism in secret (or who was falsely accused of such practice) was now within the reach of the Inquisition, which before his baptism had no power over him. He was worse than a heretic: he was a relapsed heretic, who 'like a dog returneth to his vomit'—a graphic Biblical metaphor that the Inquisitors were fond of quoting.[7] So the New Christian found himself, in certain ways, in a more vulnerable position than his former coreligionists: these, although subject to all the old disabilities, at least were out of reach of the Inquisition. Even a pogrom could attack both groups, especially perhaps the New Christians, who were more prosperous and more prominent in national life.

Such an absurd anomaly shocked the Inquisitors themselves, whose own logic was impeccable once their assumptions were accepted. There again the Church was faced with the 'four solutions' mentioned earlier. The segregation in ghettos as a 'sanitary measure' had already been put into practice. As to slaughter, the Church never accepted it officially, since there was always the hope of 'saving the remnant'. Only one alternative was left: expulsion, which had precedents in several European states. And it was exactly this that Torquemada strongly recommended to Their Catholic Majesties, Ferdinand and Isabella.

'ONCE MORE TO THE TENTS'

There was a story (perhaps a later invention) that the Jews tried to prevent the decree of expulsion by offering the royal treasury a 'ransom' of 30,000 ducats, While this was being negotiated in the palace, Torquemada broke dramatically into the room, threw a crucifix on the table, and indignantly upbraided Ferdinand and Isabella: 'Are Your Majesties prepared to play the part of Judas and betray the Lord once more for thirty pieces of silver?'

The story is sufficiently tragic to require these theatrical embellishments. On 30 March 1492, in the magnificent Alhambra Palace newly captured from the Muslims, the Catholic kings decreed the expulsion of all Jews from the domains:

> Don Fernando and Dona Isabel, by the Grace of God king and queen of Castile, Aragon, etc. . . . whereas we have been informed that some bad Christians were turning to Judaism from our Holy Catholic Faith, which was caused by communication between Jews and Christians . . .[8]

These 'bad Christians' were obviously the Marranos. For that reason, the edict continues: 'We ordered that the Jews be kept apart in cities, towns and villages, providing *juderías* and special quarters where they could live in their sin . . .'

It goes on to speak about the influence the Jews exerted on the New Christians (and possibly on some Old Christians as well), suggesting circumcision, giving them Jewish prayer books, 'taking to them unleavened bread and their meat killed with ceremonies', etc.

The decree ends by ordering that 'by the month of July they leave the country with their sons and daughters, man and maidservants and all their households'. Nobody should give them secret shelter 'for ever and ever, in their estates or homes, under penalty of confiscation of all their goods'.

The community were given three months to sell their goods. They had to pay exorbitant and baseless taxes but were not allowed to collect the debts owing to them. After all sorts of illegal seizures the Spanish Jews were able to sell their goods for only a fraction of the true value.

They set out at last for the embarkation ports, walking on the dusty roads in the hot July sun. The rabbis had provided musicians to encourage them, and Joseph ha-Cohen sees the tragic scene, as usual, in Biblical terms:

> All the hosts of the Lord, the exiles of Jerusalem in Spain, left that accursed country in the fifth month of the year 5252 [1492 A.D.] and from there were scattered to the four corners of the earth. From the port of Carthagena departed on the 16 of the month of Ab six great ships laded with human cattle, and the same happened in other provinces. The Jews went where the winds would take them to Africa, Asia, Greece or Turkey, countries which they still inhabit in our days. Terrible sufferings and pains fell on them, and the Genoese sailors ill-treated them cruelly.[9]

According to some estimates, between 150,000 and 200,000 Jews took part in this new forced Exodus. It was to be a vast, important Diaspora, that of the Sephardim. Many of them went to Italy, where they were to be treated with comparative tolerance until the election of the Pope of the Ghettos, Paul IV. Others enjoyed greater security in Turkish territory, where today there are still Spanish-speaking Jews. But the larger number, perhaps about 100,000, simply crossed the frontier to Portugal.

THE 'EXPULSION' FROM PORTUGAL

Apart from an isolated pogrom in Lisbon in 1449, the Portuguese Jews had been living until then in comparative peace. In 1492 Dom John II restricted the entry of refugees from Spain. The richer Jews who could pay high taxes, were allowed to settle on a permanent basis. These included thirty prominent families, with the learned rabbi Isaac Aboab, whose relative and namesake would become in the seventeenth century the first rabbi of the New World in Dutch Brazil. All the others were allowed to stay for only eight months, provided the adults paid a poll tax. The king promised at the end of that period to provide ships to take them where they liked.

The promise was not kept—or only under very bad conditions. Many of the Jews were forced to disembark in the nearest African port. Those left behind were sold as slaves. The Portuguese carried away seven hundred Jewish children to settle in the island of São Tomé, off the west coast of Africa, where most of them died in that very inhospitable climate.

In 1495 John II died and Dom Manuel came to the throne. He showed himself more humane at first and released the Jews who had been enslaved. But in 1496 he signed a marriage contract with the Infanta Isabella, daughter of Ferdinand and Isabella, and one of the clauses stipulated the expulsion of the Portuguese Jews. Manuel demurred, and consulted his advisers, but the Infanta herself sent him an ultimatum, declaring that she would enter Portugal only when the kingdom was 'cleansed' from all unbelievers.

At last the king made up his mind, and in December of the same year issued the decree of expulsion, determining that

> . . . all the Jews and Jewesses of whatever age who inhabit our domains must depart under penalty of death. . . . And we order the kings our successors, within peril of our curse, that they should never at any time or for any reason whatsoever allow any Jew to live or remain here.[10]

The time given for departure was more generous than in Spain: ten months, until October 1497. But Dom Manuel soon repented: the Jews were a good source of income for any king at the time, and perhaps he also had some religious interest in their conversion. According to one story, a Jewish apostate advised him to attack the community at its most vulnerable point—their children. Some Churchmen like the bishop Fernando Coutinho were against this. But Dom Manuel decided to put the suggestion into practice, and on Friday, 19 March 1497, a general order was given for all children between the ages of four and fourteen to be presented for baptism on the following Sunday.

It was the beginning of the Jewish Passover—'the birthday of Hebrew freedom', as Cecil Roth points out. And he says:

> At the appointed time, those children who were not presented voluntarily were seized by the officials and forced to the font. . . . The royal bailiffs did not obey their instructions too closely, frequently seizing young people of both sexes to the age of twenty. In many cases, parents smothered their offspring in their farewell embrace. In others they threw them into wells in order to save them from the disgrace of apostasy and then killed themselves.[11]

Later, Bishop Fernando Coutinho would remember such scenes as a nightmare of horror. In our own time the Nazis did not hesitate to take children away from families as if they were slaves to be sold.

At last, when the time limit was about to expire, about 20,000 Jews were assembled in Lisbon. A great number of them were kept in a palace called Os Estaos in concentration-camp conditions. Later the building was used rather suitably as the headquarters of the Inquisition, and even today (when it is the Theater of D. Maria II) devout Jews will refuse to enter it.

It was hoped that the Jews would not resist the autere prison diet, and, indeed, many of them accepted baptism. Those who were left remained in prison without food and drink until the time appointed for their departure was past. Then they were told that on account of their 'disobedience' they had forfeited their freedom and were now slaves of the crown. Faced with this fate, the majority yielded: some were dragged to the baptismal font, while others were hastily sprinkled with holy water and declared to be Christians.

The few who proved stubborn were thrown into a dungeon with the last *arrabi-mor*, or chief rabbi, Simon Maimi. After a week he succumbed to the ordeal and died, with two others. Only seven or eight survived, and they were shipped to Africa.

In short, Dom Manuel's expulsion had been a tragic farce: apart from the Jews who had died, the great majority had been forced into the category of New Christians. They had to use the same dissimulation as their coreligionists in Spain and were destined to suffer similar pogroms, the torments and autos-da-fé of the Inquisition, and to remain under the scrutiny and suspicion of their neighbours.

THE GREAT LISBON POGROM AND MORE AUTOS-DA-FÉ

Many Portuguese Jews managed to flee—to Italy, Africa, or Turkey. But the king soon issued a new edict (1499) forbidding their departure from the country without royal permission, and this prohibition was renewed several times during the sixteenth century. Later in the same reign the ban was no longer strictly obeyed, and many Jews managed to escape, particularly to the Low Countries.

From 1503 onwards there were several riots and attacks on New Christians in Lisbon. On 19 April 1506 mass was being celebrated at the Church of São Domingos to pray for the cessation of an epidemic which had started. Somebody noticed an unusual luminosity on a crucifix which stood at the altar, and soon the cry of 'A miracle!' was raised. A New Christian laughed at the idea and tried to explain that it was simply a natural phenomenon. His scepticism enraged the crowd, who considered it a blasphemy. He was dragged out of church and killed, and his body was burned in the square of the Rossio.

Meanwhile two Dominican friars were walking solemnly through the streets with an uplifted crucifix, shouting 'Heresia!' and inciting the crowds against the New Christians. This was the signal for the memorable and hideous pogrom of Lisbon in which took part not only the people of Lisbon but some French, Dutch, and German sailors. An eyewitness of the massacre, a German Christian, wrote:

> On Monday I saw things that I would certainly not have believed had they been reported or written, or unless I had witnessed them myself. Women with children were flung from the windows and caught on spears by those standing underneath, their offspring being hurled away. The peasantry followed the example of the townspeople. Many women and girls were ravished in the fanatical pursuit. The number of New Christians slain is estimated at between 2,000 and 4,000 souls.[12]

Even some 'Old' Christians who tried to restrain the rabble were killed, while others had to prove they were not circumcised in order to escape death.

The massacre brought at least one advantage. The king, enraged by the riot, ordered the punishment of the ringleaders, who were executed, including the two Dominicans. In March of the following year he lifted the restrictions on the movements of the New Christians. Many thousands took advantage of this and left, swelling the Diaspora of Sephardic Jews. It became such an avalanche that in 1521 the ban was imposed again.

In 1536, in spite of the efforts of the Jews who were trying to bribe the papal nuncio with great sums of money, the Inquisition was established in Portugal on similar lines to that of Spain. In 1540 an auto-da-fé took place: it was to be the first of a long series, spreading through more than two and a half centuries.

It is not part of this book to go over the history of the Inquisition in the Peninsula. I leave it to specialists to duscuss how many thousands were burned at the time of Torquemada or at later periods. However exaggerated some estimates may have been, there is general agreement that at least until the eighteenth century the main victims of the Holy Office were the New Christians and that no person of Jewish origin could feel secure while it existed.

The work of the Inquisition was not limited to the mainland. In 1691, for instance, there were four great autos-da-fé of New Christians on the island of Majorca. A huge *quemadero* (as it was called) was erected, with twenty-five stakes at which thirty-seven victims were burned. The thoughtful authorities took due care to hold the sacrifice on the shore, thus preventing the smell of burnt flesh from inconveniencing the inhabitants of the city of Palma.

On what causes or pretexts were these people denounced, put on trial, tortured, and executed? The archives of the Inquisition show that the least suspicion of Judaism could bring New Christians into the clutches of the Holy Office. Official edicts told informers by what signs Judaizers could be recognized: celebration of Jewish holidays, omission of the doxology 'Glory to the Father, and to the Son, and to the Holy Ghost' at the end of a psalm in church, any 'peculiar' cooking habits, and so on. If a New Christian so much as smiled on hearing the name of the Holy Virgin, he might be suspected of heresy. If a neighbour heard New Christians talking and could not understand what they were saying, he would think they were speaking Hebrew and would denounce them as Judaizers.

Cooking with oil was particularly suspect, which is ironical, since it later became almost universal both in Spain and Portugal. In *Candide* Voltaire (incidentally, an extreme anti-Semite) mentioned as victims of the Inquisition 'two Portuguese who on eating a chicken had taken away its fat'.[13] This is no satirist's fiction, for the archives of the Inquisition abound in such trivia. For instance, a certain Elvira del Campo was tried and tortured by the Inquisition of Toledo in 1567–69 for 'not eating pork and putting on clean linen on Saturdays'. This is an extract of the account of her torture:

> One cord was applied to the arms and twisted and she was admonished to tell the truth but she said she had nothing to tell. Then she screamed and said: 'I have done all they say'. . . . Another turn was given and she said: 'Loosen me a little that I may remember what I have to tell. . . . I did not eat pork, for it made me sick; I have done everything; loosen me and I will tell the truth'.[14]

In the end, after further torture on the frame, she broke down completely and managed to escape burning after a full confession of Judaism.

It may be said that the Inquisition was 'effective' since it practically eradicated Judaism from the Peninsula. The autos-da-fé continued throughout the seventeenth century and most of the eighteenth. Although the numbers of victims gradually declined in the towns, the Inquisition fiercely attacked the countryside, and in Portugal remote districts like Beira and Trás-os-Montes suffered heavily.

In 1751, with the Portuguese government in the hands of the Marquis of Pombal, the power of the Holy Office began to be broken. Even so, a natural catastrophe could still awaken anti-Jewish prejudice, as had occurred at the time of the Black Death in Europe. In 1755 the famous Lisbon earthquake destroyed a part of the city, including the Palace of the Inquisition. This sign of divine wrath demanded a scapegoat, and, as Voltaire said in a famous passage of his *Candide:* 'On fit un bel auto-da-fé pour empêcher les tremblements de terre'.[15]

In spite of this the decline of the Inquisition went on, and the last public auto-da-fé in Portugal took place in 1765. In Spain the Inquisition had a longer life, although the proportion of Jewish victims had become practically nil in the last phase. The Holy Office was abolished several times and then reinstituted. Its last victim seems to have been a teacher accused of 'deism' in 1826. In 1834 Queen María Christina abolished the Inquisition for ever.

SPANISH AND PORTUGUESE RACIALISM

It should be stressed that the campaign against the Marranos or Jewish *conversos* was not only 'religious' but soon acquired racial implications. In fact, as time went on, discrimination against the New Christians tended to increase in both Spain and Portugal. It began with guilds and orders of chivalry and extended to colleges and other institutions. Even some towns would not receive people of Marrano blood.

About the middle of the sixteenth century the statutes relating to *limpieza de sangre* (cleanliness or purity of blood) came to be legally enforced in Spain. Even the religious orders accepted the statutes, with the temporary exception of the Jesuits. Their founder, St. Ignatius of Loyola, ignored them and even chose a friar of Jewish origin, Diego de Lainez, to succeed him as general of the order. But in 1592 the Jesuits yielded and from that time onwards excluded Marranos.

Again, the Marranos of the Balearic Islands, although apparently good Catholics, were subjected to strict segregation in a kind of ghetto and were called *chuetas* (a local name for swine) or *individuos de la calle* (people of the street).

The racialist statutes were not always strictly enforced, but people were often asked, on applying for a post or membership in an organization, to submit evidence that they had no Jewish ancestors for three or more generations (the similarity with the Nazi 'Nuremberg Laws' is obvious). As many noble families were now 'tainted' through intermarriage with Marranos, some plebeians (like Sancho Panza in *Don Quixote*) would proclaim their 'pure blood' with pride and say that it was better to be a genuine 'Old Christian' than a *hidalgo* (nobleman).[16]

In Portugal racial discrimination was made stricter after the country became part of the Spanish Empire. So from 1588 onwards all New Christians were 'officially and legally excluded from all ecclesiastical, military, and administrative posts'.[17] Later this was extended to many professions, including all university and college posts. The Portuguese used an expression similar to the Spanish one for purity of blood (*limpeza de sangue*) and did their best to apply discrimination throughout their empire. Again it was the Pombal regime late in the eighteenth century that led to the abolition of all such discrimination, coinciding with the liberal trends of the time which led to Jewish emancipation in the West.

Ironically enough, many Spanish and Portuguese (particularly the latter) were upset by the reputation they had in Europe of living in countries permeated by Judaism. It was commonly thought that Spain and Portugal were full of Jews or half-Jews, and at one time, as we have pointed out, the words 'Portuguese' and 'Jew' were regarded as synonyms. This idea became strong in countries which were at war with Spain or had suffered from Spanish domination, like France and Italy. But it was already in evidence at the time of Erasmus, who wrote in a letter: 'If the Jews abound in Italy, in Spain there are hardly any Christians'.[18] Luther once exclaimed: 'I would prefer to have the Turks as enemies than the Spaniards as suzerains; the majority are Marranos, converted Jews'.[19]

The Portuguese were also called by Erasmus a 'race of Jews' (*illud genus judaicum*). The belief persisted for a long time, and a Portuguese diplomat, Dom Luis da Cunha, writing in 1736, observed with annoyance that his fellow countrymen were still thought of as Jews.[20] In view of the rivalry between the two Peninsular peoples, it is not surprising that the Spanish should try to throw mud at their neighbours with crude proverbs such as 'a Portuguese was born of a Jew's fart'.

Perhaps the best comment on this is a popular Portuguese story that sounds rather modern and at any rate may be taken as an indication of a more tolerant outlook. It was said that at one time King Joseph of Portugal was seriously considering a proposal made by the Inquisitors that all New Christians in the country should wear white hats as a new kind of Jewish badge. Next day his minister the Marquis of Pombal entered the royal cabinet with three white hats and explained that one was for the king, one for the Grand Inquisitor, and the third for himself.

REMNANTS OF JUDAISM IN THE PENINSULA

There was a grain of truth in such beliefs, for apart from the undoubted presence of the Jewish element in the Iberian population, there were also secret remnants of Judaism. When the Inquisition had been abolished in the 1830s, an adventurous Englishman, George Borrow, travelled in the Peninsula as a missionary, distributing Protestant Bibles. In his book *The Bible in Spain* (first published in 1843) he tells of a fascinating meeting he had had with a mysterious Jew called Abarbenel (the name, with variants, was common among the Sephardim). He revealed to Borrow that he was descended from an important Jewish family and was the heir of a great fortune: 'I have coins of silver and gold older than the times of Ferdinand the Accursed and Jezebel [Queen Isabella]; I have also large sums employed in usury'.[21] Abarbenel also told him that there were a number of New Christians among the Catholic clergy in Spain who had never entirely abandoned their Jewish faith, including an archbishop: 'There are many such as I amongst the priesthood, and not amongst the inferior priesthood either. . . . There is one particular festival of the year at which four dignified ecclesiastics are sure to visit me'.

George Borrow adds that he had some confirmation of this from a rather ignorant, extremely anti-Jewish priest who already at this time tended to consider Judaism, Freemasonry, and Lutheranism much the same sort of thing. In his opinion there was 'plenty of Judaism among the priesthood':

> No lack of it, I assure you, Don Jorge. I remember once search-ing the house of an ecclesiastic who was accused of black Juda-ism, and after much investigation, we discovered beneath the floor a wooden chest, in which was a small shrine of silver, en-closing three books in black hogskin, which, on being opened, were found to be books of Jewish devotion, written in Hebrew characters. . . . And on being questioned, the culprit made no secret of his guilt, but rather gloried in it, saying that there was no God but one, and denouncing the adoration of Maria Santis-sima as rank idolatry.[22]

These stories of George Borrow have been considered rather fanciful. But it is a fact that surprising relics of crypto-Judaism have been found at least in Portugal. One curious example was that of the Portuguese consul at Holyhead, Anglesey (United Kingdom), who on his death as recently as 1885 left instructions to be buried in the local Jewish cemetery. More impressive was the discovery made in 1917 by a Jewish engineer from Poland, Samuel Schwarz. In a remote district of northern Portugal, Bel-monte, he came across an isolated group of crypto-Jews who had forgotten their Hebrew except for one important word:

> They had not heard of the language, and doubted its existence. At last an old woman, whom the rest treated with particular deference, asked him sceptically to repeat some prayer in the tongue for which he claimed such sanctity. . . . He recited the Jewish confession of faith . . . 'Hear, O Israel! The Lord our God, the Lord is one'. As he pronounced the name of God—*Adonai*—the woman covered her eyes with her hands—the tradi-tional formality, intended to shut out all outside distractions during the recital of this verse. When he had finished, she turned to the bystanders. 'He is indeed a Jew', she said authoritatively, 'for he knows the name of *Adonai*'.[23]

It is interesting to see a woman playing a prominent part in such a masculine religion: she was even called 'priestess' (*sacerdotisa*). The encounter resembles the discovery of other exotic Jewish outposts described in Chapter 4.

The present Jewish communities in both Portugal and Spain are of more recent origin. Probably because of their small number modern anti-Semitism has not been very active in the Peninsula.[24] Fascist ideas found a favourable terrain there, and it would not be fanciful to see in the twin regimes of Salazar and Franco the heirs of that oppressive fanaticism which fostered the Inquisition and did so much to impoverish life in the Peninsula and make it so gloomy and full of conflict.

9

The Wandering Jew
and the New World

And the Lord will scatter you among all peoples, from one end of the
earth to the other. . . . And among these nations you shall find no
ease, and there shall be no rest for the sole of your foot; but the Lord
will give you a trembling heart, and failing eyes, and a languishing
soul; your life shall hang in doubt before you; night and day you shall
be in dread, and have no assurance of your life.

—Deut. 28:64–66

THE MYTH OF THE LOST TRIBES

As we saw in the last chapter, Columbus' expedition received royal approval in the same month, March 1492, that 'Their Catholic Majesties'
expelled the Jews from Spain. But even in the fateful journey made under
the sign of the cross some Marranos did take part. It is even suggested
that Columbus himself came from a Jewish family, but this is merely a
conjecture. Some Jewish scholars are prone to grant certificates of Israelite
descent to famous characters.

With the arrival of the Jews in the New World, some thought that the
Diaspora would achieve its fullest extent. The circle would be closed, and
the prophecy of the Sibylline Oracles would be fulfilled: 'And you shall
fill all the lands and all the seas; and each shall be outraged by your
customs'.[1]

The seed of Israel would be scattered all over the world, and some rabbis,
far from interpreting this in the sense of the terrible curses in Deuteronomy, tended to consider it part of the divine plan. Rabbi Eleazar says in
the Talmud: 'God dispersed the Jews in order to make proselytism
easier'.[2]

This idea was also connected with the Messianic hope. The apocalyptic
Book of Daniel—placed by the Christians among the Prophets—seemed

to predict that salvation would come with the completion of the Diaspora. Inspired by such ideas, some Jews who went to America thought that the Indians might well be descendants (however 'degraded') of the lost Ten Tribes of Israel. It seems that they were among the first to propagate this curious myth, which is still current today. For instance, it is an integral part of the Mormons' fantastic mythology.

About the middle of the seventeenth century, when Messianic beliefs were very much in evidence, the myth became popular among the Portuguese Jews of Amsterdam, apparently spread by a New Christian called Antonio de Montesinos. He claimed to have discovered in Quito (now the capital of Ecuador) Indians who were descended from the tribes of Levi and Reuben and who practised various Jewish customs. The prominent rabbi Menasseh ben Israel, also a Portuguese Jew, expounded a similar idea in a Messianic treatise called *The Hope of Israel*, which was published in Latin and Spanish. In fact, the author had it printed on the first Hebrew press established by himself at Amsterdam. Again, the petition he addressed to Cromwell a little later (1655) pleading for the readmission of the Jews to England was partly based on such apocalyptic beliefs. The rabbi held that, England being literally 'the end of the earth' (*Angle-terre*, 'angle' interpreted as a corner), it was necessary that the Jews should also reach it in order to fulfil the prediction. Once that happened, the Messianic deliverance would come.[3]

THE WANDERING JEW

By that time another apocalyptic legend had become very popular in Europe—that of the Wandering Jew. It bears all the signs of a great folk myth, in that it has obscure beginnings and then grows and develops, reflecting various levels of symbolism, some deeper than others. It may have had its early beginnings around the year 1000, popularly awaited as the year of the glorious Second Coming, or the millennium. As usual on such occasions, there were rumours about the appearance of the Antichrist. Soon this was connected with the nebulous figure of a Jew, whom some identified with Malchus, the high priest's servant whose ear Peter had cut off with his sword. Perhaps the events of the First Crusade and the militant fervour they produced helped to develop the myth. Joseph Gaer says:

> When the men of the First Crusade returned from the Holy Land laden with booty and relics, they brought back with them also a host of conflicting tales about a Deathless One who was doomed to wander over the earth until the Day of Judgment.[4]

This Immortal or Wandering Jew came to have various names and was not always identified with Malchus. As we have seen, the idea of collective guilt and of the accursed people was already well established in Christian minds. In a bull dated 1208, Pope Innocent III reminded his flock that one of the first stories in the Bible was about a criminal condemned to wander:

> God made Cain into a vagabond and a fugitive upon the earth, but marked him, making his head tremble lest he be killed [Gen. 4:12–15]. Thus the Jews against whom the blood of Jesus Christ calls out, although they are not to be killed, so that the Christian people may not forget the divine law, must remain vagabonds upon the earth, until their faces be covered with shame and they seek the name of Jesus Christ the Lord.[5]

In fact, the first written version of the legend was recorded not long after Innocent III, in the *Chronicle of St. Alban's Abbey* in England and completed about 1250. In its essentials it is very similar to the later, more popular version, except that the Wandering Jew is called Cartaphilus or Joseph. The narrator is the Archbishop of Greater Armenia, who claims to have met Cartaphilus and told the story at a meeting of English bishops and monks.

In later centuries the myth seems to have spread throughout Europe in several shapes and variations. In a Flemish version the Wandering Jew is called Joannes Buttadeus (John who smote God). A more attractive name, this time in Portuguese, is João Espera-em-Deus (John who expects God). But it was in Germany, the land of anti-Semitic myths, that the story became crystallized in its more popular form.

According to this version, a student of Wittenberg University called Paul von Eitzen (later bishop of Schleswig) met in Hamburg on Easter Sunday a very tall and gaunt old man, with a long beard and white hair, who told him his story. His name was Ahasuerus (or Ahasverus), a rather strange choice, for it is that of the legendary king of Persia in the Book of Esther (usually identified with Artaxerxes).

He had lived in Judaea at the time of Christ and had been one of the Jews who considered Jesus a false Messiah and who joined the crowd chanting 'Crucify him!'. After the trial he went back home and called his family to watch the passage of Jesus on his way to Golgotha. Ahasuerus waited in front of his house and placed his little son on his shoulder so that he might see better. Jesus approached, stumbling under the weight of the cross, stopped to rest a little in front of the Jews's house, and leaned against the wall. (Note that in the popular representations it is always Christ who carries the cross, contrary to the Gospel narrative where the bearer is Simon of Cyrene.) Ahasuerus turned to Jesus rudely and shouted, 'Go on, Jesus, go on! Why do you tarry?' (According to other versions, he pushed Jesus brutally or spat on him, thus giving rise to the story of the man who had 'smitten God' = Buttadeus.) Jesus looked him in the eye and said, 'I shall go and rest, but you shall know no rest—tarry till I come back'. At that moment Ahasuerus put his son down and followed Jesus, witnessing the whole Crucifixion. Since then he had been wandering everywhere for many centuries and found no rest.

In this version of the story, as in fact in several others, the Wandering Jew (*der ewige Jude*, or 'Eternal Jew', in German) is a virtuous, melancholy man, who is often praying—the typical repentant sinner. Wherever he goes, he is treated with respect and even reverence. In a way he is sacred because he lies under a curse or taboo. There are obvious echoes of other myths—Cain, Oedipus, or the Ancient Mariner.

In this new German version the story spread everywhere in the West and became immensely popular. After the early oral period it was also written down. A pamphlet published in 1602 at Leyden by a certain Creutzer soon went through forty-six editions in German and was translated into several other European languages. The Eternal Jew of the Germans was called *le Juif errant* by the French, *l'Ebreo errante* by the Italians, the 'wandering Jew' by the English, *o Judeu errante* by the Portuguese. It was not long before several people claimed they had seen or met the mysterious old man in Brussels, Paris, Munich, and other cities in Europe. In some cases it looks as if charlatans took advantage of the myth to make money and attract attention.

Between 1818 and 1830 the Wandering Jew is supposed to have visited London. Apparently his last appearance was in 1868, in Salt Lake City, Utah, to a Mormon, as one would expect. In the modern era of reporters, photography, and radio he seems to have become much more elusive.

If the original character of the story is obviously anti-Jewish, there is no doubt that other, deeper elements entered into the formation of the myth, something that Jung would have called the 'collective unconscious'. Hence the fascination the story has exerted. Poets understood its deeper meaning and, as often happens, the story was metamorphosed. Ahasuerus is the man of mysterious wisdom: he knows much because he has suffered much, like Oedipus, who became a prophet, or the Ancient Mariner, who was given 'strange powers of speech'.

The theme of the story is the human search for peace and God. Ahasuerus has to do penance because he denied someone peace and rest, and so he is deprived of peace. From this point of view the myth is a remarkable variation on the subject of conversion and repentance. There is also compassion in it, because one feels that the sinner will be forgiven. In fact, he cannot find rest in the things of this world because only God (Christ's second coming) can satisfy his thirst.

So it is not surprising that the Wandering Jew should have fascinated so many poets (Schlegel, Shelley, the Brazilian Castro Alves, who was philo-Jewish), novelists, and playwrights. If Shakespeare gave a certain no-bility to the character of Shylock, the Wandering Jew had a better fate—he was transfigured: to many people he became a pro-Jewish symbol, epitomizing the long sufferings of the persecuted people. But that is not rare in human history. The cross, for instance, was changed from a symbol of degradation into one of faith and love, and then again it became the sign of dark fanaticism and cruelty under the Crusades and the Inquisition.

And, perhaps Jewish and Christian Messianism have encouraged one another. Perhaps the legend of the Wandering Jew had some early connection, however distorted, with Jewish hopes. At the end of a long period of trials and wanderings ('the pangs of the Messiah'), when the Diaspora had reached the four corners of the earth, the Expected One would come at last and lead his people back to the Holy Land: it would be a repetition, on a much larger scale, of the traditional forty years of wandering in the wilderness after the Exodus.

In fact, although the Messianic hope may have a deeper, more spiritual meaning, both Christians and Jews waited in vain: the Messiah never came, nor did the Second Coming take place. For the Zionists, it is true, the era of the Wandering Jew is over. Although only a minority 'went back' to Palestine, the creation of the state of Israel constitutes, in a way, the end of a long period of wandering.

ANTI-SEMITISM AS A CAUSE OF MIGRATIONS

If one looks at these centuries as a whole, they seem to show us a series of migratory waves, under the spur of periodic persecutions, in which the Jews have traced on the map very involved itineraries.

Anti-Semitism is like an epidemic which appears here and there in successive outbursts, declining in one place and reappearing with sudden virulence in another. Even when it does not lead to pogroms and mass expulsions, it remains latent, endemic, always liable to new outbursts. And the Diaspora flowed and ebbed, following its unpredictable march.

First came the migration to the East. Under the spur of persecutions in Western Europe at the time of the Crusades, and later during the Black Death, expelled from England (1290) and from France (1306, 1394), the Jews emigrated to Eastern Europe, particularly to Poland, establishing there some of the largest and most flourishing centres of the Ashkenazim.

In the sixteenth century an era of comparative peace and prosperity in the East (including especially the Ottoman Empire) coincided with persecution in the West—Spain, Portugal, and even Latin America—in the same way that the Golden Age enjoyed by the Sephardic or Western Jews until the fourteenth century contrasted with pogroms in other European countries.

Expelled from Spain, persecuted by the Inquisition and Pope Paul IV, the Sephardim scattered to many parts of the world in what has been called the 'Marrano Diaspora'. But even before this there were Jewish communities in India, China, Ethiopia, Central Asia, and Turkestan.

In 1648 a terrible wave of pogroms destroyed the stability of the Ashkenazim in Poland (see Chapter 10), and this caused a new flow to the West. Meanwhile, a growing number of Jews were seeking refuge in more tolerant countries like Holland, Britain, and North America, and this to some extent followed the new maritime and commercial predominance first of the Dutch and later of the English.

Over two centuries later, beginning with the murder of Tsar Alexander II in 1881 (see Chapter 11), there would be a flight of Russian Jews to the West on a much larger scale, again as a result of a series of pogroms. As we shall see later, the Russian Jews would suffer again at the time of the civil war. It was this enormous Diaspora which to a large extent determined the ethnic composition of Jewish communities in the West, ensuring the numerical predominance of the Ashkenazim of Eastern origin. A great number of them sought 'the land of opportunity' in America, particularly New York, just as they concentrated in Alexandria in antiquity. The growth of the American community was very fast. According to estimates, there were in the United States about 250,000 Jews in 1870, a million and a half in 1904, and about four and a half million in 1930.

Finally came the last great wave of the Diaspora as a result of Hitler's persecution and systematic slaughter. In numbers, quality, and repercussions it was a very important one, but it did not considerably alter the composition of Jewish communities outside Nazi-occupied Europe. The three countries with the greatest Jewish population are now: the United States, with about six million; the Soviet Union, with perhaps something like three million; and Israel, with two and a half million. Argentina comes next, with half a million, and then Britain, with about 410,000.

INTOLERANCE IS 'BAD BUSINESS'

This brief summary of movements within the Diaspora shows not only the obvious influence exerted by outbursts of anti-Semitism on Jewish migrations but also their importance as factors in economic, social, and cultural changes. It is quite clear that persecution, apart from being intrinsically evil, in many ways also harms and impoverishes the country that practises it.

The case of Spain and Portugal is typical. Jews and Moors were important and productive minorities from both the economic and cultural point of view. The expulsion of about 200,000 Jews from Spain in 1492, the flight of many New Christians from the Peninsula later, then the persecution of the Moriscos and their expulsion from 1609 onwards (about half a million in number)—all this seriously disturbed the life of both countries and no doubt was a factor in their decline. There is a story that the Turkish sultan Bajazet II, on receiving Jewish refugees from Spain, said, 'This is a very unwise king who impoverishes himself in order to make me rich'.

Another good example was Catholic persecution of the French Huguenots, particularly after the revocation of the Edict of Nantes by Louis XIV in 1685. There was mass emigration, and it is estimated that about 350,000 managed to escape, most of them to England, to Brandenburg (part of the later kingdom of Prussia), and to the always welcoming Holland. Many Huguenots were skilled artisans, particularly in weaving (in certain areas in medieval times 'weaver' was almost synonymous with 'heretic'), and so the industry of all these countries profited with the settlement of the refugees. The English historian Lipson says, in fact, that the French Huguenots 'helped to build up the industrial supremacy of England'.[6]

As to the Huguenots of Brandenburg, they played an important part in the growth of the wool industry and also in the iron and steel industry. Francesca Wilson says: 'It is one of the bitter ironies of history that it was a French king who helped to build up the nation which was destined to become the most dangerous enemy of his country'.[7]

Nonconformists and rebels, whether in religion or politics, and therefore those who are able to withstand persecution, tend to be among the more energetic and capable individuals in a given community: these are the people who generally prefer to leave the country of their birth and face the risks of emigration. The traditional virtues of initiative, perseverance, and diligence, often attributed to Jewish immigrants and given as a cause for their success, also exist in other ethnic groups (who often emigrate, admittedly, for reasons that have nothing to do with persecution) and are not specifically Jewish.

In short, countries that insist on 'one God, one faith, one baptism', or succumb to oppressive regimes, often risk the loss of part of their elite, while those which open their doors to persecuted minorities very often benefit from the influx of energetic and skilled groups.

THE INQUISITION IN BRAZIL

While the Jews were being persecuted in Poland in 1648, they enjoyed a period of freedom in Brazil under the Dutch and, in fact, established the first synagogue in the New World. As we have seen, Portugal was the weaker and less fanatical partner of the inquisitorial axis, and Dom Manuel I was forced to follow his neighbour's policy more or less as Mussolini had to adopt Hitler's anti-Semitism. The expulsion of the Portuguese Jews ended up in practice as forced baptism, and given the outlook of the time, its logical outcome had to be the bloody campaign to eradicate Judaism, which poisoned the life of the country and its colonies for two and a half centuries.

The heyday of the Inquisition coincided with Spanish and Portuguese colonization of America. And, as was only natural, the New Christians were bound to seek in the New World places where they would be far from the long arm of the Inquisition (not to mention chances to make a fortune). There is no doubt that on the whole they were less persecuted in Latin America than in the Peninsula. But this was largely due to greater distances and lesser vigilance. Even so, the Inquisition went on with its gruesome work in Mexico and Peru, while in the case of Brazil it was part of the Portuguese policy of centralization that even suspects of Judaism had to be sent across the sea to Lisbon in order to go through the long inquisitorial procedure, which might mean years in prison.

In 1535 Portugal adopted the practice of transporting criminals to Brazil, and this category included people suspected of Judaism. There is little doubt that many of these practised their religion in secret. But with the Spanish annexation of Portugal vigilance was tightened, and in 1580 the bishop of Bahia (then the Brazilian capital) was given inquisitorial powers. In 1591 Bahia received the first visit (*visitação*) of the official commissioners.

The minutes of this visit [8] record a good number of denunciations and confessions, although the total number of supposed Judaizers sent to Lisbon was not large. One of the victims was an old lady aged eighty called Ana Rois. The 'Jewish practices' her informers accused her of show the minute character of the Inquisition. She confessed, for instance, that she used to place her hands on her grandsons' heads in order to bless them; and that after her son's death she had abstained from eating meat during the first eight days of mourning. She would also swear by her father's or husband's soul. Ana Rois added that she had no idea that these or other customs were Jewish, and she had always believed in Christ and in the Church.

This did not help her at all, and the old woman was sent all the way to Lisbon to be put on trial. There she was thrown into prison in 1593 and died not long after. This did not prevent the Inquisitors from 'relaxing her in statue', according to their picturesque language; i.e., her corpse was burnt as that of a heretic. The account implies that the 'old Jewess' was something of a witch.

In 1593 the same commissioner, Furtado de Mendonça, came to Olinda, the capital of Pernambuco, then the centre of one of the most prosperous provinces of Brazil. The minutes of the visit mention a good number of 'Judaizers', some of them rich sugar planters. There was talk of a synagogue, probably improvised at somebody's home, and it was even said that the Jews possessed a *Sepher Torah*—a book of the Law.

SOME JEWISH MARTYRS IN BRAZIL

One of the victims of the 1593 visit was a New Christian teacher called Bento Teixeira Pinto, who often figures in histories of Brazilian literature as the first native poet. He was the author of a very inferior imitation of Camoens' *The Lusiads*, the first epic poem to be written in Brazil.

Teixeira Pinto was accused, among other things, of refusing to hold classes on Saturdays, and owning 'forbidden books', of translating the Bible into Portuguese (a serious offence in Catholic countries at the time), of swearing by the Virgin's pudenda, and of discussing religious questions with laymen and friars. It is interesting that he was never put on trial for the murder of his wife, whom he had killed for adultery: but this was perfectly in order according to the code of the time, which considered blood the only detergent for blots on a husband's honour (literary critics may think that Teixeira Pinto's worst crime was to have written that epic poem).[9]

The unhappy poet was arrested at Olinda in 1595 and despatched to Lisbon, where he arrived early in 1596. After a long term of jail and prolonged questionings, he ended by confessing Judaism (apparently without torture). He was condemned to life imprisonment and always to wear the sanbenito, or penitential habit, but died in jail not long after, in 1600: the same year, one might remember, when the philosopher Giordano Bruno was burnt at the stake in Rome for heresy.

Another contemporary Brazilian writer, Fernandes Brandão, apparently a more talented one, was also accused of Judaism, but there was not enough evidence to send him to Lisbon. The fact that these two writers were both New Christians shows the high cultural level of the Jewish element in the colony. The Brazilian historian Oliveira Lima goes as far as to say that the Portuguese who settled in Brazil were 'very largely Jews, who represented the best element economically at the time and who wanted to flee the fanaticism that raged in the Peninsula'.[10]

THE JEWS IN DUTCH BRAZIL

In 1618 there was a further visit to Bahia of the Holy Office's commissioners, and the story was much the same, with the usual accusations of Jewish practices against a number of individuals. Here we find the first mention of Dutch connections, particularly with Amsterdam, which was then the great haven for the Portuguese and Spanish Jews.

The Dutch Calvinists could claim a common enemy with these refugees because they had achieved their independence only after a long and bloody fight with Catholic Spain. The Union of Utrecht, signed in 1579, had proclaimed freedom of worship in the territory of the republic—one of the first European countries to do such a thing. By 1624 there were in Amsterdam about eight hundred Jews, most of them from Portugal, organized in three synagogues. From 1611 onwards, following the old Alexandrian tradition of the Septuagint, these Sephardic Jews printed a Spanish version of the Hebrew Bible. Its first edition had come out in Ferrara, Italy, in 1553, and seems to have been the first published translation of the Bible in that language. Several copies of this 'Ferrara Bible',[11] as it was called, were smuggled into Brazil, and the inquisitorial commissioner of 1618 was aware of the fact.

The Jews who had settled in Amsterdam and other cities in the Low Countries took part in the enterprises of the Dutch, who were soon to become the foremost commercial power in Europe. Taking the offensive in its struggle against Spain, Holland began to consider attacking Brazil, which since 1580 had been part of Philip II's huge Spanish Empire. When the West India Company was formed in Amsterdam in 1621, eighteen Jews contributed capital. But the enterprise was very far from being what modern anti-Semites would call a tool of 'international Jewry': of a total of seven million guilders, it seems that the Jewish merchants contributed only 36,000, rather a minute fraction.

However, in their planned attacks on Brazil, the Dutch could count on another kind of help: a 'fifth column' of New Christians in Bahia and Pernambuco. At a conference in The Hague in 1623 one of the Dutch leaders pointed out this advantage and proposed that complete freedom of worship be proclaimed in the territories about to be conquered.

In 1624, when the Dutch conquered and held Bahia for a short time, most of the population abandoned the town, but there were some Jews among those who remained. Later the suspicions of the Portuguese and Spanish authorities considerably exaggerated Jewish participation in the event. When Bahia was reconquered in the following year, a number of 'collaborators' were hanged, including a New Christian.[12]

A more successful expedition was sent against Pernambuco. When it was being planned, the regulations approved by the General States of The Hague included an important clause:

> The liberty of Spaniards, Portuguese and natives, whether they be Roman Catholics or Jews, will be respected. No one will be permitted to molest them or subject them to inquiries in matters of conscience or in their private homes; and no one should dare to disquiet or disturb them or cause them any hardship—under the penalty of arbitrary punishments or, depending upon circumstances, of severe or exemplary reproof.[13]

This seems to have been the first proclamation of religious freedom in Latin America and, one might add, on the whole American continent. It is well known that religious minorities like the Quakers suffered severe discrimination and persecution in the American colonies during the seventeenth century—in fact, considerably more than the Jews when they began to settle there.

When the Dutch conquered Pernambuco in 1630 and then went on to occupy most of northeast Brazil, their religious tolerance, although far from perfect, came tolerably near the terms of that decree. It is true that the Jesuits were expelled from the colony, but there is no doubt that there was much greater freedom of worship than under the Portuguese and Spanish.

With the Dutch expedition came several Jews as soldiers. As soon as Dutch rule was consolidated, many New Christians of Pernambuco threw off disguise and practised Judaism openly. As their numbers were increased by newcomers, they decided to set up a congregation in Recife, which the Dutch were building up as their capital. The new synagogue was given the name of Zur Israel, 'Rock of Israel', which seems to be an allusion to the name of the town (Recife means 'reef' in Portuguese). It began to function at least by 1637.

THE FIRST SYNAGOGUE IN THE NEW WORLD

Menasseh ben Israel, one of the most prominent rabbis of the time and a Portuguese Jew living in Amsterdam, seriously considered coming to Recife in order to lead the new community. It would suit well his Messianic ideas that the Diaspora had to reach the ends of the earth before the expected liberation came. But he changed his mind, and it was another Portuguese Jew, Isaac Aboab da Fonseca, who came to Brazil in 1642, together with other Jewish immigrants.

According to Wisnitzer, the Jewish community of Recife may have reached about 1,400 inhabitants, not a small proportion of the white population. The street where the synagogue building was situated came to be called Rua dos Judeus (Street of the Jews) and the site of the house has been located. It is regrettable that no plaque has been set up to commemorate the first synagogue in the Americas.

In spite of the comparative religious tolerance of the Dutch rulers, soon there were signs of anti-Jewish feeling. The Jews were prospering as merchants, and some of them were rich sugar planters. Their knowledge of languages was a considerable asset: Dutch and Portuguese could not understand each other at the outset, and once more the Jews filled their old function as interpreters. But as soon as conquerors and conquered began to talk to each other, they realized they had something in common—the anti-Jewish tradition they shared. And it is interesting to see Roman Catholics and Calvinists making common cause against the Jews and even addressing protests to the authorities, particularly to John Maurice of Nassau, who governed the colony from 1636 to 1644.

The complaints were both religious and economic. It was said that the Jews made disparaging remarks about the Christian religion and practised their cult too openly and noisily, sometimes holding processions which shocked the Christian population. There was even talk of Jewish prose-lytism. They were accused of 'unfair competition' in trade and of attempt-ing to monopolize certain branches: also of forcing their Negro slaves to work on Sundays. There was nothing very strange about that, because their day of rest was, naturally, Saturday. In fact, it is known that some gave their workers both days off—a very modern weekend. Others, on the con-trary, were very strict as slaveholders, and must have been like the Jewish and Dutch planters in Surinam (Dutch Guiana), who provoked several slave rebellions.

It is difficult to say to what extent such complaints were merely the ex-pression of the deep anti-Semitic prejudice of the time, or whether in fact there were some aspects of Jewish behaviour which caused more specific re-sentment. In any case, the question is not very important, as we know that such things are typical of prejudice: to point at certain traits of character or behaviour and to resent them just because they belong to the group dis-criminated against. It is quite likely that some Jews were working off their own resentments and behaving arrogantly, after a long period of suppres-sion and dissimulation. Brazilian plantation society was based on exploita-tion whichever way you looked at it, and the Dutch invasion had only made it a little more complicated by diversifying the composition of the ruling classes.

However, the Dutch authorities yielded a little to pressure and banned Jewish processions as well as the opening of new synagogues. Some fanati-cal Calvinist ministers even attempted to have the Jewish cult forbidden altogether, just as they were obstructing John Maurice's conciliatory policy towards the Catholic Portuguese. Obviously, this would have been a fla-grant breach of the proclamation of religious freedom. But apart from a few incidents there was no great change in Dutch policy, nor were there violent outbursts of anti-Semitism.

The Brazilian Jews were thus left in peace and had some share in com-munity life. Many served in the local militia and were usually exempted from duty on the Sabbath. On the other hand, they were not eligible to sit on local councils (*conselho dos escabinos*): in other words, as in an-cient Alexandria, they were not full citizens. At that time, to be a Christian (and in most cases to be a member of the established Church) was still an essential requirement of citizenship, in both Protestant and Catholic coun-tries.

When the Brazilians rebelled against foreign rule, the Jews gave full support to the Dutch side, for they knew that any Portuguese restoration would be against their interests. They provided both soldiers and money for the defence of Recife, which became increasingly threatened as the Dutch retreated. When a Dutch ship broke the blockade and brought provisions to the besieged, Isaac Aboab celebrated the event by writing a long poem in Hebrew—the first recorded composition in the language in the New World.

DISPERSION OF THE JEWS OF PERNAMBUCO

But Dutch Brazil was doomed and with it the Jewish community of Recife. In 1654 the besieged capitulated and northeast Brazil was once again under Catholic rule, which meant a return of the Inquisition. To the Jews it was 'Once more to your tents, O Israel!' Most of the Recife community withdrew with the vanquished Dutch. It was yet another Diaspora.

Many of the Jews from the Recife community went back to Amsterdam, but others sought new opportunity in the Caribbean. Some went to Jamaica, which in the following year (1655) came under English rule. Even today most of the Jewish community of the island is of Portuguese origin. To Barbados, the earliest British colony in the West Indies, went Abraham of Mercado, one of the elders of the Recife synagogue, and his son, David Raphael, both physicians. The Sephardim of Barbados are now extinct, but the synagogue building and the Jewish cemetery still exist, the latter with many inscriptions in Portuguese.

In 1655 Benjamin da Costa, another refugee from Pernambuco, settled in Martinique (then occupied by the Dutch) and with a few other Jews and Negro slaves started sugar plantations on a large scale. As West Indian sugar came to be a strong competitor to that of Brazil, this is another good example of the economic consequences of intolerance.

Yet other Jews went to French Guiana and later to Surinam, where under Dutch protection they founded a community of some importance. In upper Surinam they started large-scale sugar plantations, and the region came to be known as Joden Savanne (Savannah of the Jews). Between 1690 and 1722 there was a series of slave rebellions which, although suppressed, led to the abandonment of the settlement. Meanwhile, the Jewish community in Paramaribo, the capital, remained.

But the most fateful consequence of the Pernambuco Diaspora was to be in North America. In that same year of 1654 when the Dutch were expelled from Brazil, twenty-three Jews from Pernambuco arrived in New Amsterdam: they were greeted by a German or Polish Jew who had arrived a few months earlier. The local governor, Peter Stuyvesant, was obviously as anti-Jewish as the Calvinist ministers in Recife and would not allow the refugees to settle. In September he sent a letter to the Amsterdam chamber of the Dutch West India Company saying:

We have, for the benefit of this weak and newly developing place and the land in general, deemed it useful to require them [the Jews] in a friendly way to depart; praying also most seriously in this connection, for ourselves as also for the general community of your worships, that the deceitful race—such hateful enemies and blasphemers of the name of Christ—be not allowed further to infect and trouble this new colony.[14]

Peter Stuyvesant did not get his way, and in the following year he received a letter from the governor of the company, dated 26 April 1655, saying that it would be unfair that such faithful allies who had lost so much in the Brazilian venture should be denied refuge in a Dutch colony. So the Brazilian Jews were allowed to remain, 'provided that the poor amongst them shall not become a burden to the community, but be supported by their own nation'.[15]

This was the humble beginning of what was to become the largest urban Jewish community in the world, for New York accounts for nearly one-third of the six million Jews in America. Soon the refugees from Brazil founded the K.K. Shearith Israel (Remnant of Israel) synagogue, which still exists.

Finally, yet another group of the Brazilian Diaspora took part in an event which was to prove equally important: the readmission of the Jews to England. In 1655 the rabbi Menasseh ben Israel, who, as we have seen, had thought of going to Brazil, presented a petition to Cromwell asking his permission for the re-entry of Israelites into England, which had been closed to them since 1290. Cromwell was in favour of the idea, but there were many who were against it, and it was not possible to obtain a formal permission in writing. Nevertheless, when a few Jews who lived clandestinely in London began to practise their religion openly, the government tacitly allowed them to do so. They were soon joined by others from Amsterdam, all of Portuguese and Spanish origin. Their synagogue was given the name of K.K. Shaar ha-Shamayim (Gate of Heaven).

In 1701 this congregation, which had grown in numbers and become more prosperous, dedicated a new building for the synagogue at Bevis Marks (City of London), which is today the oldest in the country. When I visited it in 1960, I realized that several of the founding members had also been members of the Rock of Israel in Recife.

But it is obvious that the Diaspora of 1654 did not spell the end of the Brazilian Jews, for it was limited to Pernambuco. Some remained even there, especially those who had not 'Judaized' openly. In the south many New Christians played an important part in the diamond trade. The Inquisition remained active, although to a lesser extent than in Portugal. It has been estimated that between 1591, the date of the first 'visit' from the commissioners, and 1763 about four hundred New Christians were shipped to Lisbon on charges of Judaism.[16] In 1702 and 1712 there were a good number of imprisonments, and in 1739 the Inquisition executed perhaps its most illustrious victim: the famous playwright Antonio José da Silva, popularly known as Antonio José 'o Judeu' (the Jew). When he was still a student at the University of Coimbra, he had been arrested and tortured by the Inquisitors, together with his mother. At last in 1739, while some of his comedies were being staged in Lisbon, Antonio José was taken to an auto-da-fé, where he was garrotted before being burnt at the stake.[17]

Several writers were, therefore, victims of the Portuguese Inquisition, showing once more that intolerance and anti-Semitism (as was to be seen on a much larger scale with the 'brain drain' and flight of intellectuals from Nazi Germany) are also 'bad business' in a cultural sense.

10

From Reformation to Revolution

I confess that I have not the nerves to enter their synagogues. Old prejudices cling about me. I cannot shake off the story of Hugh of Lincoln. . . . A Hebrew is nowhere congenial to me. . . . I boldly confess that I do not relish the approximation of Jew and Christian, which has become so fashionable.

—Charles Lamb, 'Imperfect Sympathies', *Essays of Elia*

LUTHER: FROM PRO-JEWISH TO ANTI-SEMITE

The Reformation, with its emphasis on the Bible and revival of the Old Testament spirit, was closer to Judaism than Roman Catholicism. As we have seen, some Protestant countries like Holland and Britain, and later America, were more tolerant towards the Jews. But this does not mean that anti-Semitism had suddenly disappeared among Protestants, and you have only to read Peter Stuyvesant's letter to his superiors to see that prejudice was very much alive.

The case of the first great reformer, Martin Luther, is interesting because, like Muhammad, he began with great good will towards the Jews. He seemed to think that the new Church, cleansed and purified, might well bring Israel to its fold at last. His pamphlet *Jesus Christ Was Born a Jew* (*Dass Jesus Christus ein geborener Jude sei*), published in 1523, is a vigorous defence of the Israelites against Christian persecution and shows some understanding of the relations between the two groups:

> Our imbeciles, the papists and the bishops . . . have treated the Jews as if they were dogs, not men. They have done nothing but persecute them. The Jews are the blood relatives, the cousins and brothers of Our Lord . . . [they] belong to Jesus Christ much

more than we do. Hence I beg my dear papists to call me a Jew, when they are tired of calling me a heretic . . .

So long as we use violence and lies and accuse them of using Christian blood to eradicate their own stink, and I do not know what other absurdities; so long as we keep them from living and working among us, in our communities, and force them to practise usury—how can they come to us? [1]

The violent, sneering language is typical of the man. Two years later, in 1525, he would turn in a similar style against the rebellious German peasants, saying that they should be killed like 'mad dogs'. Later it would become clear that his apparent tolerance and understanding of 'the Jewish problem' hung on his hope of converting them. Once they proved 'obstinate', Luther could not see much good in them. It is true that a few Jews were converted to his Reformed Church, but only a tiny number, while, on the contrary, some Bohemian Protestants, apparently under Jewish influence, went as far as to keep the Sabbath and to have themselves circumcised. This upset Luther greatly, and later he began to write anti-Jewish pamphlets, like *Against the Jews and Their Lies* (1542) and the even more violent *Schem Hemaphoras*. Here are samples of the former:

No one wants them. . . . This is proved by the fact that they have often been expelled by force: from France (which they call *Tsarpath*), where they had a downy nest; recently from Spain (which they call *Sepharad*), their chosen roost; and even this year from Bohemia, where, in Prague, they had another cherished nest; finally, in my own lifetime, from Ratisbon [Regensburg], Magdeburg, and from many other places.

Luther goes almost right back to the traditional view that the Jews are sworn enemies of Christianity:

Know, O adored Christ, and make no mistake, that aside from the Devil, you have no enemy more venomous, more desperate, more bitter, than a true Jew who truly seeks to be a Jew.

In the *Schem Hemaphoras* he takes up again the comparison with Satan:

It is as easy to convert a Jew as to convert the Devil. A Jew, a Jewish heart, are as hard as wood, as stone, as iron, as the Devil himself. In short, they are the children of the Devil, condemned to the flames of hell.[2]

He unearthed against them all the old charges he had ridiculed, and even hinted 'that they misused their medical art to do secret harm to Christians'.[3] With the exception of pogroms, Luther recommended the usual

anti-Jewish measures—expulsion, confiscation of goods, burning of synagogues, forced labour, and so on. His propaganda was not in vain, for
thanks to his influence the Jews were expelled from important German
states—Saxony, Brandenburg, and Silesia. A host of imitators followed, repeating the old medieval accusations like the 'torture' of the consecrated
host, ritual murder, and so forth. Late in the sixteenth century and again
in the seventeenth century a number of anti-Semitic pamphlets were produced, with such extravagant titles as *A Brief Catalogue of the Horrible
Jewish Blasphemies; The Sack of Jewish Serpents; Inflamed Poison of the
Dragons and Furious Bile of the Serpents; Jewish Practices, a Study of
Their Impious Life*, and so on.[4] One can see that the Nazi newspaper *Der
Stürmer* and the pamphlets that Hitler said he bought in Vienna had a
long tradition behind them.

As to popular outbursts, they were less frequent and less murderous than
in the Middle Ages, but still they did occur. In 1616, for instance, a crowd
led by a pork butcher attacked the gates of the Frankfurt ghetto and managed to enter it in spite of an improvised resistance by the Jews. None were
killed and only a few were beaten up, but the populace sacked and burned,
destroyed the sacred scrolls of the synagogues, and did not forget to burn
all documents relating to debts. The Jewish community left the city, and
some time later Worms followed the example of Frankfurt.

The Jews could clearly see the connection between anti-Semitic pamphlets and the attacks they suffered, and at a later period made efforts,
occasionally successful, to stop their publication. A good example of this
was the case of Eisenmenger, a German professor of Oriental languages,
who, about 1700, wrote a pamphlet entitled *Judaism Unmasked*, reviving
all the old charges of ritual murder, poisoning of wells, and so on. The
work was being printed at Frankfurt, and the Jewish community of that
town, aware of it and fearing for their safety, asked for the help of the
Jews of Vienna. Thanks to their influence as bankers, the latter were able
to put pressure on the court, and the emperor Leopold I banned the distribution of Eisenmenger's pamphlet.[5] It was an early, isolated instance of
anti-racialist legislation.

SUPPRESSION OF JEWISH LITERATURE

Most often, as one would expect, suppression or censorship of Jewish
writings was the rule. The burning of books—which was going on in Chile
under a brutal military regime only recently—was not a Nazi invention. In
Paris in 1240 wagonloads of precious Hebrew manuscripts were publicly
burnt. The Talmud in particular was so fiercely persecuted, because of alleged references to Jesus Christ,[6] that many of its ancient manuscripts completely disappeared. In some countries, such as Italy, it could only be

printed in expurgated editions. This is not surprising, since for a long time vernacular versions of the Bible were also forbidden in Catholic countries. In Franco's Spain until recently any Protestant Bibles found in the country were confiscated.

One should remember that until the great humanist movement in Europe it was difficult to find non-Jewish Europeans who knew Hebrew. The situation only changed towards the end of the fifteenth century, when a number of Western scholars not only acquired a new enthusiasm for Greek learning but began to appreciate and protect Hebrew literature. Luther himself learned Hebrew from a manual published by the eminent Johann Reuchlin, the first to introduce the language into the curriculum of the University of Ingolstadt.

In 1509–10 the learned world saw the curious spectacle of a baptized Jew called Pfefferkorn—*plus royaliste que le roi*, as often happens—clamouring for the destruction of Hebrew books, while the Christian Johann Reuchlin wanted to save them.[7] Pfefferkorn, supported by the Dominicans, to whom he was attached, had obtained from the emperor Maximilian an order authorizing the destruction of all Hebrew books belonging to the Jewish communities of Cologne and Frankfurt. The Jews appealed against the order, and Reuchlin was asked for his opinion. His verdict was that most Hebrew books contained neither heresy nor blasphemy and should not be burned. The only exception in his view was the *Tol 'doth Yeshu* (The Generations of Jesus), a very crude and distorted version of the Gospel story, an obvious product of Jewish resentment against Christianity which for many centuries circulated among the Jews.[8] The emperor accepted the verdict and cancelled the order, but the controversy raged for several years and involved a large part of learned Europe. As Box says: 'On one side were ranged with Reuchlin the humanists, on the other the clericals with the universities of Louvain, Cologne, Erfurt, Mayence and Paris'.[9]

Luther, who in 1509 had gone back to Erfurt to take a new degree, supported Reuchlin and not only defended Hebrew literature but declared that the conversion of the Jews should be left to God—not to aggressive proselytism. It was a far cry from his later anti-Semitism. But in the end the Reformation dispute influenced the controversy, for Pope Leo X in 1520 decided against Reuchlin.

'THE DELUGE' IN POLAND

As we have seen in Chapter 7, a great number of Jews, trying to escape from the Black Death pogroms (1348–49), fled to Poland. They were predominantly Ashkenazim, i.e., German Jews who spoke a form of medieval German which developed into Yiddish, just as later the Sephardim spoke Ladino (Spanish) or Portuguese. They were not the first to arrive:

for some time German Jews had been moving east, and it is quite possible that at an earlier period Jewish groups had migrated to Poland from the kingdom of the Khazars.

To an agricultural country, essentially consisting of two classes—nobles and serfs—the Jews brought their experience of a more advanced community. They became commercial agents to the Polish lords, bankers, merchants, and small tradesmen. Several kings of Poland, like Boleslav V (1264) and Casimir the Great (1364), granted them charters which included considerable privileges. In fact, their influence seems to have begun so early that some Polish coins of the eleventh and twelfth centuries bear Hebrew inscriptions.

In some ways they were a state within a state and their privileges provoked the protests of the Church. Persecution was rare, but in 1484 the Jews were expelled from Warsaw, and later from Cracow. These setbacks had little effect on the status of the community, which remained high. A papal legate called Commendoni, visiting the country about 1565, was surprised by the great number of Jews and their prosperity:

> They do not live in abasement and are not reduced to menial trades thereby. They own land, engage in commerce, study medicine and astronomy. They possess great wealth and are not only counted among respectable people but sometimes even dominate them. They wear no distinctive insignia, and are even permitted to bear arms. In short they have all the rights of citizens.[10]

The legate's surprise is in itself an eloquent testimony of the terribly degraded and restricted life of the Western Jews in their ghettos.

The structure of Polish society was particularly oppressive, and no doubt many Jews, as commercial agents and merchants, profited from such exploitation. Polish proverbs from that time can be taken as evidence of the feelings of the poor: 'We peasants are always in misery: we must feed the noble, the priest and the Jew'. Or, 'What the peasant earns, the noble spends and the Jew profits by'.[11]

Besides, Poland had become too large: during the sixteenth and part of the seventeenth centuries it ruled not only Lithuania but what is now western Russia, including the rich Ukraine. It was in fact the Ukrainian peasants, rising in rebellion against the Polish lords and their Jewish agents, who began the disastrous period of troubles known as 'the Deluge'. The revolt was led by the Cossack chieftain Chmielnicki, who made violent proclamations against the Jews and carried out a series of hideous massacres. Entire communities were exterminated, and contemporary Jewish chronicles estimate the total at hundreds of thousands, or even half a million. This is now considered an exaggeration, but Simon Dubnov may be right in thinking that the Polish disaster produced greater loss of life (perhaps 100,000) than the Western pogroms at the time of the Crusades or during the Black Death.

The Cossack rebellion was only the beginning. A war followed between Poland and tsarist Russia, with Swedish intervention, and for about ten' years there was almost constant conflict. In the end Poland was ruined, having lost over half its population, while its Jewish community, at the time perhaps the largest, the most secure, and the most prosperous in the world, was shattered and impoverished. Their ancient rights were gradually abolished, and the Jews, as in other parts of Europe, withdrew into a secluded and intensely religious life, which gave rise to important movements like Hasidism. 'The Deluge' of 1648–58 remained in the Jewish collective memory as one of their great historical disasters, comparable even to the fall of the First and the Second Temple.

Although many Polish Jews, as we have already mentioned, fled to Hungary and elsewhere, it was not easy to find a safe place at the time, unless it was in the Ottoman Empire. In the seventeenth century a large part of Europe was closed to the Jew by the barriers of anti-Semitism. While the Inquisition raged in the Peninsula, Spanish domination had been extended to a considerable part of Italy, and as a result the Jews were expelled from the kingdom of Naples (1510, more definitely in 1541) and from the dukedom of Milan (1591). They could live in the Papal States, but under the ghetto regime and all the other restrictions laid down by Pope Paul IV.

In France there was papal territory, but in the rest of the country the Jews did not exist officially, although there were probably clandestine groups. In Austria and in the complicated tangle of German states there were repeated expulsions, although often followed by readmissions. To England, as we have seen, the Jews only returned in 1656.

On account of this and other factors, Poland remained, in spite of the Deluge, the most important centre of Judaism. And when we remember that a large part of the country was later to be absorbed by the Russian Empire, it will be seen that the Slav centre of the Diaspora was the source of many of the most important Jewish communities of the present: thence came the majority of the American Jews and also the founders of the state of Israel.

THE JEWS IN TSARIST RUSSIA

When the ancient Polish kingdom began to be partitioned among its powerful neighbours (1772), the lion's share fell in the end to its traditional rival and enemy to the east—tsarist Russia. And if the Poles were to distinguish themselves for their fierce anti-Semitism, the Russians were not very far behind. In fact, it can be said that the tsarist empire began under the sign of opposition to the Jews.

At the time of Ivan III in the fifteenth century there was a curious and obscure incident of 'Judaizing' in Russia. According to contemporary chronicles, the 'heresy' had been brought to Novgorod about 1470 by one or several Jewish 'missionaries'. From there it spread to Moscow, involving members of the royal family and priests of the Orthodox Church. It is quite possible that there was direct or indirect Jewish influence, showing once more the latent force of Jewish proselytism. But this 'heresy' was not strict Judaism, because its followers, although circumcised, still claimed to be followers of Jesus: they rejected the Trinity and the divinity of Christ and broke the images, or icons, like the Byzantine iconoclasts. In short, it was an intermediate sect like the ancient Ebionites.

In any case, its repression contributed significantly to Russian anti-Jewish feeling. In 1504 Ivan III had the main leaders burnt and, in order to avoid further 'contaminations', banned the entry of Jews into the territory of Moscow. Ivan III was also the first Russian prince to claim imperial status as a successor of Byzantine emperors and to proclaim Moscow a 'third Rome'. The tsars would also inherit the anti-Jewish policy of the Byzantine Caesars.

Poliakov comments that the Russian rulers maintained this policy with surprising consistency. For instance, in 1550 Ivan IV ('the Terrible'), the first to use officially the title of 'Tsar' (a Russian form of 'Caesar', in German *Kaiser*), received a request from his ally, King Sigismund Augustus of Poland, to admit Jewish merchants into Moscow. His reply was in very strong terms:

> We have already written you several times, telling you of the vile actions of the Jews, who have turned our people away from Christ, introduced poisonous drugs into our state, and caused much harm to our people. You should be ashamed, our brother, to write us about them. . . . In other states, too, they have done much evil, and for this have been expelled or put to death. We cannot permit the Jews to come into our state, for we do not wish to see any evil here.[12]

But when the tsarist empire began to expand towards the west, it acquired territories where for centuries there had been Jewish communities: particularly eastern Poland and the Baltic states. Peter the Great (1689–1725), in whose reign many of these conquests were made, tolerated the presence of the Jews in the new provinces. His successors, the tsarinas Catherine I, Anne, and Elizabeth, adopted a different policy and published several decrees expelling the Jews from the Ukraine and Little

Russia. Even Catherine II ('the Great'), with her reputation as an 'enlightened despot' and living in a century of liberal policies and revolution, confirmed the acts of her predecessors in the very first year of her reign, 1762: the same year was marked by a large-scale pogrom in Uman (Polish Ukraine). It was in Catherine's reign that the partitions of Poland took place and the country finally disappeared from the map.

From 1772 onwards the tsars followed the policy of confining the Jews to the 'Pale of Settlement', and Russia would be the last country in Europe to emancipate its Jewish community.

THE JEWS IN THE PAPAL STATES

Another part of Europe that long resisted the winds of change was the Papal States. Until Italian unification in 1860 (completed by the occupation of Rome in 1870) the popes controlled a very large territory. As we have seen, after Paul IV the condition of the Jewish community greatly deteriorated. One of his successors, the fanatical Pius V, besides eradicating the last vestiges of Protestantism in Italy, expelled the Jews from his States (1569), but for commercial reasons they were allowed to stay in Rome itself and in Ancona.

His successor, Gregory XIII, instituted the so-called *predica coativa*— a weekly proselytizing sermon which the Jews were forced to attend. There were stewards with canes at the church ready to flog any who showed obvious signs of inattention, such as nodding. A comical detail is that some Jews used to stop their ears with cotton wool, and when this was discovered the attendants began to examine them before they entered.

It is clear that the greater intolerance towards the Jews was partly the result of the bitter religious conflict at the time of the Counter Reformation. Gregory XIII, for instance, ordered a medal to be struck to celebrate the Massacre of St. Bartholomew in France (1572) and also started the famous Index of forbidden books.

If compulsory sermons were a petty nuisance, there was in Rome an earlier and revolting custom which savours of Nazi methods. As part of the famous races that took place on the Corso, aged Jews were forced to run every day during Carnival. They 'were given a dinner of rich food and strong wine just before the race, in order to increase their distress and the amusement of the spectators'.[13]

This degrading spectacle was only abolished in 1688, when Pope Clement IX exempted the Jews from competing in exchange for an annual tribute. Even then, on paying the money to the Keeper of the City, the Jewish spokesman had to prostrate himself while the official put his foot on the Jew's neck and said *Andate!* (Go!).

The condition of the Roman ghetto was particularly bad and unhealthy, and most Jews earned a precarious living as dealers in old clothes and other second-hand goods. Dr. Ramazzini, a pioneer in the study of occupational diseases and the founder of industrial medicine, took a close look at life in the Roman ghetto in his book *De morbis artificum*, published in 1700. He began by exploding the myth of the *foetor judaicus*: 'It is wrong for a stench to be regarded as natural and endemic to the Jews; that which the lower classes spread among them is due to the closeness of their homes and to poverty'.

He goes on to describe how many Jewish women ruined their eyesight by mending clothes far into the night in a poor light (this long before Thomas Hood wrote his famous 'Song of the Shirt' about the English seamstresses). As for the men, Dr. Ramazzini adds:

> They sit all day long in their booths stitching clothes, or stand looking for customers to whom they can sell old rags. Hence they are mostly cachectic, melancholy and surly, and there are few even of the more wealthy who do not suffer from the itch.[14]

THE BEGINNINGS OF EMANCIPATION

Men like Dr. Ramazzini were the pioneers of the new Age of Enlightenment, which was to bring in new attitudes towards the Jews, although papal Rome and tsarist Russia long remained obdurate. Even before 1700, Germany saw the emergence of the *Hofjuden* (court, or protected, Jews), wealthy and powerful men who acted as financiers or administrators for the rulers of the German states. They lived outside the ghetto, sometimes in sumptuous palaces, enjoyed special privileges, and wore fashionable Western dress. The most famous among the court Jews was, of course, Joseph Süss-Oppenheimer, whose story Lion Feuchtwanger dramatized in his novel *Jud Süss* (1925). Süss was until his spectacular fall the most powerful man in the state of Württemberg. In 1738 he was the victim of a scandalous trial, being accused among other things of fornication with Christian ladies (a serious offence at the time), and was finally hanged. His execution was greeted with great celebrations in anti-Semitic circles and became the occasion for a new spate of pamphlets.

In 1670 the Jews were expelled from Lower and Upper Austria, including Vienna, thanks to the influence of the emperor Leopold's Spanish wife Margaret Theresa. They crossed the frontier to Germany, and some were admitted into Brandenburg, from which they had been excluded. This was in fact the origin of the important Berlin community, and, apart from those in Poland, the German Jews were to be the most numerous in Europe. But the expulsion of 1670 was far from permanent, for a few years later they were again readmitted.

In 1744–45 another Habsburg empress, Maria Theresa, decreed the expulsion of the Moravian and Bohemian Jews, including the important community of Prague (the reason was suspicion of treason during the war with the French). Graetz relates:

> The Jews of Prague, more than 20,630 souls, were obliged in the depth of the winter, hurriedly to leave the town and to suffer in the villages; and the royal cities were forbidden to harbour any of those who passed through.[15]

But here one can see the change in the climate of opinion. Even some of the Austrian Catholic clergy were against the decree. The Jewish communities of England and Holland were strong enough to make representations to their governments, and the English and Dutch ambassadors interceded with the court of Vienna. There was also intervention by the Jews of Frankfurt, Rome, and Venice. Finally, Maria Theresa allowed the Jews to remain in Bohemia and Moravia, but those of Prague had to depart. Some years later, however, they were readmitted on payment of a heavy fine and under considerable restrictions.

Ironically enough, it fell to Austria later, under an 'enlightened despot', to lead the way in Jewish emancipation. But the first Western country to grant full citizenship to its Jews was the English colonies in America. An act approved by Parliament in 1740 allowed naturalization to all Protestants, Jews, and Quakers after seven years' residence.[16] Only the Catholics were excluded. So when the United States became independent under the principle that 'all men are created equal', the Jews were already full citizens in most states, although in some they lived under restrictions which were lifted only in the following century.

In Austria, Maria Theresa's successor, the emperor Joseph II, pioneered important liberal reforms, including the partial emancipation of the Jewish community. His decree of 1781 abolished a number of restrictions to which the Jews were subjected, including the *Leibzoll* (body, or capitation, tax) and the compulsory wearing of beards. Another edict, the *Toleranzpatent* of 1782, laid down general rules for placing the Jews on equal footing with Christians, although full citizenship was still not envisaged.

That Joseph's philanthropy was 'sincere if rather fierce' (Graetz) was shown by a decree of 1787 which ordered the Jews to adopt a German surname instead of the Hebrew name that hitherto had been considered sufficient. This was, in a way, a measure of assimilation, and as many Jews delayed in making the required registration, the Austrian officials made an arbitrary choice for many of them.

THE REVOLUTIONARY TIDE

For the West and a large part of the world the landmark was clearly the French Revolution. In theory, at least, the Declaration of Human Rights removed at one stroke the disabilities of the Jewish community, most of which was in fact concentrated in the German-speaking provinces of Alsace and Lorraine. In September 1791 the National Assembly formally approved Jewish enfranchisement, not without some opposition.

The atmosphere of generous, exuberant fraternization, typical of egalitarian revolutions, was also apparent in matters of religion. The newspaper *Chronique de Paris* reported in February 1792:

> Already at the celebration of the 14th July, first at Bischwiller and later at Bischeim [both places in Alsace] Catholics, Lutherans and Jews were closely united in their patriotic enthusiasm. At the Church, the Protestant temple and the synagogue, patriots of all religions assembled in turn, presided over by the vicar, the parson and the rabbi.

At Strasbourg, the Alsatian capital, an aged Jew said to be over ninety called Abraham Dreyfus—a name that was one day to become famous in the history of French anti-Semitism—was elected president of the 'primary' municipal assembly, to great applause. And the *Chronique de Paris* again wrote with enthusiasm:

> This venerable gentleman, who with his long beard reminded one of the patriarch of the same name, was embraced by all the members of the Assembly. On blessing him, people were reminded that for fifty years he had been the benefactor of native place. . . . The other Jews, turned into citizens overnight, were welcomed by the Christians with fraternal cordiality, well worthy of our sacred constitution.[17]

In these healthy waves of fraternal emotion, many people thought that it was possible to overthrow in a few years age-old barriers of hatred and suspicion. But it would be ungenerous to follow the fashionable tendency of looking down on all this enthusiasm as naïve. In fact, there is no doubt that the revolutionary fervour (which would spread to many other countries and reappear in the first days of the Russian Revolution) had very important practical results, including a speeding up of Jewish emancipation. Everywhere in the wake of French revolutionary armies new liberal regimes were established, which abolished the ghettos. In Holland under French rule the Jews were fully emancipated in 1796, and in the following year some of them were elected to the National Assembly—perhaps the first in any European country.

Bonaparte's Italian expedition took the revolutionary tide beyond the Alps. In 1797 the end of the Republic of Venice and the resignation of the last doge coincided with the abolition of the original ghetto, which had given its name to all others. Its gates were pulled down and burnt at a public ceremony in the midst of popular rejoicing. The ghetto of Rome was also abolished, in 1798, but it would be re-established some time later. On the other hand, in cities like Senigallia and Pesaro the upheaval of the French invasion was the sign for attacks on the ghettos, apparently the only ones in Italian history.[18]

The tide of reaction begun by the Congress of Vienna in 1815 undid many of the achievements of the revolutionary era. The old restrictions were reimposed in several countries, and the work had to begin all over again. In 1819 there were many attacks on the Jewish communities in Germany, stirred by the cries of *Hep! Hep!* and *Jude, verreck!* (Jew, die like a beast). It all began with student riots at Würzburg and spread to several other towns in Franconia, like Frankfurt, where the house of the Rothschilds was attacked. Even neighbouring Denmark was affected, but this seems to have been the last occasion before the Nazi period when such large-scale attacks were carried out in Western Europe against the Jews.

Meanwhile, in Europe as a whole, the tide of reaction was little more than a prolonged rearguard action, quite comparable to the crumbling opposition that can be observed in our century against the full emancipation of coloured peoples, whether in South Africa or America. The pressure for equal rights and for a more just society continued to mount, and many Jews, newly come out from the ghettos, joined in the work with vigour. The new liberal spirit was spreading to the churches, although official Roman Catholicism, not to mention the Eastern Church, long remained obdurate. It is not surprising that many Jews, anxious for integration, should join one or other of the churches or baptize their children, often without much religious conviction. But there were also some sincere conversions.

Another field in which they began to play a part, often a prominent one, was in the radical, progressive, or revolutionary movements of the nineteenth century. Liberalism, syndicalism, socialism—in all these movements there were Jews doing active work and sometimes laying down their lives. The tradition has continued to this day, and in studies made of the political opinions of Jewish communities there is always a high proportion of those who hold 'progressive' or 'left-wing' points of view.[19]

Jews often point out with pride that some of the most revolutionary ideas of our age—such as Freud's psychoanalysis, Karl Marx's communism, and Einstein's relativity—were the creation of Jewish minds. It is said that many of the young pioneers full of idealism who arrived in Palestine early in the twentieth century to start socialist communities had Marx's *Das Kapital* in one hand and Freud's *The Interpretation of Dreams* in the other.[20] But it should be remarked that men like Marx, Freud, and Einstein were all good examples of what Isaac Deutscher called 'the non-

Jewish Jew', i.e., people who repudiate the narrow separatist tradition of Judaism.

It is not surprising that the forces of reaction soon found a new pretext for anti-Semitism: that the Jews were deliberately disrupting and poisoning the world with 'subversive ideas'. It was like the myths of the Black Death in a sublimated form.

The years 1830, 1848, 1870–71, 1917–18 are the landmarks of the revolutionary age which during the nineteenth century had Paris as its main focus. In 1830 the people of Rome overthrew the walls of the ghetto, although restrictions continued in the period of reaction that followed under Pope Pius IX, including the baptism of Jewish children, as in the notorious case of Edgardo Mortara (see Chapter 6). Compulsory sermons were stopped only in 1846.

In 1849 the Jews achieved full emancipation in Denmark. In 1858 the first Jewish Member of Parliament, Lionel Rothschild, was finally admitted to the British House of Commons. In fact he had been elected several times but had not been allowed to take his seat because of the obligation to take the oath of allegiance on the Christian Bible. In 1862 the Jews were granted full civic rights in several German states, and this was extended throughout the country with the proclamation of the Second Reich in 1871.

In 1870 papal Rome was conquered by Italian troops. The pope lost all temporal power and until the time of Mussolini became 'the prisoner of the Vatican'. Thus one of the oldest Jewish communities in Europe, whose history we have followed since the time of Caesar, finally gained its emancipation. At that time one could say that, except for tsarist Russia and some Muslim states, the long Dark Ages had ended for Israel.

To the west the revolutionary trends had given rise to the new Latin American nations, freed from the two declining imperial powers, Spain and Portugal. In countries like Brazil and Mexico there were Catholic priests who became nationalist leaders, and some of them were executed for their part in insurrections: this in striking contrast with the obscurantism of Spanish and Portuguese clergy, of which contemporary visitors like George Borrow could provide good evidence.

For instance, when Brazilian representatives were debating their first independent constitution in 1824, several Catholic priests supported full freedom of worship and wanted to amend the original bill, which denied it to the Jews:

Father Muniz Tavares . . . declared that religious freedom was 'one of the most sacred human rights' and said: 'By invoking force as an aid to faith, intolerance placed courage on the side of doubt'. God, he added, did not want to be worshipped by force

nor through bloody sacrifices like the massacre of St. Bartholomew in France; nor through the flames of the fires kindled by
'that hideous tribunal of the Inquisition'. . . . He was supported
by Father Rocha Franca, who pleaded full civil rights for the
Jews, whose religion, he said, had been the handmaid, if not the
mother, of Christianity. The Virgin, John the Baptist, Elijah and
Jesus himself had all been Jews.[21]

Naturally, there were others in the Church with an entirely different
outlook, but it is interesting to see these Brazilian priests condemning the
Inquisition in such outspoken terms, something that the Vatican has always failed to do. Later on was to see the Brazilian romantic poet Castro
Alves, quite apart from his passionate denunciation of African slavery,
writing a poem on Ahasverus the Wandering Jew, proclaiming himself a
'Hebrew' in spirit, and falling wildly in love with a Jewish actress.

It was the age of rhetoric and lyrical outpourings against tyranny, when
Byron died for Greek independence and Shelley thundered from Italy
against the Peterloo Massacre in England. It was widely thought that
once the old despotisms were overthrown, freedom and harmony would
reign everywhere, and those fraternal embraces between Christians and
Jews at the Strasbourg assembly would be repeated in all countries. It was
a noble and wonderful vision, and still is, like the 'dream' of Martin
Luther King. But it underestimated the force of old prejudices and mental
conditioning.

Let us move on to the end of the century. The year is 1889. The countries of Western Europe dominate a good part of the world, and everywhere in the West there is a firm belief in progress, in reason, and in the
stability of the world the Europeans have created. In Germany there is a
new kaiser on the throne who is about 'to drop the pilot', Bismarck, while
America has just elected her twenty-third president. In India there is a
new movement called National Congress, but the British Empire seems
to be very strong and secure. In Brazil a group of generals and civilians are
about to overthrow the only monarchy in the New World. In the Habsburg
empire, where the heir to the throne has just committed suicide, a child
is born to Catholic parents in the little Austrian town of Braunau. There
is nothing very particular about him, no omens or prophecies are recorded before or on the date of his birth, 20 April. But his name is
Adolf Hitler.

II

Anti-Semitism as
a Political Movement

I believe that I am acting in accordance with the will of the Almighty
Creator: by defending myself against the Jew I am fighting for the
work of the Lord.

—Adolf Hitler, *Mein Kampf*, end of chap. 2

A NEW PHENOMENON?

As the word anti-Semitism was coined just over a century ago, and many
people became aware of its destructive effects only recently, it is natural
that it should often be considered a modern phenomenon: particularly
when we think of the widespread ignorance not only of Jewish history but
of prejudices in general.

Most people are afraid of taking a good look at their own minds and at
the attitudes of others. You have only to think of the deep fear of mental
illness, and this in spite of the popularization of psychiatry and a great
number of books and other literature on the subject. It is easy and comfortable to dismiss what happened in Nazi Germany as just a fit of collective madness that is not likely to occur again: perhaps as an accident
that only occurred because a few European leaders let things slip and did
not stop Hitler while there was still time. As Father Flannery writes: 'The
inclination to regard Hitler as a latter-day aberration with little or no
roots in the past or connection with the present is still widespread, and
thus the problem is not faced'.[1]

Obviously, if Hitler was a monster, his monstrosity has identifiable roots
in our history, in our society, and in the last analysis in ourselves. And if
he turned against Christianity, many Christian students of the problem
now recognize that the Church bears considerable responsibility for anti-
Semitism: James Parkes and Bernhard Olson, among the Protestants, and

166

Father Flannery, among the Catholics, are some of those who have done valuable work in this respect.

Nor do I see much reason for establishing a distinction between a medieval, 'religious' anti-Semitism and the modern anti-Semitic movement which has sought inspiration rather in racialist ideas or economic interpretations of history. It is impossible to draw a firm line between the two. For instance, we have seen that in Portugal and Spain the Jews were not fully accepted even after baptism, and racialist ideas of 'purity of blood' (*limpieza de sangre*) were enforced long before Hitler's 'Nuremberg Laws'. In tsarist Russia, well into the twentieth century, a 'medieval' and apocalyptic anti-Semitism was blended with the very modern myths of the *Protocols of the Elders of Zion*. Ritual murder trials were still taking place, in Russia as well as in the Austro-Hungarian Empire, and even in America a Jew in Atlanta was lynched on the suspicion of having murdered a young girl.[2] In Catholic countries as diverse as France, Austria, Yugoslavia, or Argentina, the anti-Semitic movement has had powerful support among the more reactionary clergy and laymen.

In his book *The Last Three Popes and the Jews* the Israeli writer Pinchas Lapide has tried to defend Pius XI and Pius XII against the charge of silence or even complicity with anti-Semitism, and more particularly with the Nazi slaughter of Jews. And he quotes these words of Pius XI: 'Anti-Semitism is inadmissible; spiritually, we are all Semites'.[3]

It appears that the pope said this in the year of Munich, 1938, a little before the 'first' Nazi pogrom (the 'Night of the Broken Glass'; see Chapter 12). But Lapide also points out that until that very year the Jesuit newspaper of Rome, *La Civiltà cattolica*, was still printing vicious anti-Jewish propaganda in its columns, and even recommending measures of 'segregation and identification suitable to our time': i.e., the Jewish badge and the ghetto, which Pope Paul IV had made official nearly four centuries earlier. It was only then, in 1938, that Pius XI seems to have put a stop to this kind of propaganda, after his encyclical *Mit brennender Sorge* (With Burning Sorrow) against Nazi racialism.

With more relevance, his successor Pius XII was accused—by a German playwright in a controversial play, amongst others—of not having raised his voice publicly against the Nazi extermination of the Jews. But what could one expect of a pope who sent his congratulations to General Franco for the latter's victory in the Spanish civil war, at the very moment when the *Caudillo* was massacring his defeated political enemies? Nor should one forget that a large part of the German clergy, both Protestant and Catholic, fully supported the Nazi regime. On the other hand, many Jews still remember with deep gratitude the help and sanctuary given them during persecution by a number of priests and religious orders. We have also seen that even in the pogroms of the Crusades Jewish communities were sometimes effectively protected by bishops.

THE RISE OF MODERN ANTI-SEMITISM:
THE JEWISH BANKER AS A THREAT

Naturally, to state the essential historical continuity of the phenomenon (and, in my view, the basic similarity of its roots) is not to deny the variety of its manifestations. It was only to be expected that modern anti-Semitism should seek other arguments and rationalizations more suitable to the outlook of the time.

One must also consider the enormous help the movement received from modern resources of propaganda. Compare what Apion and other anti-Semites could do in ancient Alexandria or Rome with the quick diffusion of anti-Semitic literature in the twentieth century: within a few years the *Protocols of the Elders of Zion* had been translated into a number of languages and sold many thousands of copies. Not only that, but the anti-Semites could found societies and parties, organize popular meetings, edit newspapers with vicious cartoons satirizing the Jews, put up candidates for Parliament, and print pamphlets: in short, use all the resources and freedoms of a modern democratic society in order to undermine it with hatred. It is already a commonplace of history to say that the triumph of the Nazis in Germany was very largely due to their masterly use of all the contemporary methods of propaganda.

Although, as I have said, there is no firm dividing line, what we may call 'modern anti-Semitism' began to emerge about the middle of the nineteenth century: just when Jewish communities were achieving their emancipation almost everywhere in the West. It was partly a protest against this emancipation, and partly a hostile reaction to the various roles the Jews were playing in the deep social and economic changes of the time. The growth of cities and industry, the growing power of capitalists and bankers, the decline of traditional patterns of behaviour, the fear and insecurity generated by all these changes: anti-Semitic propaganda would concentrate all these floating anxieties and frustrations on an easily identifiable scapegoat—the Jew. And he was no longer the oppressed victim of the ghetto: he was making his way in this new world, helping to change it, and often taking the lead as a banker, a captain of industry, a press chief, or a political leader. Naturally, it was these prominent people who obsessed the anti-Semites, not the thousands of Jews who like everybody else were earning a precarious living at some work or trade, whether in Vienna, Odessa, or New York.

Each group could see in the Jew a personification of the things he dreaded or hated most. To the aristocratic conservatives, representatives of the old landed classes, everything 'liberal' or 'radical' was declared to be Jewish. To those who hated the new cities and looked back nostalgically on the old agricultural way of life, the Jews were the rootless nomads who exploited everything and settled nowhere. To some of the forerunners of modern socialism the Jew might even appear as the personification of the heartless capitalist.

Perhaps the first figure to impress itself on the imagination of the modern anti-Semite was that of the millionaire Jewish banker. This was very largely due to the spectacular success of the house of Rothschild. As we have seen, the name was derived from the sign of a 'red shield' on their family house in the ghetto of Frankfurt. By the 1820s the sons of the founder, Mayer Amschel, had established prosperous banking branches in London, Paris, Vienna, and Naples. This became the prototype of the power of 'international Jewry', exploiting and sucking the world dry through the power of money, like the tentacles of an octopus.[4]

The type of the rich, unscrupulous Jewish banker already appears in Balzac's *La Comédie humaine* as Baron Nucingen. And one of the first anti-Semitic works of this period also came out in France: it was *Les Juifs, rois de l'époque*, by A. Toussenel, first published in 1845.

In many ways it is an odd book, rather untypical of anti-Semitic literature. Toussenel was a faithful disciple of the socialist Fourier (also an anti-Semite), whose ideas inspired several American communes, and much of his work is not about the Jews at all but about the right to work, agricultural and industrial reforms, and so on. He explains (a little apologetically) that he uses the word 'Jew' as a general, non-ethnic term for banker, capitalist, or exploiter: 'tout parasite improductif, vivant de la substance et du travail d'autrui' (every unproductive parasite, who lives from another's substance and work).[5]

This becomes a little clearer (or odder) when Toussenel says that 'qui dit juif dit protestant' (who says Jews says Protestant) and includes under the concept of capitalistic Jew the English, the Dutch, and the Genevese, who are the object of his special antipathy as bankers.[6] As Protestants, inspired by the Old Testament, they all follow Jewish ways (and so do the Americans, who are added later for good measure).

According to Toussenel, the Jews are rootless parasites (others, including Hitler, would develop the same theme): 'Le juif n'est jamais que campé sur le sol qu'il habite. Quand il achète des terrains, ce n'est pas pour y faire du blé, mais pour y semer des boutiques'.[7]

But, he hastens to add, the same applies to the English, American, and Dutch merchants. After long, rambling chapters on all sorts of subjects (the power of the Rothschilds is not forgotten), he closes the book with a series of appeals. The address 'au peuple' ends with these slogans: 'Mort au parasitisme! Guerre aux juifs! Voilà la devise de la révolution nouvelle!'[8]

As one would expect, there is much valid criticism of French society in the book, but Toussenel spoils it all by his obsession with the Jews and his muddled, Pickwickian concept of 'juif'. Perhaps the best comment on him is the often quoted epigram by Bebel (co-founder of the German Social Democratic party): 'Anti-Semitism is the socialism of fools'.[9]

DISRAELI'S FREE GIFT TO THE ANTI-SEMITES

The Jew who becomes an anti-Semite—a very understandable phenomenon—is not a rare occurrence: we have only to think of converted Jews like Pfefferkorn who turned into fanatical persecutors of their former religion. Conversely, other Jews have helped anti-Semitism by an unrestrained propensity for exalting the Jewish people.

It is unlikely that Toussenel was a reader of English novels. If he had been, he might have come across a book published in London the year before his own—1844: the novel *Coningsby*, written by a baptized Jew called Benjamin Disraeli, who would one day become a famous statesman. Curiously enough, in that same year another baptized Jew by the name of Karl Marx, whose influence in the world would far surpass that of Disraeli, also published a pamphlet, *A World without Jews*, which is anything but friendly to Judaism.[10]

About halfway through Disraeli's long Victorian novel the hero, Coningsby, meets a kind of Jewish superman called Sidonia who is descended from a Marrano Spanish family. (Disraeli's grandmother came from a prominent Portuguese Jewish family). He has all the aristocratic pride of the Sephardim, but he is also a highly idealized character, the all-round man of nineteenth-century romanticism—a Count of Monte Cristo and a Byronic hero rolled into one. The power and wealth of his family of bankers is obviously modelled on that of the Rothschilds: Waterloo had made the Sidonias one of the greatest capitalist enterprises in Europe.

In a long conversation with Coningsby Sidonia reveals the extent of 'secret' Jewish power in Europe and propounds what is in fact a racialist doctrine in Jewish terms—years ahead of Gobineau, Chamberlain, and all the Aryan mythology that inspired National Socialism:

> The fact is, you cannot destroy a pure race of the Caucasian organisation. It is a physiological fact; a simple law of nature, which has baffled Egyptian and Assyrian kings, Roman emperors, and Christian Inquisitors. No penal laws, no physical torture, can effect that a superior race should be absorbed in an inferior, or be destroyed by it. The mixed persecuting races disappear; the pure persecuted race remains.[11]

This sounds odd coming from an 'assimilated' Jew who married an English lady, and the ludicrous idea of the Jews being a 'pure race' (Disraeli called them 'Mosaic Arabs') shows that the book moves in a world of fantasy. But there is more to come:

> The first Jesuits were Jews; that mysterious Russian diplomacy which so alarms Western Europe is organised and principally carried on by Jews. . . . [They] almost monopolize the professorial chairs of Germany. . . . You never observe a great intellectual movement in Europe in which the Jews do not participate.[12]

Sidonia goes on to tell Coningsby that a few years earlier he had to travel to four European capitals in order to raise a loan for the tsar through various branches of his banking family: and found that in all four countries he visited—Russia, Spain, France, and Prussia—the minister he had to deal with was invariably a Jew. Then comes the famous sentence that was to be quoted again and again in anti-Semitic literature: 'So you see, my dear Coningsby, that the world is governed by very different personages from what is imagined by those who are not behind the scenes'.[13]

Here one clearly sees the picture of Jewish financiers or bankers pulling the strings and manipulating governments like puppets. It so happens that of the politicians Disraeli mentions by name only Mendizábal (Spanish minister of finance for a short period) was of Jewish—or rather Marrano—descent: in fact, Spanish cartoonists used to picture him with a huge tail, recalling the old belief in the *judio rabudo*.[14] Disraeli—who as prime minister would be caricatured as a Jewish pedlar—was obviously giving free rein to fantasies of world power and indulging in his own ethnocentric pride and vanity. Sidonia is partly a projection of his own image—of what he would like to be (and, in a way, became). Nowadays it is still common for Jewish writers to make somewhat exaggerated claims not so much for financial power but for Jewish genius and contributions to culture. But one can well understand the eagerness with which anti-Semitic propagandists were later to seize on these fanciful passages as a heaven-sent piece of evidence: freely provided, one might add, by a Jew who was to become prime minister of the greatest imperial power of the time and pull off such financial coups as the purchase of the Suez shares (with money from his friends the Rothschilds), which gave Britain control of the canal.

In fact, by the time the anti-Semites had 'discovered' the power of the Rothschilds, their comparative importance had declined and they had become only one of several great banking firms in Europe. This is typical of the way prejudices work: they often use real facts, but magnify them out of all proportion and fail to take into account the nuances and quick changes that are occurring all the time. For instance, bankruptcies were not rare at the time, with disastrous losses among the public. As James Parkes points out:

> On both sides of the picture there were, of course, Jews. But only when they were among the first group [the bankers] were they remembered; and their role was so exaggerated that *all* financial scandals were assumed to be Jewish, and to be part of a vast web, with the Rothschilds in the centre, for the exploitation and impoverishment of Christian Europe.[15]

After Toussenel the theme was to be developed in a wider context by the French Catholic Henri Gougenot des Mousseaux, who in 1869 published his *Le Juif, le judaïsme et la judaisation des peuples chrétiens*. This is more in the main stream of anti-Semitism, for he goes back to the medieval accusations, while raising new themes—particularly the corrupting power of the 'Jewish press': one that was to become a favourite hobby-horse of anti-Semites, from Wilhelm Marr to Adolf Hitler. But Mousseaux's book involved more ambitious, apocalyptic ideas, and therefore has a more proper place in the following chapter. Incidentally, he seems to have been the first to make use of Disraeli's *Coningsby* and quoted the key passage on the title page of his book.

In that same year of 1869 a French diplomat and writer, the Comte de Gobineau, was in Rio de Janeiro representing France at the court of the Brazilian emperor Pedro II (they were to become great friends, and Gobineau was to accompany Dom Pedro on his European travels). Between 1853 and 1855 the count had published a monumental four-volume work entitled *Essai sur l'inégalité des races humaines*.[16] Ironically, it was a Frenchman and a Germanized Englishman (Houston Chamberlain) who were to give German racialism its ideological basis.

Strictly speaking, Gobineau does not belong to the history of anti-Semitism. Far from being anti-Jewish, he rated the contribution of the Jews to history and culture very highly. But (like Disraeli in this respect) he did think that all mixing of races produced decline, and declared that the purest whites (the 'Aryans') were superior to both the 'Semites' (who had deteriorated through the infusion of 'black blood') and the 'Hamites' (who were entirely 'saturated' with it). Although Gobineau himself was pessimistic about the racial future of Germany—and, indeed, of the whole white race, which, in his view, was doomed—his mythology was to be taken up with enthusiasm and developed by other apostles of racialism, particularly anti-Semitic Germans like Wagner.[17]

In 1870 Gobineau left Rio for Paris in a hurry, to witness the overwhelming defeat of France at the hands of the Prussians (no doubt, in his view, a sign of racial weakness). In the following year, in the famous Hall of Mirrors in the Palace of Versailles, the Second German Reich was proclaimed. Very soon its founder, Bismarck, was to use anti-Semitism as a political weapon for the first time in recent history.

THE ANTI-SEMITIC MOVEMENT IN GERMANY

In 1873, after a period of intense economic development and frantic speculation, Germany went through a serious financial crisis and there was a great crash on the Berlin exchange. It was not a disaster on the scale of 1929, which would create mass unemployment and in the end lead to the Nazi seizure of power. But many people suffered, and there were several Jewish bankruptcies: it would have been very strange if the Jews were not involved, for since emancipation they had taken part in all fields of national life.

In that same year a journalist called Wilhelm Marr published a short book, little more than a pamphlet, with the pompous title *The Victory of Jewry over Germanism* (*Der Sieg des Judenthums über das Germanenthum*). Little is known about the author: there is even a story that he was the baptized son of a Jewish actor. In the book Marr admits a personal grudge: he had lost a job on a newspaper through 'Jewish influence'. Resentments of this nature are common among militant anti-Semites, and one may compare Hitler's professional failures in Vienna.

Marr wrote his pamphlet 'from a non-denominational point of view' and claims to make a clean break with any religious or pseudo-religious motivation. To him it is no longer a question of faith but of race—of 'blood'. He even admits that in the Middle Ages the Jews may have been unfairly persecuted as scapegoats. What obsesses him is a conviction of defeat: *Finis Germaniae!* With their diabolical cunning, their control of finance and the press, the Jews were gaining the mastery everywhere and the future belonged to them. In Germany they had set up 'a social-political dictatorship', Austria was in their hands, and in the West stood 'poor Jew-ridden France' and England ruled by Disraeli, 'a German-hater *comme il faut*': 'France had in the last seven years a Jewish dictator and a Jewish triumvirate, England a Jewish premier, and Germany has become the Jewry's Eldorado'.[18]

Here Marr is indulging in the game of 'smelling Jews in high places', which was to become more popular and even wilder among anti-Semites (again, one might blame Disraeli for starting it). He reveals in an earlier passage that the 'Jewish' rulers of France alluded to are Gambetta, Jules Simon, and Adolphe Crémieux. Gambetta was of Italian origin and there is no evidence that he was of Jewish descent. The radical leader Jules Simon (prime minister from 1876 to 1877) was not a Jew—not everybody with such a name is one. In fact, Marr got only one right. Crémieux (minister of justice in 1870–71) was both the acknowledged leader of the

French Jewish community and a prominent politician on the left: he was among the first French Jews to be elected to the Chamber of Deputies (in 1842) and founded in 1858 the Alliance Israélite Universelle. This organization did good work defending Jews against persecution, but was soon to be pointed out by the anti-Semites as the centre of a sinister conspiracy.

Later, of course, Jewish descent would be invented for all kinds of prominent figures, such as Lenin or the German Social Democratic leader Karl Kautsky.

Marr's pamphlet, however, introduced a more subtle and cunning brand of anti-Semitism. Giving up the crude old slanders, it appealed to feelings of envy and frustration and painted a picture of a minority growing in power and wealth. But the 'reasonableness' was only apparent: just as before, the Jews was still being magnified as a creature endowed with mysterious and dangerous powers. Marr's defeatism was also a false and theatrical reaction. From now on whoever felt resentful or defeated in Germany had an excellent scapegoat: *plus ça change plus c'est la même chose.*

Marr's little book became a best seller and within six years went through no less than twelve editions: that must have been ample compensation for his failure as a journalist. Following up his success, the author launched an ephemeral newspaper and in 1879 founded an Anti-Semitic League. This seems to have been the first organization of the kind in the world, and the coining of the word 'anti-Semitism' is also attributed to Marr.

But in the previous year, 1878, the campaign against the Jews had already been used as a politico-electoral weapon. Chancellor Bismarck, the ultra-conservative creator of the Second Reich, had so far worked in alliance with the National Liberal party, and with their help had just conducted a fierce and petty anti-Catholic campaign, the notorious *Kulturkampf.* But he disliked such liberal doctrines as free trade: in fact, he hated everything that smacked of progressive ideas. So he decided to give up the attempt to govern through a parliamentary ministry. In June 1878, following an attempt to assassinate Kaiser Wilhelm I, Bismarck dissolved the Reichstag and launched a violent electoral campaign, aimed at discrediting his opponents.

The formula was quite simple. Everything the Prussian conservatives hated—such as liberalism and, even worse, socialism—was declared to be *Reichsfeind* (inimical to the Reich). These doctrines were also tainted by frequent association with Jews. Rather conveniently, two of the most prominent National Liberal leaders, Lasker and Bamberger, happened to be Jews. So anti-Semitism was a very good weapon for discrediting the liberals. It was no coincidence that at the same time Bismarck was also attacking the socialists and succeeded in getting the Reichstag to outlaw the Social Democratic party.

The trick worked in the 1878 election, and the National Liberals lost thirty seats. By another Machiavellian *volte-face* Bismarck now reconciled himself with the Catholics and their Centre party. Anti-Semitism was a good rallying point for Bismarck's conservatives and an important section of Catholicism, and in the Rhineland the fanatical priest Augustus Rohling was conducting a violent campaign against the Jews through his newspaper. In 1871 he had published a book called *Der Talmudjude* (The Jew of the Talmud), which was little more than a repetition of the old accusations and legends collected by Eisenmenger in his *Judaism Unmasked* (see Chapter 10).

On the Protestant side the anti-Semitic movement found a leader in Adolf Stoecker, a Lutheran court chaplain, who was given full official support. He was particularly useful because, like Toussenel, he claimed to be a socialist and saw in the Jews the exploiting capitalists. In that same year of 1878 Stoecker founded the Christian Social Workers' party (later renamed Christian Social party) and in 1881 was elected to the Reichstag, where he supported the conservatives. Stoecker's attempt to woo the German workers away from the Social Democrats was a failure, but his anti-Semitism attracted many supporters among the middle classes. In some ways this Adolf was a forerunner of Hitler, and one might remember that the full name of the Nazi party was the National Socialist Workers' party.

Meanwhile, other leaders were emerging in Berlin, without any sympathy for and often hostile to Christianity: people like Bernhard Förster, who married Nietzsche's sister, Elizabeth, and in the 1880s went off with her to found an 'Aryan colony' in Paraguay called Nueva Germania. When this failed, he committed suicide, but Elizabeth Förster-Nietzsche lived to see Hitler in power and acknowledged him as the heir of her brother's philosophy. Other anti-Semitic agitators were Heinrici and Sonnenberg, who together with Förster conducted a campaign on the popular level, with boycotts, satire, and frequent attacks on Jews. Sometimes they would challenge them to duels, with fatal results.

Both Förster and Heinrici were schoolteachers and, like others, helped to spread the anti-Semitic virus (together with racialist and militaristic ideas) among the new generations. Heinrich von Treitschke, who was professor of history at Berlin University from 1874, helped matters along; his lectures were immensely popular, and even General Staff officers and officials of the Prussian establishment attended them. Treitschke was a fanatical apostle of Prussian military might and state authoritarianism, and a determined enemy of socialism. He exalted war and thought that 'martial glory is the basis of all the political virtues'. To cap all that, he was violently anti-Semitic and coined the slogan 'The Jews are our misfortune' (*Die Juden sind unser Unglück*), which would one day be used everywhere by the Nazis in their demonstrations. Apart from his lectures, Treitschke edited an influential periodical and was also a member of the Reichstag.

With all this orchestration from pulpits, schools, universities, and the streets, the anti-Semitic movement worked up to a climax in 1881—also the year when the first pogroms took place in Russia. Signatures were collected for a monster petition to Bismarck, asking among other things for the political disfranchisement of all German Jews (which was to be carried out half a century later by Hitler) and the banning of all further Jewish immigration from Eastern Europe. Over 200,000 signatures were collected, but after this the affair rather petered out.

The brilliant Portuguese novelist and satirist Eça de Queiroz, who was watching all this from England, reported on it for a Brazilian newspaper. Remembering what had happened once in his own country, he smelled in Germany 'a hateful odour of auto-da-fé', and was indignant that the English weekly *Spectator* should echo the German attacks with a series of anti-Jewish articles. And he wrote:

> In the Middle Ages, every time the oppressed lower classes showed signs of rebellion, the Church and Princes hastened to warn them: 'We can see you suffer, but it is your own fault. The Jews killed Our Lord, and you have not punished them enough'. . . . The trick never failed. . . . It is just what Chancellor Bismarck is doing now, with civilized moderation. Germany suffers and murmurs: the prolonged financial crisis, a series of bad harvests, high taxation . . . all this exasperates the middle class. . . . Therefore, for want of a war, the Prince von Bismarck distracts the attention of famished Germans by pointing at enriched Jews. Naturally, he does not mention the death of Jesus Christ. But he talks about the Jew's millions and the power of the synagogue.[19]

Of course, it is a bit oversimplified, but like a few others Eça de Queiroz was shrewd enough to see the basic scapegoat mechanism at work. It was the old cry again: *Der Jud ist Schuld!* (It's the Jew's fault!) To Bismarck himself, as he confessed later, anti-Semitism was no more than a convenient weapon: if it came his way, he saw no objection to using it.[20] In reply to the monster petition, the tight-lipped government announced, to Eça's indignation, that *'for the present* there was no intention of altering the legislation relating to the Jews'. Once his political objectives had been achieved, Bismarck believed in letting sleeping dogs lie.

But the harm to the country and to the new generation was still being done: new seeds were being sown for the later 'harvest of hatred'. Year by year students were being taught to worship the idol of German military might and the collective image of an invincible Germany, which perhaps could only be defeated by 'the enemy within'.

We ended the previous chapter with the landmark of 1889, when Hitler was born and Kaiser Wilhelm II, a fanatical believer in that idolatry, was firmly on the throne. Ten years later, in 1899, a book was published that was to fan the flames of German racialist pride and whose author was to become a devoted admirer first of the kaiser and later of Hitler. It was yet another portentous German work, *The Foundations of the Nineteenth Century*, by Houston Stewart Chamberlain. It was published, very appropriately, in Munich, for it was to become the racialist Bible of National Socialism.

Chamberlain, the son of a British admiral, had become enamoured of everything German and was later to marry the daughter of another of his heroes, Wagner. The basic philosophy of his book, although propounded with imagination and a certain brilliancy, is almost childishly simple: everything good in civilization came from the Aryans, particularly from the Teutons. The Jews, whom he considered a pure race, had made a mainly negative contribution to civilization and were a dangerous enemy of the Aryans. Chamberlain was following the anti-Semitism of his hero Wagner. And as Jesus Christ had been one of the great figures of history, it was obvious that he could not have been a Jew: 'The probability that Christ was no Jew, that he had not a drop of genuinely Jewish blood, is so great that it almost amounts to certainty'.[21]

It was from schools and universities pervaded by such distorted racialist doctrines that thousands of Germans would come, who fought in two world wars and who were to be the instruments of the Nazi crimes against humanity.

POLITICAL ANTI-SEMITISM IN AUSTRIA

In the Austro-Hungarian Empire, a conservative monarchy like the Second Reich but much less strong, anti-Semitism was also to play a part in the clash between reactionary and progressive forces. In fact, Pulzer says that Vienna may 'claim to be the cradle of modern political anti-Semitism',[22] as Alexandria was for anti-Judaism in the ancient world.

As in Germany, there was strong opposition to Jewish emancipation and the anti-Semitic movement was made up of several elements. First there was the Catholic right, which was represented by several vociferously anti-Jewish papers. Its followers considered the Jews 'the party of subversion' and responsible for all revolutionary ideas.

But anti-Semitism was also popular among the artisans and lower middle class of Vienna, who feared competition from Jewish immigrants and exaggerated their importance. According to Pulzer, two events helped to make it important politically: first, the financial crash of 1873, which affected Vienna as well as Berlin, and, secondly, the Russian pogroms, which, apart from setting an example of violence, also swelled the flight of Jewish refugees into Austria.

At that time the anti-Semitic movement was beginning to acquire international ramifications. For instance, the Austrian archduchess Maria Theresa, wife of the Count of Chambord, pretender to the French throne, sent a friend to Germany in 1881 to collect anti-Semitic material and literature. Meanwhile, the imperial government was persuaded to appoint to the chair of Hebrew at the University of Prague the notorious anti-Semitic priest Augustus Rohling, whom we have already met as the author of *Der Talmudjude*. As we shall see in a moment, Rohling was so busy hating the Jews that he did not have much time to brush up his Hebrew.

In April 1882 an opportunity arose for rehearsing the hackneyed medieval defamation that his book helped to spread. At the town of Tisza Eszlar, in Hungary, a girl called Esther Solymossi was reported missing. A Hungarian deputy who was connected with Maria Theresa's anti-Semitic group, Geza Onody, hastened to accuse the local Jews of ritual murder; they were supposed to have got her blood to make matzos, as the Jewish Passover was near. The beadle of the synagogue was arrested, together with other Jews, and the case dragged on for a long time, encouraged by the finding of a body, which in the end turned out not to be the missing girl at all. In the end the crown prosecutor withdrew from the case for lack of evidence.

The fiasco helped to discredit anti-Semitism in Hungary, but as usual the promoters of the campaign went on exploiting it. In the same year, 1882, a German called Pinkert organized in Dresden the so-called First International Anti-Jewish Congress. At the meeting hall he put up a large oil painting of the missing Hungarian girl, a young barefoot peasant, the alleged 'innocent victim' of Jewish hatred.

Meanwhile, the anti-Semitic conservatives continued their campaign in Vienna and even paid an agitator who went round the working-class suburbs spreading the story that the collapse of the Tisza Eszlar trial had been due to bribery by Jewish capitalists. James Parkes says:

> For some months it looked as though they would succeed. It is
> the only case during the whole period in which the Socialist party
> of any country came near to falling into the trap of believing that
> 'the Jews' were the enemy they should be fighting.[23]

The situation was saved by the local rabbi, Dr. J. Bloch, who bravely intervened to counteract the malicious propaganda. Going over to the offensive, Bloch made such violent attacks against Rohling (now Canon Rohling), accusing him of ignorance, and challenging him to translate an unseen Hebrew text, that the priest was forced to bring a suit for libel. It seemed like a re-enactment of the old medieval disputes between the Church and the synagogue. But this time the rabbi received the support of Christian experts, like the prominent Professor Delitzsch of Leipzig. In the end, in 1885, Rohling was forced to withdraw his charge and had to pay a large penalty for costs. But his utter discredit did not prevent his book *The Jew of the Talmud* from continuing to circulate—even further afield, in countries like France and Russia.

Meanwhile, the Austrian anti-Semitic movement had found two effective leaders—the more radical and extreme Schönerer and Dr. Karl Lueger, who was to prove the more successful of the two. Schönerer, a nationalist and a dissident member of the Liberal party, drew up a new programme of social reform (the Linz Programme) and in 1885 included as a basic clause 'the removal of Jewish influence from all sections of public life'. As to Lueger, in 1887 he joined the newly formed anti-Semitic Christlich-sozialer Verein (Social Christian Union, or party). By 1889 the manifesto of a United Christian group was demanding the exclusion of the Jews from many professions and trades and the restriction of immigration.

Their main triumph was to come in the 1895 elections to the Vienna city council, when Lueger's Social Christian party won two-thirds of the seats and he was elected mayor. This victory was helped by Pope Leo XIII, who, impressed by Lueger's success in attracting the working classes to Catholicism, ordered the withdrawal of a pastoral letter the Austrian Church had drawn up against anti-Semitism. The Austrian emperor, who viewed Lueger's radical views and methods with suspicion, was harder to convince, and it was only two years later, in 1897, that he allowed the new burgomaster to take office.

THE YOUNG HITLER IN VIENNA

Lueger was burgomaster of Vienna for thirteen years: this means that until just before World War I an anti-Semitic party governed one of the largest European capitals. But this fact had another sinister consequence. It was to this centre of anti-Semitism that in 1907 came the eighteen-year-old Adolf Hitler. There he spent crucial years of his development until 1913, when he moved to the cradle of the Nazi movement, Munich.

There is not much point in discussing, as some have done, whether Hitler 'caught' anti-Semitism in Vienna or whether he was already an anti-Semite when he came from Linz, as stated by his companion Kubicek. Anti-Semitism is not an infection contracted at one given moment, and it is obvious that Hitler had the stereotypes inculcated by the upbringing of his time. The moving forces of his personality—the deep hostility and resentment, ready to seek an outside 'enemy'—must have been already well developed. But he was probably right when he claimed later, in *Mein Kampf*, that Vienna had been his hard school. In the Habsburg capital he was the *déclassé*, the ambitious young man with artistic pretensions who had been rejected by the School of Fine Arts, who lived in hostels and doss houses, acting out his frustrations and fantasies of power in constant arguments and violent preaching.

In Vienna Hitler admired Lueger's cunning and learned from his methods. For the burgomaster anti-Semitism was a convenient weapon and not much else. For the extremist from Linz it was a question of life and death. Vienna had the role of focusing and concentrating his resentments. One cannot take very seriously Hitler's claim that he had never heard the word 'Jew' at home. But his account of the 'discovery' is a revealing one:

> One day, when passing through the Inner City, I suddenly came across an apparition [*Erscheinung*] in a long caftan and wearing black sidelocks. My first thought was: is this a Jew? They certainly did not have this appearance in Linz. I watched the man stealthily and cautiously, but the longer I gazed at this strange countenance and examined it section by section, the more the first question took another shape in my brain: is this a German? I turned to books for help in removing my doubts. For the first time in my life I bought myself some anti-Semitic pamphlets for a few coins.[24]

This is a very telling account of seeing somebody as 'a stranger', as 'wholly other'. Characteristically, Hitler stresses the peculiar dress and the physical traits, points at him with his finger: 'See how strange he is!' It is a very irrational and deep conviction, like that of an English working-class woman I once heard telling about an incident with a West Indian: 'He was black as coal, black as coal!' It is the appearance of the member of the hated group that becomes an object of loathing. As in individual antipathies, people say, 'I can't even bear to look at him—he makes me sick!'

Hitler does not fail to mention the myth of the 'Jewish stench' and says that he 'often grew sick to my stomach from the smell of these caftan-wearers'.[25] This becomes all the more ironical when one learns that, according to companions who knew him in those years as a vagabond, Hitler himself wore a long, shabby overcoat very much like a caftan, which had been given him by a Hungarian Jewish dealer in old clothes. He had a dirty, unkempt aspect, and a fellow artist, Hanisch, says that he looked like 'an apparition such as rarely occurs among Christians'.[26] It is revealing that Hanisch uses the same word that Hitler applied to the Jew he 'discovered' in Vienna.

In Hitler's mind the supposed Jewish uncleanliness corresponded to an even greater moral degradation, and here, as with Nazi propaganda at the time of the genocide, he had to resort to animal imagery:

> Was there any form of filth or profligacy [*Unrat, Schamlosigkeit*], particularly in cultural life, without at least one Jew involved in it?

> If you cut even cautiously such an abscess, you found, like a maggot in a rotting body, often blinded by the sudden light, a little Jew [*ein Jüdlein*]! [27]

To Hitler 'the dark Jew' seems to have been a symbol of degradation on whom he projected anything that in his blindness he was unable to acknowledge in himself. Another passage of *Mein Kampf* shows this clearly: 'With satanic joy in his face, the black-haired Jewish youth lurks in wait for the unsuspecting girl whom he defiles with his blood [*mit seinem Blute schändet*], thus stealing her from her people'.[28]

This is an allusion to the myth of 'racial pollution' we shall mention later (see Chapter 12). It is in this context that Hitler brings in the charge that the Jews had introduced Negroes into the Rhineland (the Senegalese troops of the French army; see Chapter 1) with the 'secret thought and clear aim of ruining the hated white race by the necessarily resulting bastardization (*Bastardierung*)'.

In the end he says he came to hate Vienna:

> I detested the conglomeration of races that the imperial capital exhibits, I detested that mixed crowd of Czechs, Poles, Hungarians, Ruthenians, Serbians, Croatians and so on, and in the midst of all that eternal mushroom of mankind—Jews and more Jews. To me the big city appeared as the personification of incest' [*eine Verkörperung der Blutschande*].[29]

To a Freudian psychoanalyst such a confession would be almost too good to be true. Just think: Hitler left Vienna for Munich in 1913, and the first volume of *Mein Kampf*, where this passage occurs, was published in 1925. By this time psychoanalysis was well known and hotly debated in many countries (and no doubt considered by the anti-Semites as yet another example of the corrupting Jewish influence). The famous Oedipus complex had been described in 1899. So this madman was having such reactions about Freud's own Vienna under the very nose, as it were, of the founder of psychoanalysis. And to make the case more obvious, Hitler was strongly attached to his half sister, Angela, and probably had an incestuous relationship with her daughter, Geli, who later committed suicide, apparently to escape from the liaison with her uncle.[30]

The strong suspicion that Hitler suffered from some sexual perversion that he was ashamed of led Gordon Allport, together with a group of psychoanalysts, to present his case as 'a classical example of direct projection':

> It seems clear that Hitler identified his own baser nature with the Jews, and in condemning the latter evaded the necessity of pointing the accusing finger at himself. The historical consequences . . . have been pointed out by Gertrud Kurth, who writes: 'The

torrent of apocalyptic horrors that engulfed six million Jews was unleashed in the futile endeavour to exterminate that incestuous, black-haired little monster that was Adolf Hitler's Mr. Hyde'.[31]

This psychoanalytic interpretation is very suggestive, and perhaps more convincing than some Freudian theories (including Freud's own wild and absurd speculations about Moses and early Jewish history). Although it strikes one as an oversimplification—the Jews were not slaughtered just because the Führer was ashamed of his incest fantasies—the psychoanalytical concept of projection is a very valuable contribution to the understanding of prejudices and one that has been generally accepted.

There is no evidence that Hitler knew anything about Freud or psychoanalysis when he lived in Vienna. His knowledge and information about the world was certainly one-sided and patchy, as is usually the case with such political fanatics. But it is nevertheless ironical to think that the two lived in the same town, and that the young paranoiac (to use a label that is perhaps the least inappropriate) could have consulted the great Jewish psychiatrist.

A quarter of a century later, in 1938, Freud would very reluctantly leave Vienna because Hitler's anti-Semitic dream had at last come true: he was now to purge his native country of that 'eternal mushroom of mankind' and to wipe out the blot of *Blutschande* (incest) in Vienna. But anti-Semitism was nothing new to Freud. He remembered how indignant he had been in 1868, when his father, Jacob, had been told by a man in the street, 'Jew, get off the pavement!' The man had thrown Jacob's cap in the gutter, and he accepted the humiliation without hitting back.[32] Later, at the time of Lueger, Freud himself, already a prominent doctor, had been denied a post at the university because he was a Jew.

THE POGROMS OF TSARIST RUSSIA

Before World War I there were three powerful 'Caesars' on the European continent: the two German kaisers of Germany and of Austria-Hungary, and the tsar of Russia. These three great monarchies were all bulwarks of authoritarianism and militarism, and in some ways their interests were so close that Bismarck's diplomacy had succeeded for a time in cementing their alliance in the so-called *Drei Kaiser Bund* (League of the Three Emperors). Of the three the most backward and authoritarian was undoubtedly tsarist Russia. It was also the only one where the Jews lived under severe restrictions and whose government followed an openly anti-Semitic policy.

In the nineteenth century Russian anti-Semitism might be described as essentially 'medieval', in the sense that it was rationalized in 'religious' terms. But its propagandists soon learned to use other ideas which had originated in the West, and by the time of World War I they had managed to blend the two main themes, and ultra-ring-wing Russians would be among the most militant Jew-baiters in Europe.

As we have seen, the millions of Jews of the huge tsarist empire were confined to the 'Pale of Settlement' in western Russia established by Catherine II in 1772. They suffered more in periods of reaction, as during the reign of Nicholas I (1825–55), when it is estimated that no fewer than six hundred *ukases* (decrees) were enacted concerning the Jews. Perhaps the one that caused most hardship was the law about military conscription, promulgated in August 1827. For the first time Jewish young men were subject to military service, which then extended over a period of twenty-five years. But in order to prepare the young Jews for the army (and, obviously, to force assimilation or conversion), the law required that they should start at twelve, or in some cases at an earlier age. As one would expect, conditions of service were brutal and the boys were often flogged. They were forbidden to speak Yiddish or to practise their religion, and had to attend Orthodox Christian services. In some cases such pressure achieved results and a number of Jewish boys accepted baptism, but most resisted and not a few committed suicide.[33]

This oppressive law was repealed under the liberal rule of Tsar Alexander II (1855–81). Among other reforms (like the liberation of the serfs), the Russian Jews were freed from some restrictions and were able to enter professions such as the law.

The liberal trend came to an abrupt stop when the tsar was murdered by anarchists in March 1881. It was easy to pretend that the Jews were implicated in the plot and that there were sinister forces at work. Soon the West was to learn the significance of a new word which the Russian language was to give to the international vocabulary: *pogrom* (in English the term only came into general use about 1905).

Few people knew that all over Europe massacres of Jews had been frequent in the Middle Ages, and even later. In modern Russia there had been some sporadic pogroms, in 1820, 1859, and 1871, all of them in Odessa.[34] But they could not be compared in scale to those of 1881 and later.

The trouble began in Kirovograd (then called Elisavetgrad) in the Ukraine. After an argument about the old accusation of ritual murder the Jewish owner of a tavern ejected a drunken Russian. There was a rumour that the Jews were attacking Russians, and a riot began which was checked by the police. Next day the attack was resumed, and this time the authorities did not intervene. Then it spread to larger towns like Kiev and Odessa, and in several places the police and troops gave open assistance to the attacking mobs. Pogroms were recorded in no less than 160 places in south Russia. At Christmas there was a further wave of attacks, followed by a series of widespread fires in the Pale of Settlement. There is some evidence that these, like many of the pogroms, were instigated or organized by a secret band of tsarist officials calling themselves the 'Sacred League'.

Far from punishing the culprits, the tsarist government enacted in 1882 the famous 'May Laws', which further tightened the net of restrictions under which the Jews lived:

> No new Jewish settlers were allowed in the villages and hamlets of the Pale; Jews could not own or manage real estate or farms outside the cities of the Pale; Jews were not allowed to do business on Sunday or other Christian holidays.[35]

Local authorities were also empowered to expel 'depraved elements', on the pretext that they were corrupting the peasants with the sale of vodka. This could only result in the impoverishment of many Jews, who had to concentrate in the towns. At the same time, all efforts were made to bar the entrance of young Jews to schools, universities, and other teaching establishments.

The soul of the persecutory campaign, the Russian Torquemada, was the procurator of the Holy Synod, Pobyedonostzev, who as the tutor of the new tsar, Alexander III (and later also of his successor, Nicholas II), became a very powerful figure. In 1898 he told a Jewish delegation that the problem would be 'solved' in this way: one third of the Russian Jews would be killed, another third 'converted', while the remaining third would emigrate.

Emigration, as we have seen, became the choice of a growing number of Jews, who constituted perhaps the greatest migratory movement of their long history.

Many others—and some of the most energetic and intelligent—threw themselves with fervour into various revolutionary movements whose aim was the overthrow of the tsarist regime, while still others were to lead the Zionist movement. And as was inevitable, this contributed to reinforce the identification of the Jews with all 'subversive' forces in the eyes of the more conservative.

In 1891 orders were given to expel a large proportion of the Jews who lived in the major towns outside the Pale. The Moscow community suffered most: two-thirds—about 20,000 Jews, mostly artisans—had to leave. Only the older and more prosperous Jewish residents were allowed to remain. One curious detail is that Jewish women could live in the great cities, and even enter a university, if they held the infamous 'yellow ticket' of a prostitute, which every reader of *Crime and Punishment* will remember. Many took advantage of this and were 'prostitutes' only in name.

At the close of the century the pogroms started again in the Ukraine.

One of the worst took place in Nikolaev during the Easter of 1899 and lasted three days.

The new century began badly for Russia. In 1902 there was famine and an epidemic of cholera, and 1904 brought the disastrous Russo-Japanese war, which led to the 1905 revolution—'the general rehearsal for 1917', as Lenin called it. There is no doubt this time that the tsarist government, and particularly the minister of the interior, Plehve, were responsible for directing popular animosity against the Jews and instigating attacks. In 1903 an accusation of ritual murder sparked off the rumour that the tsar had ordered a general massacre. A pogrom broke out at Kishinev—again at Easter time—and terrible atrocities were committed against the Jewish community there. One of its organizers was a man called Krushevan, who in the same year was to publish the notorious *Protocols of the Elders of Zion* in his anti-Semitic paper *Znamia* (Banner).

From 1905 onwards the pogroms were usually organized by an ultra-reactionary organization with official backing—the Union of the Russian People, popularly known as the 'Black Hundred' (*Chornaia Sotnja*). They followed a definite pattern:

> Someone, supposedly of course a Jew, would fire upon a patriotic procession carrying a portrait of the tsar, and the mob, infuriated, would fall upon the Jewish population. The pogrom usually lasted three or four days, while the police professed their helplessness to check the fury of the crowd.[36]

Bloody pogroms of this sort occurred at Zhitomir, Odessa, Bialystok, and Sedlez (Siedlce). It is estimated that within four years there were massacres in 184 cities, with possibly a total of 50,000 victims. It should be pointed out that the Jews were not the only targets: the Black Hundred aimed at terrorizing all opposition, particularly the revolutionaries and Social Democrats.

In 1911 the murder of a boy by a gang of criminals led to the fabrication of another ritual murder accusation against a Jewish worker called Mendel Beilis. He was arrested, and the case dragged on for two years. Finally, in spite of a blatantly prejudiced judge, a jury of twelve peasants acquitted Beilis.

The ritual murder case, like the earlier pogroms, aroused world opinion, and at the end of 1911 the American government broke its commercial treaty with Russia on account of her persecution of the Jews. It is an interesting parallel with the present situation.

For us, who have become somewhat callous after the Nazi concentration camps, it is not very easy perhaps to have an idea of the shock the Russian pogroms caused in the world and in the Jewish community itself. One should remember that people were living in an age of liberal optimism and faith in progress. The great Western cities saw the arrival in their thousands of Russian Jews, many utterly destitute, clothed with the traditional caftan and the fur cap (*streimel*). Such a migration had never been seen in modern times. They were not like ordinary immigrants, seeking better opportunities: they were a living proof of persecution. Russia was not the only source: many were fleeing from Rumania, where anti-Semitic persecution was rife (in 1895 an Anti-Semitic League had been founded in Bucharest).

It is estimated that between 1881 and 1905 about a million Jews emigrated from Eastern Europe: 700,000 from Russia, 200,000 from Austria, and 100,000 from Rumania. Of these the great majority went to the two main English-speaking countries, trusting their traditions of tolerance and also attracted by the fame of America as 'the land of opportunity'. According to calculations, about 850,000 went to the United States, 100,000 to Britain, and the remainder to other countries (particularly Germany and Austria-Hungary where, as we have seen, the anti-Semites were seeking to restrict immigration). The two largest South American countries, Brazil and Argentina, received their quota of Jewish immigrants, so many that for a long time in both countries it was usual to call all Jews 'Russians'. By the time the 1914 war broke out, nearly two million Eastern European Jews had emigrated.

But a certain number would seek another solution: the return to Palestine. In 1882, one year after the first wave of pogroms, a Russian Jew, a doctor, and a scholar called Leo Pinsker published an anonymous pamphlet in Berlin with the title *Auto-Emancipation: An Appeal to His People*.[37] Pinsker made a penetrating analysis of the Jewish situation and described anti-Semitism as a 'demonopathy'. He thought it was incurable: Jewish emancipation was no solution, and the Jews would be the victims of persecution as long as they had no national home. Dr. Pinsker was not thinking of Palestine, but he recommended a national organization very similar to what eventually emerged with the First Zionist Congress fifteen years later.

FRANCE: THE DREYFUS AFFAIR

In the last quarter of the nineteenth century France was almost the only republic in Europe to uphold at least in appearance the old ideals of 1789, which had promoted, among other reforms, Jewish emancipation. But the Third Republic was rather shaky, vulnerable, and deeply divided by class struggle and ideological conflict. In fact, it was in some aspects rather comparable to the Weimar Republic which Hitler overthrew. Both had emerged after humiliating defeat in a war, followed by a bloody revolutionary uprising: in France there was the Commune, considered by the

Marxists a first muddled attempt to establish a Communist regime, and in Germany the rebellion of the Spartacists. Both uprisings had been suppressed in a bloodbath. Both regimes faced the hostility, if not open sabotage, of reactionary pressure groups: the army, with its aristocratic caste of officers; the monarchists, who considered the republic an ephemeral interlude; and—particularly in France—a large part of the clergy and the 'clericals'. Finally, both the French and German right wing were strongly pervaded with anti-Semitism, and both tended to see in the new republic a manifestation of the Jewish spirit and of its hostility to 'Christian institutions'.

The foremost French anti-Semitic propagandist at the time was Édouard Drumont. In 1886 he published a book in two volumes entitled *La France juive*. His theme was by now a familiar one: the Jews had always been guilty of most of the misfortunes and corrupting influences in French life. If the Jews were enemies, then (almost) every enemy was a Jew, and Drumont—like the German anti-Semites and the Nazis later—did not hesitate to attribute Jewish descent to quite a few individuals. As Lueger himself had said, 'I decide who is a Jew' (*Wer ein Jud' ist, das bestimme ich*). Compare the ease with which people label others as 'Communists' in political witch-hunts, or as 'Trotskyites' or 'deviationists' in Communist regimes.

Drumont was particularly obsessed with the corrupting power of money, in the hands of Jewish bankers and financiers. For instance, the bankruptcy of the Union Générale, a bank that had been started as 'a Christian enterprise', was attributed to Jewish machinations. The notorious Panama scandal (1892–93), which ruined a number of people and in which some Jews were involved, was held up as yet another proof of Jewish corruption. Drumont led the campaign through his newspaper *La Libre Parole*, which was started in 1892 (he had also founded an Anti-Semitic League in 1889).

In 1894 *La Libre Parole* announced with éclat that there was treason in the French General Staff: an officer was selling military secrets to a foreign power (Germany). By a curious 'coincidence' he was the only Jewish officer on the General Staff: Alfred Dreyfus.

Dreyfus came from a prosperous Alsatian family and bore a similar name to that of the 'venerable patriarch' who had presided over the Strasbourg assembly during the French Revolution. The main evidence against him was an unsigned letter (the famous *bordereau*, or memorandum) which was claimed to be in his handwriting. The proceedings against him were hasty and highly irregular: he was tried in secret, convicted, and sentenced to life imprisonment in the 'tropical hell' of Devil's Island off the coast of French Guiana.

The case unleashed a violent outburst of anti-Semitic feeling, and the cry of 'Judas!' was heard all over France. Drumont and his followers were able to hold up the case of Dreyfus as clear evidence of Jewish disloyalty.

In the following year, 1895, Colonel Picquart, the new director of French counter-espionage, communicated to the head of the General Staff his strong suspicions that the real culprit was a French officer of Hungarian origin, Major Esterhazy. The army chiefs did everything to avoid the reopening of the case, and Picquart was transferred to Tunisia. But Dreyfus's relatives were untiring in their efforts and soon they had several prominent supporters. The Jewish writer Bernard Lazare published a pamphlet on the affair, the radical politician Clemenceau (later to become prime minister) also took up his defence, and Émile Zola wrote his famous article 'J'accuse' in Clemenceau's newspaper.

Now, 'the honour of the army' had to be defended at all costs, to the sacrifice of everything including truth. A series of judicial farces followed: Major Esterhazy was formally tried and acquitted, Picquart was arrested, and Zola, convicted of libel, had to flee to England to a chorus of 'Death to Zola! Death to the Jews!'

By that time 'L'Affaire', as it came to be called, had become a *cause célèbre* both in France and abroad, and led to an unprecedented polarization of opinions. It was now deeply affecting the political life of the nation. The Dreyfusards (supporters of Dreyfus) attracted all liberal and progressive elements—radicals, socialists, and so on—while the anti-Semitic anti-Dreyfusards had on their side most of the right wing—monarchists, militarists, and clericals.

At first the advantage lay with the anti-Dreyfusards, who used this opportunity to capitalize on anti-Semitic propaganda. By 1898 there were nineteen openly anti-Semitic deputies in the French Assembly, including Drumont himself, elected in that same year. In short, as in Germany and Austria, the anti-Semitic movement had become definitely political.

But it was also in 1898 that the course of events began to favour the Dreyfusards. Esterhazy, expelled from the army for dishonesty, fled to England and admitted to a reporter that he had forged the *bordereau*. A certain Major Henry confessed he had forged other documents in order to strengthen the case against Dreyfus, and committed suicide. A change of government took place in 1899, and the new cabinet, led by the radical Waldeck-Rousseau, forced the reopening of the case. A new court-martial was held, and, amazingly enough, it found Dreyfus guilty and gave him a ten-year sentence in view of 'extenuating circumstances'. A few weeks later he was pardoned: he had spent five years on Devil's Island.

It was only in 1906 that justice was finally done: a court of appeals annulled the earlier sentence, and Dreyfus was fully rehabilitated and also awarded the Légion d'Honneur. This time, at the solemn military ceremony, instead of shouts of 'Judas!', people cried 'Vive Dreyfus!' and 'Vive la verité!'

In the whole of human history it would be difficult to find such a clear example of 'the scapegoat'—chosen because Jews were always scapegoats: the monstrous condemnation of an innocent man while the real culprit went free. Perhaps all the devious plots and intricacies of the Dreyfus case will never be fully revealed, but its main lesson is obvious enough.

The consequences of 'L'Affaire' were far-reaching, and not only for France. The Jewish communities, already shaken by the Russian pogroms, were given a further shock. One of the press correspondents who reported on the Dreyfus case was Theodor Herzl. He became convinced, like Leo Pinsker, that there was no safety even for assimilated Jews, and the only solution lay in a Jewish national state. The First Zionist Congress, which he inspired and organized, took place just before the turning point of the Dreyfus affair, in 1897.

For France the division between Dreyfusards and anti-Dreyfusards deepened the rift between the 'two Frances'. It was a crushing defeat for the right wing and the enemies of the republic, and the new government began its anti-clerical attack which disestablished the Roman Catholic Church. As Father Flannery admits, the Church had seriously compromised itself with anti-Semitism:

> Its influence on public life permanently declined; and anti-clericalism became an integral part of the government. The main cause of the decline was undoubtedly the almost fanatic support given the army by the large majority of Catholic opinion, particularly the Catholic press. Because of this unfortunate commitment, the Church became more than ever identified with reaction and anti-Republicanism.[38]

Of course, there were also Catholics on the Dreyfusard side (Colonel Picquart was one), but the clergy as a whole was anti-Dreyfusard, and some priests expressed anti-Jewish sentiments quite comparable to those of the medieval rabble-rousers. One said that he would like a 'rug of Yiddish skin'. Catholic periodicals like *La Croix* welcomed the looting of Jewish houses in Algiers (a focus of fierce anti-Semitism which had elected Drumont as a deputy) and the stripping of Jewish women in the street. The Jesuit newspaper of Rome, *La Civiltà cattolica*, joined the anti-Dreyfus campaign and wrote in 1898:

> The Jew was created by God to be a spy wherever treason was being plotted. . . . The real judicial error was that Jews should ever have been granted French citizenship. That Law must be

abrogated, not in France only, but in Germany, Austria, and Italy. The Jews are masters of the Republic, which is not so much French as Hebrew.[39]

When in the 1930s France had to face the Nazi regime, her divisions deeply undermined her ability to resist. The reactionary factions at the end of the nineteenth century (whose followers never gave up their belief in Dreyfus's guilt) had as their successors the Fascist or monarchist groups, like the Cagoulards of the period between the wars. The slogan 'We would rather have Hitler than Blum' became popular with many people in the French right wing. Léon Blum, who was to become both the first socialist and the first Jewish prime minister of France, had helped Jean Jaurès in the Dreyfusard campaign. On the other hand, the Frenchmen who perpetrated the great Vichy betrayal were brothers in spirit of those who crucified Dreyfus. Some, like Marshal Pétain, were well advanced in their army career at the time of L'Affaire. Vichy may well be called, in the words of Wilhelm Herzog, 'the revenge of the anti-Dreyfusards'.[40]

But the repercussions of L'Affaire did not stop there. It was in Paris, at about the same time, that a group of Russian secret police had the idea of forging 'documents', this time not to incriminate a man but to defame a whole people.

12

The Sign of the Swastika

Svastika   *m.* auspicious mark, conducive to well-being.
—From a Sanskrit dictionary

THE IDEA OF THE SECRET SOCIETY

When I began to study psychiatry and became interested in delusions and paranoid cases in general, I came across a patient who had been in hospital for many years. He thought he was being persecuted by powerful secret societies who had managed to get him into hospital. As a talisman he wore on his lapel a couple of badges of his own design, which, according to him, stood for two *good* societies—the orders of the Knights Templar and the Knights of Malta.

This rigid duality between good and evil forces, which I found in several cases of this kind, and the delight in badges and insignia are typical features of what one might call the paranoid mentality, whether individual or collective, and go back to very old and archaic symbols. In the Book of Revelation, which owes much to Daniel and other Jewish apocalyptic works, there are marks and signs, like the famous 'mark of the Beast' and the number 666 (Rev. 13:16–18). The latter has usually been interpreted as applying to a persecuting Roman emperor, probably Nero or Domitian, but it is significant that both the Antichrist and the Beast should have been identified at different times with various European rulers. In the nineteenth century it was mainly Napoleon, and during World War II there were calculations 'proving' that the number 666, with a certain amount of good will, could very well be applied to Hitler.

The fact that National Socialism was fundamentally anti-Christian (Nietzsche, whom the Nazis rather unfairly claimed as their philosopher, had rejected both Judaism and Christianity as 'Semitic' religions, the product of a 'slavish mentality') did not prevent it from using symbols and ideas of Christian origin. Even the slogan 'the thousand-year Reich' was in fact derived from the Book of Revelation.

National Socialism was very largely the enactment of delusional fantasies: the difference was that while my patient acted out his delusion in hospital, Hitler found millions of partners on the stage of history. From this point it is not difficult to go a bit further and to recognize that a very large part of what we call 'real life' or 'the facts' (as Pirandello tried to show in his *Henry IV*) is no more than the enactment of such fantasies.

The delight in rituals, uniforms, and insignia shown by Fascist and militarist organizations goes back to very primitive levels of development, and in fact secret societies with their rituals, masks, or badges have been found in many tribes. If 'the enemy' has his own magic and secret power, then one must call upon other, more powerful forces. From the early days of Christianity, with its stories about Simon the Magician, we can trace a duality between the Church and its 'dark side'—'white-' and 'black magic'. The contrast between the two rituals even went as far as to create the idea of a 'Black Mass' centred on the Devil and on the denial of all Christian symbols.

We have already mentioned the conflict between the Jewish *Tol 'doth Yeshu* and some Apocryphal Gospels on the Christian side. In the former the magic power is conferred on 'the name of the Lord', and Judas is the 'good magician' who overthrows the 'bad magician' Yeshu (Jesus). In the Apocryphal Gospels the pattern is basically the same, with the difference that Jesus vanquishes Judas with his miracles, just as Moses defeated the Egyptian priests and Elijah the priests of Baal.

A similar Manichaean duality is found in the mythology that passes as 'national history' in most countries and also in certain kinds of fiction: in both we find the black-and-white contrast between heroes and villains.

If I believe there is a secret plot against me and my people, it is only natural to try and make a stronger counterplot. My patient, isolated in his delusion, protected himself against the 'secret societies' by calling upon the help of the Templars and the Maltese Knights. The Nazis, who saw almost everywhere the sinister hand of 'international Jewry', tried to fight the Star of David with the swastika and in fact formed an international alliance with various anti-Semitic groups.

There never was any Jewish conspiracy to 'dominate the world', but there has been what Norman Cohn has called an 'anti-Semitic international' aimed at doing every possible evil to the Jews. Its activities were quite manifest not many years ago, at the time of Eichmann's trial, through planned anti-Jewish campaigns in several parts of the world.

Another irony is that the Nazi genocide turned out to be one of the decisive factors that led to the foundation of the state of Israel. Without anti-Semitism it would be difficult to conceive such a development. As often happens, the frantic effort to exorcise a ghost ends up by producing something very like it.

SOME MODERN FORERUNNERS OF THE 'PROTOCOLS'

As we have seen in earlier chapters, the idea of a secret plot developed by the forgers of the *Protocols of the Elders of Zion* was not very new. Over two thousand years ago some Alexandrian writers spread the story of a Jewish secret oath to do all possible evil to the Greeks. In the Middle Ages and later many people came to believe that the 'synagogue of Satan' was a devilish organization aimed at harming Christians and Christianity —through magic arts, usury and exploitation, the poisoning of wells at the time of the Black Death, or the torture and ritual murder of children.

These medieval myths had not died out and were still current in many parts of the world, but they were declining in the new atmosphere of 'enlightenment'. On the other hand, the very fact that people thought a little naïvely that they had outgrown old prejudices and superstitions left them rather vulnerable to acquiring new ones, or rather new forms of old prejudices. In their optimistic belief in 'the light of human reason' they often showed a marked ignorance of the more hidden powers of the mind, whether destructive or creative. Naturally, this ignorance did not apply to the great poets, artists, or religious minds, who were deeply aware of both these sides. They knew that myths and prejudices grow in the dark, like dreams or the delusions of the mentally ill.

In the nineteenth century, with its social and economic changes, there were in Europe a great number of people who felt threatened or insecure when faced with the growth of democracy, freedom of thought, egalitarianism, industry and capitalism, and so on. As usual, they tended to blame the supporters of the new ideologies—the 'radicals', the Jacobins, the 'atheists', or, later in the century, the socialists and anarchists. But this was not always satisfactory, and somehow the idea of a secret or hidden conspiracy came to appeal to a growing number of people.

In 1797, when the storm of the French Revolution was very recent, a French Jesuit, the Abbé Barruel, had an inspiration: it was the Freemasons who were behind everything. But the conspiracy was a little more complicated and there was a plot within a plot. The real leaders behind the Masons were the Templars, those shock troops of the Church Militant, in fact strongly anti-Jewish, whom my hospital patient had called to his aid.

It did not terribly matter that the Templars had been destroyed in 1314 by Philip the Fair of France and by a subservient pope, mainly with the aim of confiscating the order's wealth. Philip attacked them after expelling the Jews from the country, and the trial of the Grand Master and other leaders was the prototype of modern political purges, with a whole array of charges including witchcraft, heresy, and sexual perversions. But the Abbé Barruel, ignoring this troublesome historical fact, was certain that the Templars had survived as a secret society, devoted to the abolition of all monarchies, the overthrow of the papacy, and the proclamation of unrestricted freedom for all peoples. The French *philosophes* of the eighteenth century, like Diderot, Voltaire, and d'Alembert, had all belonged to a secret academy affiliated with the Freemasons. But the real leaders of this rather complicated network were yet another group—the 'Illuminati'. This society, a rival of Freemasonry, had been dissolved in 1786, but one could always argue that they had continued to exist secretly.

Until the publication of his book on the secret societies—a massive work in five volumes—the Abbé had not thought much about the Jews, whom he hardly mentions. But in 1806 he received a letter from Florence allegedly written by a certain Captain Simonini, a mysterious person whom nobody had ever met, who opened his eyes to 'the Jewish danger'.

Simonini, whoever he was, revealed to the Abbé that once he had pretended to be of Jewish descent to a group of Piedmontese Jews. They had promptly disclosed to him, with surprising trustfulness, all the secrets of the conspiracy. The Jews were in fact the masterminds of the whole network of secret societies, including not only the Freemasons and the Illuminati but also the notorious Assassins, a kind of Muslim Mafia that had existed at the time of the Crusades.

But the plot did not stop there. The Jews had deeply infiltrated the clergy, and Simonini swore that in Italy alone there were over eight hundred Jewish priests, including bishops and cardinals. In Spain they were also strong (one may compare George Borrow's stories about crypto-Jews in the Spanish Church). Very soon they would be able to elect a pope. Everywhere Jews disguised as Christians were reaching positions of power and wealth. Their ultimate aim was to own all the land and to achieve complete control:

> . . . in less than a century they would be masters of the world . . . they would abolish all other sects and establish the rule of their own sect, turning Christian churches into so many synagogues and reducing the remaining Christians to a state of absolute slavery.[1]

The essential idea of the *Protocols* is here, though not yet with all its refinements. For the first time the Jews appear as allies of the Freemasons (that special bugbear of the Catholic Church), a theme that would later be used and reprinted a number of times by the anti-Semitic movement.

The Abbé Barruel welcomed this idea with open arms, and before his death in 1820 he had imparted to another Jesuit, Father Grivel, a much improved version of the great Jewish-Masonic plot. In his view all Europe was honeycombed with Masonic lodges (later, of course, people would talk of Communist cells), and the whole network was directed by a supreme council of twenty-one members, of whom nine were Jews. On top of it all stood the supreme despot, the Grand Master, who had power of life and death over all members.

'THE RABBI'S SPEECH' AND THE MASONIC PLOT

Much could be written on anti-Semitism in Western literature from the nineteenth century to our own times. But one important source was no doubt the novel *Biarritz*, written by the German Hermann Goedsche in 1868 under the English pseudonym of 'Sir John Retcliffe'. One of the crucial scenes takes place at night 'in the Jewish cemetery in Prague'. Thirteen figures muffled in white veils appear around a tomb. They are the representatives of the twelve tribes of Israel, with an extra delegate representing 'the unfortunates and exiles'. The meeting is presided over by a Levite, but from the tomb a blue flame appears and the Devil's voice is heard greeting the heads of the twelve tribes of Israel. Each one is in charge of one department of society and reports on what he has been doing to promote Jewish domination of the world. At the end they arrange another meeting in a hundred years' time, when their descendants will be able to announce achievement of the plan. But success is certain, for 'the future is ours' (*unser ist die Zukunft*). The Levite addresses them as 'sons of the Golden Calf' (*Söhne des goldenen Kalbes*), and as the meeting adjourns a huge 'shapeless golden animal figure' (*eine goldene unförmliche Thiergestalt*) emerges from the tomb, symbolizing the materialistic power whom the Jews have always worshipped.[2] But without the participants' knowledge there were two hidden witnesses watching everything —a German scholar and a baptized Jew, who swore to do everything in their power to defeat the diabolical plan.

The Russian anti-Semites were the first to use this lurid fantasy as a genuine document and to publish it in pamphlet form. Later all the 'reports' of the cemetery scene were combined into a single speech, and this required a change of scenery. It was presented as *The Rabbi's Speech*, supposed to have been made by a chief rabbi at a secret meeting.

In this shortened form it became very popular and was published in many countries (later it was reported that the imaginary 'Sir John Retcliffe' had been murdered by the Jews, and he was revered as a martyr). Its essential idea remains the same: the Jews must rule the world through the power of money. They must also use the press, and the authors of the 'document' did not forget the element of sexual jealousy:

> We must demand marriage between Jews and Christians. Israel will only be the gainer, even though there be an admixture of impure blood to a certain degree. Our sons and daughters will marry into renowned and powerful Christian families. We give

money and thus have influence. . . . Another thing is that we respect the Jewish woman and we enjoy the forbidden pleasure with the women of our enemies. We have money, and for money we can get everything. A Jew must never make a daughter of his own race his mistress. If he should desire to sin against the Seventh Commandment he should content himself with Christian girls.[3]

It would be tedious to give here a catalogue of the anti-Semitic literature which preceded the *Protocols*. But it is interesting to note that the theme of a Jewish-Masonic alliance remained popular, at least with Roman Catholic reactionaries. We have already mentioned the book by Gougenot des Mousseaux—*Le Juif, le judaïsme et la judaisation des peuples chrétiens* (1869). He also adopted the idea of the Jewish-Masonic plot, but went further than the Abbé Barruel into sheer Manichaeism and tried to trace the conspiracy to its earliest origins. Mousseaux thought he had found it in diabolism or the deliberate worship of evil practised by the sons of Cain. Starting at this source, he was able to trace a long 'apostolic succession' from the sons of Cain to the Chaldeans, from the Chaldeans to the ancient Jews, and then successfully to the Gnostics, the Manichaeans, the Assassins, the Templars, and finally the Freemasons. But throughout this long chain the Jews had always been the leaders of diabolism through their knowledge of the Kabbala (Jewish esoteric mysticism, which the anti-Semites tended to look upon as part of black magic):

> The representatives on earth of the spirit of darkness, V*os ex patre diabolo* [The devil is your father (John 8:44)], they were the providential ministers and Grand Masters of occultism. Every society of mystery and disorder has adopted as leaders the Jewish Kabbalists as the leaders and hereditary guardians of all doctrines suited to their occult aim.[4]

Mousseaux's ideas were frankly apocalyptic, for he also announced the imminent coming of the Antichrist, who would be proclaimed Messiah by the Jews in the midst of a great European war.

The apocalyptic theme was taken up again by the French Abbé Chabauty, who in 1881, just when the great pogroms began in Russia, published his massive book *Les Franc-Maçons et les juifs*. His ideas were not very original: Satan, through the Jewish-Masonic plot, was preparing the way for the coming of a Jewish Antichrist and Jewish domination of the world. Chabauty did not confine himself to writing books: he also edited a provincial newspaper called *L'Anti-Sémitique*.

It was also about this time that the Jesuit newspaper of Rome, *La Civiltà cattolica*, began a fierce anti-Jewish campaign as part of its anti-

Masonic propaganda (later, significantly, it also joined the anti-Dreyfus camp). The Roman Jesuits did not hesitate to use the old discredited stories of ritual murder. Here is a sample from the issue of 21 January 1882, in a supposedly 'enlightened' Europe: 'Every year the Hebrews crucify a child . . . in order that the blood be effective, the child must die in torment'.[5]

The attacks of *La Civiltà cattolica* were only stopped (presumably by Pope Pius XII) in the Hitlerite era, in 1938.

THE 'PROTOCOLS' IN ACTION

One of the striking features of anti-Semitic literature is the poverty of its imagination, the dull, strip-cartoon character of its products. It becomes more obvious when contrasted with a genuine popular myth like the Wandering Jew, which has depth and poetry like the best fairy tales.

Perhaps the final proof of the anti-Semites' lack of originality is the fact that its most widespread 'document', which has been compared to the Bible for the number of its editions and translations, is nothing but a case of plagiarism. It is not even an original forgery like some apocryphal religious writings. In fact, the affair of the *Protocols of the Elders of Zion* reads like a detective story and is infinitely more interesting than the text itself.

The first appearance of the *Protocols* seems to have been in a St. Petersburg newspaper called *Znamia* (Banner), in August-September 1903. The date has some importance, because the editor of the paper, Krushevan, was a militant anti-Semite, who some months earlier had instigated the pogrom at Kishinev in Bessarabia (see Chapter 11).

I do not propose to deal here in any detail with the *Protocols*. Like *The Rabbi's Speech* they are essentially a Machiavellian project (and the word itself gives a clue to its origin) of world domination by the Jews. To achieve that end, all possible means are to be used: in fact, some of the methods recommended are very similar to those openly proposed by Hitler in *Mein Kampf*, and he himself admitted, as we shall see, that he had taken more than a hint from the *Protocols*.

All the traditional institutions must be overthrown—monarchies, churches, and so forth. (The aim of this is obvious—to tar with the Jewish brush all reforming or radical tendencies.) So the Jews must propagate all 'subversive' doctrines—liberalism, republicanism, socialism, communism —and demoralize and corrupt all Christian peoples with wars, armament races, strikes, revolutions, and so on. Assassination of important leaders, inoculation with dangerous diseases, all this will contribute to increase chaos and disorder. And finally the secret organization of the 'Elders of Zion' will be ready openly to assume the direction of the world, which in fact they already control in large part behind the scenes, through financial power, the press, and so on. The Gentiles will be enslaved and a despotic regime will be established, with a single religion—Judaism—and having at its head a descendant of the house of David.

Soon other editions were to appear in pamphlet form, and in the revolutionary year 1905 a Russian writer called Sergey Nilus, all taken up with visionary and apocalyptic ideas, included the *Protocols* in a new edition of his book *The Great in the Small: Antichrist Considered as an Imminent Political Possibility*.

How had the editors got hold of the mysterious *Protocols*? They all said that the 'document' had been translated from the French into Russian, which was, after all, quite true, but then the explanations began to diverge. At first it was claimed that the *Protocols* had been copied from the secret archives of the 'Central Chancellery of Zion' in France—a high-sounding name for an entity nobody had ever heard of, for the simple reason that it had never existed. Then Sergey Nilus contradicted himself: in a new edition of the *Protocols* in 1917 he stated categorically that they had been 'presented to the Council of Elders by "the Prince of the Exile", Theodor Herzl, at the time of the First Zionist Congress, summoned by him at Basel in August 1897'.[6]

This new version was later adopted by most editors and propagandists of the *Protocols*. It had the advantage of linking the supposed 'document' to a genuine, militant Jewish movement, which officially launched the idea of a state of Israel. Among so many absurdities, it is hardly necessary to point out that the language of the whole Zionist Congress had been German, while the original of the *Protocols* was in French.

In 1905, when Nilus published his book, Krushevan and other fanatical anti-Semites were forming the so-called Union of the Russian People, which organized many of the pogroms of the time and also the murder of liberal leaders. The Union was in some aspects a forerunner of the Fascist movements which emerged after World War I in several countries.

In the same year Tsar Nicholas II read the *Protocols* and at first was much impressed. But when the Union of the Russian People asked for government subsidies in order to use the *Protocols* in its anti-Semitic campaign, the minister of the interior ordered two police officials to carry out an inquiry into the source of the document. Apparently the result was so unfavourable to the authenticity of the *Protocols* that the tsar did not accede to the request of the Union leaders. But obviously none of this was disclosed at the time.

In February 1917 the first Russian Revolution forced the tsar's abdication, and in October the Bolsheviks took power. To the lunatic fringe on the extreme right this was seen as the expected coming of the Antichrist: the diabolical jewish conspiracy had triumphed, at least temporarily. Just as previously many Catholics tended to see the hand of Freemasonry behind every liberal revolution, now it was easy to point at the Jews inside the Bolshevik party: at Trotsky, whose real name was Leo Bronstein, at Zinoviev, Kamenev, and others. In fact, there were many more Jews in the socialist groups who opposed the Bolshevik take-over, like the Mensheviks and the Social Revolutionary party: so much so that Stalin (who later would liquidate most of his Jewish comrades and follow an anti-Semitic policy) is reported to have once joked, 'We must make a pogrom of these Jewish Mensheviks!'

In 1918 began the long and terrible civil war that would bring appalling losses, not least to the Russian Jews. In the ruthless struggle between 'Reds' and 'Whites' terror would be applied by both sides, but the 'Whites' took the opportunity to carry on with their pogroms.

In that same year a dramatic incident would link the Russian imperial family, the anti-Semitic movement, and the sign of the swastika. In July the Czech army, acting in alliance with the tsarists, captured in its advance from the east the town of Ekaterinburg (now Sverdlovsk). There they found the corpses of the tsar and his family, who had been shot a few days earlier by the Bolsheviks so as to prevent them from being used by the enemy.

Among the objects belonging to the tsarina three bedside books were found: the Bible, Tolstoi's *War and Peace*, and *The Great in the Small*, by Sergey Nilus, including, as we have seen, the *Protocols*. It is no coincidence that the favourite books of that neurotic and superstitious woman all had apocalyptic matter. In *War and Peace* the very first paragraph identifies Napoleon with the Antichrist and Nilus' book, of course, was entirely inspired by such ideas.

But that was not all. The empress Alexandra was German, at least on her father's side. In the embrasure of a window in the room occupied by her and the tsar she had drawn a swastika. It is known that she made much use of this symbol as an amulet and wore a jewelled swastika.

In fact, the Nazis were not the first to associate it with German racialism. Long before the 1914 war the Austrian writer Guido von List had proclaimed that the swastika was an essentially German symbol and stood for the purity of 'the Germano-Aryans' against Jewish contamination. Some Russian monarchists were aware of this, with the difference that in their eyes it was the Holy Orthodox Church, the tsar, and Pan-Slavism that had to be defended. As Norman Cohn says:

> . . . the discovery of the Empress's swastika together with the copy of Nilus came as a revelation from on high. This, they believed, was a testament from their dead Empress; and what it said was that the reign of Antichrist was beginning, that the

Bolshevik revolution was the supreme assault of the Satanic powers, that the imperial family had been destroyed because they represented the divine will on earth—and that the forces of darkness
were incarnated in the Jews.[7]

Anti-Semitism could be more effective with martyrs of its own, and when
they were not forthcoming one could always invent them. When a story
of ritual murder was spread, the cry would be, 'They've killed an innocent
child!' When Tsar Alexander II was murdered, then people cried, 'They've
killed Our Father!' Our Father was originally Jesus Christ, but in Russia
there was this charismatic figure—'Little Father' (*Batyushka*). In 1918, as
in 1881, revenge had to be exacted from his supposed murderers.

The *Protocols* became very popular among the narrow-minded officers,
brought up on authoritarian ideas, who fought in the White armies. The
Ukrainian nationalists, led by Simon Petlyura, were also strongly anti-
Semitic, as they had been in the days of the Deluge in the seventeenth
century, and carried out pogroms. But the civilian crowds also took a hand,
as in Lemberg and in Vilna. Nor should we forget that other Horseman of
the Apocalypse—hunger. Herbert Agar mentions an incident which tends
to be forgotten in histories of World War I:

> The worst doom of all was that of the Jews in unoccupied Russia
> —in the part of the Pale which the Germans never reached. The
> Pale itself was abolished, for all practical purposes, by 1916, so
> that the Jews could be got out of the way. Half a million were
> deported by the Russian army at the beginning of the war, under
> conditions which recall the German death-trains of 1942–45. They
> were not, however, sent to be murdered, but merely to starve in-
> conspicuously in some place where they were no trouble to the
> soldiers.[8]

But besides this there were systematic pogroms by the White armies
and their followers. Rough estimates have been made of 100,000 to 150,000
dead and many more wounded. The pogroms may have been worse than
those of 1881 and 1903, which caused a greater sensation in the world. To
get an idea of the losses suffered by the Eastern European community during the 1914–18 war and the Russian civil war of 1918–20, we have only
to remember that of an estimated total of 15 million Jews in 1915, two-
thirds, i.e., about 10 million, lived in the three great monarchies—Germany, Austria-Hungary, and tsarist Russia—and of these the Russian Pale
of Settlement accounted for no less than 7 million.

The fiercest *pogromshchicki* (pogrom makers) seem to have been the
Cossacks, who in the Ukraine went on a rampage of murder and rape. A
Russian journalist who witnessed their activities in Fastov, near Kiev, in
September 1919, gives an idea of what was happening:

They [the Cossacks] were also stopping Jews in the streets. Sometimes they would simply ask, 'A Yid?' (Zhid) and put a bullet
through his skull. . . . Many of the killers were drunk. . . .
About the second or third day they began to set fire to Jewish
homes. The reason for this was that the *pogromshchicki* wanted
to destroy the traces of their worst crimes. In one house on the
corner of Torgovy Square, for instance, were fifteen corpses, including many young girls who had been killed after being raped.
They set the house alight to cover up those crimes.⁹

HOW THE 'PROTOCOLS' SPREAD

One might well remember that several powers—like Britain, France, and
Japan—were at that time giving effective help to the White armies and
therefore supporting the side that committed such atrocities. When the
improvised Red armies, galvanized by Trotsky (a Jew with no interest in
Judaism or Zionism) and other leaders, defeated all attacks, the vanquished
tsarist officers fled to Germany, France, and other countries. And in this
new kind of Diaspora they began to scatter everywhere the seeds of anti-
Semitism, newly inspired by the *Protocols*.

There were many people, including some old anti-Jewish campaigners,
who warmly welcomed the new reinforcement. Seventy years earlier, Karl
Marx (and everybody knew he was a Jew) and Engels had begun their
Communist Manifesto with these famous words: 'A spectre is haunting
Europe—the spectre of Communism'.

In 1917 and the following years the spectre was indeed in many people's
minds. In Germany and Hungary there had been attempts to establish
Communist regimes. Fear very often does not discriminate, and many
found it more comfortable to believe that Bolshevism was part of 'a Jewish
conspiracy' than an element in the interplay of social forces that had to
be understood. In postwar Germany, full of tensions and economic problems and, what is more, with a long tradition of anti-Jewish writings and
violence, the new propagandists found fertile ground for their activities. In
1920 two Russians, both of whom had been militant in the Black Hundred
and one of them a former tsarist officer, launched the first edition of the
Protocols in Berlin. It was immediately a great success, particularly with
the middle classes. By 1933, when Hitler rose to power, there had been no
less than thirty-three editions or reprints of this translation alone. But
there were several others, besides commentaries and miscellaneous anti-
Semitic writings.

In Germany during the 1920s meetings and lectures promoted by the
anti-Semites were frequent, and university teachers and students flocked to
them. The leaders of the defeated Second Reich also welcomed the myth
of a Jewish conspiracy. Ex-Kaiser Wilhelm II, exiled in Holland, became

convinced that he had lost his throne through the machinations of the 'Elders of Zion'. General Ludendorff, who in 1923 was to become involved in Hitler's Munich *Putsch*, openly proclaimed that German defeat had been plotted by 'international Jewry': this was the famous, impudent lie that the invincible German army had been the victim of 'a stab in the back' (*der Dolchstoss in den Rücken des Heeres*).[10] Anti-Semitism became therefore an important plank in the platform of the right wing for their fierce campaign against the Weimar Republic. One of the most active groups in anti-Semitic propaganda was, of course, the National Socialist party.

In fact, the plotting and the campaign of lies were mostly carried out by these extremist nationalist groups, and political assassination was one of their weapons. In 1919 Kurt Eisner, the Jewish leader of the Bavarian republic, was murdered in Munich by a well-known anti-Semite, Count Anton Arco-Valley. A more sensational murder was that of Foreign Minister Walter Rathenau, who was killed in 1922 by a group of right-wing terrorists after signing the Rapallo Treaty with the Soviet Union. In an article written before World War I but printed in book form in that same year, 1922, Rathenau had deplored the fact that financial affairs in Europe were controlled by a small group of people and wrote: 'Three hundred men, all of whom are known to one another, guide the economic destinies of the Continent and seek their successors among their followers'.[11]

The anti-Semites, beginning with Ludendorff, promptly concluded that, as Rathenau himself was a Jew, he must be one of the three hundred and that these were in fact the mysterious 'Elders of Zion'. It is hardly necessary to point out that the original article did not mention Jews at all.

In the 1920s the *Protocols* were translated into a number of languages and eagerly welcomed as 'evidence' by many anti-Semitic groups in the West. In the United States Henry Ford allowed his newspaper the *Dearborn Independent* to publish a series of articles on the 'Jewish world-conspiracy' based on the *Protocols*, and in the same year (1920) they were issued in book form with the title *The International Jew: The World's Foremost Problem*. As Norman Cohn says:

> Half a million copies of the book were put into circulation in the United States. Moreover, it was translated into German, Russian and Spanish; in due course a shortened version of it was to become a stock item in Nazi propaganda. All in all *The International Jew* probably did more than any other work to make the *Protocols* world-famous.[12]

Naturally, there was reaction in several countries, and in America a declaration was published against anti-Semitic propaganda, signed by a number of prominent personalities and writers headed by Woodrow Wilson. In the

1930s the most prominent anti-Semite in the United States was Father Charles Coughlin, but there were also at one time a large number of Fascist organizations conducting anti-Jewish propaganda, like the Silver Shirts and the German-American Bund.[13]

In 1927, several years after the *Protocols* had been exposed as a forgery, Henry Ford publicly dissociated himself from the anti-Semitic movement. But by that time *The International Jew*, using the prestige of his name, had been published in many countries, and in Germany the Nazis refused to withdraw the book from circulation.

With or without the help of Ford, the *Protocols* continued their prosperous career. In Poland, at war with the Soviet Union, leading Catholic bishops openly identified Bolshevism with the Jews and described it as 'the embodiment and incarnation of the spirit of Antichrist on earth'.

In France monarchist and anti-democratic groups like Action Française actively promoted the dissemination of the *Protocols*. In 1920 Monsignor Jouin, an old campaigner against 'the Judaeo-Masonic conspiracy' and founder of the *Révue internationale des sociétés secrètes*, set out to write a massive work in five volumes devoted to a detailed translation and commentary of the available versions of the *Protocols*. He finished the task in seven years at the age of eighty-two and seemed to regard this *magnum opus* as almost as important as a comprehensive commentary on the Bible.

In England, where conservative circles were also alarmed by the 'Red peril', Lord Alfred Douglas, a distinguished poet notorious for his liaison with Oscar Wilde, edited an anti-Semitic weekly which made much use of the *Protocols*. The Russian correspondents of right-wing newspapers—like the *Morning Post* and *The Times* itself—sent alarming despatches 'confirming' that Bolshevism was in fact the product of a Jewish conspiracy. In May 1920 *The Times* published a long article on a recent English translation of the *Protocols* and expressed its alarm in no uncertain terms:

> What are these *Protocols*? Are they authentic? If so, what malevolent assembly concocted these plans, and gloated over their exposition? Are they a forgery? If so, whence comes the uncanny note of prophecy, prophecy in parts fulfilled, in parts far gone in the way of fulfilment? . . . Have we, by straining every fibre of our national body, escaped a 'Pax Germanica' only to fall into a 'Pax Judaica'? [14]

THE 'PROTOCOLS' UNMASKED

That a newspaper of such standing and reputation, in a stable country like Britain where anti-Semitism had not been very active or violent, should publish such an article is a measure both of the effectiveness of anti-Semitic propaganda and of the panic created by the revolutionary wave. But a year later *The Times* had to recant: more than that, thanks to the efforts of its correspondent in Constantinople, Philip Graves, it fell to the newspaper's credit to be the first to unmask the *Protocols* as a blatant forgery.

The story is very strange and reads like a cross between a spy thriller and the discovery of some important manuscript. A Russian monarchist— a 'Mr. X', whose name has never been disclosed—revealed to Philip Graves the results of his own researches. He had been studying the *Protocols* for some time and at first believed in their authenticity. But a few months earlier he had bought a batch of old books from a former officer of the tsarist secret police, the Okhrana. Among them was a small French volume without title page and with the word 'Joli' printed on the leather back. The only indication as to the date of publication was in the Preface, which said 'Geneva, 15 October 1864'. Mr. X began to turn the pages of the book and soon noticed the similarity between certain passages and the French edition of the *Protocols*. He set out to compare the two works in detail and became convinced that the obscure book was indeed the source of the famous 'document' which was going round the world as positive proof of a Jewish conspiracy to rule the earth.

Armed with this precious clue, Philip Graves went to the British Museum Library—that famous Reading Room where a hundred years ago Karl Marx had carried out his research for *Das Kapital* and where people like Bernard Shaw and Lenin had also studied socialism. He had no trouble in identifying the book and the author. The mysterious 'Joli' was the French journalist Maurice Joly, and the title of his book was *Dialogue aux enfers entre Montesquieu et Machiavel* (Dialogue in Hell between Montesquieu and Machiavelli). The author had written it in 1864 as a satire against the regime of Napoleon III in France, but his purpose was so obvious that he was quickly arrested and the whole edition confiscated. As a result, the *Dialogue* was a very rare and obscure work, and the forgers who plagiarized it thought they were quite safe to do so. They were not far wrong, as the forgery escaped detection for a number of years. It was only a very lucky accident that brought it to light.

In the original satire Montesquieu defends liberal and democratic ideas while 'Machiavelli' (who stands for Napoleon III) propounds with vigour the old cynical doctrine that the masses are helpless and ignorant, democracy an absurdity, and the only effective government is a strong, despotic one in which the ruler pursues his aims without any scruples. What the forgers of the *Protocols* seem to have done was simply to attribute to an imaginary 'Elder of Zion' the arguments put forward by 'Machiavelli'. But as it was in their interests to discredit democracy, they also used some material from 'Montesquieu', presenting liberal ideas as a Jewish trick to disguise their own tyrannical design. It is thought that about two-fifths of the *Protocols* is a direct borrowing or adaptation from the *Dialogue,* while the rest consists of variations on the same ideas, with additions addressed to the Russian public.

In fact, those who have spent time and effort in the somewhat tedious task of comparing the two books generally agree that Joly's work is a satire of literary value, while the *Protocols* is a hurried patchwork, sometimes inconsistent and contradictory. As to its central idea of a secret Jewish plot, it is not original either, for it derives, as we have seen, from Goedsche's novel *Biarritz* and its adaptation, *The Rabbi's Speech.*

The publication of Philip Graves' articles by *The Times* in 1921, followed up by later research, discredited the *Protocols* in the eyes of many people who were or might have been taken in by their crude propaganda. It did not convince many anti-Semitic militants. They soon invented a theory that Maurice Joly himself had been a Jew and so Philip Graves' discovery proved nothing. This was accepted and elaborated by many others. Anybody who has talked to patients afflicted with delusions of persecution soon realizes that they are not amenable to reasonable argument. But the same applies to strongly prejudiced people, and any attempt to hold some sort of debate with them lands one in all sorts of blind alleys. To grapple with a closed mind, unless one takes care to keep one's balance, can be a very frustrating experience and give you a feeling close to mental asphyxiation.

Here is, for example, a dialogue (if it can be called that) with Hitler as reported by the German industrialist Hermann Rauschning, who for some time financed the Nazi party. It took place a few years before Hitler became chancellor:

> 'I have read the *Protocols of the Elders of Zion*—it simply appalled me [Hitler says]. The stealthiness of the enemy, and his ubiquity! *I saw at once that we must copy it—in our own way, of course* . . .'
>
> 'Don't you think', I objected, 'that you are attributing rather too much importance to the Jews?'
>
> 'No, no, no!' exclaimed Hitler. 'It is impossible to exaggerate the formidable quality of the Jews as enemy'.
>
> 'But', I said, 'the *Protocols* are a manifest forgery. . . . It is evident to me that they can't possibly be genuine'.
>
> 'Why not?' grunted Hitler.
>
> He did not care two straws, he said, whether the story was historically true. If it was not, its intrinsic truth was all the more convincing to him. [The italics are mine.] [15]

This is probably a good illustration of the way Hitler's mind (and that of people like him) worked—on a level of mythology which was impervious to objective analysis. But there are myths and myths, and those who insist on accepting only Gradgrind's world of 'hard facts' also end up in another heresy and another type of 'closed mind': they refuse to see that there are very important truths that cannot be expressed in 'objective terms' and can only be personally experienced and then perhaps indicated through symbols.

But to return to the *Protocols*, the next question was: Who had been the forgers? The fact that the copy bought by Mr. X had belonged to a former officer of the tsarist secret police was in itself a significant clue. The mystery is not entirely clear, but it seems that one Rachkovsky, head of the Okhrana outside Russia, was one of the key figures, perhaps with the complicity of Sergey Nilus. It is possible that the *Protocols* were forged in the late 1890s in Paris, just at the height of the Dreyfus affair. It happens that one of the copies of Joly's book in the Bibliothèque Nationale in Paris contains some suggestive markings which correspond to some of the passages borrowed by the forgers of the *Protocols*.

In a way it is fitting that the responsibility for this malignant plot should have been traced to a secret police—a worthy forerunner of the Gestapo, the OGPU and its successors, or Salazar's notorious PIDE. It was only natural that an unscrupulous police, eager to smell plots everywhere, should attribute to others the use of its own Machiavellian methods. And, again, it was part of the same logic that Hitler should, by his own admission, follow the recipes of the *Protocols*.

Meanwhile, anti-Semitic groups in a number of countries, often helped and subsidized by Hitler's regime (through organizations like the W*eltdienst*, or World Service), went on printing editions of the *Protocols* as if nothing had happened. They usually had lurid covers, like those of cheap horror novels. The symbol most often used was the serpent of 'international Jewry' coiling itself round the world: a good example of this was the Brazilian edition published in the 1930s by the 'Integralist' (Fascist) leader Gustavo Barroso.

'The cycle of the symbolic snake' is mentioned in the text of the *Protocols* (Protocol No. 3), and it is stated that 'when the ring closes all the states of Europe will be locked in its coils as in a powerful vise'.[16] Sergey Nilus had elaborated this idea and traced the earliest plans of Jewish domination to King Solomon himself in 929 B.C. (the date is wrong for a start). He also drew a map showing the historical stages in the progress of the Jewish snake: the first in 429 B.C. with the death of Pericles in Athens, the second with Augustus in Rome in 69 B.C. (again a wildly inaccurate date), then successively with Charles V in Spain, Louis XVI in Paris, the British Empire in 1814 after the fall of Napoleon, Berlin in 1871 after the German victory over France, and St. Petersburg in 1881 (the tsar's murder). The end was very near and would come with 'the return of the snake's head to Zion' (i.e., Jerusalem).

The use of this old, archetypal symbol is interesting and might well provide a clue to some of the deeper fears of the anti-Semites. The serpent that eats its own tail, or *Uroboros* (Greek = tail-devouring),[17] is an important cosmic symbol and appears in several mythologies. Some Greek philosophers thought circularity was something inherent in the universe and that human life was an attempt to 'close the circle'. In a way the possibility of world domination had been implicit since the emergence of the first empires, and the title 'King of the Universe' was actually used by Akkadian and Assyrian rulers. We have already seen how important the idea of the *oikoumene* was in antiquity and how many religious Jews gave great significance to the Diaspora 'closing its circle' round the earth. In fact, the anti-Semites used these Jewish hopes and speculations as supposed 'evidence' for schemes of world rule.

The Catholic scientist and philosopher Teilhard de Chardin saw in the present stage of human history a decisive climax of convergence which had already 'crossed the equator'. 'What we call civilisation', he wrote, 'is weaving its web around us with a terrifying rapidity'.[18] We all know, now more than ever, the alarming feeling of being caught in this web, in a 'runaway world', as some have called it. The historical process is impersonal, no matter how we might interpret it. But the anti-Semites, who are usually people who fear and hate change, felt it as a deep threat to their psychological security and found relief in giving a name to their fear. We might therefore suspect that the 'symbolic snake' closing the circle round the world expresses their panic fear of a tremendous, very real historical process that has been dissolving old institutions and tribal feelings.

THE SWASTIKA TAKES OVER

We now come to the climax of the modern wave of anti-Semitism, which used the forged *Protocols* as one of its main weapons. The story of Nazi extermination of the Jews is so well documented and has so often been told that I do not think it necessary to go over it in detail.

The attack began soon after the new regime was established, with violence against individual Jews particularly by members of the uniformed Nazi SS (*Schutzstaffel*), boycott of Jewish shops, and dismissal of Jewish civil servants. In 1935 came the 'Nuremberg Laws' forbidding marriage and extramarital intercourse between Jews and 'Aryan' Germans, the employment in Jewish households of German women under the age of forty-five, and the raising by Jews of the Reich flag. Under a new citizenship law restricting civil and political rights (such as they were) to 'Aryan' Germans, the German Jews were entirely disfranchised.

So far there was nothing very new or unprecedented, and Hilberg has drawn useful tables showing that most Nazi anti-Jewish legislation had close parallels in medieval laws.[19] Although the Nazis repudiated Christianity, their anti-Jewish propaganda drew on 'Christian' ideas and symbols. For instance, in a speech to the Hitler Youth, Julius Streicher referred to the Jews as 'this people which has wandered about the world for centuries and millennia, marked with the sign of Cain'. With typical Nazi disrespect for the truth, he claimed that Christ—'the greatest anti-Semite of all time'!—had said the Jews were children of the Devil.[20]

Even before extermination became official policy, the German Jews were submitted to all sorts of humiliations and restrictions. There were public notices in a number of towns saying, JEWS NOT WANTED HERE. In many places Jewish families could not even get milk for their children. Even traffic notices were used to give vent to a macabre anti-Semitism, such as this one at Ludwigshafen:

DRIVE CAREFULLY! SHARP CURVE!
JEWS 75 MILES AN HOUR! [21]

In November 1938 a young Polish Jew murdered a minor official of the German Embassy in Paris. This became the pretext for a pogrom which was not really the outcome of popular indignation but carefully planned and instigated by Goebbels. In the so-called *Kristallnacht* (Night of the Broken Glass) the notorious party Brownshirts of the SA (*Sturmabteilung*) set out systematically to burn down all Jewish synagogues in Germany. A number of Jews were also killed, although the authorities only admitted the death of thirty-six. There was great loss of property, and the Nazi government also imposed a punitive fine of one billion marks on the Jewish community. Himmler took the opportunity to throw about 20,000 Jews into concentration camps. Those who held Polish passports were abandoned on the frontier with Poland, during the winter, and the Polish government refused to admit them.[22]

Meanwhile the exodus had begun, in spite of all the obstacles created by the authorities. Many Jews had the misfortune of emigrating to European countries which were later occupied by the Germans and were therefore caught in the general slaughter.

As the Jews were considered to have acquired their goods dishonestly, it was held that all Jewish property belonged by rights to the Reich and all means were used to expropriate it. All Jews who emigrated had to pay a heavy 'Reich Flight Tax', and through this and other measures the Jewish community, which by 1939 was reduced to half its original size, was already impoverished. During the war there were further measures, like the concentration in ghettos or Jewish streets, the compulsory wearing of the Yellow Star (again an imitation of the medieval Jewish badge), forced labour, and special wage regulations. Under rationing restrictions the Jews were not entitled to a number of food items, and even Jewish children had their milk ration cut and were allowed skim milk only. These were, of course, starvation measures.

From here to slaughter it was a 'logical' step, and the Nazis had some method in their madness, although in fact even Hitler for a long time hesitated before the final decision. The phrase 'Final Solution of the Jewish question' (*Endloesung der Judenfrage*) seems to have been first used in an order signed by Göring on 31 July 1941. The date is significant, for the Third Reich had just begun its ruthless campaign against Soviet Russia, and there had always been a tendency to equate 'Jew' and 'Bolshevik'.

It was to be a 'crusade' in which both Slav Communists (a 'lower race') and Jews were to be slaughtered without pity. But there was an important difference between the pogroms of the medieval Crusades and the genocide perpetrated by the German Nazis. This was no 'popular' outburst of violence. It was minutely organized with all the efficiency of a modern state and all the resources of modern technology, down to the utilization of anything that could be extracted from the victims—gold from tooth fillings, collection of artificial limbs, and even fat to make soap. Again, the Nazi leaders did not dare to do it openly, and it was only towards the end of the war that the true extent of the holocaust began to be known.

The total number of victims is usually estimated at around six million, but Gerald Reitlinger [23] in his comprehensive study of the subject has arrived at a lower estimate while admitting a wider and more realistic margin of error: the minimum would be about 4,200,000 and the maximum over 5,700,000. These divergences, of course, affect neither the enormity of the crime nor the essence of the facts.

Although the 'Final Solution' was kept secret and those who took part in the 'operation' considered it bad form to talk about it, attempts were constantly made to keep up anti-Jewish propaganda and to justify what was being done. The Jews were incessantly reviled as mortal enemies of the Third Reich, and the war itself was supposedly being waged by international Jewry. Roosevelt, Churchill, Stalin, and all the Allied war leaders were no more than tools of the Jewish conspiracy. At a time when hundreds of thousands of Jewish children were being slaughtered, a Nazi called Helmut Schramm published a book entitled *The Jewish Ritual Murder: A Historical Inquiry* (1943). It was simply a revival of the old medieval legend, but Himmler was enthusiastic about it. He ordered investigations of 'ritual murders' of children in Rumania, Hungary, and Bulgaria, and even suggested using cases of missing children in Britain 'so that we can report in our radio broadcasts that in the town of XY a child is missing and that it is probably another case of Jewish ritual murder'.[24]

How far was this kind of propaganda effective? An observer, Muller-Claudius, conducted inquiries among party members in Germany on two occasions: first after the pogrom of November 1938, and then during the war in 1942. The most striking result of the first poll is the large proportion of people (63 percent) who were indignant at the anti-Jewish attacks. Only 5 percent thought violence justified because 'terror must be met with terror'. In 1942 the proportion of persons who showed any concern for the fate of the Jews had gone down to 26 percent, while the indifferent constituted the majority. There was a similar low proportion (5 percent) of fanatics who accepted the extermination of the Jews as necessary.[25]

These results, although based on a small sample and not very conclusive, at least show that Nazi propaganda had not really been effective with the great majority. Anti-Semitism was very widespread in Germany, but most anti-Semites were prepared to accept only certain restrictive measures: nothing like genocide was contemplated. As to the increase in the reaction of indifference, one should remember that intimidation is very effective in a dictatorship and that moral concern for others demands a high level of mental and spiritual development. Under the stress of war and insecurity, not to mention the corrupting and distorting influence of a regime like the Third Reich, moral standards are bound to decline.

THE MYTH OF 'RACIAL POLLUTION'

Finally, what could be said about the state of mind of the Nazi leaders? It is significant that as Nazi policy became more refined in its brutality, the image of the 'Jew' in their minds became progressively degraded, like a kind of portrait of Dorian Gray. To begin with, the Jew was only sub-human, a lower race without real character or morality, although Hitler, as we have seen, compared the Jews to maggots and mushrooms in *Mein Kampf*.

Later, in his obscene newspaper *Der Stürmer*, Julius Streicher was to explore all variations on the theme of 'racial pollution'. For instance, there was a popular (but entirely unfounded) belief that the children from a woman's second marriage could 'inherit' some characteristics of her first husband. Streicher drew his own conclusion from that and write in a semi-medical journal called *German People's Health*:

> One single cohabitation of a Jew with an Aryan woman is sufficient to poison her blood for ever. Together with the 'alien albumen' she has absorbed the alien soul. Never again will she be able

to bear purely Aryan children. . . . They will all be bastards. . . . Now we know why the Jew uses every artifice of seduction in order to ravish German girls at as early an age as possible, why the Jewish doctor rapes his female patients while they are under anaesthetics.[26]

At about the same time *Der Stürmer* published the picture of a girl being strangled by a man with obvious 'Jewish' features, with the caption:

CASTRATION FOR RACE POLLUTERS. ONLY HEAVY PENALTIES WILL PRESERVE OUR WOMENFOLK FROM A TIGHTER GRIP FROM LOATHSOME JEWISH CLAWS

This 'our womenfolk' (like 'our boys' or 'our girls') is an obvious appeal to tribal jealousy and possessiveness.

Besides adopting the *Protocols* as a schoolbook, the Nazis also used some of the crude propaganda from *Der Stürmer* to indoctrinate German children. These are extracts from a short story entitled 'Poisonous Fingers', which was published in a children's book:

Inge sits in the reception room of the Jewish doctor. She has to wait a long time . . . she glances through the papers on the table but is too nervous to read: she remembers what her mother has told her and again and again her mind reflects on the warnings of the leader of the League of German Girls. A German girl must not consult a Jew doctor. Many a girl who went to a Jewish doctor to be cured has met with disease and disgrace. . . . Then the door opens. The Jew appears. She screams. In terror she drops the paper. Horrified she jumps up. Her eyes stare into the face of the doctor, and his face is the face of the Devil. In the middle of the Devil's face is a huge crooked nose. Behind the spectacles gleam two criminal eyes. Around the thick lips plays a grin that means, 'Now I have you at last, you little German girl!'

And then the Jew approaches her. His fat fingers clutch at her. But now Inge has got hold of herself. Before the Jew can grab her she smacks his fat face with her hand. One jump to the door. Breathlessly she runs down the stairs and escapes from the Jew's house.[27]

This is pure strip-cartoon world with a touch of Red Ridinghood, but note that the medieval image of the Devil is also there. The insistence on physical traits, like 'fat fingers', 'crooked nose', is as crude as that of anti-Negro racialism. The Negro is also the dangerous rapist, the oversexed beast. Even recently in Britain racialist propaganda has tried to identify

West Indian immigrants with prostitution and venereal disease, just as Hitler and Streicher did in the case of the Jews.

As the war went on and the 'Final Solution' gathered momentum, the image of the Jew in the mind of the Nazi leaders went down on the zoological scale: they became the 'worms', the 'germs', the 'bacteria', which had to be liquidated. Himmler said in a speech that to get rid of the Jews was 'a matter of hygiene', like delousing. Again, in 1940 when the Warsaw ghetto was established, the Nazis invoked yet another reason to justify it. They invented the story that the Jews were spreading an epidemic of typhus and created the formula, 'Jews—Lice—Typhus' (*Juden—Läuser—Fleckfieber*).[28] It was almost a revival of the medieval stories about the Black Death.

In April 1943 the victims, almost without weapons, rebelled in desperation against their tormentors, and the German army had to take the Warsaw ghetto as 'a heroic military operation'. Some time earlier a film had been made showing the conditions in which the Jews lived there. Its aim had been to point out the degraded existence of the 'subhuman race' and so to demonstrate the truth of anti-Semitic propaganda. But the result was so hideous that it seems that even the Nazis did not dare to show it publicly. Later, with the Allied victory, the film was seized and became a living proof of the crimes against humanity committed by the Third Reich.

The Warsaw ghetto, like the concentration camps and the rest of the Nazi machinery of repression, was created in order to degrade and humiliate a group of people. The name 'ghetto' is still being applied today, not without reason, to various kinds of slums or shanty towns where Negroes or coloured people live in degrading conditions, in countries like the United States, Brazil, or South Africa. And, of course, racialists can always point to them as evidence of the Negro's racial inferiority.

13

And It Goes On . . .

Above all, I enjoin the Government and the people the duty of up-
holding the racial laws in all their severity and mercilessy resisting the
universal poisoner of all nations, international Jewry.
— Adolf Hiltler's Political Testament (last words)

NEW OUTBREAKS OF THE EPIDEMIC

January 1945: The Soviet troops occupy Warsaw at last. From the bunkers,
from the concentration camps, from hiding-places in villages and forests,
a few dozen people emerge in rags, half starved. There are some two hundred altogether—all that is left of a Jewish community that was at one
time one of the largest in the world.

Very soon these survivors of extermination were the target of violent
anti-Semitism among the Poles, who themselves had been the victims of
Nazi racialism and brutality. 'What, still so many Jews?' they asked. 'We
thought the Germans had been more efficient'. And it did not stop there:
one of the survivors was arrested for speaking Yiddish in public.[1]

In the following year, on 4 July 1946, a real pogrom took place at Kielce,
in which forty-one Jews were killed and sixty wounded. This was the last
straw: the Polish community became convinced that there was no future
for them there, and by the end of the year 120,000 had left the country.
It seems strange indeed that so many had escaped from the 'Final Solution', but many had fled to Russia during the German invasion and had
now come back in the wake of the Soviet troops.

November 1945: Tripoli, the capital of the former Italian colony of
Libya, is under occupation by the British troops who had won the desert
war. The city's Greek name is evidence of its long history: Tripoli (literally, 'triple town') was founded by the Phoenicians, and there must have
been Jews there at least since the heyday of Alexandria. At the time of
the last war there were about 35,000 Jews in Libya, of whom about two-
thirds lived in Tripoli. Many of them were merchants and traders, and the

213

whole community was autonomous in matters of education and religion. The Italians had conquered Libya from the Turks in 1911, but neither Fascist anti-Semitic legislation nor the arrival of Rommel's German army during the desert war had affected the Libyan Jews. But suddenly in November 1945 they were the target of an unexpected pogrom. Herbert Agar comments:

> Just as a passing herd of cattle can infect the earth with foot-and mouth disease, so the German armies would seem to have poisoned the desert sands with the germ of Jew-killing.
> The pogrom lasted only two days because the British troops were diligent in suppression. Thirty children and a hundred adults perished; seven synagogues, five hundred shops and three hundred and fifty private houses were destroyed: a small affair compared to Ukrainian or Polish efforts, but the results were startling. This pogrom marked the end of creative Jewish life in Libya.[2]

In 1948, the year when the state of Israel was founded, there was a second, less destructive pogrom, but by that time the Libyan Jews, like those of Poland, had lost all hope of remaining. More fortunate in their comparative proximity to their new country, they emigrated en masse to Israel. By 1952 no less than 32,000 had left Libya. Something similar has happened in other Muslim countries where local anti-Semitism—often mild or latent—has been exacerbated by the hatred provoked by the long Arab-Israeli conflict in Palestine.

The case of the former French colonies in North Africa, particularly Algeria, is interesting because of the curious political changes and polarizations that have taken place there. Since the last century the French colons in Algeria had been a strongly chauvinistic and anti-Semitic community. Édouard Drumont, the anti-Semitic leader at the time of the Dreyfus affair, was a deputy for Algiers. When the Vichy regime was established in 1940—representing the right-wing groups who were the heirs of the anti-Dreyfusards—it had firm support among the colons in North Africa. And it is interesting to note that the Resistance movement, which in 1942 staged a rising in Algiers and co-operated with the Allied invasion, included a strong Jewish element.

Then came the long-drawn-out, bloody colonial war in Algeria, in which the French paras and colons committed many atrocities against the Algerian FLN. A few Algerian Jews co-operated with the Muslim FLN, while in France most Jewish students, together with a large number of intellectuals and journalists, sided with the Algerian liberation movement against the colons of the notorious OAS.

On the other hand, in the Suez war in 1956 there was the ill-fated, shocking alliance between Israel and the governments of France and Britain set on protecting their colonial interests.

Yet when Algeria at last won her independence, most of the Jewish community (estimated at 130,000) chose to emigrate to France, fearing the local repercussions of the Arab-Israeli conflict. The same trend occurred in Tunisia and Morocco, with the result that the Jewish community in France, which Nazi slaughter had reduced to about a third (from 300,000 to 100,000), was doubled in number and also changed its character considerably.

A more curious change was that of the formerly anti-Semitic *colons* and French colonials, who out of anti-Arab hatred became supporters and often admirers of Israel.

ONCE MORE THE ANTI-SEMITIC INTERNATIONAL

Christmas Eve 1959: A synagogue in Cologne, West Germany, is found desecrated with swastikas. Later incidents elsewhere showed that this was no mere hark-back to the Nazi era. There was a genuine international wave of anti-Semitic vandalism, which, according to one calculation, affected forty countries. By March 1960 the Anti-Defamation League of B'nai B'rith had recorded hundreds of incidents in 236 American cities:

> Eighty-four percent of these incidents involved the construction and display, through various means, of swastikas and/or anti-Jewish epithets and slogans; 11 percent involved mail, telephone, and personal threats; and 5 percent of the incidents consisted of physical damage (other than mere defacement) of personal and community property.[3]

As we shall see later, the wave also affected South American countries, particularly after the Eichmann trial.

Although at least in America most of the offenders were maladjusted teen-agers, there are clear signs of a planned, concerted effort which seem to indicate the existence at the time of some sort of international organization.

With the fall of the Third Reich a number of Nazis fled to many countries, and not all of them went to Argentina like Eichmann. This may be compared to the dispersion of White Russian officers which helped to disseminate the *Protocols*. Some of the Nazi refugees did not remain inactive but joined various Fascist or semi-Fascist movements which emerged in a number of countries, often under some sort of camouflage. Others offered their services to centres of Arab anti-Israeli propaganda and were accepted.

In the 1950s and 1960s some Fascist organizations used the convenient cover of European Union to express their racialist ideas. Anti-Semitism has by no means disappeared among them, but in view of its discredit it is not often openly admitted. In Britain, for instance, the heirs of Mosley's Fascists have turned against the coloured immigrants (Indians, Pakistanis, and West Indians) and formed movements like the National Front, with its slogan 'Stop Immigration, Start Repatriation'. But the painting of anti-Jewish slogans on walls is frequent enough and the swastika is also popular.

It is difficult to follow all the ramifications and camouflages of contemporary Fascism, which has proved to be a true chameleon. In the 1960s James Parkes was able to trace its connection with another 'Diaspora' —that of frustrated settlers and colonials who had lost their comfortable niches in newly independent African countries and could no longer 'lord it over the niggers':

> Frenchmen dispossessed from North Africa, Belgians from the Congo, Dutchmen from the East Indies, Englishmen from Kenya and East Africa or the Middle East may find themselves allied with the schoolboys and students who placed plastic bombs for the French Secret Army, or the OAS.[4]

In Britain the latest anti-Semitic gambit has been a crude attempt to dismiss as an exaggeration the Nazi genocide and to claim that the figure of six million 'was deliberately invented by the Zionists' in order to extract concessions from the British government over Palestine and compensation from West Germany.[5]

ANTI-SEMITIC TRENDS IN SOUTH AMERICA

> Uniformed Nazis on the rampage in the central shopping area of a big city; the public burning of a Jewish flag; the shouting of anti-Semitic slogans, and the crash of splintering glass; a Jewish girl student abducted from the university precincts, to be released later with a swastika carved on her breast; a dazed youth wandering the streets after torture, and the same symbol of hate branded into his forehead and cheek. This is not a description of scenes in pre-war Berlin. They happened in the 1960s, in Buenos Aires.[6]

Thus Barnet Litvinoff begins his chapter on Latin America in his book A Peculiar People, a general survey of the Jewish world.

Perhaps it is not very difficult to understand why Argentina should have been the only Latin American country with a violent, militant anti-Semitism. First of all, it has the second largest Jewish community in the Americas: the total is not much under half a million, with the majority (perhaps 380,000) concentrated in Buenos Aires.

Naturally, the visibility of a large colony makes it more vulnerable to prejudice, as in the case of ancient Alexandria or modern Berlin. Secondly, Argentina also has a good percentage of German immigrants, like the south of Brazil: before World War II the number of Argentinians of German descent was estimated at about a million. When Hitler came to power in Germany, his Foreign Office gave special attention to the organization of National Socialism in South America, and a special league was founded under the name of Volksbund für Argentinien (Folk League for Argentina). This network was considerably more militant than among German immigrants in Brazil, whose organization was dismantled by the Brazilian police after the Vargas regime broke off relations with the Axis powers in 1942.

In fact, the economic crisis of 1929 and the ideological conflicts of the time had political repercussions in both countries, as elsewhere in Latin America. In Brazil the popular revolution of 1930 could be described as 'left of centre', and it was only later that it developed into the Vargas dictatorship—a curious blend of 'populism' and semi-Fascism. In Argentina the 1930 military coup was led by right-wing generals, whose leader was José Uriburu, an admirer of Mussolini and of German militarism and an anti-Semite. Although he had to give way to another general in 1932, anti-Semitic propaganda was rife in the country. In 1939, when war broke out (during which Argentina remained neutral), a crowd estimated at about ten thousand made a great demonstration at the Plaza San Martin, in Buenos Aires, shouting, 'Death to the British pigs! Death to the Jews!' As among the Brazilian Fascists, anti-Semitism was combined with Anglophobia and to a lesser extent anti-American feeling, and naturally people of German descent took a leading part in the movement. In the 1930s the anti-Semites even published a newspaper called *Clarinada*, which resembled Streicher's *Der Stürmer*.

In 1943 came another military coup which included pro-Nazi and anti-Semitic elements. The new minister of education in particular, Martinez Zuviria, was a very popular writer under the pseudonym of Hugo Wast, and some of his novels were anti-Jewish. Perón, the new leader who emerged a few years later, had an ambiguous attitude to the Jews. He did try to conciliate the Jewish community, but he was more sympathetic to Nazi refugees, whom he welcomed in larger numbers than Jewish immigrants.

Throughout this period anti-Semitic propaganda remained active in the country, not only among Argentinians of German descent but among right-wing groups, including Catholics.

In 1958, three years after the fall of Perón, a new ultra-nationalist society was founded with the name of Tacuara; one of its leaders was a young relative of General Uriburu, the dictator of 1930. It was Tacuara that organized a violent anti-Semitic campaign in the 1960s, particularly after the capture of Eichmann by Israeli agents in Argentina (1960). The disturbances began at the University of Buenos Aires with attacks on Jewish students. Groups of hooligans also invaded synagogues during services, and attacked buses carrying Jewish children to school.

The campaign reached its climax in 1962 with Eichmann's execution in Israel: to the Argentinian anti-Semites he became something of a national hero. Tacuara organized a violent demonstration in the centre of Buenos Aires, but these excesses led to the imprisonment of over eighty of its leading young members, and in 1963 the government banned the society. The anti-Semitic campaign was still carried on by other extremist groups, like the Guardia Restauradora Nacionalista and the Legión Nacionalista Contrarrevolucionaria (the latter founded in 1970), but at least the violence died down. After the Six-Day War, South American anti-Semites tended to ally themselves with Arab propagandists.

In Brazil the Eichmann case also gave rise to attempts to whip up anti-Jewish feeling, but these were sporadic and amounted in most cases to painting slogans on walls. This must have been part of the organized international campaign, for the seeds sown by the earlier Integralist (Fascist) Action had failed to produce a really aggressive anti-Semitic movement in Brazil.

The Vargas dictatorship (1937–45) only showed anti-Jewish tendencies in its immigration policy: prospective immigrants had to fill in a form which included an entry on 'race', and there is a persistent story that Brazilian consulates abroad had orders to restrict Jewish immigration. But it is interesting to note that in 1939 Artur Hehl Neiva, in an official report to the Brazilian Council for Immigration and Colonization, condemned anti-Semitism and favoured Jewish immigrants.[7]

Neiva even defended the Jews against the allegation that they tended to be 'subversive elements'. This was partly due to the fact that after the Communist-led rebellion in 1935 a German of reputedly Jewish origin called Harry Berger had been arrested together with the Brazilian Communist leader Prestes (Berger and his wife were brutally tortured by the police of Rio de Janeiro). A wave of anti-Communist hysteria was then sweeping Brazil, giving rise to witch-hunts, which were to be repeated after the military coup of 1964.

I have already mentioned the earlier activities of the Brazilian Integralists (Greenshirts), who supported the Vargas dictatorship but were later banned by him. One of their leaders, the writer Gustavo Barroso, not only published a special Brazilian edition of the *Protocols* but wrote the book *Brazil a Bankers' Colony*, exploiting the fact that the country had for a long period been tied to a foreign debt contracted with Rothschild's in London.[8]

On the credit side, one should not forget that a group of thirty-five

Brazilian writers and intellectuals was one of the first in the West to publish (in 1933) a collective condemnation of anti-Semitism.[9]

Elsewhere in South America anti-Jewish propaganda has on the whole
been sporadic and of little significance: as usual, it has been the weapon of
extremist right-wing movements. One interesting example is the attempt
to exploit the fact that there were Jews among the leaders of the Allende
left-wing regime in Chile. In August 1973, a little before the military coup
that overthrew the government, a letter published in the newspaper *La
Segunda* recommended that two hundred of 'the criminals of Jewish race
be hanged on the lampposts of Santiago'.[10]

The Chilean army was trained in the German tradition, and the present
military regime has acquired an evil reputation for its Nazi-like brutality
(there have even been bonfires of books in Santiago). In a recent American book it has even been suggested that it might 'permit Jews to be made
scapegoats' of the bad economic situation of the country.[11] But so far this
has not happened and seems rather unlikely.

ANTI-SEMITISM IN THE SOVIET UNION

The history of anti-Semitism is full of ironies, but it is difficult to match
this one: while Nazi propaganda equated Jew with Bolshevik and in that
spirit Hitler launched his crusade against Russia, the Soviet Union was
itself pervaded with anti-Semitism. Could one really believe that the Russian Revolution had wiped out centuries of anti-Jewish prejudice?

The beginnings, it is true, were very auspicious. The war, as we have
seen, had done away with the old Pale of Settlement, and after the first
revolution (in February 1917, or, according to the new calendar, March)
the Jews found themselves entirely emancipated. An early decree of the
Provisional Government abolished 'all restrictions based on class, religion
and nationality'.[12] The Bolshevik government which took power after the
October (November) revolution confirmed this and abolished all anti-
Nazi laws, which under the tsars had exceeded a total of five hundred.

There were many militant Jews in the socialist parties, and in the ruling
Bolshevik (now Communist) party itself anti-Semites aboard could point
to such prominent figures as Trotsky (Leo Bronstein)—easily the most
important leader after Lenin—Kamenev, Zinoviev, Sverdlov, and Yoffe.
But there were even more Jews in the other socialist parties (like the Jewish *Bund*) which opposed the Bolshevik take-over.

Litvinov, who was also Jewish, relates in his journal that at first Trotsky
was reluctant to accept the post of chairman of the Council of People's
Commissars: 'They would say: "The Soviet Government is in the hands
of the Jews". Ilich [Lenin] laughed and replied: "They say in any case
that we are all Yids!" ' [13]

Under the new regime a number of publications appeared exposing and condemning anti-Semitism as a counter-revolutionary weapon.[14] The very fact that it was thought necessary to issue such warnings shows that anti-Jewish prejudice was very much alive; and, indeed, there is plenty of evidence for it in the early years of the regime—some time after the terrible pogroms carried out by the tsarist 'Whites' during the civil war. In the Crimea, for instance, the peasants protested against the local settlement of Jews, and in the factories there were many incidents. One must remember that the Jewish community were now taking up occupations which for centuries had been barred to them.

On the other hand, it cannot be said that even under Lenin the regime treated the Jews the same as other ethnic minorities. For instance, they were not allowed to organize their own Communist party, and the official boards in charge of Jewish affairs, the Yevsektsiyas, through Bolshevik Jews like Esther Frumkin, made it clear that assimilation under a socialist society was the final aim. Communism being a kind of religion, it was 'a jealous god' that did not tolerate other creeds, and 'Judaism suffered perhaps even more than Christianity'.[15] While Yiddish culture was tolerated and even encouraged for a time, both the teaching of Hebrew and religious instruction were forbidden. This had never happened even under the tsars.

Much worse was to come under Stalin. His notorious purges involved not only most Jewish Bolshevik leaders, like Zinoviev, Kamenev, Radek, and of course Trotsky himself, but all the heads of the Yevsektsiyas. 'Jewish nationalism' became a serious 'deviation' and offence, and many Jewish intellectuals and teachers were arrested. During the 1930s all the Yiddish schools were closed down, and in 1937 the last Yiddish newspaper in Moscow stopped publication.

While paying lip-service to the campaign against anti-Semitism and showing favour to some Jewish intellectuals (the writer Ilya Ehrenburg was one of the most prominent), Stalin became more anti-Jewish in practice, particularly after the non-aggression pact with Nazi Germany (this was in fact heralded by the sacking of the Jewish Maxim Litvinov, for years Soviet foreign minister and famous as an advocate of disarmament and collective security). There was then a further purge of Jewish officials, including diplomats. Stalin went as far as to prevent the Soviet press from reporting any Nazi crimes against the Jews: this policy had the tragic result of leaving the Russian Jews (particularly those of the Ukraine and White Russia) without any warning of the fate that was to overwhelm them when the German invasion finally came. In fact, the local population often helped the Nazis to round up and exterminate the Russian Jews.

Partly to counterbalance the attractions of Jewish emigration to Palestine, the Soviet government created in remote Siberia, on the frontier with Manchuria, the Jewish Autonomous Region (or Oblast) of Birobidzhan (1934), which had been open to Jewish settlement since 1928.

Severely affected by the 1936 purges, it has never enjoyed real cultural autonomy, and today the Jewish population there (under 20,000) is heavily outnumbered by Russians and other groups.

After the war the situation of the Jews under the Soviet regime deteriorated instead of improving. In fact, there is now convincing evidence that Stalin—who, like Hitler, had pronounced paranoid tendencies—was himself an anti-Semite. For instance, Litvinov's journal reveals incidents where the Russian dictator used violent language against what he called 'that Zionist rabble', and makes this comment: 'Of course Koba's [Stalin's] anti-Semitism is the sequel to the support given by the majority of Jews in our party to Trotsky and the opposition. But I have in fact noted that Koba felt some inherent hostility towards us'.[16]

In 1948 Stalin ordered the MVD (then the name of the Soviet political police) to arrest no fewer than 431 leading Jewish personalities (writers, artists, officials), under the accusation of being 'nationalist bourgeois Zionists' and 'agents of American imperialism'. Most of them died in concentration camps, and one group was secretly executed in 1952. Later, after Khrushchev's famous speech at the Twentieth Party Congress in February 1956, a number of Jewish writers were rehabilitated.

But Stalin's most 'medieval' anti-Jewish blow—harking back to the days of Ivan the Terrible—was to come in January 1953, two months before his death. It was perhaps (as some have interpreted) a sign of his own mental deterioration. This was the famous 'Doctors' Plot'. *Pravda* suddenly revealed that a number of doctors (the total number varied and was given at one time as fifteen), among whom there were six Jews, had been arrested for criminal and subversive acts on behalf of Jewish organizations abroad and as part of 'a world Zionist conspiracy'.[17] Using their medical profession, they had plotted to kill a number of Soviet leaders, and had already been responsible for the death of several, including Zhdanov (a close associate of Stalin, responsible for severe interference with and suppression of cultural activities, who in fact had died in 1948).

Khrushchev later revealed that the 'Doctors' Plot' was to have been a pretext for a mass deportation of Jews to Siberia, but he (probably with the help of Kaganovich, the only remaining Jew among the Old Bolsheviks who had escaped all purges) persuaded Stalin to cancel the plan. Later the imprisoned doctors were released and allowed to go back to their profession.

Anti-Semitic witch-hunting was not limited to the Soviet Union. A few months before the 'Doctors' Plot', in November 1952, thirteen prominent leaders of the Czechoslovak Communist party were declared guilty of various crimes and hanged in a prison in Prague. Ten of them were Jews, the most prominent being Rudolf Slansky, secretary-general of the party and one of the key figures in the Communist take-over of the country in 1948.

They were accused of being 'Zionist agents' among other things, and of having 'arranged with a Freemason physician to shorten the life of President Gottwald'.[18] There is no doubt that this brutal anti-Jewish purge was carried out on instructions from Stalin.

Under Khrushchev's so-called 'thaw' and destalinization, the situation improved at first, and thousands of Jews were released from prison. But it soon became apparent that the campaign against Judaism and Zionism was to continue. It has been estimated that under Khrushchev the number of synagogues in Russia was reduced from 500 to under 100. Under his successors it dropped to 62, almost half of them in the Asian republics.[19] Although the practice of Judaism has certainly declined as in other countries, one must remember that according to the official census there are over two million Jews in the Soviet Union (and this may be an underestimate). There is no doubt, therefore, that through this and other restrictions the Soviet government has been trying to squeeze Judaism out of existence. As Joshua Rothenberg says: 'The intention was to "silence to death" a living organism by *creating the illusion that it did not exist— until such time as it would in fact cease to exist'*. [Author's italics.] [20]

It might be argued that this is not really anti-Semitism but an integral part of Communist anti-religious policy, which has been more or less consistently applied to all denominations since the days of Lenin. This is partly true, but the campaign against Judaism is usually entangled with anti-Jewish and anti-Zionist themes, which brings it well in line with the main anti-Semitic tradition. For instance, a book published in 1963 by the Ukrainian Academy of Sciences under the title *Judaism without Embellishment* 'depicted Judaism as fostering hypocrisy, bribery, greed, and usury', and linking it with Zionism, Israel, Jewish bankers, and Western capitalists.[21] The text was 'embellished' with crude anti-Semitic caricatures. In 1964, after many protests from abroad, the book was condemned by a Communist party organ and withdrawn from circulation.

But perhaps the most striking feature of anti-Semitism during the Khrushchev period was the frequency with which Jews were tried for economic offences, particularly foreign-currency charges. These cases were prominently reported in the Soviet press, and although the defendants were not explicitly labelled as Jews, the reports made a point of printing a revealing patronymic (like Abramovich) and mentioning their connections or relatives in Israel or the United States. Sometimes, as in the Vilna trial in 1962, rabbis were said to be involved and the local synagogue was reported to have been used for illicit deals in foreign currency. In several of these press reports the headlines and whole tone tended to stress Jewish greed for money and gold—the age-old theme of anti-Semitic propaganda.

That such trials still take place was recently shown by the case of Dr. Mikhail Shtern, who was sentenced to eight years for bribe-taking and swindling. After his conviction he was reported to have shouted, 'Shame on all who sow hatred towards Jews!' [22]

There is also evidence for discrimination against Jews in the Soviet Union, particularly in government, administrative, and party bodies, where their participation has steadily declined, and also in admission to universities. This is no doubt helped by the fact that Soviet law officially recognizes a number of nationalities within the union, and Jews are usually described as *Yevrei* in their internal passports (*Yevrei*, or Hebrew, is the 'respectable' designation, while *Zhid*, like 'Yid', has remained an offensive term).[23]

We move now into the very recent period, about which I do not have to say much, as it is a matter of common knowledge to all who follow developments with any degree of interest. After the Six-Day War the situation of the Jews in Russia became more deeply involved not only with Soviet policy towards the Israel-Arab conflict but also with dissent and rebellion in Eastern Europe and in the Soviet Union itself. In both Poland and Czechoslovakia some of the 'liberal Communist' leaders were Jewish, and the Soviet government used the anti-Semitic weapon in its repressive policy.

As regards the movement of protest and dissent in Russia itself, it is interesting to note that several writers and intellectuals who have taken a leading part in it are Jews: Boris Pasternak himself; Yuli Daniel and his wife, Larissa; Paul Litvinov, the grandson of Maxim Litvinov; Piotr Yakir; and a number of others. Once again, as in the days of the tsars, a number of Russian Jews are joining in the struggle for freedom and for humanizing an oppressive regime.

The 1970s, as is well known, have been marked for striking and exciting developments, in which the Soviet Jewish community has adopted increasing militancy. The whole question has come out into the open, with demonstrations both inside and outside Russia. Progress has been made at least in the question of emigration, which has been the burning issue. The situation of the Jews in the Soviet Union has come to occupy an important place in international affairs and become a bargaining point for *détente* negotiations. Here again we seem to be following the nineteenth-century tradition, when the treatment of minorities was already an important issue in international relations. But the interdependence of all these issues and problems has increased immeasurably, and so have both the danger and promise they offer.

ZIONISM AND ANTI-SEMITISM

Strictly speaking, the Arab-Israeli conflict lies outside the scope of this book, as it is essentially a territorial struggle, and I do not propose here to deal with its complexities. Historically, it is comparable to the frequent wars in ancient times between the Jews and neighbouring tribes like the Philistines, Moabites, or Amalekites.

And yet there is nothing 'chemically pure' in history, and issues tend to get entangled with one another. The stimulus that led to the foundation of the state of Israel was, very largely, anti-Semitic persecution in Europe. On the other hand, it was almost inevitable that the Arabs, in their propaganda war against Israel, should resort to any weapons within their reach.

Any account of these aspects of the conflict must begin with the fact that for centuries Arabs and Jews lived at peace in Palestine under the Ottoman sultans. Turkish rule may have been oppressive and corrupt in many ways, but it did not lead to aggressive anti-Semitism. One of the most balanced Israeli writers, Uri Avnery, fully admits this:

> The depth of bitterness and hatred throughout our Semitic region seems bottomless. Yet it is a comparatively new phenomenon, the outcome of the recent clash of our peoples. Nothing like European anti-Semitism ever existed in the Arab world prior to the events which created the vicious circle.[24]

Although Jewish communities did suffer persecution in some Muslim countries (Iran, Yemen, and even Spain under the Almohades), this was really caused by religious intolerance, and there was nothing comparable to the ingrained anti-Jewish prejudice in the West. Certainly there have been a number of anti-Jewish pronouncements in Arab literature—beginning with the Quran itself (although it also praises the Jews). But the tendency was to present them as a poor, wretched, humiliated people, all on account of their being rejected by God: 'The "humiliation and wretchedness" of the Jews were presented by the Muslims as a proof of the falsity of the Jewish faith, while the righteousness of Islam was demonstrated by its wordly success'.[25]

One may argue that this line was also frequently taken by the Christians from the very beginning with their controversies with Judaism, and in fact it goes back to the Bible itself, particularly to the curses in Deuteronomy (see Chapter 6). But the popular Christian image of the Jews as a powerful, dangerous threat, endowed with magical or secret powers, is absent among the Muslims.

When the modern conflict with the state of Israel began and rapidly increased in bitterness, Arab governments and organizations began to resort to anti-Semitic propaganda. In fact, this was very largely borrowed from the West (occasionally, as we have seen, by hiring former Nazi propagandists), and when it appeared it was officially inspired. For instance, in 1956 an Arab edition of the *Protocols of the Elders of Zion* was published in Cairo by the UAR Information Services. In 1958 Nasser said in an interview to an Indian paper:

It is very important that you should read it [the *Protocols*]. . . .
It proves beyond a doubt that three hundred Zionists, each of
whom knows all the others, govern the fate of the European continent . . . and that they elect their successors from their en-
tourage.[26]

As one can see, the phrase is not from the *Protocols*, but a repetition,
almost word for word, of Walter Rathenau's statement (see Chapter 12),
which did not refer to the Jews at all but had been presented as 'evidence'
of Jewish domination by the anti-Semites.

Arab writers also made use of the ritual murder (or 'blood libel') accusation and collected cases which had taken place in the Middle East, including the famous Damascus trial in 1840. Some went so far as to justify Nazi
crimes against the Jews, arguing that Hitler only acted in self-defence, protecting his country and Europe from the crimes and threat presented by
Jewry; or, alternatively, that Jewish propaganda had exaggerated out of
all proportion the Nazi slaughter in order to derive political advantages
from it, while other peoples had suffered much more under the Germans.
Some of the Arab press also condemned the Israelis for kidnapping Eichmann, and a Jordanian newspaper in Jerusalem sent him this message of
encouragement: 'Find consolation in the fact that this trial will one day
lead to the liquidation of the remaining six million'.[27] There were also
heated protests when the Vatican Council announced its proposal to
exonerate the Jews from collective guilt for the death of Jesus (see Chapter 5).

It is difficult to say how much all this has influenced the Arab peoples
themselves, but the Israeli writer Harkabi rightly stresses that, especially
in Egypt, anti-Semitic propaganda is officially inspired and 'can therefore
be controlled, directed and halted if the authorities so desire, especially if
it proves to lead to criticism abroad'. And he adds:

Arab anti-Semitism is the outcome of political circumstances . . .
it is not a cause of the conflict but a product of it. The Arabs
did not oppose Jewish settlement for anti-Semitic motives; their
opposition aroused anti-Semitic emotions among them.[28]

More disturbing perhaps is the Arab alliance with and support of anti-
Semitic groups in the West. This connection has been public in a few
cases, and one may quote the example of a leader of the Argentinian
Tacuara who visited Egypt as a guest of the Arab League.

People of pro-Arab sympathies who oppose Israeli claims (and these
sometimes include Jews) tend to be left wing, and so one sees quite a
different atmosphere from the recent past, when most anti-Semitic groups
were Fascist or extreme right wing. But although some of these pro-Arabs
may come dangerously near a new form of anti-Semitism, the obvious point

must be stressed that to favour the Arab case or to oppose Israeli policies has nothing to do with being anti-Jewish. Some contemporary Jewish writers, in an excess of zeal and concern, sometimes tend to see anti-Semitism (or a new form of it) where it does not really exist.

In this, as in several other aspects, Israel (and, indirectly, the Jewish communities in the world) is paying the penalty for its own success and 'respectability'. In spite of some limited Arab success in the last war, Israel is still the top dog, and popular sympathy tends to go to the underdog. It is also supported by the United States—not exactly a way of ingratiating the Israelis in many parts of the world. It has become much too easy for the cruder type of left-wing propaganda to link Zionism with American imperialism. More thoughtful Israeli writers like Uri Avnery have seen the danger of this dependence and look forward to a future—much too difficult to envisage at present—when Israel might well re-think and re-orient her position in the world.

But it is not only a question of the Jews losing sympathy in the world and 'worsening' their image. Certainly the success of Israel (and I am thinking here not so much of her military survival as of her success in human and social terms) has been a great source of inspiration and confidence, not only for Jews but also for non-Jews. For one thing, it gave the lie to the anti-Semitic claim that the whole Jewish people is an urban, parasitic excrescence no longer capable of striking roots anywhere. And yet Israel is also something new and unexpected—even for some visiting Jews who may be puzzled or repelled by things they see and feel. As Avnery says: 'Zionism created something which it never consciously intended, a new nation. And by its very success, Zionism has become obsolete'.[29]

Again, this was a triumphant demonstration of the falsity of anti-Semitic myths. It is significant that to both Hitler and Stalin (men who in their formative years hardly travelled at all and who could only speak their own national languages) the alleged cosmopolitan character of the Jews was one of their most objectionable and 'dangerous' traits. Hitler boasted that in Vienna he 'turned from a weak cosmopolitan (*Weltbürger*) into a fanatical anti-Semite'.[30] Over a century ago the anti-Semite Gougenot des Mousseaux paid (not without sarcasm) this tribute to the Jews:

> The Jew is, by his essence, the most indestructible people on earth, and therefore the best endowed . . . for *foreign missions,* which are facilitated by *his wonderful gift for speaking the languages of all nations.* Thus, from the physical and intellectual point of view, the Jew, that remarkable cosmopolitan, is . . . the most *universal,* that is the most *catholic* man one can conceive, for that is exactly the meaning of the word (*katholikos*)! [Author's italics.] [31]

Like all such generalizations, of course, that one too ignored the complexity of the matter—for instance, the existence of many provincial types of Jews. It is also absurd to claim that some groups are better at learning foreign languages than others.

Driven by anti-Semitism, the Jews—or rather, a section of them—have succeeded, after an interval of over two thousand years, in founding a national state: and with it they have been drawn into one of the bitterest and most prolonged conflicts of modern history. But the issue is even deeper and more tragic, for it meant a recrudescence of the nationalist fever. It was perhaps Isaac Deutscher who best touched the core of the problem, when he write:

> The world has compelled the Jew to embrace the nation-state and to make it his pride and hope just at a time when there is little or no hope left in it. You cannot blame the Jews for this; you must blame the world. But Jews should at least be aware of the paradox and realize that their intense enthusiasm for 'national sovereignty' is historically belated. . . . They have taken possession of it only after it has become a factor of disunity and social disintegration.[32]

And, one might add, a factor for maintaining and exacerbating all kinds of prejudices, something that is obviously happening in the course of the Arab-Israeli struggles. It is one of those conflicts that seem to be almost insoluble in the terms in which they are presented, and a living proof of what Deutscher asserts—the destructive nature of nationalism and of the nation-state in the contemporary world. For the root of the matter seems to be that certain groups of people consider themselves to be, above everything else, Israelis or Arabs, and not human beings. In the Postscript I shall have something to say about this issue, which in my view is central to the whole question of dealing with prejudices.

14

Final Reflections
on Prejudice

It is just possible that a further transformation is possible if men can come to experience themselves as 'One of Us'. If, even on the basis of the crassest self interest, we can realize that We and Them must be transcended in the totality of the human race, if we in destroying them are not to destroy us all.

As war continues, both sides come more and more to resemble each other. . . . Shall we realize that We and Them are shadows of each other? We are Them to Them as They are Them to us. When will the veil be lifted?

—R. D. Laing, *The Politics of Experience*

'THE OTHER'

'What is the cause of anti-Semitism?' When people ask this question, it is clear in most cases what they expect. They want something limited that can be pinned down, preferably something external to themselves. In a similar way, when we go to a doctor, we want to be told that the cause of our symptoms is something external that can be removed (like a germ) or some definite trouble that can be put right by some sort of medicine. We want to be reassured that there is nothing basically wrong with us, nothing that might require a drastic change of habits or way of life.

Clearly, the need for reassurance also works on the collective level, and we want to be told that our country or our group is 'all right'.

Most modern students of the problem now recognize that there is nothing like a single cause or even a number of causes of anti-Semitism. There is no simple formula that can explain it as an isolated phenomenon, such as economic resentment, religious prejudice, or even psychoanalytic interpretations like hostility to 'the bad father', and so on.

Obviously, even a superficial examination of the question shows that religious history has been an important factor. The way Christianity broke

228

with Judaism, the development of the Passion story, and the idea of the collective guilt of the Jewish people as murderers of Christ—all this was a very powerful element in the emergence and reinforcement of anti-Semitism.

But in a way this was no more than a rationalization, like the modern identification of Jews with Communists or the supposed Jewish conspiracy to dominate the world. We can understand the mechanism of projection by which Jews have been made scapegoats. But why should people need to have 'enemies' or scapegoats at all? How does it all begin?

Research has shown that, although stereotypes and prejudices are always acquired, they are inculcated very early with the first awareness of distinctions between 'We' and 'Them'.[1] For instance, here is an American Jewish schoolgirl answering questions:

> I'm Jewish. I know all about it. . . . Jews are the best people, mother says. You know I'm a Jew. . . . I'm not allowed to go [to church]. Only synagogue. Churches ain't no good. Synagogue is better. Catholics don't like Jews. Make fun of Jews. I don't care if they don't like me. . . . Jews are good and nice. . . . My teacher's a Jew [accurate].[2]

This girl's attitude was tense and defensive because she found herself the only one in a class of Italian children. This shows how in a world of mutually exclusive categories the identification with a collective entity brings some comfort and reassurance. 'Jews are good' is like saying 'My family are good', 'We are good people', 'He is OK'. On that level 'good' is what you know, what you are familiar with. In London—as in other modern towns, I suppose—it is common to see slogans such as 'Hendon Vandals OK' scribbled up by teen-age gangs.

But if my group is 'good' or 'OK', then it necessarily follows that at least some of the others are less good, or bad ('Nigger crap', 'Kill the wogs' scribbled on walls). As in the slogan chanted by the sheep in Orwell's *Animal Farm*, 'Four legs good, two legs baaad!'. If I have to 'belong' to some group and identify myself with it, then it necessarily follows that I must exclude others as strangers. If I make positive generalizations about my own group, if I say we are good, better, or best, then I must also make negative generalizations about the others.

As people grow up and enlarge their field of experience, they tend to realize that such generalizations are really emotional: for instance, they become able to evaluate their parents and the other members of their family on a more objective basis and are less tied to their needs of emotional reassurance. But do they really learn to transcend the other primary ties to ethnic group or to nation? Not in most cases, perhaps.

I am assuming here (no doubt many people will disagree) that one of the signs of mental or spiritual maturity is precisely this: to transcend all collective identification, to realize that all human groupings are in a way 'conventional', and that in the last analysis there is no such thing as a 'stranger': or, as the psychiatrist R. D. Laing puts it, 'We are Them to Them as They are Them to us'.

To the anti-Semite, on the other hand, the Jew is the 'enemy", the irreducible 'Other': irreducible because he refuses to look inside himself (and others) so as to experience the essential human unity. In that respect, the messages of all higher religions are at one. *Tat tvam asi* (Thou art that) is one of the basic precepts of the Hindu Vedanta. In a similar way, to the real Christian the neighbour is Christ, who is beyond all barriers. Any mental exclusion destroys the fundamental experience of unity.

In the Mosaic precept 'Thou shalt love thy neighbour as thyself' (Lev. 19:18 [most Christians seem to forget that in his preaching Jesus was quoting, not coining a new saying]), the Hebrew word that we translate as 'neighbour' (*re'a*) also means 'the other'. Equally significant is the commandment to treat 'the stranger [*ger*] who sojourns with you . . . as the native among you . . . you shall love him as yourself; for you were strangers [*gerim*] in the land of Egypt' (Lev. 19:34; cf. Deut. 23:7 for attitudes to Egyptians and Edomites). This implies a recognition of the famous Golden Rule, 'Do as you would be done by', and also that the concept of the stranger or the Other is essentially relative.

The inability to realize this must lead to some sort of demonology: the Other easily becomes the Devil, on whom people project everything they consider evil. Most modern political myths—and not only Hitlerism—developed some sort of demonology. In fact, 'Satan' simply means 'the enemy' (a popular name for the Devil in several languages); and to begin with, the Hebrew word, as used in the Bible, was a common noun. The concept of the Devil or Lucifer as a personalized entity only appeared later in Judaism, and was taken over by both Christianity and Islam (Arabic *Shaitan* = Satan).

The more one represses, the more barriers of fear one puts up, the more 'enemies' and 'demons' appear outside, and the most persecuted one feels. The Devil is the Other, that which I refuse to recognize. Medieval society was obsessed with Jews, witches, or heretics as 'enemies'. In the same way, modern political regimes which are based on some sort of ideological conflict need an 'enemy' as the necessary condition for their existence: they have to create the myth (which may become a reality) of a sinister plot against what they believe in—whether it is conducted by the Jews, the Communists, the Trotskyites, or 'the subversives'. Some historians tend to apply rules of common sense to situations which are not 'logical' or to create false problems like 'Why did Hitler invade Russia when it was so obviously against the interests of Germany?' The answer is that the Nazi regime was based on conflict and could exist in no other way. The rulers of modern states are, admittedly, a little saner than Hitler, but it is obvious that their actions or decisions are much of the time influenced by irrational prejudices and anxieties. As some have said, they look very often like the actions of somnambulists.

As we saw in the first part of this book, anti-Jewish feeling began with the more or less general features of hostility against 'the stranger'. The Jews were 'different', they had peculiar customs. Their religion and dietary habits represented a barrier to assimilation. Now, the wish to assimilate a minority (or the minority's wish to get assimilated) is in the last instance due to fear and anxiety. 'Who are these people in our midst? What do they want? Could it be they mean us harm?' This is probably a very basic, animal re-action, which may be compared to the habit of sniffing every strange crea-ture or the hostility shown whenever territory is trespassed upon.

This sort of tribal hostility to strangers is deeply ingrained in peoples who consider 'civilization' an integral part of their collective image, like those of Europe: it is expressed, for instance, in strong colour prejudices, which are particularly marked in northern Europe and North America, and which are often related to sexual anxieties and jealousy.[3]

We have also seen the importance of smells in anti-Semitism and other ethnic prejudices. 'These people have a bad smell' is a way of saying 'Their smell is different from ours'. Similarly, 'They have no manners' often means 'Their manners are different from ours'. Montaigne defined the bar-barian as the one who thinks that his customs are the only civilized ones. Another aspect of this barbarism or provincialism, as I shall try to show later, is to think that 'my religion is the only true one'.

The differences of smell are very largely due to differences in diet and food habits. But just as dogs sniff each other, human beings, who still live on a rather primitive level of fear and suspicion, need a series of rituals which act as mutual reassurance as to the character and intentions of one's neighbour. Things like the handshake, the exchange of greetings (the Jew-ish *shalom* or the equivalent Arabic *salaam* is a declaration of peace, show-ing that the other is not an enemy), eating or drinking together, having a 'joking' relationship, sharing in rituals and festivals—all this reduces the feelings of strangeness and reinforces solidarity. It is obvious that the ten-dency of the Jews to preserve their own rituals (which in most cases ex-cluded others) was likely to provoke or reinforce the primitive reaction of bafflement or hostility in face of the stranger. Again, the tendency to pre-serve their original language (Yiddish in Poland and Russia or other coun-tries) could only strengthen this.

On the other hand, individual Jews—and in some cases whole groups of them—have been carried away by an anxiety for assimilation and tried to wipe away any 'Jewish traits'. In not a few cases they have become anti-

Semitic or (in the days of religious intolerance) implacable persecutors of their former coreligionists. We have come across a few examples of this—Pfefferkorn in Germany and Jerome of Santa Fe and Pablo de Santa Maria in Spain—but there were many others.[4]

In modern times it is ironical that it was just in the country where anti-Semitism was to lead to the most frantic hysteria of hatred—Germany—that the Jews (or at least a section of them) made special efforts to become 'perfect Germans'. In his very perceptive book on the German-Jewish relationship, Leschnitzer shows how they, who had dropped Yiddish some time ago, regarded the Eastern European Jews with contempt:

> But there was more to it than this. Whenever an unseemly liveli-
> ness, a too eager gesticulation betrayed their own Jewish friends,
> set them somehow apart from their milieu, they were ready to
> condemn that tone and gesture as 'objectionably Jewish'.[5]

The very anxiety betrayed in this process seems to show that deep down they felt the threat of the virulent German nationalism and wanted to escape from it. But this is just one of many similar cases where the minority—as in animal camouflage—tries to identify with the majority down to the adoption of its own chauvinism.

EXCLUSION AND THE CONCEPT OF THE GUEST

Human groups vary a great deal in the degree of their suspicion or exclusion of strangers. Sometimes the name they give themselves means 'the men' or 'the true men', while the human character is (partly) denied to the outsider. The human, the 'civilized' character lies in *my* group: outside is chaos, disorder, the barbarians (somewhat like the popular Christian idea of Hell, which is 'outside' or 'down below').

Exclusion is seen to operate in the Bible from its earliest myths, in the pairs of opposites: Cain and Abel, Ham and Shem, Esau and Jacob, or even Saul and David. There is always one who is accepted and one who is rejected (the story of Joseph breaks this pattern somewhat, as it ends with a reconciliation; hence its deeper and more satisfactory character). Exclusion or rejection was to find its full expression in the Christian idea of 'the true people of Israel' (*Verus Israel*): the 'insiders' (the Jews) were now to be rejected, while the 'outsiders' (the Gentiles) became accepted.

In the parables of Jesus, which in fact inspired this conception, the wicked are excluded from the Messianic banquet in the vision of 'the last things'. There would be an ultimate separation between the just and the sinners, the sheep and the goats. Or take the practice of excommunication —derived, as we have seen, from the synagogue—which is an exclusion from 'eating together'.

The Hebrews themselves were aware of the Egyptian feeling of superiority towards all foreigners—a feeling they may have inherited (see, for instance, Gen. 43:32). 'Gentile' (*goy*) is a term of exclusion, as *barbaros* was with the Greeks (probably meaning originally 'babblers', 'people who cannot speak properly', i.e., those who don't speak Greek). Even the more tolerant Hindus applied the term *mleccha* to outsiders (non-Aryan, or barbarian).

The unfamiliar often looks confused and shapeless at first (and therefore frightening) to those who are more anxious and less secure. As John Dewey wrote:

> Foreign languages that we do not understand always seem jibberings, babblings, in which it is impossible to fix a definite, clear-cut, individualized group of sounds. All strangers of another race proverbially look alike to the visiting stranger.[6]

The tendency to exclude may become stronger, paradoxically, when reinforced by a religion which transcends narrow ethnic loyalties. In all three 'Semitic' religions (Judaism, Christianity, and Islam) the outsiders, or 'infidels', are in a way outside the pale: they can only be considered properly 'human' if they enter the fold. During the heyday of Christian unity the statement 'I am a Christian' tended to mean 'I am a human being'. English dictionaries (Oxford, Webster) give as current meanings for Christian 'a human being', 'a decent, respectable person', i.e., somebody who dressed and behaves in an acceptable way (one remembers Hanisch's comment about Hitler's appearance in Vienna).

Talking about the well-known British ethnocentrism, the Hungarian humorist George Mikes writes: 'The verb *to naturalise* clearly proves what the British think of you. Before you are admitted to British citizenship you are not even considered a natural human being'.[7]

The counterpart to the exclusion of strangers has been the great tradition of hospitality. Significantly, it has tended to assume a sacred, religious character. The stranger who is received in somebody's home is invested with a special protection. The Greeks, for instance, talked about Zeus Xenios (Zeus protector of guests), and in the Bible 'the stranger in your midst', the *ger*—a word which, as we have seen, came to be used in the sense of proselyte—is sometimes enrolled with 'orphans and widows' as worthy of special protection.

Equally significant is the old folk theme, which assumes many variations, that the foreigner who appears poor and unprotected is a divinity in disguise (or an angel from the Lord), or again 'the beggar prince', as in the *Odyssey*. This might be considered, perhaps, an intimation of the Christian (and Buddhist) ideal of human fraternity. In the Gospels Jesus identifies himself with all outsiders and pariah groups (publicans, prostitutes,

Samaritans, lepers), as in this famous passage: 'I was a stranger and you welcomed me, I was naked and you clothed me, I was sick and you visited me, I was in prison and you came to me' (Matt. 25:35–36).

Centuries before modern depth psychology, as I have already pointed out, Jesus had a full understanding of the mechanism of projection, and his famous simile of the mote and beam has been used in psychological phraseology. He knew very well the motives that lay behind those fingers pointing at the Samaritans, the publicans, or the adulteresses, and the craving to judge and condemn or to be 'holier than thou'.

In every high religion all primary ties and identifications are abandoned and transcended, and the native land becomes as strange a place as any other. To the religious soul the only true home is the world of the spirit (the paradise that is lost and found again). Apocryphal sayings attributed to Jesus exhort the Christian to be like a pilgrim or a wanderer (a theme that has been repeated, with many variations, in Christian works of devotion): 'Life is a bridge, do not build houses on it'. That remarkable anonymous writing, the *Epistle to Diognetus*, describes the way of life of the early Christians:

> They live in their native countries, but like aliens. . . . Every foreign land is a country to them, and every native country a foreign land. . . . They live on earth, but are citizens of heaven. . . . The Jews make war on them as on foreigners, the Greeks persecute them.[8]

This deep feeling of alienation was part of Christian spiritual dynamics at the time, but gradually faded when the Church became the established religion of the empire. Christianity was bound to transcend all tribal and national loyalties, and follow Paul's splendid proclamation, which I have already quoted: 'There is neither Jew nor Greek, there is neither slave nor free, there is neither male nor female; for you are all one in Christ Jesus' (Gal. 3:28).

The early Christians—often recruited from 'outsiders' or marginal groups—came to the new faith through a deep experience of conversion, which was regarded as a new birth and a radical change of mind and life. The situation changed when many people came to accept Christianity as the 'regular thing', as the faith of their parents and their native countries. This was in many ways a different religion (in fact, a betrayal or distortion of original Christianity), and it was inevitable that it should take over the old ethnic loyalties, the old prejudices and exclusions. In the end the word 'Christian' became yet another label which divided people and put up barriers.

But the Jews themselves, who for many centuries lived as 'outsiders' or minorities in many parts of the world, also had a deep experience of alienation. For instance, what Leo Pinsker said about the Jew at the end of the last century may well be compared to the passage from the *Epistle to Diognetus* quoted above:

> He is, in very truth, the stranger *par excellence*. For the living, the Jew is a dead man, for the natives an alien and a vagrant, for property-holders a beggar, for the poor an exploiter and a millionaire, for the patriot a man without a country, for all classes a hated rival.[9]

THE RIGHT NOT TO BELONG

But what about those human beings, of whatever origin, who no longer want to play this old, dreary game of 'we' and 'them'? Both the anti-Semite and the more narrow-minded or ethnocentric Jew are alike in one thing: they tend to regard 'the Jews' as a monolithic community whose members are always (or should be) unswervingly loyal. This has never been so in the past (you have only to skim the Bible to realize it), and it is not so now.

The 'international' or cosmopolitan Jew—the type most feared and abhorred by modern anti-Semites—is often the one who breaks with Jewish traditions altogether, who rebels against them in order to develop more freely. His experience of 'alienation'—of 'not belonging' anywhere—makes him transcend all categories, all the straitjackets in which both Gentiles and Jews want to imprison him. This 'non-Jewish Jew', as Isaac Deutscher called him, is often a true world citizen. He does not give up loyalty to Judaism in order to become 'a good German' (as in the case so well observed by Leschnitzer) or 'a good American'. His motive is not fear or craving for security, but a deep aspiration for freedom and human universality.

In their understandable concern with the 'freedom to be a Jew' and to practise Judaism, some Jews tend to forget or overlook an equally precious freedom: the freedom to stop being a Jew, which is as important as the freedom to give up any nationality, religion, or loyalty in the world. That freedom is not exactly denied but obstructed by the blind—one might say blasphemous—assumption that every Jew is or should be proud of his Jewishness, that every American is or should be in love with America, that every Englishman should think that 'British is best', and so on: and if they are not, then there is something very wrong, peculiar, or disloyal about them all.

For instance, it is not rare to find in books written by Jewish authors commendation of a prominent personality for having 'remained faithful to his Jewish origins' or an implied condemnation of somebody who on the contrary 'estranged' himself from his people. It is also well known that a number of Jews in Western countries only keep up with certain observances (such as closing a shop on the Sabbath) for fear of being criticized or ostracized by their Jewish neighbours. And naturally there is the chronic anxiety in many Jewish families that one of the children may marry a Gentile.[10] These are just a few examples of the well-known pressure to conform to the norms of a group.

As one would expect, whenever Judaism or Jews have been persecuted, Jewish solidarity tends to increase, while long periods of tolerance may lead to a loosening of bonds and in some countries to assimilation. Anti-Semites are always complaining of Jewish 'clannishness' (they have been doing so since Tacitus); they do not seem to realize that their activities are the best way to reinforce that clannishness.

I have already quoted (in Chapter 4) Bernard Lazare's observation that 'the anti-Semites do the work of philo-Semites'. He also wrote:

> The ethnologic prejudice is universal, and even those who suffer from it are its most tenacious upholders. Anti-Semites and philo-Semites join hands to defend the same doctrine, they part company only when it comes to award the supremacy.[11]

Lazare also pointed out the typical contradiction of anti-Semitic nationalists: they blamed the Jews for not assimilating and at the same time did their best to prevent their assimilation in the future.

ANTI-SEMITISM AND MODERN PSYCHOLOGY

Lazare's book *L'Antisémitisme, son histoire et ses causes* (first published in 1894), which tends to be somewhat ignored nowadays, was in fact the first serious, thorough study of the subject. Writing before the two world wars (he died in 1903 after joining the Zionist movement), Lazare shows little or no awareness of the deeper psychological mechanisms involved: I doubt whether the word 'scapegoat' is ever mentioned in his book. But he applied scholarly research to the subject, and many of his observations —particularly on nationalism and cosmopolitanism—remain valid and important. In any case, his attempt to face the problem from a wider and more detached point of view represented a marked progress compared to that of Leo Pinsker, who dismissed anti-Semitism in despair as a hereditary, incurable 'psychic aberration'.[12]

As one would expect, more intensive research on anti-Semitism and prejudices in general came only after World War II, mainly prompted by the Nazi holocaust. Studies of prejudiced individuals, often inspired by psychoanalytic ideas, led to the now classic concept of Adorno's 'authoritarian personality', which, in spite of criticism from some sectors, remains a valid and fruitful one. One of the earliest studies was that carried out among stdents of the University of California (76 women and 24 men) by Frenkel-Brunswik and Sanford.[13] The differences between the more and less prejudiced groups were striking:

> The girls who were high in anti-Semitism were, on the average, well groomed, of higher than average income, greatly interested in social standing, conservative, from socially mobile families, ethnocentric. All of them said they liked their parents and subscribed to statements that indicate obedience to authority. The girls low in anti-Semitism were more nondescript in appearance, less at ease socially, more willing to talk about themselves and to make critical appraisals of their parents.[14]

The study concluded that those with anti-Semitic trends tend to be conformists and show a great deal of 'social anxiety' at the appearance of any social deviation. They have little insight into themselves and tend to project undesired traits onto other people.

The two California research workers joined Adorno and Levinson in writing *The Authoritarian Personality*. The most important result of this basic study is that people who tend to be prejudiced are not just anti-Semites or anti-Negro: they reveal a whole series of corresponding attitudes in the family, at work, in human relations in general, and in fact in all their attitudes to religion, politics, and so on. Prejudiced people tend to be hierarchical, authoritarian, and exploitive, and their whole orientation in life 'may well culminate in a political philosophy and social outlook which has no room for anything but a desperate clinging to what appears to be strong and a disdainful rejection of whatever is relegated to the bottom'.[15]

Most revealing is the correlation observed between high scores on prejudice and tendencies like 'rigidity of outlook (inaccessibility to new experience), intolerance of ambiguity (they want to know the answers), pseudo-scientific or antiscientific attitudes, suggestibility and credulity'. The more tolerant, on the other hand, 'show more flexibility of judgement, greater tolerance of ambiguity, a more scientific-naturalistic explanation of events, and greater autonomy and reliance'.[16]

A striking confirmation of the importance of the personality factor was provided by Hartley. He asked a group of university students to mark their reactions to no less than thirty-five racial, national, religious, and economic groups. The scale used included five intermediate steps between the two extremes of acceptance ('Would you marry one of them?') and rejection ('Would you exclude them from the country?'). Among the thirty-five there were three imaginary groups—Danireans, Pireneans, and Wallonians—and yet he found (in confirmation of his hypothesis) that the more prejudiced individuals also tended to object to these groups while the less prejudiced were also tolerant towards them.[17]

Ackerman and Jahoda studied the connection between anti-Semitism and a more limited group—emotionally disturbed patients under intensive psychoanalysis. Although the sample was small, their findings were more or less in line with those of the previous research workers: they found 'an exaggerated surface conformity beneath which lurks a primitive, untamed hostility'.[18]

Studying a working-class district in East London, James Robb found evidence of the usual anti-Jewish stereotypes: Jews 'are clannish', have too much money, or are Communists ('90 percent Communists are Jews', said one man).[19] There was also a tendency grossly to overestimate their numbers, and one worker even said there were five million Jews in Britain (the accurate figure is around 410,000).

As to personality, Robb found that the anti-Semitic workers were more pessimistic about the future and anxious about themselves; several of them were obsessed with an idea of general deterioration. They tended to have few relationships outside the family circle and on the whole gave an impression of 'narrow, constricted, poorly organized personalities', often with paranoid traits. By contrast, the tolerant types were more optimistic, had a wider social life, and tended to make much less use of stereotypes in their general comments. Robb also found that 'tolerant people are much more critical of their parents than anti-Semites'.[20]

The history of anti-Semitism provides a great deal of confirmation of such studies. We have seen that many leading anti-Semites were also strongly prejudiced against other human groups and showed obvious signs of ill-balanced, disturbed personalities. Martin Luther, H. S. Chamberlain, Hitler, and several of his associates were in many ways good examples of the authoritarian personality.[21] The superstition of several Nazi leaders—particularly the belief in astrology—also finds a parallel in some of the research work we have just mentioned. And we have seen the marked pessimism of propagandists like Wilhelm Marr.

But this is also true in a more general way, where we have little or no knowledge of the personalities involved. For instance, Poliakov stresses that in medieval and early modern Europe witch-hunters were also Jew-hunters,[22] and we all know that witch-hunting has continued, only with different targets. It has also been claimed that in 'true' witch-hunting (in both European and African communities) there has been an important element of anti-feminine aggression.[23] So what is now termed a 'male chauvinist' tends to be a chauvinist in other ways, as shown, for instance, by the strong anti-feminist trend in German anti-Semitism (and in Fascism in general), both in its first wave in the Second Reich and under National Socialism.[24]

One of the best examples of this connection is the case of Otto Weininger, an Austrian Jew who became an anti-Semite and published his extravagant *Geschlecht und Charakter* (Sex and Character) in 1903. He committed suicide shortly after at the age of twenty-three. His book is obsessed with the male-female polarity, which overspills into his racialist ideas. Here is a typical quotation:

> The true conception of the State is foreign to the Jew, because he, like the Woman, is wanting in personality. . . . As there is no real dignity in women, so what is meant by the word 'gentleman' does not exist among the Jews.[25]

This obviously unhappy man shows once again the relation between emotional disturbance and prejudice. And yet there is the obvious fact—which writers like Ackerman and Jahoda fully admit—that many disturbed or frustrated people are not strongly prejudiced and many anti-Semites are not particularly disturbed or obviously neurotic. Prejudice is a complex phenomenon and cannot be tackled just from a psychological or psychoanalytic point of view. In their recent analysis Simpson and Yinger have distinguished four approaches or levels of explanation, which may be accepted as a useful framework for a 'theory of prejudice'.

The first level corresponds to the question we have already dealt with: What kinds of people tend to be prejudiced and what psychological needs do prejudices tend to 'satisfy'?

The second level lies in the structure of society, in economic and political conditions, and particularly in its 'power arrangements'. To what extent is prejudice against minorities being used to preserve the existing power structures? Simpson and Yinger write:

> Such use of prejudice is seldom rational and conscious; it is hidden, as we shall see, by many protective beliefs. . . . It is easy to say that prejudice is nothing but a way of getting an economic advantage, that it is forced on the great majority by the propaganda of a small ruling group who profit mightily from it. The exaggerations of the proponents of such a view, however, must not blind us to the accumulated evidence that prejudice *is* an economic and political weapon.[26]

This is quite clear from the study of European anti-Semitism in the nineteenth and twentieth centuries, when it was often used by the ruling classes and by the political right in general to fight or discredit movements or parties of liberal, radical, or socialist character. This could be done openly or in more subtle and hidden ways.

So prejudice against a minority, which by itself is a symptom of closed minds, is often used to keep a certain society closed or to prevent it from opening itself. This has been closely bound up with the development or failure of democratic institutions, as the example of Germany eloquently shows. In the 1848 revolution the democratic forces were defeated both in Germany (where a number of Jews among the revolutionaries were killed) and in the Austrian Empire, while in France, Britain, and other European countries democracy was making intermittent if slow progress. German nationalism, which came comparatively late, assumed a virulently racialist form, and the democratic forces were never strong enough to counterbalance it.[27] In Russia democracy had even less of a chance, and that is why a form of anti-Semitism is still being used to help keep the Soviet society a closed one.

Naturally, extreme situations of crisis are also an important factor in unleashing more aggressive forms of prejudice, as witnessed by the pogroms of the Black Death in medieval Europe, those of tsarist Russia from 1903 onwards (bad economic conditions, war, revolution, and the deliberate use of anti-Jewish hatred as a safety valve of popular resentment), or again the wave of anti-Semitism that followed the 1929 depression.

The third approach or level of explanation is the cultural inheritance of a group, which obviously includes all sort of attitudes and stereotypes. The importance of this factor is obvious in the case of anti-Semitism; we have seen throughout this book the continuity of the anti-Jewish tradition from Hellenistic and Roman times to the Christian era and then to modern anti-Semitism. Throughout this long period many people were using anti-Jewish hatred to 'satisfy' certain psychological needs, and powerful ruling groups were also using anti-Semitism as a weapon. But all this was greatly facilitated by the fact that the Jews were a traditional target and that Christianity emerged and developed in militant conflict with Judaism.

Finally, there is the fourth factor: the minority itself which is the target of prejudice. To the anti-Semite, of course, the Jews and their character are the only cause, while we might almost say, with Sartre, that anti-Semitism causes the Jews, in the sense that it has certainly strengthened Jewish solidarity. Just as in the past relentless Christian persecution of the Jews reinforced anti-Christian and anti-Gentile feelings among the Jews, modern anti-Semitism gave rise to Zionism. Zionism in its turn produced Arab aggression, and to fight Arab aggression Israel had to become 'Sparta in the Levant' (Barnet Litvinoff). Now Israelis and Arabs are locked in the vicious circle of mutual aggression and hatred, and the Arabs do their best to stir anti-Semitism in the rest of the world. So the chain of mutual exclusions, prejudices, and hatred goes on in an apparently unending spiral.

PRIDE AND PREJUDICE AS DRUGS

The destructive and explosive effects of prejudice in social life should now be obvious to most people. Its effect on the prejudiced person may not be so blatant and yet is clear enough.

In their study of anti-Semitic patients, Ackerman and Jahoda pointed out that prejudice seems to fulfil a need and to give them some sort of satisfaction, but it does not solve any of their problems. In fact, the craving to criticize and condemn others, to attack them verbally or physically, or just to feel superior to them and hold them in contempt seems to act very much as a psychological drug: it requires repeated and often higher doses because it leads to no lasting satisfaction. National pride (or any form of collective or individual pride) can be highly intoxicating—as abundantly shown not only by Germany in the Nazi era but also at the height of European jingoism before World War I.

For both the individual and the community, prejudices and stereotypes have another important negative effect which is often overlooked: they block or discourage genuine interest in all sorts of human groups, and therefore act as inhibitors of growth and development. They are like a black shutter over a window. In fact, this could be compared to the way a drug or a poison acts in a living organism: by combining with certain basic substances it blocks certain essential metabolic reactions.

GOING BEYOND LABELS

Prejudices as we know them are just one very obvious form of 'thinking with labels': and this is the result of a defective method of education which tends to leave people at this very immature stage of development. As I said in the beginning, the way to fight anti-Semitism (or any other similar prejudice) is not to try and replace 'bad labels' with good ones: it is not to persuade people (and particularly the young) that 'Jews are OK' or 'Black is beautiful'. It is essentially to stimulate people to reach a stage of understanding where labels are simply dropped because they are no longer required: in fact, labels or stereotypes are merely a substitute for real inquiry and real understanding. As Nietzsche said, 'Every word is a prejudice'.

I meet a girl in London and she says, 'Oh, you come from Brazil—is it a nice country?' Of course, I know this is just the sort of conversational gambit that people are always coming up with for lack of something more substantial. She knows next to nothing about Brazil, and her question (which is not a real question) does not express genuine curiosity. I know I would be a pedant if I said, 'Please rephrase your question. The statements "Brazil is a nice country" and "Brazil is not a nice country" are so vague as to be utterly meaningless: as meaningless on that level as "Dick is a good boy" or "My mother smells nice—I like her". These are all signs of emotional approval, or reassurance'. One goes back to the Jewish schoolgirl saying, 'Jews are the best people, mother says. . . . Jews are good and nice'.

When you observe people (including yourself) 'thinking' in terms of labels, it is very revealing to see their minds busily cataloguing and card-indexing a person in terms of social status, profession, nationality, race, income, educational level, and so on. But of course this does not only happen when meeting strangers. Most of us tend to apply labels to our friends, to our relatives, and, what is more, to ourselves. Statements like 'My wife is very emotional' or 'I am lazy' may express an awareness of something real, but they may also be a blockage to real understanding and therefore very similar to ethnic or racial prejudices. There are many people who imprison themselves and others inside these labels. The classic case of the young man who accepts his parents' estimate of himself as a 'failure' (and therefore usually fails at what he tries) is comparable to that of the Jew—rare nowadays—who (at least emotionally) accepts the 'truth' of anti-Semitism and therefore rejects all that seems 'Jewish' in himself.

The label is a mark of either acceptance or rejection: either the medal for bravery or the Jewish Yellow Star, the sanbenito of the Inquisition, the dunce's cap for the 'stupid' boy, the scarlet letter for the adulteress. To be puffed up with pride or to be overcome with shame—both are emotional blocks to real understanding.

It is a well-known fact that the people who 'succeed' (in a real sense) as doctors, nurses, social workers, administrators, and so on, are those who are quietly receptive, who have the patience and calm to avoid hasty judgements and deepen their understanding. This is what a Buddhist monk writes about cultivating what he calls 'bare attention' for knowing and shaping the mind:

> Owing to a rash or habitual *limiting, labelling,* misjudging and mishandling of things, important sources of knowledge often remain closed. Western humanity, in particular, will have to learn from the East to keep the mind longer and more frequently in a receptive, but keenly observing, state—a mental attitude which is cultivated by the scientist and the research worker, but should increasingly become common property.[28]

It is hardly necessary to point out that strongly prejudiced people betray at every moment the lack of this ability, in the rash, disturbed, and over-hasty way in which their minds work. The crude mistakes and confusions of fact (apart from outright lies and dishonesty) constantly made in anti-Semitic and anti-Negro propaganda are an obvious example of that.

Postscript
Towards the End of Babel?

'This is Britannus, my secretary. . . . He is a barbarian, and thinks
that the customs of his tribe and island are the laws of nature'.
—Bernard Shaw, *Caesar and Cleopatra*

We are now become so much Englishmen, Frenchmen, Dutch-
men . . . that we are no longer citizens of the world. . . . An ex-
emption from prejudice . . . ought to be regarded as the character-
istical mark of a gentleman; for let a man's birth be ever so high, yet
if he is not free from national and other prejudices, I should make
bold to tell him, that he had a low and vulgar mind. . . . And in
fact, you will always find that those are most apt to boast of national
merit, who have little or no merit of their own to depend on.
—Oliver Goldsmith, *The Citizen of the World*

THE AGE OF BABEL

Babel (in Hebrew 'the gate of God') means the same as Babylon which became a symbol and a byword for all that is worst in human cities. The
Book of Genesis gave Babel another meaning which we have generally
accepted:

> And the Lord said: 'Behold, they are one people, and they have
> all one language; and this is only the beginning of what they
> will do. . . . Come, let us go down, and there confuse their
> language, that they may not understand one another's speech'
> (Gen. 11:6–7).

The myth of Babel, like that of the lost paradise, seems to testify to a
dim but very deep conviction: that in a very remote beginning (or perhaps
on a different level, beyond time and space) human beings 'had been' in
some way in closer touch with the divine power and also closer to one
another.

Myths are not history, but in these days we are becoming less arrogant than our rationalist grandparents and beginning to realize that there may be some truth and wisdom in many ancient myths.

As far back as human history can reach, we have lived in the age of Babel, which is also the age of violence (Gen. 6:11). Babel, of course, means not just diversity of language but lack of real communication and understanding, which, we are also beginning to realize, is the 'normal' condition among human beings. However destructive and frustrating this condition might be, it was bearable as long as human communities were reasonably remote and only loosely interconnected. We could say that mankind was still in the period of 'scattering' that Genesis mentions (11:9) and people could get away from one another.

This period, however—long by historical standards but very short in terms of biological evolution—has now come to an end. (Curiously enough, just as the first book of the Christian Bible announces the beginning of Babel, the last, the Apocalypse, proclaims: 'Fallen, fallen is Babylon the great!' [Rev. 18:2].) We live in one interdependent world, a world which, in the expression of Teilhard de Chardin, *'s'enroule'* or *'se replie sur soi même'* (rolls up or folds in upon itself).[1] We are now being more and more implacably forced to 'get on' with one another. All the human problems, all the results of ramshackle or faulty social structures, are coming to a head and giving rise to almost unbearable strains. And yet people who refuse to see the 'signs of the times', or are too frightened even to think of them, still cling to old ideas of stability and still hope that somehow mankind will muddle through with the Neolithic patterns of old Babel.

The more perceptive are fully aware of this paradox, one of the many that stand out in the present situation: the technical means of communication have never been so advanced, and yet in terms of human understanding—even of language—we are shockingly primitive and underdeveloped. Some modern art—through the theatre, television, the cinema, or the novel—reflects this painful discovery that we are strangers to one another and to ourselves.

The very obsession with violence, morbid as it may be, is itself part of this process of awakening. The question whether or not violence is on the increase is not really essential to the issue. In the past, periods of marked lawlessness tended to be interpreted as 'an age of troubles' that was somehow inevitable. Now people seem to be facing much more deeply the central problem and asking, 'Why violence at all?' In the period of human 'scattering' aggression was not so important because its repercussions were limited, while now they involve the whole human mass. To make a crude comparison: three thousand years ago a war between the Philistines and the Israelites was a limited affair in Palestine, which would hardly affect countries like Greece or Italy, let alone India or China. Now the Israeli-Arab conflict might at any moment precipitate a world war, and the consequences it has already produced are obvious to everyone.

The term 'genocide' may be new, but the phenomenon is not. Conquering peoples like the Assyrians and Mongols practised ruthless slaughter of human groups, and the Europeans, in their predatory age, exterminated whole peoples like the Caribbeans and Tasmanians. But the fact that in the twentieth century six million Jews were killed by the German Nazis because they were Jews marked our age with a new, burning consciousness of the problem.

The development of modern psychology and social psychology has been stimulated by all this. For the first time prejudice and human aggression have become subjects of scientific research. Meanwhile, there has been a growing interest in methods for shaping and integrating the human mind, for people are beginning to understand that Babel, like the Kingdom of God, is within us (as well as outside) and that we must conquer it there, It has been a sobering lesson for Western pride to discover that in India and the Buddhist countries some people have for centuries been practising certain methods of spiritual development from which we have much to learn. More than that: this kind of cross-fertilization has already begun to overthrow age-old barriers of religious prejudice, and nobody can predict the spiritual revival or synthesis that may well be on the way

In short, we can no longer live with Babel, because it means either destruction or a new age of darkness. Nevertheless, it is clear that we (or most of us) will resist change to the utmost—both inner and social change. And we have seen that prejudice is both the cause and the weapon of this resistance. We have seen, for instance, that the opening up of society and of human minds was regarded by those who dreaded change as the action of dark, sinister forces: and this found expression in the myth of world domination by secret societies which were often said to be masterminded by Jews.

THE FIGHT AGAINST PREJUDICE

A great deal of valuable work has been done on methods for reducing prejudice, and I do not propose to deal with it here in detail.[2] Anti-racialist legislation, manipulation of concrete situations, work of enlightenment in schools, analysis of schoolbooks in history and religious education—all this has been tried with useful results.

And yet it all looks a bit like patchwork, like striking at the heads of a Hydra that keeps sprouting new ones. Cannot the fight against prejudice be turned into something more radical, into a new, positive way of looking at and thinking about human relations? Martin Luther King realized this towards the end of his life when he said:

For years I laboured with the idea of reforming the existing institutions of society, a little change here, a little change there.
Now I feel quite differently. I think you've got to have a reconstruction of the entire society, a revolution of values.[3]

Whoever is distressed or shocked by racial discrimination or violence
and does something about it, however limited, is implicitly agreeing that
human life has a meaning, that history has a meaning (a notion that professional historians have been studiously ignoring as if it were some sort
of pornography). But history can only have a meaning if we accept it as a
creative process in which the old prophetic tradition has its place and the
great visions and dreams of mankind are once again accepted as something
deeply important and not as irrelevant hallucinations.

Immediately after World War II and in later years there was a lot of
talk about 'educating for world citizenship', and no doubt UNESCO (long
before it came to be used, as apparently it is now, in a campaign against
Israel) carried out much useful and inspiring work. Meanwhile, both old
and new countries have (with some honourable exceptions) been busily
educating not for world citizenship but for the old Babel. Israel was
founded by highly educated, cosmopolitan Jews, and yet this is what Uri
Avnery writes about the teaching of history in Israel today:

The victory of Islam, the Crusades, the Mongol invasion . . . all
these, with the ruins and edifices they left behind, seemed irrelevant, even illegal, interruptions in the history of Eretz-Israel,
the land of Israel. History, as taught today in Israeli schools, has
very little to do with all these happenings. It follows the history
of the Jews as seen through Zionist eyes, leaving Palestine with
the destruction of the Temple and returning with the first aliyah.[4]

Perhaps this was to be expected after the Nazi holocaust and the Arab
attacks. But it helps neither Israel nor the world.

Israelis will doubtless argue that they are not teaching their children to
hate the Arabs as no doubt the Arabs have been teaching theirs to hate the
Jews. But if our aim is to do away with prejudice, it is naïve and short-
sighted to think that it is enough to abstain from spreading negative
ideas about other peoples. To perpetuate Babel you do not have actively
to hate: it is enough (and in some ways more effective) to ignore and to
exclude.

In fact, by teaching history 'as seen through Zionist eyes', the Israelis
are no more than following what Western nations have been doing for
some time—and no doubt being imitated by the newly independent Asian
and African countries. In Britain history still means by and large British

and imperial history, as in America it is mainly American history, and so on.

Official religious education—in so far as it still takes place—is perhaps even more one-sided and provincial. If many people still think that theirs is the only 'true' religion (or, at any rate, the best), then it is even easier to exclude all the others: this is greatly facilitated by the fact that many of the people in charge of this sort of education seem to have little curiosity, or none at all, about the fascinating phenomenon of human religion.

It is true that many efforts are being made to correct this appalling ignorance and to give people a less one-sided picture. I could mention, for instance, some excellent religious programmes shown on British television, which are inspired by a truly ecumenical spirit. Incidentally, they may help to fight prejudice by enlightening people about the religious practices of Indian and Pakistani immigrants.

And yet Christian education, which still helps to spread anti-Jewish prejudices, can go on in the blissful ignorance that Hindu and Buddhist hermits and monks long antedated St. Anthony of Egypt or St. Benedict. It is also easy, in teaching Judaism, to either ignoring Jesus Christ or treat Christianity as an irrelevance, although some recent books written by rabbis have markedly improved in this respect. Islam used to be better placed in this respect, as the Quran paid reverence both to Moses and to 'Isa ben Mariam' (Jesus the son of Mary), but now, as one would expect, many Muslims have been busy turning anti-Zionism into a holy war. We also know the glaring distortions and omissions of education in most Communist countries and in countries committed to anti-Communism.

PROVINCIALISM AND WORLD CITIZENSHIP

The principle of exclusion or omission, I repeat, is as important, if not more so, than active dislike or hatred. In terms of education and life it means barring or discouraging curiosity, shutting out avenues of inquiry and enrichment of life. As we saw in the last chapter, the prejudiced personality is often an impoverished, restricted one in terms of cultural, social, and emotional development.

By and large—although no doubt there have been striking improvements —people are still given a very restricted, provincial view of the world they live in. I stress the importance of history not only because my training and approach are historical but also because of its obvious importance for the whole question of national and racial prejudice.

In the Introduction I quoted Father Flannery as saying that 'the pages Jews have memorized have been torn from our histories of the Christian era'. But this is in fact a very general phenomenon: people are given mostly isolated and one-sided scraps, and this is greatly helped by the frantic specialization that has been plaguing historical studies (as, indeed, all science and education).

Léon Poliakov chose the following quotation from James Baldwin as the motto of the third volume of his *Histoire de l'antisémitisme:*

> What happened to the Negro in this country is not simply a matter of *my* memory or *my* history: it is a matter of *American* history and *American* memory. As a Negro, I cannot ignore or deny or overlook it, but the white American necessity is precisely to ignore, deny and overlook it. Now what I would like to see happen in some way is *a fusion between what I remember and what you remember.*[5]

One might well ask how many schools in Europe, America, or even Asia give children any account of Negro Africa (which was absurdly supposed not to have any history) and of African slavery. But the fusion Baldwin envisages has to be enlarged so as to comprise the whole world. People laughed when the Nazis proclaimed 'an Aryan physics' purged of Einstein's relativity or when Lysenko invented 'a Soviet biology' independent of Mendelian genetics. But is a history from a European, American, Zionist, or Arab point of view any less absurd?

If you believe in fighting prejudice, then I think you have to accept that 'education for world citizenship' is a practical proposition and not just an empty slogan: in fact, the *only* practical proposition, for the alternative, it seems to me, is an increasingly destructive and alienating Babel.

To be or to become a world citizen (which is in fact the original Greek meaning of the now emasculated term 'cosmopolitan', so hated by the anti-Semites) is not to accept a vague, pious concept of human fraternity. It means to transcend all national, ethnic, divisive labels and to give one's loyalty to the only thing that has not become too narrow: to mankind as a whole, whether seen in religious or purely humanist terms.

Barely stated like that, it may appear to many as something terribly remote or utopian. And yet it has a very practical application which is already being carried out by many people, even if they are not necessarily thinking in terms of world citizenship.

This application can be effected both in the study of human culture and in the understanding of human beings, and in both cases national and racial labels can be transcended.

For instance, instead of the provincial scraps with which most people are being fed now, they can be told the real history of mankind, which is an infinitely more dramatic and exciting story not only of conflict and division but of endless blendings and combinations of different traditions. Instead of the childish and dreary game of staking claims and counter-claims to this or that invention for one's own ethnic group, students can practise the more mature exercise illustrated by Ralph Linton in his classic *The Study of Man*. He began by saying: 'There is probably no culture today which owes more than 10 per cent of its total elements to inventions made by members of its own society.[6]

Then Linton proceeded briefly to trace the probable source of every habit or product used by an average American citizen from the moment of getting up to that of going to bed:

> When our friend has finished eating he settles back to smoke, an American Indian habit, consuming a plant domesticated in Brazil in either a pipe, derived from the Indians of Virginia, or a cigarette, derived from Mexico. . . . While smoking he reads the news of the day, imprinted in characters by the ancient Semites upon a material invented in China by a process invented in Germany. As he absorbs the accounts of foreign troubles he will, if he is a good conservative citizen, thank a Hebrew deity in an Indo-European language that he is 100 per cent American.[7]

Such exercises are useful in cultivating attitudes of non-identification and critical inquiry towards the habits of one's own social group, making them appear in their proper perspective of non-permanence and change-ability. In a similar way, anthropological studies are no longer conducted on the barbaric assumption of Western supremacy that Bernard Shaw attributes to Britannus in *Caesar and Cleopatra*. For instance, an anthropologist like Margaret Mead was able, with some objectivity, to compare dating among American teen-agers with courtship habits among Pacific islanders.

WORLD CITIZENSHIP IN RELIGION

Linton's mention of the 'Hebrew deity' shows that a similar method can be applied to religious education and to fostering new attitudes to religion. Just as there is no 'pure race' or 'pure culture', so there is no such thing as an entirely original religion, and they have all been influenced by each other and by cults now extinct. Christianity came out of Judaism, just as Buddhism was an offshoot of Hinduism. But the development of Judaism itself cannot be understood out of its Oriental context. Jesus can be looked upon as a great Jewish rabbi and prophet, just as Buddha was a great Indian yogi (and both are revered by many Hindus as divine incarnations). And yet this does not destroy the originality of either.

It is now the fashion among Jewish scholars to try to show that after all there was not such a great difference between the teaching of Jesus and that of the early Talmudists and that Jesus was very much a devout

Jew of his own time. Certainly Jesus was a Jew (in both religious and ethnic terms), just as Buddha was an Indian, Plato a Greek, and Beethoven a German. But no real understanding of people—let alone of gigantic figures who utterly transcend these categories—can be achieved by just labelling them. You cannot get away from the fact that Jesus produced a tremendous religious revolution because he was something more than a Jew of his time, because he was not just a Gamaliel or a John the Baptist.

To label individuals (whether 'ordinary' people or geniuses) is really to cut them down to size, to try and get away from the wonder and mystery of their individuality, which puzzles and even frightens us because we can pin it down. In fact, it is a form of blasphemy: as Bernard Shaw put it, the 'violation of that sacred aura which surrounds every living soul like the halo surrounding the heads of saints'.[8] It is perhaps that mysterious sin that Jesus himself called 'the sin against the Holy Ghost'.

In the last chapter I mentioned the findings of some psychologists that link strongly prejudiced personalities with their uncritical attitude to their parents. 'What was good enough for my father is good enough for me.' This applies to customs, habits, ways of thinking, and, of course, to religion, which is often 'the religion of our forefathers'. But if I must not go beyond my father, that means that nobody else should either. Hence the violent feelings of hatred, alarm, or envy directed at the innovator; feelings which could be put something like this: 'How dare he go beyond what my father did when I myself accepted it as a limit?'

To come back to the religious problem, the crucial question is that every religion has somehow to explain the existence of all the others (since none of them has made the others disappear). The belief 'Mine is the only true religion—all the others are false' (comparable to 'Our ways are the only really civilized ones') is not really as strong and widespread as some people think. In the more intolerant form in which we know it, it is more characteristic, as I have tried to show, of Judaism, Christianity, and Islam. Hindus and Buddhists may believe that their own religion is the best one, but religious persecution has been a very rare phenomenon in the history of India. As we have also seen, it is one of the few countries in the world where a Jewish community like the Bene Israel has lived for centuries without any interference.

In the third century B.C. the great Indian emperor Ashoka (who became a pacifist after his conversion to Buddhism) was the first ruler in the world to proclaim (in edicts that are still standing) complete religious tolerance and reverence for all beliefs. Yet (in the West at least) Ashoka is comparatively little known, and his fame cannot stand comparison with that of power-mad rulers like Caesar, Napoleon, or Frederick the Great.

Over two thousand years later another Indian came to the West to preach something more than tolerance—a new form of religious universalism. It was Swami Vivekananda, the dominant figure of the first World Parliament of Religions, assembled in Chicago in 1893, and also the first Indian master to teach Yoga in the West. He spoke in these terms:

> May he who is the Brahman of the Hindus, the Ahura Mazda of the Zoroastrians, the Buddha of the Buddhists, the Jehovah of the Jews, the Father in Heaven of the Christians, give strength to you. . . . The Christian is not to become a Hindu or a Buddhist, nor a Hindu or a Buddhist is to become a Christian. But each must assimilate the spirit of the others and yet preserve his individuality and grow according to his own law of growth. . . . The Parliament of Religions . . . has proved . . . that holiness, purity and charity are not the exclusive possession of any church in the world, and that every system has produced men and women of the most exalted character'.[9]

These words were not mere pious wishes; indeed, they have proved prophetic. We are living in a truly ecumenical era (one may remember the fascinating history of this word, which I mentioned in Chapter 3): not merely in the narrower sense of a more or less official movement inside institutional Christianity, but in the much deeper sense of a new spiritual search which transcends all labels and organizations. The mutual assimilation and cross-fertilization that Swami Vivekananda's great vision predicted are really taking place. Just as in the days of intense ferment in the Roman Empire which gave rise to Christianity, many people are turning to the spiritual schools of the East—Yoga, Buddhism, Sufism—while their representatives are coming to the West both to teach and to assimilate what is useful. It is a far cry from the old days of intolerance when one sees a Jesuit enter a Zen monastery in order to learn Buddhist meditation or a Cistercian monk like Thomas Merton travel to India or Thailand to study Indian and Buddhist spirituality.

Speaking at Calcutta, Merton claimed that 'communication' at this level is no longer a difficult problem:

> We are well on our way to a workable interreligious lexicon of key words—mostly rooted in Sanskrit—which will permit intelligent discussion of all kinds of religious experience in all the religious traditions. This is in fact already being done to some extent, and one of the results of it is that psychologists and psychoanalysts, as well as anthropologists and students of comparative religion, are now able to talk a kind of lingua franca of religious experience.[10]

As one who has been for some time engaged in this kind of work, I can warmly endorse what he says.

When it comes to the struggle of oppressed groups, again one sees both Martin Luther King in America and the Catholic archbishop Dom Helder Camara in Brazil (who has become a champion not only of the oppressed poor in Latin America but of the whole Third World) finding inspiration in Gandhi's non-violent methods. Gandhi in his turn was influenced not only by Christianity but also by the ideas of men like Tolstoi, Thoreau, and Edward Carpenter. The increasing interest for radical reform and socialist ideas in religions like Christianity and Buddhism is another sign of the times.

In religious or spiritual terms, we can perhaps understand what being a world citizen means: it means being as open as possible to a full range of religious experience. He is one who claims the whole religious inheritance of mankind, who is able to be inspired by the Sermon on the Mount or the Bhagavad Gita, by the Psalms or the Buddhist scriptures, by the journal of George Fox or the Quran. It does not necessarily mean that he can understand and assimilate all these great religious works and traditions (much as a music lover may have his preferences and limitations), but at least he can free himself from restrictive prejudices or barriers—in the field of national cultures as well as in that of religion.

THE END OF THE NATIONAL IDOL?

Nowadays, with the decline of organized religion, religious prejudice and religious identification are much less of an obstacle to world citizenship than nationalism. In spite of growing interdependence, the national category remains very strong.

This is not the place to discuss the future of the nation-state as an institution, but one thing seems clear: as long as people identify themselves emotionally with their country or nation, and are taught and encouraged to do so, there will be national and racial prejudices. It is obvious that all the modern forms of anti-Semitism have been ultra-nationalistic: one of the constant charges against the Jew is that he is not 'a good German' or 'a good American', just as in ancient Alexandria he was accused of not being 'a loyal Alexandrian'.

I am not trying to deny that much can be done, and has been done, to reduce the more virulent forms of racial prejudice within the present framework. And yet we know that this is just the tip of a huge iceberg of ignorance, mental underdevelopment, and 'thinking with labels'. It is these blocks that keep Babel as it is, and, as we know or should know, there are powerful forces trying to perpetuate Babel because the coming of a new world would mean the end of their wealth and power.

On the other hand, all sorts of things are happening to make national boundaries and 'my country right or wrong' more and more obsolete.

Travelling and emigration have become much more widespread, and there is an ever increasing number of 'professional nomads'—scientists, technicians, engineers, and so on—who go from one country to another and sometimes cannot be said to have a 'home' anywhere. Again, countries are changing so fast, and their population with them, that the world is becoming an ever stranger place to live in and at the same time drearily uniform. The process of cultural uniformity that we noticed in parts of the Roman Empire in Chapter 3 is now occurring in all the cities of the world and at an ever quickening pace.

If somebody asks for a direction in one of the larger cities, it is very likely that the answer will be, 'I'm sorry, I'm a stranger here too'. In a way, this may be taken as a symbol of the position in which mankind finds itself.

Certainly, attachment to home and country has been for centuries a very strong force, and still is to many millions of people all over the world. It has inspired many positive things—poetry, music, and other forms of art. But the feelings 'I belong here' or 'I am a stranger here' have nothing permanent in them, and in a world of increasing alienation they tend to become blurred. If we wanted to exaggerate a little, we could say that we are all becoming strangers.

Will these changes tend to weaken the force of the prejudices against 'the stranger'? Or will the alienation itself act as a negative force and seek a scapegoat, as it has already done in the case of anti-Semitism (the theory that hatred of Jews is partly a projection of hatred of cities)? It is very difficult to say. But one thing is certain: these changes are likely to increase in pace and become more and more marked. It may well be—although this is only a speculation—that we are approaching the end of that stage of man's development marked by attachment to territory. (In that sense the Nazi cult of 'blood and soil' [*Blut und Boden*] may well have been the last desperate attempt to delay this implacable process.) In other words: the long Neolithic period may be coming to an end, and with it we may have at last to shed its tribal mind, of which the cult of national flags, anthems, and military uniforms, brought to its frenzied pitch by Fascism, is the last, more virulent, stage.

It is significant that in most of the great religions there has been the tradition of the monk or hermit who leaves home and gives up all attachments. He has no abode and makes his home anywhere: 'Foxes have holes, and birds of the air have nests; but the Son of man has nowhere to lay his head' (Luke 9:58).

Is it utopian to imagine a future when human beings will feel at home everywhere, just because they have lost the attachment to a particular place? Is it utopian to conceive a mankind of real world citizens who will claim for themselves the whole human inheritance and not just an isolated section of it? Then people will have left behind the period of tribal prides and prejudices as that of a long adolescence.

This is a very old vision, which does not conflict with all great dreams of liberation—whether Theodor Herzl's dream or Martin Luther King's dream. If it is a false vision, then our outlook is bleak indeed.

As I write these last lines, Arab terrorists have just made another attack on Israel and killed 'perfect strangers'—tourists at a hotel in Tel Aviv. But let me add something which has not made headlines. A few weeks ago I spent a short period in a London hospital ward where the nursing and domestic staff was drawn from a dozen countries, representing all the main racial groups of mankind (they included a lovely dark girl from a country the Africans call Zimbabwe and which will one day, after liberation, lose its ill-fitting name of 'Rhodesia'). We were all 'strangers' to one another, and yet we were all drawn together by this very intimate experience of looking after and being looked after (the nurse is the universal mother and sister). There were occasional verbal misunderstandings because the standard of English varied somewhat, but I did not feel then that I was in Babel.

London, March 1975

Notes

INTRODUCTION

1. *New Statesman*, 31 Dec. 1965, pp. 1028–29.
2. Edward H. Flannery, *The Anguish of the Jews* (New York: Macmillan, 1965), p. xi.
3. Letter of a Hungarian Jew quoted at the end of Herbert Agar, *The Saving Remnant* (London: Hart-Davis, 1960), p. 249.

1. IN THE BEGINNING

1. On one occasion the Mufti of Jerusalem (then the religious leader of the Palestine Arabs) visited Rosenberg, who promised him to ban the use of the word 'anti-Semitism'. Léon Poliakov and Josef Wulf, *The Third Reich and the Jews*, translated from the German (Barcelona: Seix Barral, 1960), p. 306.
2. Gordon W. Allport, *The Nature of Prejudice* (Reading, Mass.: Addison-Wesley, 1954), pp. 6ff. For other definitions see Howard J. Ehrlich, *The Social Psychology of Prejudice* (New York: Wiley, 1973), pp. 3–4.
3. See Cecil Roth, *A History of the Jews in England* (Oxford University Press, 1964), pp. 143ff. Marlowe's anti-Semitic play *The Jew of Malta*, rather inferior to Shakespeare's, was staged in London between Lopez's trial and his execution.
4. See V. G. Kiernan, *The Lords of Human Kind* (London: Weidenfeld & Nicolson, 1969), p. 237. This is a very instructive book about Western attitudes towards 'colonial peoples' in the imperial age.
5. The story was that a Negro sentinel at Essen had smashed the skull of a German boy with the butt of his rifle and proceeded to eat the brains. It appeared in a 'serious' paper, the *Deutsche Allgemeine Zeitung*. See Leopold Schwarzschild, *World in Trance* (London: Hamish Hamilton, 1945), p. 143. It is amusing to recall that Swift, in his savage satire *A Modest Proposal* (1729), proposing that the problem of overpopulation and hunger in Ireland might be solved by slaughtering Irish babies for human consumption, mischievously attributed his culinary information to 'a very knowing American of my acquaintance'.
6. For instance by Bernhard Olson, *Faith and Prejudice* (New Haven: Yale University Press, 1963). (See Chap. 6, note 6.) Charles Y. Glock and Rodney Stark, *Christian Beliefs and Anti-Semitism* (New York: Harper & Row, 1966).
7. Margaret Mead, article in *Fundamental and Adult Education*, ed. UNESCO, 12, No. 3 (1960), 109. About national and ethnic prejudices in

schoolbooks see J. A. Lauwerys, *History Textbooks and International Under-standing* (Paris: UNESCO, 1953).

8. Jean-Paul Clébert, *The Gypsies,* translated from the French *Les Tziganes* (Harmondsworth: Penguin Books, 1967), pp. 250–54 (persecutions). Clébert shows that popular mythology has sometimes associated Gypsies with Jews. According to a legend current in Germany, the Jews who had been persecuted at the time of the Black Death (1348) had taken refuge in caves and kept hidden there for a long time. After learning a number of new skills, they had reappeared in the guise of Gypsies. In 1782 forty-five *Zingari* in Hungary were charged with cannibalism and tried. The emperor Joseph II (the same who promoted the emancipation of the Jews) ordered an inquiry, but the Gypsies had already been executed. For the extermination of Gypsies under Nazi rule see Raul Hilberg, *The Destruction of the European Jews* (New York: Quad-rangle, 1962), pp. 641–42.

9. It was also during this period that the Samaritans, i.e., the remnants of the extinct kingdom of Israel, were set apart as a schismatic or heretical group. Some five hundred of them are now left, largely concentrated at Nablus (ancient Shechem, now in the part of Jordan occupied by Israel). They fol-low a kind of Jewish ritual, and the Samaritan Bible is a special version of the Torah or Pentateuch. In language and culture they are very similar to the Arabs, while racially two distinct types are found—one predominantly dark and the other fair. It is clear that at the time of Christ there was marked intolerance and mutual prejudice between Samaritans and Jews, which sometimes exploded in violent quarrels. Jesus tried to counter the unfavourable stereotype of the group among the Jews with his famous parable of the Good Samaritan (in a passage of John's Gospel he is accused of being a Samaritan himself [John 8:48], as in the Middle Ages and later one would say 'heretic' or 'Judaizer', or nowa-days 'nigger-lover' or 'Jew-lover'. Under Christianity the Samaritans were the victims of prejudice and persecution as much as the Jews. In the Byzantine Empire, during the reigns of Justin and Justinian, there were rebellions, forced conversion, and other disturbances. It is interesting to note that at this time many Samaritans were money-changers, so that the two words became synon-ymous, just as 'Jew' and 'usurer' did later.

10. Josephus, *The Wars of the Jews,* VII.6.6 The tax was collected with great strictness during the reign of Domitian (who succeeded Titus, the con-queror of Jerusalem). As Suetonius recalls: 'As a boy, I remember once attend-ing a crowded Court where the Procurator had a ninety-year-old man stripped to establish whether or not he had been circumcised' (*Life of Domitian,* 12). His successor, Nerva, proudly claimed, on a coin inscription, to have abolished such abuses (*fisci judaici calumnia sublata*), but the *fiscus judaicus,* in fact a poll tax, continued to be collected at least until the fourth century.

2. ALEXANDRIA, THE CRADLE OF ANTI-SEMITISM

1. The events at Alexandria are related by Philo in his pamphlet *Against Flaccus* and the episode of Caligula's statue in *Embassy to Gaius* (both in the

Loeb edition, Vols. IX–X, translated by F. H. Colson, 1942). Josephus gives his version in *The Antiquities of the Jews*, XVIII.8 and *Wars*, 11.10. See Robert H. Pfeiffer, *History of New Testament Times* (New York: Harper, 1949), pp. 37–38.

2. *Maran atha* ('Our Lord, come!' or 'Our Lord comes!') in I Cor. 16:22–24. See Richard N. Longenecker, *The Christology of Early Jewish Christianity* (London: SCM Press, 1970), pp. 121ff. One may remember a more harmless parody: in 1876, when Queen Victoria assumed the title of Empress of India, Tenniel (the famous illustrator of Lewis Carroll's *Alice* books) caricatured Prime Minister Disraeli as a Jewish pedlar inviting the queen to exchange 'old crowns for new'.

3. For instance, the incident related by Josephus during the administration of Cumanus: a Roman soldier, during the Passover at Jerusalem, mocked the festival by raising his tunic, 'turning his backside towards the Jews and making a noise as indecent as his attitude' (*Wars*, II.12.1; *Antiquities*, XX.513). At about the same time another soldier tore up a scroll of the Torah (*Wars*, II.12.2).

4. Philo, *Embassy to Gaius*, XVIII.120.

5. In his attractive but fanciful novel *Claudius the God*, Robert Graves makes Agrippa secretly plan to proclaim himself Messiah and to become independent of Rome. But his impious vanity on hearing himself compared to a god attracted divine punishment and he was struck by a mysterious, fatal disease. (For his death see *Josephus, Antiquities*, XIX.8.2, and Acts 12:19–23.) It is relevant to note that Agrippa's sudden death in 44 A.D. was mourned by many Jews and greeted with joyous celebrations by the Gentiles of Caesarea and Sebaste (Samaria)—an outbreak of anti-Jewish feeling comparable to the Alexandria pogrom a few years earlier. The soldiers stationed at Caesarea took the statues of Agrippa's daughters (or, according to another version, the princesses themselves) into brothels and set them up on the rooftops where 'they abused them to the utmost of their power, and did such things to them as are too indecent to be related' (Josephus, *Antiquities*, XIX.9.1).

3. JUDAISM AND ANTI-JUDAISM IN THE ROMAN EMPIRE

1. Suetonius, *Life of Vespasian*, 4.

2. Josephus, *Antiquities*, XVI.6.8.

3. Josephus, *Wars*, III.16.4 (cf. VII.3.3). Many Jews would see in the Diaspora a divine punishment for disobedience of the Law, already prophesied in the terrible curses of Deuteronomy (28:37ff. and particularly 64–68; cf. 4:26–28 [see Chap. 6]). Although basically this part of the Torah probably dates from the seventh century B.C., some modern scholars believe that the passages about the Dispersion were written at the time of the Babylonian exile (middle of the sixth century to the fifth). It will be noticed that the Dispersion is presented as an accomplished fact in Deut. 30:3 (see Robert H. Pfeiffer, *Introduction to the Old Testament* [New York: Harper, 1948], pp. 186–87). Philo explains the Diaspora more optimistically: because of the great number

of Jews that no single country can contain, 'they live in many of the most attractive areas of Europe and Asia, both on the islands and the mainland' (*Against Flaccus*, 7). Later, Jewish dispersion would be interpreted in Messianic terms, and it was believed that once it had been completed over the whole earth the Messiah would come (see Chap. 9).

4. Polybius, *Histories*, I.3.4. In the beginning of his *Library of History* Diodorus Siculus also writes that the historian may deal with the whole *oikoumene* as if it were a single state or city. One can see that the concept of universal history popularized by H. G. Wells is not all that new. The ideal of the 'world citizen' (see Postscript) first emerged during the Hellenistic period, with Diogenes the Cynic and others.

5. Pfeiffer, *New Testament Times*, p. 189.

6. In *Antisemitism in the United States*, ed. Leonard Dinnerstein (New York: Holt, Rinehart & Winston, 1971), p. 41ff.

7. See II Maccabees 4:9–15. The phrase of I Maccabees that some Jews at that time 'made prepuces for themselves' (1:15) can only mean that they submitted to plastic surgery. Paul also mentions this in I Cor. 7:18. See Emil Schürer, *The History of the Jewish People in the Time of Jesus Christ* (Edinburgh: Clark, 1973), Vol. I, p. 149, note 28.

8. As in Herodotus, I.131.3 and I.199.3.

9. Tacitus, *Histories*, V.4. We may compare this chapter to Herodotus' classical description of the Egyptians, also strongly emphasizing their peculiarity (but with a positive interest and none of the Roman writer's hostility) and the things they do 'contrary to the whole world' (II.35ff). Note particularly the concern with cleanliness, the practice of circumcision, food precepts, aversion to contact with foreigners and refusal to eat with them (cf. Gen. 43:32), dislike of pigs and banning of pork. It is clear that the Hebrews, on leaving Egypt, carried with them not only stolen objects (Exod. 12:35–36) but a great many Egyptian habits and customs (see Josephus, *Against Apion*, II.113.141).

10. Josephus, *Against Apion*, II.8.95.

11. Ibid., II.6.65.

12. Tacitus, V.5.

13. Ibid., V.9.

14. Ibid., V.5.

15. *The Merchant of Venice*, I.3.28–30.

16. Matt. 10:5. In the incident with the Canaanite woman there is apparent contempt in the words, 'It is not fair to take the children's bread and throw it to the dogs' (Matt. 15:26), which may be compared to the famous saying, 'Do not give dogs what is holy, and do not throw your pearls before swine' (Matt. 7:6). In rabbinic literature dogs and swine are common terms of contempt for Gentiles. It was an ironic reversal that they should be later used to express the growing anti-Judaism by Christians (as in the names *Marranos* and *Chuetas* [see Chap. 8]).

17. Tacitus, V.5.

18. Herodotus, II.104; Josephus, *Against Apion*, I.22.169–71.

19. Tacitus, V.8. That is what Bickerman has called the anti-Semitic inter-

pretation of the Maccabaean rebellion (Pfeiffer, *New Testament Times*, pp. 9–10).

20. Rom. 16:3–16. Of the names mentioned, seven are Roman, one Hebrew, and the remainder Greek. But some of the Latin and Greek ones may have belonged to Jews.

21. Tacitus, V.8; Quintilian, *Institutio oratoria*, III.7.21. For the incident relating to Marcus Aurelius see Ammianus Marcellinus, *Rerum gestarum*, XXII.5.4–5; Théodore Reinach, *Textes d'auteurs grecs et romains relatifs au judaïsme* (Paris, 1895), pp. 352–53, note 3.

22. G. K. Morlan, in *Journal of Genetic Psychology*, 77 (1950), 257–65; Allport, *Nature of Prejudice*, p. 137. Allport mentions the connection between garlic and Italians in the United States and points out that in some cases prejudice can lead to something very much like olfactory hallucinations. This might work as a conditioned reflex: if a certain group is associated with a specific smell, the presence of an individual belonging to it could produce the corresponding smell. According to George Orwell, the Burmese say that Europeans smell 'of corpses'. He also caused a certain shock in England when he openly wrote in *The Road to Wigan Pier* (1937) that according to many middle-class people 'the working classes stink'.

23. Josephus, *Against Apion*, I.26.228ff.

24. Ibid., I.12.60.

25. Tacitus, V.5. Cf. Josephus, *Against Apion*, II.14.148; Juvenal, *Satires*, XIV.103ff.

26. Josephus, *Against Apion*, II.10.121.

27. Pfeiffer, *New Testament Times*, p. 190.

28. III Maccabees can be found in some editions of the Apocrypha (in Greek). In fact, it has nothing to do with the Maccabees and is considered a work of fiction set in the reign of Ptolemy IV, Philopator (221–204 B.C.). It relates an imaginary threat against the Jews in Egypt. At the instigation of some anti-Jewish ministers, the king decreed their extermination, and they were about to be trampled to death by elephants on the race course at Alexandria when God saved them miraculously. In the end the king's anger is turned against his friends, and the Jews are honoured instead of killed. It is significant that they were also allowed to kill their apostate brethren, to the number of three hundred (III Macc. 7:10–15). See Otto Eissfeldt, *The Old Testament: An Introduction*, trans. Peter R. Ackroyd (Oxford: Blackwell, 1966), p. 581 (with bibliography); Pfeiffer, *New Testament Times*, pp. 203–6. Some writers (including Simon Dubnov) have considered the story genuine.

29. Pfeiffer, *Introduction to the Old Testament*, p. 747.

4. JEWISH PROSELYTISM AND ASSIMILATION

1. See Elena Cassin, *San Nicandro: The Story of a Religious Phenomenon*, translated from the French (London: Cohen & West, 1959). On reviewing this book for the *Jewish Chronicle* (21 Aug. 1959), Robert Graves reported that when he visited Israel he found that a number of Sabbatini had gone back to Italy, but I have been informed that that is not the case.

2. For the use of *proselytos* in the Greek Bible see, for instance, Deut. 5:14; Exod. 12:49. Many references in the New Testament: Acts 2:10; 6:5; 13:43; etc.

3. If a Christian became a convert to Judaism and persisted in his new faith, his hair and beard would be shaved, he would be publicly whipped, and finally he would be given up as a serf to anybody the king chose.

4. See Arthur J. Zuckerman, *A Jewish Princedom in Feudal France, 768–900* (New York: Columbia University Press, 1972), pp. 204ff.

5. Roth, *History of the Jews in England*, p. 149.

6. Article 'Proselytes', in the *Encyclopaedia Judaica* (Jerusalem, 1971), pp. 1192–93. Among these proselytes 'females outnumber males five to one'.

7. An allusion to II Kings 17:24–28; 'Proselytes', p. 1186.

8. Tacitus, V.5.

9. Juvenal, XIV. 96–106.

10. 'The customs of that most accursed nation (*sceleratis summae gentis*) have gained such strength that they have been recorded in all lands; the conquered have given laws to the conquerors'. Quoted from Seneca, *De superstitione*, in St. Augustine, *The City of God*, VI.II. See Salo W. Baron, *A Social and Religious History of the Jews* (New York: Columbia University Press, 1952–58), Vol. I, p. 191.

11. Josephus, *Wars*, II.20.2. The whole passage deserves to be quoted, as it gives an example of a pogrom at the time of the rebellion: 'At this time the people of Damascus, learning of the destruction of the Roman force, were eager to exterminate the Jews in their midst. As they had them cooped up in the Gymnasium for a long time now, taking this precaution as a result of suspicion, the task appeared perfectly simple; but they were afraid of their own wives, who had almost all gone over to the Jewish religion, so that their chief anxiety was to keep them in the dark. Accordingly they fell upon the Jews, crowded together and unarmed, and though they numbered 10,500 they slaughtered them all in one hour without any trouble' (trans. G. A. Williamson [Harmondsworth: Penguin Books, 1972]).

12. Article 'Circumcision', in *Encyclopaedia Judaica*; Richard Lewinsohn, *Histoire de la vie sexuelle*, trans. L. Lamorlette (Paris: Payot, 1957), pp. 36–37. The alleged medical reasons in support of this practice are better hygiene of the penis and the prevention of cancer, which seems to have lower incidence among Jews and Muslims. Nowadays, however, there is strong medical reaction against 'prophylactic' circumcision, on account of its likely traumatic effect.

13. Josephus, *Against Apion*, II.39.282.

14. F. H. Colson, *The Week* (Cambridge University Press, 1926), pp. 14ff., 39.

15. Horace, *Satires*, I.9.69. There are several other references to the Sabbath in Roman authors: Ovid, *Ars amatoria*, I.75.415; Tibullus, I.3.17–18; Juvenal, III.10ff.; VI.156ff.; XIX.96, 106. For analysis and comment see Colson, *The Week*.

16. Tacitus, V.1.

17. W. Montgomery Watt, *Muhammad at Medina* (Oxford University Press, 1956), pp. 198–99.

18. The supposed letter from the king of the Khazars to Hasdai ibn Sha-brut is given in Edmond Fleg, *Anthologie juive* (Paris: Gallimard, 1939), Vol. II, p. 10. On the Khazars: D. M. Dunlop, *The History of the Jewish Khazars* (Princeton University Press, 1954). There is also a chapter by the same author in *The World History of the Jewish People*, Vol. XI, *The Dark Ages*, ed. Cecil Roth (London: W. H. Allen, 1966), pp. 325–56.

19. Philippe Julian, *The Snob Spotter's Guide* (London: Weidenfeld & Nicolson, 1958), pp. 103–4.

20. Bernard D. Weinryb, 'Jewish Immigration and Accommodation to America', in *The Jews: Social Patterns of an American Group*, ed. Marshall Sklare (Glencoe, Ill.: Free Press, 1960), p. 12.

21. For the prejudice of the German Jews see Adolft Leschnitzer, *The Magic Background of Modern Anti-Semitism: An Analysis of the German-Jewish Relationship* (New York: International Universities Press, 1956), p. 11. He says, 'The Berlin Jews looked down on those country cousins with contempt. The earlocks and kaftans struck them as funny, and they did not hesitate to laugh'. For the attitudes of the Baghdadis towards the Bene Israel see Schifra Strizower, *The Children of Israel: The Bene Israel of Bombay* (Oxford: Blackwell, 1971), pp. 3, 44–47.

22. Strizower, *Children of Israel*, p. 5. See also Barnet Litvinoff, *A Peculiar People* (London: Weidenfeld & Nicolson, 1969), pp. 228 ff. Thousands of members of these Indian communities have now emigrated to Israel.

23. Article 'Peru', in *Standard Jewish Encyclopaedia*, ed. Cecil Roth (London: W. H. Allen, 1959; printed in Israel). For the smaller Jewish communities in general see Schifra Strizower, *Exotic Jewish Communities* (London: Thomas Yoseloff [World Jewish Congress], 1962).

24. Howard Brotz, *The Black Jews of Harlem* (Glencoe, Ill., and London: Free Press, 1964).

25. Andre Spire, transcribed in Fleg, *Anthologie juive*, Vol. II, pp. 174–75.

26. Strizower, *Children of Israel*, p. 3.

27. Bernard Lazare, *L'Antisémitisme, son histoire et ses causes* (Paris: Chaillot, 1934; first published 1894), pp. 391–92; p. 358 in the English translation.

28. Allport, *Nature of Prejudice*, p. 150.

29. A. A. Roback, *A Dictionary of International Slurs* (Cambridge, Mass.: SCI-Art Publishers, 1944), p. 152.

30. '. . . l'antisémitisme est une conception du monde manichéiste et primitive où la haine du Juif prend place à titre de grand mythe explicatif'. Jean-Paul Sartre, *Réflexions sur la question juive* (Paris: Gallimard, 1954), p. 179.

31. Eissfeldt, *The Old Testament*, p. 66.

32. Athenagoras, *Legatio pro Christianis*, 1–3, in *A New Eusebius: Documents Illustrative of the History of the Church to A.D. 337*, ed. J. Stevenson (London: SPCK, 1968), p. 71.

33. Quoted by Seymour B. Liebman, *The Jews in New Spain* (Coral Gables, Fla.: University of Miami Press, 1970), p. 25.

34. Leonard P. Broom, Helen P. Broom, and Virginia Harris, 'Characteris-

tics of 1,107 Petitions for Change of Name', *American Sociological Review*, 20 (Feb. 1955), 33–39. The importance of this percentage is better appreciated when it is compared to the proportion of Jews in the population of Los Angeles (about 236,000 in nearly 4 million at the time, and therefore 6 percent). Discrimination in hotel room reservations: S. L. Wax, 'A Survey of Restrictive Advertising and Discrimination by Summer Resorts in the Province of Ontario', *Canadian Jewish Congress: Information and Comment*, 7 (1948), 10–13; quoted by Allport, *Nature of Prejudice*, p. 4.

35. Foreign minorities are often identified by their accents, but this does not often happen with Jews. One might recall the proverbial story of 'Shibboleth' in Judges 12:5–6, in which the regional pronunciation of this word ('Sibboleth') by the tribe of Ephraim was used as a test word to identify the Ephraimites, who were immediately killed. It has an exact parallel in the massacre of the Flemish merchants during the English peasant revolt (1381), when they were asked to pronounce 'bread and cheese'. Anyone who tended to say something like 'brod und kase' was taken to be Flemish and killed. Or again, in the Gospels Peter is identified as a Galilean, and therefore a follower of Jesus, by his accent (Matt. 26:73 and parallels in Mark and Luke).

5. THE ROOTS OF CHRISTIAN ANTI-SEMITISM

1. '*Iudaeos impulsores Chresto assidue tumultuantes Roma expulit*'. Suetonius, *Life of Claudius*, 25.4. C. H. Dodd, *The Epistle of Paul to the Romans*, (London: Collins, 1959), p. 20. See also Dio Cassius, XXXVII.17; LX.6. Jews in Rome at the time of Nero: Josephus, *Antiquities*, XX.8.11; Acts 28:17.

2. See particularly Edwyn Bevan, *Christianity* (London: Butterworth, 1938), pp. 13–14. *Christos* comes from the verb *chriō* = to smear, to anoint. As far as I know, the first Biblical use of *Christos* is in Samuel and Kings to translate *Mashiah*, as applied to the anointed king of Israel. For instance, David recoils rather shocked at the idea of 'touching the Anointed of the Lord' (Greek *Christos Kyriou*; I Sam. 24:7). Cf. Eusebius, *Ecclesiastical History*, I.3.7.

3. Acts 24:5. For the use of the word *hairesis* ('heresy') in the New Testament see for instance Acts 5:17; 15:5, etc.; also Josephus, *Wars*, II.8.1. Even in the fourth century Eusebius calls the Christian Church 'the Most Holy Sect' or *hairesis* (*Ecclesiastical History*, X.5.22).

4. The usual Hebrew term corresponding to 'heresy' is *Minuth*, while *Natzarim* ('Nazarenes') became the normal designation applied to Christians (compare the derogatory term 'Galileans' used by the emperor Julian).

5. For the killing of Zechariah, II Chron. 24:20–22. Uriah and Jeremiah: Jer. 26:7–24. General description of persecution: Heb. 11:35–38.

6. 'Every devoted thing is most holy to Yahweh', Lev. 27:28. Cf. Num. 18:14; 21:2–3 (a people reserved for destruction); Deut. 7:25–26 (idols and 'abominations' of the Gentiles considered anathema); Deut. 13:15–17 (a 'heretical' city condemned to destruction). Incident of the condemned Amalekites whom King Saul spares: I Sam. 15:1–22.

7. Quoted in Pinchas Lapide, *The Last Three Popes and the Jews* (London:

Souvenir Press, 1967), p. 81. In 1959 Pope John XXIII ordered that the words *perfidi Judaei* (treacherous Jews) and *Judaica perfidia* be struck off the Good Friday liturgy (cf. *la perfide Albion* and *fides Punica* [Punic bad faith], the anti-Carthaginian slogan used by the Romans). See Glock and Stark, *Christian Beliefs and Anti-Semitism*, p. xix.

8. See Pfeiffer, *New Testament Times*, pp. 55–56; Joseph Klausner, *Jesus of Nazareth*, trans. Herbert Dandy (London: Allen & Unwin, 1947), pp. 194, 214, 276. Cf. John 7:49: 'But this crowd, who do not know the Law, are accursed'. While the disciples of Jesus and John the Baptist were very largely from among the poor, the Pharisees tended to belong to the middle class and the Sadducees to the upper classes (Josephus, *Antiquities*, XIII.10.6; Pfeiffer, *New Testament Times*, p. 56; Klausner, *Jesus of Nazareth*, p. 217).

9. *Anguish of the Jews*, p. 30. On the other hand, it is interesting that of the four Gospels John is the only one who says that Jesus was arrested by Roman soldiers, a version which has been accepted (in my view wrongly) by several historians, including Brandon. Official Catholic concern with John's 'anti-Semitism' is shown in the recent declaration by the Vatican (January 1975). It says that the term 'the Jews' in the fourth Gospel should be interpreted as meaning either 'the leaders of the Jews' or 'the adversaries of Jesus' (See text of declaration in the London weekly *Catholic Herald*, Friday, 10 January 1975).

10. See also Acts 11:2 and 21:17–26 (Jacob pointing out to Paul the great number of Jews converted to Christianity). See A. D. Nock, *St. Paul* (Oxford University Press, 1953), p. 111.

11. In the 'great persecution' against the Church related in Acts 8:1, it is significant that no mention is made of the apostles. On this passage: Charles Guignebert, *Le Christ* (Paris: Michel, 1948), pp. 128–30. The names of the 'Seven Deacons' who represent the Hellenists are all Greek, and one of them is called 'Nicholas, a proselyte from Antioch' (Acts 6:5; see Chap. 4 for the large number of proselytes in that town).

12. C. Delisle Burns, *The First Europe* (New York: Norton, 1948), p. 502.

13. Eusebius, *Ecclesiastical History*, III.27.2,4; cf. V.8.10 and VI.17.

14. Baron, *Social and Religious History*, Vol. II, p. 135.

15. *Martyrdom of Polycarp*, XVIII. 1, in Stevenson, ed., *A New Eusebius*, p. 24.

16. Tertullian, *Apology*, 40.2, in *A New Eusebius*, p. 169.

17. Text in Josephus, *Antiquities*, XIX.5.3. In another letter from Claudius found among Egyptian papyri, he adopts a more severe tone to the Jews. After condemning the recent violence, which he describes as downright war, Claudius tells the Alexandrians to show themselves 'forbearing and kindly towards the Jews' and respect their religious customs. On the other hand, he warns the Jews 'not to agitate for more privileges than they formerly possessed', not to send a separate embassy as if they belonged to a different city, and not to force their way into some of the public games. They live in a city which is not theirs, and therefore they should not try and introduce Jews from Syria or other parts of Egypt; otherwise they would be punished 'as fomenters of what is a general plague infecting the whole world [*oikoumene*]' (A. S. Hunt and C. C. Edgar,

Papyri: Non-Literary Selections, Loeb Classical Library [London: Heinemann, 1934], Vol. II, No. 212, pp. 78ff).

6. THE CHURCH MILITANT AND THE JEWS

1. Julian, *Epistles*, 53 (to the people of Bostra, in 362 A.D.); *Documents of the Christian Church*, ed. H. Bettenson (Oxford University Press, 1956), p. 31.

2. Ambrose, *Epistles*, 29; quoted in Henry H. Milman, *The History of the Jews* (London: Dent, 1939), Vol. II, p. 197.

3. Text of bull in *Documents of the Christian Church*, ed. Bettenson, pp. 159ff.

4. The story is told in Baronius, *Annales ecclesiastici*; quoted in Milman, *History of the Jews*, Vol. II, p. 201.

5. Both passages (*Patrologia*, ed. Migne) quoted by Léon Poliakov, *The History of Anti-Semitism*, trans. Richard Howard (London: Routledge & Kegan Paul, 1974), Vol. I, p. 25.

6. About the accusation see Chap. 5 and Flannery, *Anguish of the Jews*, passim. Just as UNESCO has been studying national stereotypes and prejudices in schoolbooks, something similar has taken place in a few countries as regards the teaching of religion. In the United States some of these studies were carried out on behalf of the American Jewish Committee in various Protestant churches and Jewish and Catholic schools. In his book *Faith and Prejudice*, Dr. Bernhard Olson, a Methodist clergyman who teaches at a theological school, showed that current religious texts propagate strong anti-Catholic and anti-Jewish prejudices. For instance, one Biblical commentary said: 'The Gospels illustrate how bitterly Jesus was hated by the Jews' (this is obviously false and, as we have seen, could only apply partly to John's Gospel). And again: 'The Pharisees called him Beelzebub, a revolting title, which they applied to Satan'. Here is Dr. Olson's accurate. analysis of this argument: 'The writer uses the responses of a small group of Pharisees to Jesus in a particular moment in history to project a series of generalizations: 1) from a few to all Pharisees, 2) from all Pharisees to all Jews in the time of Jesus, and 3) from all first-century Jews to Jews of any time or place'. This last generalization has been made by Christians for centuries. One should also point out the unfavourable stereotype about the Pharisees, among whom Jesus had friends, some even following Christianity.

7. See Chap. 10, note 8.

8. Grimm, *Deutsches Wörterbuch*, is quoted by Poliakov, *History of Anti-Semitism*, Vol. I, pp. 239–40. On the linguistic aspects of prejudice see the chapter 'Language and Intolerance' in Mario Pei, *The Story of Language* (Philadelphia: Lippincott, 1949); also Allport, *Nature of Prejudice*, passim. The Polish example is taken from Roback, *Dictionary of International Slurs*, p. 125.

9. The tradition of a red-haired Judas was usual in Spanish pictures. The English soldiers who fought in the Peninsular War against the armies of Napoleon were considered 'heretics' and called *rubios* partly because of their

similarity to Judas (Arthur Bryant, *Years of Victory* [London: Collins, 1951], p. 301). Judas' traditional moneybag is based on John 12:6 and 13:29, where it is said that he acted as a kind of treasurer of the group of disciples (who 'held all things in common' and obviously went on practising this form of communism after the Master's death). He was in charge of the *glossokomon*, a bag or box of money, and John (12:6) also says that Judas stole from it. The other Gospels, usually more trustworthy, say nothing about this supposed function. The Judas myth was further elaborated in the Apocryphal Gospels and in medieval legends. For instance, in the Arabic Infancy Gospel, Judas as a boy slaps Jesus on the face and soon afterward Satan comes out of him in the form of a dog (*The Apocryphal New Testament*, trans. M. R. James [Oxford University Press, 1955], p. 82, XXXV).

10. Julio Baroja, *Los Judios en la España moderna y contemporanea* (Madrid: Arion, 1961), Vol. III, p. 183. Minister of Finance Mendizábal (see Chap. 11) was caricatured with a tail, and Baroja also shows how many village communities in Spain were mocked in verses by their neighbours for being crypto-Jewish, or *Judios rabudos*—tailed Jews (ibid., pp. 215ff.).

11. Poliakov, *History of Anti-Semitism*, Vol. I, p. 143. For the connection between the goat and the *foetor judaicus* see Joshua Trachtenberg, *The Devil and the Jews* (New Haven: Yale University Press, 1945), pp. 47ff.

12. Agobard's letter to Nebridius of Narbonne, quoted by Milman, *History of the Jews*, Vol. II, p. 282. Agobard asked the emperor Louis the Pious to put into force regulations that forbade the Jews to have Christian servants. Instead of that, the emperor confirmed the privileges of the Jewish community in the south of France. Agobard and Amulo, his successor as archbishop of Lyons, are called by Cecil Roth 'the fathers of medieval anti-Semitism' (*A Short History of the Jewish People* [London: East & West Library, 1969], p. 167), but in fact they never recommended violent measures—only a stricter *apartheid* between Christians and Jews. Agobard's five anti-Jewish letters provide, in fact, valuable evidence for good relations between the two communities in Carolingian times. The Jews could own land, and many of them were merchants, travelling a great deal. They even made proselytes among Christians, which further irritated the clergy. For their self-government and *nasi* (prince) see Zuckerman, *Jewish Princedom in Feudal France*. About Agobard and the Jews see Poliakov, *History of Anti-Semitism*, Vol. I, pp. 29ff.

13. On the conscious level it is what Gordon Allport describes as 'the well-known Machiavellian trick of creating a common enemy to cement an in-group'. And he adds: 'Hitler created the Jewish menace not so much to demolish the Jews as to cement the Nazi hold over Germany' (*Nature of Prejudice*, p. 41). Although this may be true on an unconscious level, the interpretation cannot really be accepted. As we shall see (Chap. 12), Nazi anti-Semitism was not merely a 'Machiavellian trick': Hitler, Himmler, and several other leaders really believed in their delusional ideas. As to the use of rumours or panics for political ends, that also is an age-old trick. The case of the Reichstag fire in 1934 became famous and may be compared to Nero's charge that the Christians had set fire to Rome. In 1937 Julius Streicher's anti-Semitic paper *Der Stürmer* blamed the Jews for the destruction of the dirigible *Hindenburg* (Lord

Russell of Liverpool, *The Scourge of the Swastika* [London: Corgi, 1964], pp. 255–56).

14. Poliakov, *History of Anti-Semitism*, Vol. I, p. 57.

15. The incident is told in Socrates, *Historia ecclesiastica*, VII.16 (London: Bohn Library, 1853); since he lived in the fifth century, he is a contemporary source. See Milman, *History of the Jews*, Vol. II, p. 201. The story is ignored in most books about the subject, but Marcel Simon accepts it as true (*Vérus Israel* [Paris: Boccard, 1948], p. 160). Simon Dubnov interprets the case as a harmless 'Purim jest' and thinks that the supposed Christian boy on the cross was just a wooden block (*History of the Jews* [London: Yoseloff, 1968], Vol. II, p. 191). It must be admitted that this does not seem very likely, but of course one cannot be sure of the real facts. In any case, this has nothing to do with the charge of ritual murder of children, which is utterly false.

16. In Chaucer's *Prioress's Tale* a Christian child is murdered by Jews from a Jewry because he used to pass singing the hymn *O alma redemptoris mater*. But the boy went on singing even after his throat was cut, and so he revealed to his mother the well where his body had been thrown. (The similarities with children's stories of various sources are obvious.) In the narrative there is a reference to 'the serpent Sathanas that hath in Jewes herte his waspes nest' and to Hugh of Lincoln, also killed by 'cursed Jewes . . . for it nis but a litel whyle ago' (Chaucer, *The Canterbury Tales*, in *Complete Works* [Oxford University Press, 1949], B.1874–76). One may note that the *Canterbury Tales* were written after 1386, nearly a century after the expulsion of the Jews from England (1290).

17. Roth, *Short History*, pp. 190–91.

18. Milman, *History of the Jews*, Vol. II, p. 299.

19. Ibid., p. 302. Note that stoning was the punishment for blasphemers and adulterers in Mosaic law (applied in the case of Stephen [Acts 7:58] and probably also in the case of Jacob, or James, the brother of Jesus). It is a violent way of releasing a crowd's aggressive impulses. Talking about the lynching of Negroes in America, Gordon Allport says: 'This whole macabre practice . . . depends to a considerable extent upon cultural custom. Among marginal and uneducated men of certain localities there has existed the tradition of a man hunt [and] to "get your nigger" has been a permissible sport, virtually a duty' (*Nature of Prejudice*, p. 62). After seeing the recent Boston riots, one cannot doubt that the tradition is very much alive.

20. *Codex Theodosianus*, XVI, *De Judaeis*, 18; quoted by Milman, *History of the Jews*, Vol. II, p. 200.

21. Norman Cohn, *The Pursuit of the Millennium* (London: Secker & Warburg, 1957). Cohn tends to see in many of these anti-Semitic sects a delusional trend towards the 'old Jew' as a hostile father figure (pp. 69ff.; see also his *Warrant for Genocide* [London: Eyre & Spottiswoode, 1967], passim). In 1320 the apocalyptic sect of the Pastoureaux carried out several pogroms in the south of France and parts of Spain (see Chap. 8). Cohn mentions a nationalistic apocalyptic work, the *Book of a Hundred Chapters*, which presents certain striking anticipations of Nazi doctrines. The Germans are held up as a superior people whom the 'Latins' are destined to serve. The book states that

the Germans once ruled over the whole world and will do so again with even greater power. This is the myth of an ancient Germanic empire centred at Trier. National Socialism returned in many ways to these apocalyptic ideas. In talking about a 'thousand-year Reich', Hitler adopted millenarianism without Christianity, while Himmler tried to revive the traditions of the Teutonic Knights and to explore the mythical past of the 'Aryan race' (see, for instance, H. R. Trevor-Roper, *The Last Days of Hitler* [London: Macmillan, 1947], pp. 19ff.). Another apocalyptic sect was that of the Flagellants, who carried out a number of pogroms during the Black Death in 1348–49 (Cohn, *Pursuit of the Millennium*, pp. 124ff.; Philip Ziegler, *The Black Death* [London: Collins, 1969], pp. 96ff.).

7. CRUSADES, POGROMS, AND GHETTOS

1. See *Gesta Francorum* (Paris: Brehier, 1938), p. 202. Another chronicler, Daimbert, goes further than that and says that in the temple of Solomon the horses waded in blood up to their knees (quoted by Steven Runciman, *The Crusades* [Harmondsworth: Penguin Books, 1965], Vol. I, p. 287).

2. Lauwerys, *History Textbooks and International Understanding*.

3. Milman, *History of the Jews*, Vol. II, p. 307. 'And calumniated his Mother' must be a reference to the *Tol 'doth Yeshu* (Chap. 10), which contributed to spread the story of Jesus as 'son of fornication'.

4. Quoted in Fleg, *Anthologie juive*, Vol. II, p. 14. The phrase 'a nation of stern countenance' and so on is a quotation of Deut. 28:50.

5. Roth, *Short History*, p. 185.

6. Matthew Paris, *Historia Anglorum*, 11.9: 'Because of the magic arts which Jews and *some women* notoriously exercise at royal coronation'; quoted in Roth, *History of the Jews in England*, p. 19, note 1.

7. See particularly Ziegler, *Black Death*, pp. 96ff.

8. Thomas Merton, *New Seeds of Contemplation* (New York: New Directions, 1962).

9. Travelling about the middle of the twelfth century (from 1165 onwards) the rabbi Benjamin of Tudela mentions specifically the territories where the Jews could own land: notably in the south of France (Narbonne), where from Carolingian times they had enjoyed a very favourable situation (see *Early Travels in Palestine* [London: Bohn Library, 1848], p. 64).

10. In the Roman Empire the Jews lost the right to serve in the legions in the fifth century. 'Samuel Ibn Nagrela commanded the forces of Granada in the eleventh century. In the wars between Christians and Moors in the Peninsula the Jews served on both sides, and later the Marranos took part in the Spanish conquest of the New World' (article, 'Armed Forces, Jews in', *Standard Jewish Encyclopaedia*, ed. Roth).

11. For the question of usury in the Bible see Deut. 23:31; Luke 6:35. There are also prohibitions in the Talmud. On condemnations by the Church: R. H. Tawney, *Religion and the Rise of Capitalism* (Harmondsworth: Penguin Books, 1942), pp. 47–48. Jews in trade: Henri Pirenne, *Economic and Social*

History of Medieval Europe, trans. I. E. Clegg (New York: Harcourt Brace, 1956), p. 11; Burns, *The First Europe*, p. 446. Interest rates charged by usurers at the time were extremely high: in the thirteenth century the Lombards (see note 12) charged over 43 percent per annum (Pirenne, *Economic and Social History*, p. 136).

12. *Inferno*, XVII.71. The Tuscans (Florentines) themselves are accused of the same sin. It was apparently during the thirteenth century that 'Christian' usurers began to offer serious competition to the Jews. The citizens of Cahors (south of France) became so notorious in this respect that the word 'Cahorsin' became a synonym for 'usurer' (just as with 'Samaritan' and 'money-changer' at the time of Justinian [Milman, *History of the Jews*, Vol. II, p. 230]). But they were soon outstripped by the Lombards (Pirenne, *Economic and Social History*, p. 135).

13. Allport, *Nature of Prejudice*, pp. 124, 192ff. A comparative study made between groups of Catholics, Protestants, and Jews as to which of the three was most 'money-minded' showed no significant difference (Dorothy Spoerl, 'The Jewish Stereotype, the Jewish Personality, and Jewish Prejudice', *Yivo Annual of Jewish Social Science*, 7 (1952), 268–76; Allport, *Nature of Prejudice*, p. 124). On the wall of Rothenburg in Germany there was an inscription (probably dating from the sixteenth or seventeenth century) showing the caricature of a Jew with a moneybag and verses that began: 'Profit, Gier und List / Im Handeln bey mir ist . . .' (Profit, greed, and cunning are my business).

14. In the fourteenth century it was renewed in Germany under the name of *Opferpfennig*, 'as a token that the Holy Roman Emperor had inherited, from Vespasian to Titus, supremacy over the people conquered and enslaved so many hundreds of years before' (Roth, *Short History*, p. 209).

15. Milman, *History of the Jews*, Vol. II, pp. 297–98.

16. See, for instance, Eric Dingwall, *Racial Pride and Prejudice* (London: Watts, 1946); George E. Simpson and J. Milton Yinger, *Racial and Cultural Minorities: An Analysis of Prejudice and Discrimination*, 4th ed. (New York: Harper & Row, 1972), pp. 241ff. In both Rhodesia and South Africa sexual intercourse between a white woman and a coloured man is an offence which often goes to the courts. In the United States it is notorious that many lynchings of Negroes in the southern states were caused by a supposed infringement of sexual segregation. It was widely assumed that a white woman ('sacred' to the Negro) would never feel sexually attracted to a coloured man, and therefore every case tended to be regarded as one of rape.

17. Talking about the anti-Semitic campaign in Germany towards the end of the nineteenth century, Leschnitzer writes: 'In the mouths of their assailants, the word "Jew" had an ugly, terrifying sound. There was contempt in it and hatred and many other undefinable passions' (*Magic Background of Modern Anti-Semitism*, p. 87).

18. For variations in the Jewish badge see Israel Abrahams, *Jewish Life in the Middle Ages* (New York: Temple Books, 1969), pp. 295ff.

19. Quoted by Milman, *History of the Jews*, Vol. II, p. 420.

20. *Inferno*, XXXIV.117.

21. In *The Merchant of Venice* Shylock complains to the anti-Semite Antonio:

> You call me misbeliever, cut-throat dog,
> And spet upon my Jewish gaberdine (I.3.103–4).

22. Quoted in Harold Fisch, *The Dual Image: A Study of the Figure of the Jew in English Literature* (London: Lincolns-Prager, 1959), pp. 13, 15.

23. *Réflexions sur la question juive*, p. 173.

8. EXPULSIONS AND AUTOS-DA-FÉ

1. 'Digest of Columbus's Log-Book on His First Voyage', from *The Four Voyages of Christopher Columbus*, ed. and trans. J. M. Cohen (Harmondsworth: Penguin Books, 1969), p. 38.

2. Translated from the original document in Spanish transcribed in the useful appendix to José Amador de los Rios, *Historia social, politica y religiosa de los Judios de España y Portugal* (Buenos Aires, 1943), Vol. III, p. 588. The edict is also quoted in Poliakov, *History of Anti-Semitism*, Vol. II, p. 198.

3. That such a slogan of unity was very much in people's minds in Spain is shown by a painting of St. Vincent Ferrer ordering Jewish and Moorish books to be burnt. From the flames a scroll goes up with the words 'UNUS DEUS, UNA FIDES, UNA BAPTISMA'. See Melveena McKendrick, *Ferdinand and Isabella* (London: Cassell, 1969), p. 122.

4. Josephus, *Against Apion*, II.18.178. For the commandment to teach the Law to children see Deut. 6:7; 11:19. Law written in the heart: Jer. 31:33.

5. Charles Singer, 'The Nature of the Jewish Factor', in *The Legacy of Israel*, ed. Edwyn Bevan and Charles Singer (Oxford University Press, 1953), pp. 177–80.

6. Quoted in Milman, *History of the Jews*, Vol. II, p. 379.

7. 'Like a dog that returns to his vomit, is a fool that repeats his folly': Prov. 26:11; quoted II Pet. 2:22.

8. Translated from the edict in Spanish transcribed in Amador de los Rios, *Historia social*, Vol. II, pp. 585ff.

9. Cecil Roth, *A History of the Marranos* (New York: Meridian Books, 1959), p. 53.

10. Translated from the Portuguese edict transcribed in Amador de los Rios, *Historia social*, Vol. II, p. 595.

11. Roth, *History of the Marranos*, p. 58.

12. Ibid., p. 65.

13. Voltaire, *Romans et contes* (Paris: Classiques Garnier, 1955), p. 149. In fact the auto-da-fé to which he refers took place in the following year, on 20 June 1756. For the condemnation of the Spanish and Portuguese Inquisition in contemporary Europe, see Roth, *History of the Marranos*, pp. 346ff.

14. Ibid., pp. 111ff.

15. Title of chap. 6 of *Candide* (*Romans et contes*, p. 149).

16. *Don Quixote*, Part I, Book III, chap. 6. Some Spanish Catholics held beliefs that amounted to a theory of 'racial pollution' comparable to Nazi anti-Semitism (see Chap. 12). See Poliakov, *History of Anti-Semitism*, Vol. II, p. 226.

17. C. R. Boxer, *The Portuguese Seaborne Empire* (London: Hutchinson, 1969), p. 269.

18. Poliakov, *History of Anti-Semitism*, Vol. II, p. 220.

19. Ibid.

20. Boxer, *Portuguese Seaborne Empire*, p. 272.

21. George Borrow, *The Bible in Spain*, Everyman ed. (London: Dent, 1947), p. 109.

22. Ibid., p. 166.

23. Roth, *History of the Marranos*, pp. 363–64. This is a summary of the story told by Samuel Schwarz himself in his book *Os Cristãos-Novos em Portugal no século XX* (Lisbon, 1925), pp. 8–12. The book transcribes a series of Jewish prayers used by the Belmonte community and is illustrated with photographs of some of the families Schwarz met.

24. For a very detailed account of Jews and anti-Semitism in modern Spain see Baroja, *Los Judios en la España moderna*. As we shall see in Chap. 11, in the 1830s a Spaniard of Jewish origin, Juan Mendizábal, became finance minister for a short period, and Disraeli made much of this in his novel *Coningsby*.

9. THE WANDERING JEW AND THE NEW WORLD

1. Sibylline Oracles, III.271; quoted by Pfeiffer, *New Testament Times*, p. 166.

2. Talmud, *Pesahim*, 87b; quoted by Pfeiffer, *New Testament Times*, p. 190.

3. Roth, *History of the Marranos*, p. 262.

4. Joseph Gaer, *The Legend of the Wandering Jew* (New York: Mentor Books, 1961), p. 14.

5. Quoted by Poliakov, *History of Anti-Semitism*, Vol. I, p. 242, note 19.

6. Quoted by Francesca Wilson, *They Came as Strangers* (London: Hamish Hamilton, 1959), p. 28.

7. Ibid., p. 29.

8. For the original document in Portuguese see *Anais da Biblioteca Nacional* (Rio de Janeiro), 74 (1953), 213. For an account in English: Arnold Wisnitzer, *The Jews in Colonial Brazil* (New York: Columbia University Press, 1960), pp. 12ff.

9. On Bento Teixeira Pinto see José Antonio Gonçalves de Mello, *Estudos Pernambucanos* (Recife, 1960), with full bibliography.

10. Oliveira Lima, *A Nova Lusitania: Historia da colonização Portuguesa do Brasil* (Rio de Janeiro, no date), Vol. III, pp. 294–95.

11. Wisnitzer, *Jews in Colonial Brazil*, pp. 40ff. The connection between Judaism and 'heretical books' seems to have persisted in the Peninsula, for when George Borrow travelled in Spain in 1840–41 distributing Spanish Protes-

tant Bibles he was accused of spreading *libros judios,* or 'Jewish books' (see *Bible in Spain*). For earlier Spanish translations of the Bible (in manuscript), particularly that of Moses Arragel, see G. H. Box, 'Hebrew Scholarship in the Middle Ages', in *Legacy of Israel,* ed. Bevan and Singer, pp. 311–12.

12. José Antonio Gonçalves de Mello, *Tempo do flamengos* (Rio de Janeiro: José Olimpio, 1947), p. 221; Wisnitzer, *Jews in Colonial Brazil,* p. 56.

13. For the Portuguese version see *Revista do Instituto Arqueologico e Geografico de Pernambuco,* 31 (1945), 289. See also Wisnitzer, *Jews in Colonial Brazil,* p. 57.

14. *A Documentary History of the Jews in the United States, 1654–1875,* ed. Morris U. Schappes, 3rd ed. (New York: Schocken Books, 1971), pp. 1–2.

15. Roth, *History of the Marranos,* p. 293.

16. Wisnitzer, *Jews in Colonial Brazil,* p. 165; Boxer, *Portuguese Seaborne Empire,* p. 270.

17. For a full account see J. Lucio D'Azevedo, *Historia dos Christãos Novos portugueses* (Lisbon, 1921), pp. 343–45. D'Azevedo points out as a factor in the final trial the envy and annoyance caused by Antonio José's satirical farces. He was denounced by a woman slave who accused him of not working on Saturdays and keeping fasts on days not prescribed by the Catholic Church.

10. FROM REFORMATION TO REVOLUTION

1. Martin Luther, *Deutsche Schriften* (Vienna: Phaidon, 1927). See also Poliakov, *History of Anti-Semitism,* Vol. I, p. 222.

2. Ibid., pp. 217–19.

3. Richard Friedenthal, *Luther,* trans. John Newell (London: Weidenfeld & Nicolson, 1967), p. 525.

4. Poliakov, *History of Anti-Semitism,* Vol. I, p. 241.

5. H. Graetz, *History of the Jews* (London, 1891–92), Vol. V, p. 199ff.

6. All these supposed references (some of them authentic) were examined in detail by Klausner in his important work *Jesus of Nazareth,* pp. 18ff. Most of them are doubtful or ambiguous and add practically nothing to our knowledge of Jesus.

7. For the controversy see G. H. Box, 'Hebrew Studies in the Reformation Period and After', in *Legacy of Israel,* ed. Bevan and Singer, pp. 321–22. Poliakov (*History of Anti-Semitism,* Vol. I, pp. 213ff.) points out that even Reuchlin was somewhat anti-Jewish and that the Dominicans 'seem in comparison more clement'.

8. See Klausner's detailed analysis of the *Tol 'doth Yeshu* in *Jesus of Nazareth,* pp. 47–54. The title is the parody of a Biblical expression frequently used in genealogies and imitated by the Gospels (Matthew begins, 'The book of the generations of Jesus Christ', and perhaps the compiler of the *Tol 'doth* intended to mock this versicle). Klausner says that the book, banned by the censor in Russia and Poland, was then (1929) rare, but at one time had been very popular 'in Hebrew and Yiddish among the simpler-minded Jews, and even more educated Jews used to study the book during the nights of *Natal* [Christ-

mas]. . . . Our mothers knew its contents by hearsay—of course with all manner of corruptions, changes, omissions and imaginative additions—and handed them on to their children' (*Jesus of Nazareth*, p. 48). In the *Tol 'doth Yeshu* Jesus is the son of Mary's adultery with a handsome villain called Joseph Pandera, or Ben Pandera (who in other versions is a Roman soldier): the defamatory story that Jesus was a 'son of fornication' appears in one of the Apocryphal Gospels and elsewhere. It emerged very early and is mentioned by Origen (third century). In many ways the *Tol 'doth Yeshu* simply turns the Gospel story upside down. Yeshu is the villain and the blasphemer, while Judas (Yehuda Iskarioto) appears as the hero who defeats his magic arts. Yeshu is hanged in the end (not crucified) on the eve of the Passover (this version is similar to one of the Talmudic passages analyzed by Klausner [*Jesus of Nazareth*, p. 27]).

As one can see, the *Tol 'doth Yeshu* is in every way similar to the defamatory stories the Christians invented about Muhammad or the Catholics used to circulate about Luther. That Christian anti-Semitism made Christ a hateful figure to the Jews is not one of its least regrettable results. In our own days, as one would expect, there has been a gradual reassessment of Jesus and Christianity in Judaism.

9. Box, 'Hebrew Studies', p. 321. For an account of the Reuchlin dispute and Luther's attitude to it see Friedenthal, *Luther*, pp. 108–16.

10. Quoted in Poliakov, *History of Anti-Semitism*, Vol. I, p. 249.

11. Ibid., p. 256.

12. Ibid., p. 279.

13. Norwood Young, *The Story of Rome* (London: Dent, 1907), p. 269. These races were originally introduced by Pope Paul II in 1466, and in the beginning the Jewish event was a genuine competition for boys under twenty. It was only later that it degenerated into sadistic mockery. See Cecil Roth, *The History of the Jews of Italy* (Philadelphia: Jewish Publication Society, 1946), pp. 386–87.

14. Quoted in Roth, *Jews of Italy*, pp. 374–75.

15. Graetz, *History of the Jews*, Vol. V, p. 268.

16. For the text of the act see *Documentary History*, ed. Schappes, p. 26.

17. Both quotations from the French article transcribed in Fleg, *Anthologie juive*, Vol. II, p. 164.

18. Roth, *Jews of Italy*, pp. 434–35.

19. See, for instance, Werner Cohn, 'The Politics of American Jews', in *The Jews: Social Patterns of an American Group*, ed. Sklare, pp. 614ff. For Britain the *Jewish Year Book* for 1975 gives a list of Jewish MPs in the House of Commons, of which 34 are Labour, 10 Conservative, and 1 Liberal (Clement Freud, a relative of Sigmund Freud).

20. Jews from Galicia arrived in Palestine 'with no clothes, but with a copy of *Das Kapital* and *Die Traumdeutung* under their arms' (Ernest Jones, *The Life and Work of Sigmund Freud* [New York: Basic Books, 1956], Vol. III, p. 31; letter from Freud, who had been informed by Dr. Weizmann).

21. Tobias Monteiro, *Elaboração da independencia*, quoted in Artur Hehl

Neiva, *Estudo sobre a imigração semita no Brasil* (Study on Semitic Immigration to Brazil [Rio de Janeiro: Imprensa Nacional, 1945]), pp. 30–31.

11. ANTI-SEMITISM AS A POLITICAL MOVEMENT

1. Flannery, *Anguish of the Jews*, p. xii.

2. For the Leo Frank case see Leonard Dinnerstein, 'A Dreyfus Affair in Georgia', in *Antisemitism in the United States*, ed. Dinnerstein, p. 87. He also wrote *The Leo Frank Case* (New York: Columbia University Press, 1968). The murder, which had no ritual implications, was generally given a sexual motivation and has never been really cleared up (another suspect was a Negro watchman).

3. Quoted in Lapide, *The Last Three Popes and the Jews*, p. 114.

4. For a Frankfurt cartoon (1845) of Amschel Rothschild (one of the founder's sons) see Eduard Fuchs, *Die Juden in der Karikatur* (Munich: Langen, 1921), pp. 120–21. There is also a much later French caricature (end of the century) showing Rothschild grabbing the globe with clawlike hands (Fuchs, p. 208).

5. A. Toussenel, *Les Juifs, rois de l'époque*, 4th ed. (Paris: Dentu, 1888), Vol. I, p. xi of introduction.

6. Ibid., p. xv.

7. Ibid., p. xxx.

8. Ibid., Vol. II, p. 291.

9. As often happens with famous phrases, this one too has been fathered on other people. Eduard Fuchs, who quotes it as 'Der Antisemitismus ist der Sozialismus der dummen Kerle', attributes it to the Communist leader Liebknecht (*Die Juden in der Karikatur*, p. 80).

10. For some quotations of this essay see Cang, *Silent Millions*, pp. 37ff. Karl Marx's attitudes to the Jews have been analyzed by Edmund Silberner, 'Was Marx an Anti-Semite?' *Historia Judaica*, 11 (1949), 3–52.

11. Benjamin Disraeli, *Coningsby; or, The New Generation* (London: John Lehmann, 1948), p. 228. Sidonia's background is explained in detail in chap. 10, and the conversation with Coningsby takes up all of chap. 15 of Book 4.

12. Ibid., p. 229.

13. Ibid., p. 230.

14. See Baroja, *Los Judíos en la España moderna*, Vol. III, pp. 181–84, for Mendizábal's Jewish ancestry. It was rumoured that he was dismissed because Queen María Cristina objected to his 'Jewish blood', of which the minister was supposed to boast.

15. James Parkes, *Antisemitism* (London: Valentine, Mitchell, 1963), p. 72.

16. There is now a vast literature on Gobineau and other racialist writers. For a short, lively account see chap. 10 ('Gobineau and His Contemporaries') of Léon Poliakov's recent *The Aryan Myth: A History of Racist and Nationalist Ideas in Europe* (New York: Basic Books, 1974), particularly pp. 233ff.

17. About Wagner as anti-Semite see Poliakov, *History of Anti-Semitism*, Vol. III, pp. 440ff.

18. Marr, *Der Sieg des Judenthums über das Germanenthum*, 4th ed. (Berne, 1879), p. 37. It is amusing that among a number of other contemporary booklets that the British Museum Library has bound together in a single volume (Marr's is the very last), there is one by a certain S. Backhaus offering evidence that the Germans are a people of 'Semitic' origin (*Die Germanen ein semitischer Volksstamm* [Berlin, 1878]). It seems to have escaped the attention of Léon Poliakov in his thorough, fascinating study of racialist fantasies (*Aryan Myth*).

19. Eça de Queiroz, *Cartas de Inglaterra* (Letters from England), my translation from the Portuguese edition of his *Obras completas* (Porto: Lello & Irmão, no date), Vol. II, p. 533. Eça mentions with delight that old Professor Virchow rose in the Reichstag to speak for the Jews.

20. Otto Johlinger, *Bismarck und die Juden* quoted in Parkes, *Antisemitism*, p. 27. For a short account of Bismarck's tortuous manoeuvres see Erich Eyck, *Bismarck and the German Empire* (London: Allen & Unwin, 1968), pp. 223ff. Also A. J. P. Taylor's article 'Otto von Bismarck', in the *Encyclopædia Britannica*.

21. H. S. Chamberlain, *Die Grundlagen des neunzehnten Jahrhunderts*, 4th ed. (Munich, 1903), Vol. I, pp. 218–19. James Parkes relates how he met a Nazi theological student who was very surprised to hear that 'I, as a theologian, had not been taught that Jesus was a German, son of a German soldier and a Persian [i.e., Aryan] woman. He appeared, quite sincerely, to believe that this was an accepted conclusion of scholarship' (*Antisemitism*, p. 91). This preposterous invention seems to be a later distortion of the Jewish *Tol 'doth Yeshu*, which made Jesus the son of Mary's adultery (see Chap. 10, note 8).

22. *Peter Pulzer*, 'The Development of Political Antisemitism in Austria', in *The Jews of Austria*, ed. Josef Fraenkel (London: Valentine, Mitchell, 1967), p. 429.

23. *Antisemitism*, p. 32.

24. Adolf Hitler, *Mein Kampf*, official NSDAP (Nazi) ed. (Munich, 1938), Vol. I, p. 59. There is a good recent English translation by Ralph Mannheim (London: Radius Books/Hutchinson, 1972); for this passage, p. 52.

25. Ibid.: German, p. 61; Mannheim's English translation, p. 53.

26. Konrad Heiden, *Der Fuehrer*, trans. Ralph Mannheim (London: Pordes, 1967), p. 61.

27. *Mein Kampf*, p. 61; p. 53 in the translation.

28. Ibid., p. 357; p. 295 in the translation.

29. Ibid., p. 135; p. 113 in the translation (Mannheim prefers to translate *Blutschande* as 'racial desecration').

30. See William Shirer, *The Rise and Fall of the Third Reich* (New York: Simon & Schuster, 1960), pp. 131–32.

31. Allport, *Nature of Prejudice*, p. 389.

32. Jones, *Sigmund Freud*, Vol. I, p. 22. For Freud's attitude to the Jews see Friedrich Heer, 'Freud, the Viennese Jew', and Martin Esslin, 'Freud's Vienna', in *Freud: The Man, His World, His Influence*, ed. Jonathan Miller (London: Weidenfeld & Nicolson, 1972). Also Martin Freud, 'Who Was Freud?', in *Jews of Austria*, ed. Fraenkel, p. 197.

33. This was the so-called 'cantonist system'. For details see Louis Greenberg, *The Jews in Russia* (New Haven: Yale University Press, 1944), Vol. I, pp. 48ff.

34. Ibid., Vol. II (1951), p. 19.

35. Ibid., p. 30.

36. Ibid., p. 76.

37. There is an English translation (published with other writings by Pinsker under the title *The Road to Freedom: Writings and Addresses* [New York: Scopus, 1944]), from which I quote in Chap. 14.

38. Flannery, *Anguish of the Jews*, p. 187.

39. Quoted by Roger Soltau, 'The Struggle between the Two Frances', in *The Dreyfus Affair*, ed. Leslie Derfler (Boston: D. C. Heath, 1966), p. 73.

40. Extract from his book *From Dreyfus to Pétain: The Struggle of a Republic* (1947), printed in *Dreyfus Affair*, ed. Derfler, p. 76.

12. THE SIGN OF THE SWASTIKA

1. For the text of Simonini's letter see the anti-Semitic book written by the tsarist general A. Netchvolodow, *L'Empereur Nicolas II et les Juifs* (Paris, 1924), pp. 231–34.

2. 'Sir John Retcliffe', *Biarritz: A Historical Political Novel* (Berlin, 1868). This is in fact a huge series of novels in several volumes (there is a copy in the British Museum Library), and the chapter in question—'Auf dem Judenkirchhof in Prag'—occupies no fewer than fifty pages (pp. 141–93 of Vol. I). The phrases quoted are from pp. 167 and 185. As far as I know, there is no English translation of the novel, but Herman Bernstein's book, *The Truth about the Protocols of Zion* (New York: Covici, Friede, 1935), includes a translation of the whole relevant chapter, made from the Russian version of 1872 (pp. 265–84).

3. Quoted from the English version of 'The Jewish Cemetery in Prague', trans. Bernstein, *Protocols of Zion*, pp. 280–81, which is practically identical with *The Rabbi's Speech* (for which see Bernstein, pp. 285–92; Cohn, *Warrant for Genocide*, pp. 269–74).

4. Gougenot des Mousseaux, *Le Juif, le judaïsme et la judaïsation des peuples chrétiens* (Paris: Henri Plon, 1869), p. 530. At this point Mousseaux quotes in his support Éliphas Lévi, the contemporary writer on magic. Earlier in the book he devotes a long chapter to stories of ritual murder (which he calls *assassinat talmudique*) and recalls the comparatively recent case of Father Thomas (see chap. 6, pp. 184ff.), who mysteriously disappeared in Damascus in 1840 with a servant. Christian mobs accused the Jews of murder, and a number of Jewish residents were arrested and subjected to torture. There followed protests from Jewish communities in Europe, and Sir Moses Montefiore in England and Adolphe Crémieux in France intervened. Finally, the Ottoman sultan ordered the release of the Jews and proclaimed their innocence.

5. Quoted in Lapide, *The Last Three Popes and the Jews*, p. 81.

6. Bernstein, *Protocols of Zion*, pp. 30–31; Cohn, *Warrant for Genocide*, p. 69.

7. Cohn, *Warrant for Genocide*, p. 117.

8. Agar, *Saving Remnant*, p. 31.

9. Quoted in Cohn, *Warrant for Genocide*, pp. 123–24.

10. See Shirer, *Rise and Fall of the Third Reich*, pp. 31–32. That by the early 1920s this had become a current idea in Germany is shown, for instance, by Fuchs, *Die Juden in der Karikatur*, p. 78.

11. 'Dreihundert Männer, von denen jeder jeden kennt, leiten die wirtschaftlichen Geschicke des Kontinents und suchen sich Nachfolger aus ihrer Umgebung', Walter Rathenau, *Zur Kritik der Zeit* (Towards a Critique of Our Time) (Berlin: S. Fischer Verlag, 1922), p. 207. For an example of anti-Semitic use of this passage see preface to *Protocols of the Meetings of the Learned Elders of Zion*, trans. Victor E. Marsden (London: Britons Publishing Society, 1933), p. 7.

12. Cohn, *Warrant for Genocide*, pp. 158–59.

13. For brief historical accounts of anti-Semitism in the United States see John Higham, 'American Antisemitism Historically Reconsidered', in *Antisemitism in the United States*, ed. Dinnerstein, pp. 63–77; Simpson and Yinger, *Racial and Cultural Minorities*, p. 273.

14. *The Times*, 8 May 1920. The unsigned article, under the same title as that of the book, *The Jewish Peril*, is followed, ironically enough, by a report about *Dr. Weizmann on the Future of Palestine*. The author openly admits that alarm at the wave of revolutions might make such ideas attractive to many people and writes: 'The average man thinks that there is something very fundamentally wrong with the world he lives in. He will eagerly grasp a plausible "working hypothesis" '.

15. Hermann Rauschning, *Hitler Speaks* (London, 1939), pp. 235–36.

16. *Protocols*, trans. Marsden. See also the version conveniently printed by Bernstein in *Protocols of Zion*, p. 302.

17. For pictures of the *Uroboros* see Erich Neumann, *The Origins and History of Consciousness*, Bollingen series XLII (New York: Pantheon, 1954), chap. 1. Neumann is a disciple of Jung (see also his *Aion* [London, 1959], passim), and I do not necessarily accept the speculations of the Jungian school.

18. Pierre Teilhard de Chardin, *The Future of Man*, trans. Norman Denny (London: Collins, 1965), p. 43.

19. Hilberg, *Destruction of the European Jews*, pp. 5ff.

20. Ibid., p. 12.

21. Shirer, *Rise and Fall of the Third Reich*, p. 234.

22. See Lionel Kochan, *Pogrom, 10 November 1938* (London: Deutsch, 1957).

23. Gerald Reitlinger, *The Final Solution* (London: Valentine, Mitchell, 1955).

24. Quoted in Hilberg, *Destruction of the European Jews*, pp. 656–57.

25. M. Muller-Claudius, *Der Antisemitismus und das deutsche Verhängnis* (Frankfurt-am-Main, 1948), pp. 162–66; see also Cohn, *Warrant for Genocide*, pp. 210–12.

26. Quoted in Russell, *Scourge of the Swastika*, p. 256.

27. Both quotations ibid., pp. 256–57.

28. Hilberg, *Destruction of the European Jews*, p. 151.

13. AND IT GOES ON . . .

1. Bernard Goldstein, *The Stars Bear Witness* (New York: Viking, 1949); Goldstein was the Jew arrested for speaking Yiddish. See Agar, *Saving Remnant*, pp. 111–12.

2. Ibid., pp. 187–88.

3. Howard Ehrlich, 'The Swastika Epidemic of 1953–1960: Anti-Semitism and Community Characteristics', *Social Problems* (1962), quoted in Simpson and Yinger, *Racial and Cultural Minorities*, p. 277.

4. Parkes, *Antisemitism*, p. 112.

5. Report in the London *Sunday Times*, 23 February 1975, p. 4. The pamphlet, written by Richard Harwood (supposed to be working with the University of London, which denied all connection with him), was sent to all British Members of Parliament and to leading citizens of the Jewish community. It claims, among other things, that *The Diary of Anne Frank* (a well-known account of a Jewish child in Holland during the Nazi occupation) is a forgery. The Board of Deputies of British Jews asked the Director of Public Prosecutions to take action against author and publisher under the Race Relations Act, but got the reply that it would be 'too difficult to prove intent to stir up hatred'.

6. Litvinoff, *A Peculiar People*, p. 201.

7. Neiva, *Estudo sobre a imigração Semita no Brazil*, p. 200.

8. Gustavo Barroso, *Brasil colonia de banqueiros* (São Paulo, 1934).

9. *Por que ser anti-semita?* (Why be anti-Semite?), opinions from 35 Brazilian intellectuals (Rio de Janeiro: Civilização Brasileira, 1933); see also Nelson Saldanha, *Historia das ideias politicas no Brasil* (Recife: Imprensa Universitaria, 1968), p. 296.

10. Quoted in Arnold Forster and Benjamin R. Epstein, *The New Anti-Semitism* (New York: McGraw-Hill, 1974), p. 283.

11. Ibid., p. 282.

12. A. F. Kerensky, *The Kerensky Memoirs* (London: Cassell, 1966), p. 210.

13. Maxim Litvinov, *Notes for a Journal* (London: Andre Deutsch, 1955), p. 34.

14. For titles and details see Cang, *Silent Millions*, pp. 68ff.

15. Parkes, *Antisemitism*, p. 148.

16. Litvinov, *Journal*, pp. 46–47.

17. See Joel Cang's detailed account in *Silent Millions*, p. 108ff.

18. Ibid., p. 112.

19. Joshua Rothenberg, 'Jewish Religion in the Soviet Union', in *The Jews in Soviet Russia since 1917*, ed. Lionel Kochan (Oxford University Press, 1972), pp. 180–81; see also Cang, *Silent Millions*.

20. *Jews in Soviet Russia*, p. 175.

21. William Korey, 'The Legal Position of Soviet Jewry,' in *Jews in Soviet Russia*, ed. pp. 96–97.

22. *The Times* (London), 2 January 1975.

23. For the question of Jewish passports see Korey, 'The Legal Position of Soviet Jewry', and also Alec Nove and J. A. Newth, 'The Jewish Population', in *Jews in Soviet Russia*, ed. Kochan, pp. 126–29. See also Bernard D. Weinryb, 'Anti-Semitism in Soviet Russia', p. 288 in the same book, of which I have made use in this chapter. For use of the derogatory term *Zhid* in Soviet Russia, see article by Zev Katz, p. 327 of the book, and also the popular term *Abrams*, p. 305.

24. Uri Avnery, *Israel without Zionists* (New York and London: Macmillan, 1968), p. 212.

25. Y. Harkabi, *Arab Attitudes to Israel*, trans. Misha Louvish (London: Valentine, Mitchell, 1972), p. 220.

26. Ibid., p. 235.

27. Gideon Hausner, *Justice in Jerusalem* (London: Nelson, 1967), p. 346.

28. Harkabi, *Arab Attitudes*, pp. 224–25.

29. Avnery, *Israel without Zionists*, p. 156.

30. *Mein Kampf*, p. 69; p. 59 in Mannheim's translation.

31. Mousseaux, *Le Juif, le judaïsme, et la judaisation*, p. 408.

32. Isaac Deutscher, *The Non-Jewish Jew and Other Essays* (Oxford University Press, 1968), p. 41; see also pp. 123–25.

14. FINAL REFLECTIONS ON PREJUDICE

1. See, for instance, Isidore Pushkin and Thelma Veness, 'The Development of Racial Awareness and Prejudice in Children', in *Psychology and Race*, ed. Peter Watson (Harmondsworth: Penguin Books, 1973), pp. 23ff.

2. Marian Radke Yarrow, 'Personality Development and Minority Group Membership', in *The Jews*, ed. Sklare, p. 455.

3. See Philip Mason, *Common Sense about Race* (London: Gollancz, 1961), p. 91.

4. Bernard Lazare, *L'Antisémitisme* (English translation, pp. 156ff.), gives a good account of the part played by fanatical Jewish converts in anti-Jewish literature and persecution.

5. Leschnitzer, *Magic Background of Modern Anti-Semitism*, p. 11.

6. John Dewey, *How We Think*, p. 121, quoted in Walter Lippmann, *Public Opinion* (New York: Harcourt, Brace, 1922), p. 80.

7. George Mikes, *How to Be an Alien* (London: Wingate, 1950), p. 82.

8. *Epistola ad Diognetum* (Tübingen: V. Hefele, 1847), in *Patrum apostolicorum opera*, pp. 308–10.

9. Leo Pinsker, *Auto-Emancipation*, included in *The Road to Freedom*, pp. 81, 83–84. Also quoted in Greenberg, *Jews in Russia*, Vol. II, p. 71. Pinsker's book was originally published in Berlin in 1882 under the title *Auto-emanzipation: Ein Mahruf an seine Stammesgenossen* (An Appeal to His People), and signed simply, 'By a Russian Jew'.

10. See *The Jews*, ed. Sklare, passim.

11. Lazare, *L'Antisémitisme*, pp. 239–40.

12. Pinsker, *Road to Freedom*, p. 78.

13. Else Frenkel-Brunswik and Nevitt R. Sanford, 'Some Personality Factors in Anti-Semitism', *Journal of Psychology*, 20 (Oct. 1945), pp. 271–91.

14. From the summary of the study in Simpson and Yinger, *Racial and Cultural Minorities*, p. 78. For a good short account of this and other papers see also Arnold Rose, *The Roots of Prejudice* (Paris: UNESCO, 1958), p. 32.

15. T. W. Adorno and others, *The Authoritarian Personality* (New York: Norton Library, 1969), p. 971.

16. Simpson and Yinger, *Racial and Cultural Minorities*, p. 79.

17. Eugene Hartley, *Problems in Prejudice* (New York: King's Crown Press, 1946).

18. Nathan Ackerman and Marie Jahoda, *Anti-Semitism and Emotional Disorder* (New York: Harper & Row, 1950), pp. 39–40.

19. James H. Robb, *Working-Class Anti-Semite* (London: Tavistock, 1954).

20. Ibid., p. 152.

21. For an analysis of Luther's authoritarianism (and of authoritarian attitudes in general) see Erich Fromm, *Escape from Freedom* (New York: Holt, Rinehart & Winston, 1941), pp. 69ff.

22. *History of Anti-Semitism*, Vol. I, p. 153.

23. I have developed this point in my book *The Emancipation of Women* (*A Emancipação da mulher* [Porto Alegre, 1968]), which is really a history of male stereotypes and prejudices about women. For witch-hunting as a weapon against 'women's lib' in Europe and Africa see Geoffrey Parrinder, *Witchcraft* (Harmondsworth: Penguin Books, 1958), p. 57. Talking about authoritarian attitudes (and commenting on Weininger's book *Sex and Character*), J. K. Folsom and Marion Bassett write: 'It is an attitude which readily transfers itself from one object to another. It is a passionate need to believe that some human beings are inherently less worthy than others. It is almost a refusal to accept the fact that mankind is a single species, a protest against nature for not having created more useful types of animals immediately below man' (*The Family and Democratic Society* [London: Routledge & Kegan Paul, 1948], p. 633).

24. See Peter Pulzer, *The Rise of Political Anti-Semitism in Germany and Austria* (New York: Wiley, 1964), for Germany and Austria in the nineteenth century. There is a wealth of information about the reactionary attitude to women under National Socialism. See, for instance, Richard Grunberg, *A Social History of the Third Reich* (London: Weidenfeld & Nicolson, 1971), pp. 251ff.

25. Otto Weininger, *Sex and Character* (London: Heinemann, 1916), pp. 307–8. He also makes the point that 'the bitterest anti-Semites are to be found amongst the Jews themselves' (p. 304)—a relevant observation, since poor Weininger himself was consumed with self-hatred. And yet he had flashes of intuition and seems to have been aware of projection. A terribly withdrawn and schizoid personality, he was showing signs of psychosis just before his suicide. See the book written by the psychiatrist David Abrahamsen under the somewhat inflated title *The Mind and Death of a Genius* (New

York: Columbia University Press, 1946). It is interesting to recall that Weininger showed the first version of his book (presented as a Ph.D. thesis) to
Freud, who had an unfavourable opinion of it.

26. *Racial and Cultural Minorities*, p. 64.

27. This point is rightly stressed by Leschnitzer, who says that this 'permanent failure in political life is so intimately connected with a collapse of civilization' *Magic Background of Modern Anti-Semitism*, p. 75).

28. Nyanaponika Thera, *The Heart of Buddhist Meditation* (London:
Rider, 1969), pp. 35–36.

POSTSCRIPT

1. For Teilhard's illuminating concept of convergence see his fundamental
works *The Phenomenon of Man* and *The Future of Man*, both translated into
English and published by Collins in London. For the notion of 'enroulement':
Julian Huxley's introduction to *The Phenomenon of Man* (1969), p. 16. Teilhard de Chardin, *Je m'explique* (Paris: Éditions du Seuil, 1966), pp. 73, 77.

2. See, for instance, Milton Yinger and G. E. Simpson's two chapters on
'Techniques for Reducing Prejudice' in *Psychology and Race*, ed. Watson,
pp. 96, 145.

3. Quoted in the *Encyclopædia Britannica* article on Martin Luther King
(1974 ed.).

4. Avnery, *Israel without Zionists*, p. 81.

5. Quoted without source as epigraph in Poliakov, *Histoire de l'antisémitisme* (Paris: Calmann-Levy, 1968), Vol. III, *De Voltaire à Wagner*.

6. Ralph Linton, *Study of Man* (London: Peter Owen, 1965), p. 325.

7. Ibid., p. 327.

8. In the play *Too True to Be Good*, Act I.

9. Romain Rolland, *The Life of Vivekananda*, trans. E. F. Malcolm-Smith
(Almora, Himalayas (India): Advaita Ashrama, 1953), 39–40. See also 'The
Ideal of a Universal Religion', in *Speeches and Writings of Swami Vivekananda*
(Madras: Natesan, 1927), p. 362.

10. *The Asian Journal of Thomas Merton*, published by his friends after his
death in 1968 (London: Sheldon Press, 1974), p. 314.

Select Bibliography

GENERAL WORKS ON JEWISH HISTORY AND ANTI-SEMITISM

Baron, Salo Wittmayer. *A Social and Religious History of the Jews*, 2nd ed. 8 vols. New York: Columbia University Press, 1952–58.

Bevan, Edwyn R., and Charles Singer, eds. *The Legacy of Israel*. Oxford: Oxford University Press, 1953 (1927).

Encyclopaedia Judaica. Jerusalem, 1971.

Epstein, Isidore. *Judaism*. Harmondsworth: Penguin Books, 1959.

Finkelstein, Louis. *The Jews, Their History, Culture, and Religion*. 2 vols. London: Peter Owen, 1961.

Flannery, Edward H. *The Anguish of the Jews*. New York: Macmillan, 1965.

Fleg, Edmond. *Anthologie juive*. 2 vols. Paris: Gallimard, 1939.

Graetz, H. *History of the Jews*, trans. Bella Löwy. 5 vols. London, 1891–92.

Lazare, Bernard. *L'Antisémitisme, son histoire et ses causes*. 2 vols. Paris: Chaillot, 1934 (1894). Also translated into English as *Anti-Semitism, Its History and Causes*. New York: International Library Publishing Co., 1903.

Milman, Henry Hart. *The History of the Jews*. Everyman Library. London: Dent, 1939 (1830).

Parkes, James. *Antisemitism*. London: Valentine, Mitchell, 1963.

———. *A History of the Jewish People*. Harmondsworth: Penguin Books, 1955.

Pinsker, Leo. *The Road to Freedom: Writings and Addresses* (including *Auto-Emancipation*). New York: Scopus, 1944.

Poliakov, Léon. *The History of Anti-Semitism*, Vol. I, *From Roman Times to the Court Jews*, trans. Richard Howard. London: Routledge & Kegan Paul, 1974.

———. Vol. II, *From Mohammed to the Marranos*, trans. Natalie Gerardi. London: Routledge & Kegan Paul, 1974.

———. Vol. III, *From Voltaire to Wagner*, trans. Miriam Kochan. London: Routledge & Kegan Paul, 1975.

Roth, Cecil. *A Short History of the Jewish People*, new ed. London: East & West Library, 1969.

———, ed. *Standard Jewish Encyclopaedia*. London: W. H. Allen, 1959.

Valentin, Hugo. *Anti-Semitism Historically and Critically Examined*. London: Gollancz, 1936.

JEWS IN ANTIQUITY AND EARLY CONFLICT
WITH CHRISTIANITY

Brandon, S. G. F. *The Trial of Jesus of Nazareth*. London: Batsford, 1968.

Bright, John. *A History of Israel*. London: SCM Press, 1972.

Buck, Harry M. *People of the Lord*. New York: Macmillan, 1966.
Carmichael, Joel. *The Death of Jesus*. Harmondsworth: Penguin Books, 1966.
Grant, Michael. *The Jews in the Roman World*. London: Weidenfeld & Nicolson, 1973.
Guignebert, Charles. *Le Christ*. Paris: Albin Michel, 1948.
Josephus, Flavius. *Contre Apion*, Édition Budé (bilingual) by Théodore Reinach and Léon Blum. Paris, 1930.
———. *The Jewish War*, trans. G. A. Williamson. Harmondsworth: Penguin Books, 1969.
———. *Works*, Loeb Classical Library. London: Heinemann, 1926–61.
Klausner, Joseph. *Jesus of Nazareth*, trans. Herbert Dandy. London: Allen & Unwin, 1947.
Noth, Martin. *A History of Israel*. London: Black, 1960.
Pfeiffer, Robert H. *History of New Testament Times*. New York: Harper, 1949.
———. *Introduction to the Old Testament*. New York: Harper, 1948.
Reinach, Théodore. *Textes d'auteurs grecs et romains relatifs au judaisme*. Paris: Ernest Leroux, 1895.
Schürer, Emil. *The History of the Jewish People in the Time of Jesus Christ*, Vol. I, rev. and ed. Geza Vermes and Fergus Millar. Edinburgh: Clark, 1973.
Simon, Marcel. *Les Sectus juives au temps de Jésus*. Paris: Presses Universitaires, 1960.
———. *Vérus Israel: Étude sur les rélations entre chrétiens et juifs dans l'empire romain* (135–425). Paris: Boccard, 1948.

MONOGRAPHS: WORKS ON SPECIAL PERIODS OR COUNTRIES

Abrahams, Israel. *Jewish Life in the Middle Ages*, 2nd ed. London: 1932; New York: Temple Books, 1969.
Agar, Herbert. *The Saving Remnant: An Account of Jewish Survival since 1914*. London: Rupert Hart-Davis, 1960.
Amador de los Rios, José Antonio. *Historia social, politica y religiosa de los judios de España y Portugal*. 2 vols. Buenos Aires, 1943.
Avnery, Uri. *Israel without Zionists*. New York and London: Macmillan, 1968.
Azevedo, J. Lucio d'. *Historia dos Christãos Novos portugueses*. Lisbon: Livraria Classica Editora, 1921.
Baroja, Julio Caro. *Los Judios en la España moderna y contemporanea*. 3 vols. Madrid: Ediciones Arion, 1961.
Beller, Jacob. *Jews in Latin America*. New York: Jonathan David, 1969.
Bernstein, Herman. *The Truth about the Protocols of Zion*. New York: Covici, Friede, 1935.
Brotz, Howard. *The Black Jews of Harlem*. Glencoe, Ill.: Free Press, 1964.
Bullock, Alan. *Hitler: A Study in Tyranny*. London: Odhams, 1952; Penguin Books ed., 1962.
Cang, Joel. *The Silent Millions: A History of the Jews in the Soviet Union*. London: Rapp & Whiting, 1969.

Cassin, Elena. *San Nicandro: The Story of a Religious Phenomenon*, trans. Douglas West. London: Cohen & West, 1959.

Chacon, Vamireh. *O Anti-Semitismo no Brasil*. Recife: Clube Hebraico, 1955.

Clarkson, Jesse D. *A History of Russia*. London: Longmans, 1962.

Cohn, Norman. *The Pursuit of the Millennium*. London: Secker & Warburg, 1957.

———. *Warrant for Genocide*. London: Eyre & Spottiswoode, 1967.

Derfler, Leslie, ed. *The Dreyfus Affair*. Boston: D. C. Heath, 1966.

Dinnerstein, Leonard, ed. *Antisemitism in the United States*. New York: Holt, Rinehart & Winston, 1971.

Dunlop, D. M. *The History of the Jewish Khazars*. Princeton: Princeton University Press, 1954.

Fisch, Harold. *The Dual Image: A Study of the Figure of the Jew in English Literature*. London: Lincolns-Prager, 1959.

Forster, Arnold, and Benjamin R. Epstein. *The New Anti-Semitism*. New York: McGraw-Hill, 1974.

Fraenkel, Josef, ed. *The Jews of Austria*. London: Valentine, Mitchell, 1967.

Fuchs, Eduard. *Die Juden in der Karikatur*. Munich: Albert Langen, 1921.

Gaer, Joseph. *The Legend of the Wandering Jew*. New York: Mentor Books, 1961.

Glock, Charles Y., and Rodney Stark. *Christian Beliefs and Anti-Semitism*. New York: Harper & Row, 1966.

Greenberg, Louis. *The Jews in Russia*. 2 vols. New Haven: Yale University Press, 1944–51.

Grunfeld, Frederick V. *The Hitler File*. London: Weidenfeld & Nicolson, 1974.

Harkabi, Y. *Arab Attitudes to Israel*. London: Valentine, Mitchell, 1972.

Hausner, Gideon. *Justice in Jerusalem: The Trial of Adolf Eichmann*. London: Nelson, 1967.

Heiden, Konrad. *Der Fuehrer*, trans. Ralph Mannheim. London: Pordes, 1967.

Jenks, William A. *Vienna and the Young Hitler*. New York: Columbia University Press, 1960.

Katz, Jacob. *Exclusiveness and Tolerance: Studies in Jewish-Gentile Relations in Medieval and Modern Times*. Oxford: Oxford University Press, 1961.

Kochan, Lionel, ed. *The Jews in Soviet Russia since 1917*, 2nd ed. London: Oxford University Press, 1972.

———. *Pogrom: 10 November 1938*. London: Andre Deutsch, 1957.

Lapide, Pinchas. *The Last Three Popes and the Jews*. London: Souvenir Press, 1967.

Leschnitzer, Adolf. *The Magic Background of Modern Anti-Semitism*. New York: International Universities Press, 1956.

Liebman, Seymour B. *The Jews in New Spain*. Coral Gables, Fla.: University of Miami Press, 1970.

Litvinoff, Barnet. *A Peculiar People: Inside the Jewish World Today*. London: Weidenfeld & Nicolson, 1969.

———. *Road to Jerusalem*. London: Weidenfeld & Nicolson, 1965.

Madariaga, Salvador de. *Spain and the Jews*. London: Jewish Historical Society of England, 1946.

Neiva, Artur Hehl. *Estudo sobre a imigração Semita no Brasil.* Rio de Janeiro: Imprensa Nacional, 1945.

Olson, Bernhard. *Faith and Prejudice.* New Haven: Yale University Press, 1963.

Omegna, Nelson. *Diabolização dos judeus.* Rio de Janeiro and São Paulo: Record, 1969.

Poliakov, Léon. *The Aryan Myth: A History of Racist and Nationalist Ideas in Europe.* New York: Basic Books, 1974.

Pulzer, Peter. *The Rise of Political Anti-Semitism in Germany and Austria.* New York: Wiley, 1964.

Reitlinger, Gerald. *The Final Solution,* 2nd ed. London: Valentine, Mitchell, 1955.

Remedios, J. Mendes Dos. *Os Judeus em Portugal.* Coimbra: França Amado, 1895.

Roth, Cecil. *A History of the Jews in England,* 3rd ed. Oxford: Oxford University Press, 1964.

————. *The History of the Jews of Italy.* Philadelphia: Jewish Publication Society, 1946.

————. *A History of the Marranos.* New York: Meridian Books, 1959.

Rubens, Alfred. *A History of Jewish Costume,* rev. ed. London: Valentine, Mitchell, 1973.

Russell of Liverpool, Lord. *The Scourge of the Swastika.* London: Corgi, 1964.

Schappes, Morris U., ed. *A Documentary History of the Jews in the United States, 1645–1875,* 3rd ed. New York: Schocken Books, 1971.

Schoeps, Hans Joachim. *The Jewish-Christian Argument.* London: Faber & Faber, 1963.

Schwarz, Samuel. *Os Cristãos-Novos em Portugal no século XX.* Lisbon, 1925.

Shaffer, Harry G. *The Soviet Treatment of Jews.* New York: Praeger, 1974.

Shapiro, Harry L. *The Jewish People: A Biological History.* Paris: UNESCO, 1960.

Shirer, William L. *The Rise and Fall of the Third Reich.* New York: Simon & Schuster, 1960.

Sklare, Marshall, ed. *The Jews: Social Patterns of an American Group.* Glencoe, Ill.: Free Press, 1960.

Speer, Albert. *Inside the Third Reich,* trans. Richard and Clara Winston. London: Weidenfeld & Nicolson, 1970.

Strizower, Schifra. *The Children of Israel: The Bene Israel of Bombay.* Oxford: Blackwell, 1971.

————. *Exotic Jewish Communities.* London: Thomas Yoseloff (World Jewish Congress), 1962.

Synan, Edward A. *The Popes and the Jews in the Middle Ages.* New York: Macmillan, 1965.

Trachtenberg, Joshua. *The Devil and the Jews.* New Haven: Yale University Press, 1945.

Trevor-Roper, H. R. *The Last Days of Hitler.* London: Macmillan, 1947.

Wisnitzer, Arnold. *The Jews in Colonial Brazil.* New York: Columbia University Press, 1960.

Ziegler, Philip. *The Black Death.* London: Collins, 1969.

SOME SAMPLES OF ANTI-SEMITIC LITERATURE

Barroso, Gustavo. *Brasil colonia de banqueiros* (Brazil a Bankers' Colony). São Paulo, 1934.

———. *Os Protocolos dos sabios de Sião*, 3rd ed. São Paulo: Agencia Minerva, 1937.

Chamberlain, Houston Stewart. *Die Grundlagen des neunzehnten Jahrhunderts*, 4th ed. 2 vols. Munich, 1903.

Hitler, Adolf. *Mein Kampf*, NSDAP (Nazi) ed. Munich, 1938. English translation by Ralph Mannheim. London: Radius Books/Hutchinson, 1972.

Marr, Wilhelm. *Der Sieg des Judenthums über das Germanenthum: Vom nicht confessionellen Standpunkt aus betrachtet*, 4th ed. Berne, 1879.

Mousseaux, Henri Gougenot des. *Le Juif, le judaïsme et la judaisation des peuples chrétiens*. Paris, 1869.

Netchvolodow, A. *L'Empereur Nicolas II et les juifs*. Paris, 1924.

Protocols of the Meetings of the Learned Elders of Zion, trans. Victor E. Marsden. London: Britons Publishing Society, 1933. *The Jewish Peril*, a translation of Sergey Nilus' Russian edition of the *Protocols*. London, 1920.

'Retcliffe', 'Sir John' (Hermann Goedsche). *Biarritz: A Historical Political Novel*. Berlin, 1868.

Tacitus. *Histories*, chap. 5. Loeb Classical Library. 4 vols. London: Heinemann, 1925–37. (There is a new translation by Kenneth Wellesley, published by Penguin Books, 1964.)

Toussenel, A. *Les Juifs, rois de l'époque*, 4th ed. 2 vols. Paris: Dentu, 1888.

Weininger, Otto. *Sex and Character*, trans. from the German. London: Heinemann, 1916.

SOCIAL PSYCHOLOGY OF PREJUDICE

Ackerman, Nathan W., and Marie Jahoda. *Anti-Semitism and Emotional Disorder: A Psychoanalytic Interpretation*. New York: Harper & Row, 1950.

Adorno, T. W., Else Frenkel-Brunswik, D. J. Levinson, and R. N. Sanford. *The Authoritarian Personality*. New York: Norton Library, 1969.

Allport, Gordon W. *The Nature of Prejudice*. Reading, Mass.: Addison-Wesley, 1954.

Bach, H. I. 'Projection of the "Protocols": The Guilt Feeling in Anti-Semitism', *Patterns of Prejudice*, 7 (July–Aug. 1973), 24.

Banton, Michael. *Race Relations*. London: Tavistock, 1967.

Bettelheim, Bruno, and Morris Janowitz. *Social Change and Prejudice*. Glencoe: Ill.: Free Press, 1964.

Broom, Leonard P., Helen P. Broom, and Virginia Harris. 'Characteristics of 1,107 Petitions for Change of Name', *American Sociological Review*, 20 Feb. 1955), 33–39.

Dingwall, Eric John. *Racial Pride and Prejudice*. London: Watts, 1946.

Ehrlich, Howard J. *The Social Psychology of Prejudice*. New York: Wiley, 1973.

Ichheiser, G. 'Projection and the Mote-Beam Mechanism', *Journal of Abnormal and Social Psychology*, 42 (1947), 131–33.

Mason, Philip. *Common Sense about Race*. London: Gollancz, 1961.

Roback, A. A. *A Dictionary of International Slurs*. Cambridge, Mass.: SCI-Art Publishers, 1944.

Robb, James H. *Working-Class Anti-Semite*. London: Tavistock, 1954.

Rose, Arnold. 'Anti-Semitism's Root in City Hatred', *Commentary*, 6 (1948), 374–78.

————. *The Roots of Prejudice*. Paris: UNESCO, 1958.

Simpson, George Eaton, and J. Milton Yinger. *Racial and Cultural Minorities: An Analysis of Prejudice and Discrimination*, 4th ed. New York: Harper & Row, 1972.

Watson, Peter, ed. *Psychology and Race*. Harmondsworth: Penguin Books, 1973.

Index